UNLOCKING JUSTICE

THE AMERICANS WITH DISABILITIES ACT AND ITS AMENDMENTS ACT PROTECTING PERSONS WITH DISABILITIES IN COURT:

Domestic Violence • Post Traumatic Stress Disorder • Legal Abuse Syndrome
Autism Spectrum Disorders & Other Functional Impairments

> " *Using the techniques in this book may well lead a revolutionary movement toward humanizing our legal system for those most vulnerable among us – an aging population, those with non-apparent disabilities, PTSD, Traumatic Brain Injury, ADHD, Depression, Anxiety, Autism, and many other conditions. These will be the quiet heroes who went to court, faced off with an adversary, demanded fair and equal access, won their day against the System, and set legal precedent that will outlive us all.* "
>
> Philip Zimbardo, Professor Emeritus Stanford University
> Author of the Lucifer Effect and many others.

DR. KARIN HUFFER

Edited by Wilene Gremain

Cover, Illustrations, Photography and Interior Design by CoPilot Creative

The cases discussed in this book are true events. Identifying information has been altered while preserving the pertinent dynamics of ADAAA as disability and litigation intersect.

Typeset by: Service Typographers, Inc.

Library of Congress Cataloging-in-Publication Data

Huffer, Dr. Karin
         Unlocking Justice – The Americans with Disabilities Act and its Amendments Act Protecting Persons with Disabilities in court

         Includes bibliographical references.
         ISBN: 978-0-9641786-1-8

Published by Fulkort Press, LLC
www.fulkortpress.com

Printed in U.S.A.

First Edition: 2012

Dedication

To Karin Ingeborg Pearson, my Swedish Grandmother, 1902-1972, whose powerful spirit of love, loyalty, and appreciation of treasured human values bonded me to ideals of justice, daily gratitude, and love for humanity. She inspires me to serve and guides my pen.

Tack så mycket

In memory of JDH 1943-2007

Deepest Thank You To:

Jason Darwin Huffer, my son, who gave of his time, expertise in publication management, and creative graphics vision to bring the first book, Overcoming the Devastation of Legal Abuse Syndrome, to reality. He has never veered from supporting the seeds of my mission planted in that first work. He brings to Unlocking Justice his acutely clear vision, and creative brilliance honed with nearly two decades of life experience in the trenches. It is rare to have a person commit to the passion of another and go the distance. Without a closer like Jason, I could not have fulfilled this mission.

Also Thank You To:

Alan Dershowitz, Esq. Harvard Law Professor who critically reviewed my first work on Legal Abuse Syndrome (LAS). Then by publishing it in The Abuse Excuse, 1994, the concept of Legal Abuse Syndrome was critically reviewed, projected nationwide greatly enhancing peer review and acceptance of LAS as a public health problem.

Kenn Goldblatt, MA, legal researcher and educator for allowing citations and quotes from another writing project to be used in the body of this work and Appendix B. He describes himself as "a litigator without a license." He has twenty years experience participating in difficult cases across the United States in support of attorneys (some with disabilities) and assisting litigants who qualify as disabled according to the definitions of the Americans with Disabilities Act Amendments Act of 2008 and their attorneys. His experience includes both federal and state litigation from trial court filings through final appeals at every level.

Mary Alice Gwynn, PA, attorney, who perseveres for the rights of litigants with disabilities in Florida and for providing insights into the burdens born by those with impairments in the climate of the judicial system contributing to the development of this standard of care.

Don Alan "Mo" Frederick, Esq. for using the techniques in this book, critical review, proofreading, and suggestions.

Bessel van der Kolk, M.D., Psychiatrist and The Trauma Center for post conference neuroscience "Quaker Meetings" that encouraged internalization of new information encouraging creative projection of original ideas for application of trauma treatment and elegant research that has supported the concept of complex PTSD found in LAS.

Karen Stelleck, physical therapist whose exceptional level of knowledge and professionalism contributed to my ability to understand how to neurologically override trauma.

Maureen Therese Hannah, PhD, professor of psychology at Siena College in Albany, NY who brings sufferers of LAS together annually in a conference designed to address healing, survival, and systemic change.

Joan Zorza, Esq., Wendy Murphy, Esq., Nancy Erickson, J.D., MA, Meera Fox, Esq., Garland Waller, M.S., Renee Beeker, forensic disability specialist, for sustained effort that has influenced and encouraged this work.

Robert Geffner, Ph.D. ABPP, ABPN and founding president of the Family Violence and Sexual Assault Institute in San Diego, CA who annually produces the Institute on Violence, Abuse and Trauma (IVAT) where Huffer's 8-steps and the techniques in this book have been presented and testes through various addresses, plenaries, workshops, and seminars.

Juli T. Star-Alexander for her tireless work as executive director of Redress Inc. and co-researching for a decade to obtain the basic data that clarified Legal Abuse Syndrome in the context of the many litigants with disabilities whose health was negatively impacted by their litigation experience.

Chief Justice Lewis - Chief Justice Lewis of Florida stands firm for equal access for persons with disabilities, inspired, and supported this work.

Linda Smith, a worst case example of litigation stress that resulted in death causing me to work to never lose another client from preventable LAS.

Gordon S. Hale, for your passion, vast knowledge and contribution as truly one of the best educators in the country and for your twenty plus years of true friendship and loyalty.

Liliane Miller for all of your hard work, support and encouragement in this endeavor.

Judith Ray, PsyD, for your incredible insight, friendship, and undaunted passion for moving the ADA forward.

Raffaela DiBauda, RMT, CNMT, RCST, SD, for your therapeutic support in every way to keep my health, and strength at an optimum.

Patti Wilhelm, LMT for your therapeutic healing from my disabling condition.

Therese Morgan, for everything that you do, if we listed it all we would need a second book. Your true support in sickness and health is deeply appreciated.

Braxton, who brings light into the darkness and reminds us why we do what we do.

Christopher, you know who you are, and we truly appreciate your dedication and service.

Michael L. Shaffner, for your never-ending friendship, support, positive encouragement and advice.

Marc Browne, for your never-ending friendship, support, positive encouragement and advice.

C. Ann Huffer, whose legal career began with her preparing the manuscript for the first E book of Overcoming the Devastation of Legal Abuse Syndrome. She has gone on to become a certified advocate, a forensic disability specialist, an honor student in law school stretching services to litigants with disabilities nationwide.

Certain people are appreciated with anonymity – they will know who they are:

Jordan, Randy, Meryl, Rebecca, Dr. Neil...

Rubric for the Effective Use of ADAAA

CERTIFIED ADA
ADVOCATE

EC
Ethical Compliance under the Americans with
Disabilities Act Related to Invisible Disabilities

ADA
Full ability to
reference relevant
sections of the ADAAA
for equal access

DA
Working familiarity with
symptoms &
characteristics of LWD's
disability Design
Accommodations

GRL
Working familiarity with
that portion of the
state/local court rules
system relevant to your
client.

H8S
Supportive Counseling
ability to use Huffer's
8-step protocol with
symptomatic LWDs

™

*We cannot mess with each other in the wake of trauma. When people do terrible
things to each other, it is very different from accident trauma.*

-van der Kolk

CADAAs Rely on the Rubric when Planning, Observing, Anticipating, and Responding

Each chapter relates to the rubric according to the key listed below. Also listed are abbreviations referenced and defined in the chapters. While it is taught in ADA Advocacy Webinars from beginning to end, the book is not necessarily intended for reading from beginning to end. Rather it is resource and a guide with keys linking the reader to a particular counseling step, an ADA Accommodation, and/or applicable rules and laws.

This book is a tool to be used as the ADAAA is applied to invisible disabilities in many forums. It is the handbook for the ADA advocate or litigant with disabilities. It is the attorney's ADA guide for practical and ethical application and the ADA Access Coordinator's handy desk reference.

The ADAAA is a new law dispelling much bias. I forces all who use it to first do no harm and calls upon imagination and many untapped resources. *Unlocking Justice* is not esoteric. It serves professionals by approaching practical application of the ADAAA while illuminating the frustration and dissatisfaction many litigants with disabilities experience.

We can do better as professionals in America by using the techniques in this book. Citations are few inviting new research and requiring use of related research that is more than a decade old.

In this book, when you see the term "Huffer's Steps," it cues the reader that those specific therapeutic steps are customized to address the unique trauma imposed by our justice system. Largely litigation re-traumatizes by its very nature. For the purpose of this book, focus will be on persons with disabilities (PWDs) or litigants with disabilities (LWDs) and the word litigant will refer to LWDs.

EC   Ethical Compliance
ADA   ADAAA Laws
DA   Disability Accommodations
GRL   Governing Rules & Laws
H8S   Huffer's Eight (8) Counseling/Coaching Steps

Ch1	EC, H8S	**Ch7**	DA, H8S	**Ch13**	H8S
Ch2	ADA, DA, H8S	**Ch8**	DA, H8S	**Ch14**	EC, GRL, H8S
Ch3	EC, ADA	**Ch9**	GRL, H8S	**Ch15**	DA, H8S
Ch4	DA	**Ch10**	H8S	**Ch16**	ADA, DA, GRL
Ch5	ADA, H8S	**Ch11**	H8S	**Ch17**	DA, GRL
Ch6	ADA	**Ch12**	H8S		

Table of Contents

Chapter 12: Obsessive-Compulsive Hyper-vigilance (OCH): Huffer's Step-5 Regaining Creative Control 165

Chapter 13: Blaming: Huffer's Step-6 Accountability and Attribution 183

Chapter 14: Empowerment: Huffer's Step-7 Fearlessly Self-protect, Research, and Confront Ethical Challenges 199

Foreword

For the past decade I have observed and corresponded with Karin Huffer about her intricate journey into the crawlspace of traumatic human interactions with systems of authority. She chooses the most unwieldy and challenging forum for her studies, the judicial system as experienced by persons with invisible disabilities. I was intrigued that she named and researched a subcategory of Post Traumatic Stress Disorder (PTSD), Legal Abuse Syndrome, in her first book. While I publicly write and speak on the crucibles in which authority, power, and dominance blend, Karin Huffer takes this work deeper into the psyche, souls and needs of the individuals caught in litigation. Delving into a combined socio/medical/legal realm of human trauma, she has crafted a way of helping all players in the courtroom to preserve their health and the qualities humans value most.

While most researchers and professionals tend to avoid, even fear the legal system, Karin embraces it. In *Unlocking Justice: Innovative ADA Advocacy* she brings research and best practices into the courtroom and lawyers' offices using realistic application of the Americans with Disabilities Act tied to resilience-enhancing counseling protocols. Her groundbreaking rubric specifies convergence of local rules, reasonable human expectations, counseling protocols, in the context of the ADA as intended for use to ensure fairness in the judicial system.

She established almost two decades ago in her first work that disability can exist prior to litigation. However, too often stress induced impairments manifest cumulatively as litigation wears on sometimes for years. She illustrates with sound evidence how re-traumatization can trigger the constellation of symptoms that comprise PTSD of the legal abuse syndrome type. Once this happens the afflicted litigant's performance takes a downward spiral. Then, in the adversarial legal system, lawyers go in for the kill. If a person with disabilities does not have accommodations establishing equal access to the proceeding, this dynamic unleashes a biased brutality through exploitation of a disability rather than a competitive edge. ADA Advocates prevent these wars of attrition that can stealthily wipe out due process of law.

Karin advocates prevention of legal system-induced affliction followed by exploitation. Among the tools recommended in *Unlocking Justice* is a simple data analysis form that brings judicial notice to cognitive dissonance caused by lies that unfairly distress and attack the person with disabilities. I caution in my work about the fundamental attribution error that can occur when the environment affects a situation improperly influencing outcome. Litigants enter the judicial system with trust armed with truth and seeking justice. If they are placed in a courtroom facing the impossible position of defending against lies, traumatic stress neurologically renders them speechless. The very context of the power differential in the courtroom will impact them. Unlocking Justice provides methods and skills that offset the risk of unfair rulings influenced more by lies than facts. The litigant now has innovative ways to achieve equal standing in court.

Using the techniques in this book may well lead a revolutionary movement toward humanizing our legal system for those most vulnerable among us — an aging population, those with non-apparent disabilities, PTSD, Traumatic Brain injury, ADHD, depression, anxiety, autism, and the many other conditions. These will be the quiet heroes who went to court, faced off with an adversary, demanded fair and equal access, won their day against the System, and set legal precedent that will outlive us all.

Philip G. Zimbardo, Professor Emeritus of Psychology at Stanford University is a two-time past president of the Western Psychological Association, and the past president of the American Psychological Association. As an internationally recognized scholar, educator, researcher and media personality, he has won numerous awards and honors in each of these domains. He has been a Stanford University professor since 1968, having taught previously at Yale, NYU, and Columbia. Zimbardo's career is noted for giving psychology away to the public through his popular PBS-TV series, Discovering Psychology, along with many text and trade books, among his 300 publications. Zimbardo's latest books are The Time Paradox: The New Psychology of Time That Will Change Your Life (Free Press, 2008) and The Lucifer Effect: Understanding How Good People Turn Evil (Random House, 2007). Go to: http://www.thetimeparadox.com and http://www.lucifereffect.org/

Preface

The impossibly broad enterprise of creating *Unlocking Justice* felt like it would unearth many profound discoveries as I researched and wrote. After the passage of the ADAAA in 2008, I set out to create a workable method for defining and ensuring a standard of care for the many persons with disabilities who would rely on this law. The task was a first in marrying medical and legal standards of care. If medical and legal are not blended, medical diagnoses and legal requirements for accommodating persons with disabilities could result in a standoff as legal judicial personnel demand more proof of a disability while medical personnel attempt to make a somewhat round peg of disability fit in a square hole of law that, at its best, is stressful and not conducive to health. Against the advice of some who warned this book might "offend" the legal community, I forged on determined to lay a path to realistic application of the highest standard of care for the ADAAA.

The first task in this enterprise is to separate the idea of standard of care from fear of litigation. In legalspeak, when standard of care is mentioned it automatically triggers legal requirements for proving malpractice. *Unlocking Justice* elevates the concept of high standard of care from fear-provoking attachment with an imminent lawsuit to an image of a proper medical/legal level of performance. Establishing and supporting a top-notch standard of care for legal consumers proves to lessen lawsuits and improve public perception of the judiciary. Persons with disabilities or the indigent including the "new poor" do not tend to bring lawsuits particularly if they have received fair and considerate treatment.

After documenting more than twenty years of experience immersed in what many times felt like irrelevant, autocratic, and arbitrary court experiences by the sides of LWDs, I was determined to improve the path to rational problem solving. The plan required bringing science, law, counseling protocols, basic information on common impairments, and innovation together, in what seemed impossibly broad as a writing project. Yet, the massive multi-disciplinary body of knowledge converges into a simple truth. The entirety of the endeavor, jelled and congealing with historical perspective, uncovers the simplest of human needs put in what feels revolutionary but is not new in the history of human interactions. Rather it refreshes human intuition. Human beings have been guided by a basic moral code since the beginning of recorded history. Moral and ethic foundations of professions such as law and institutions like courts find they are subject to periodical compromise of human values and needs depending upon the politically controlled climate. However, history teaches that the nebulous value of ethical human behavior cycles back around with a corrective mechanism that seems hardwired in the guts of most people (not all, a small percent do not have a moral or ethical compass) .

Judith Herman, M.D., writes, "…the study of psychological trauma is an inherently political enterprise because it calls attention to the experience of oppressed people" (Herman 1997). However, the answer to psychological trauma, always that unwelcome intruder that is comorbid with human afflictions and tragedies, is only partially political. It starts with the passage of the ADAAA in 2008, a federal law that sets the stage for equality for those with impairments. But the ADAAA is but an invitation that invites each human being to reignite the spirit of intuition through improved ethical and moral behaviors. This cycle is not new to the world. History reveals that this pendulum of political dominance and coercive control swings too far. Then human intuition drives decent men and women to say, "enough" and swing the pendulum back guided by a moral compass and ethical behaviors. This cycle has been done over and over again since the beginning of man.

Unlocking Justice does more than say, "enough." *Unlocking Justice* teaches exactly how human beings can join their voices with my message learning the tasks needed to answer human intuition's drive for equality and justice supported by the ADAAA. ADA Advocates are the glue that binds ADAAA mandates to the court, the lawyers' offices under ADAAA Titles II and III to ensure that even litigants with PTSD, Traumatic Brain Injury, Dissociation from traumatic stress are shored up where their impairments would prevent them from participating in judicial processes. After intolerable experiences, the human brain "escapes." It is a built in protective mechanism. Dissociation is the very mechanism that blocks many people who need to use the judicial system from being able to do so, without an ADA Advocate.

PTSD is widely accepted as a valid diagnosis today. We now have scans that can measure the brain in trauma and precisely what occurs during dissociation. The fMRI scan takes the doubt out of argument as to the veracity of PTSD and its symptoms. Unfortunately, biased treatment of persons with disabilities extends the scope of traumatic stress disorders to secondary conditions caused by circumstances. Legal Abuse Syndrome as an etiological component of this subcategory of PTSD tells us that litigation literally can cause or exacerbate PTSD in litigants.

According to current research, the proof is in the scans. Therefore, it is time to re-evaluate the interpersonal dynamics of adversarial litigation so as to halt the judiciary as a possible public health menace. A *Journal of Traumatic Stress* article clearly illustrates dissociation in script-driven imagery responses. Litigation demands re-experiencing of an event as part of the process. If a litigant dissociates from the discussion of the issues of the cases, the person is not present at the hearing for all practical purposes. This study suggests that upon analyses of relationships between severity of posttraumatic symptoms and neural activation state re-experiencing severity was associated positively with right anterior insula activity and negatively with right rostral anterior cingulate cortex (rACC) of the brain. Avoidance correlated negatively with rACC and subcallosal anterior cingulate activity. In addition, dissociation correlated positively with activity in the left medial prefrontal and right superior temporal cortices, and negatively with the left superior temporal cortex. Therefore, actual brain involvement caused the person to mentally "leave the premises" and created severe emotional dysregulation. It is obvious that lawyers cannot be the final determiners of ADA Accommodations (Hopper, 2007). They are not medically qualified; however, with the advanced state of diagnostic ability today, the medical facts of disability and special needs cannot be ignored.

It is a new day with a new law. The ADAAA provides mandates that are intentionally nebulous insuring that no disability can be ignored. A burden was created for those who must comply with the ADAAA by it not providing more exactness as to a meaningful standard of care. A very serious result is that the burden has been shifted to the person with disabilities forcing them to undergo a vetting by court administration in order to be granted needed accommodations. *Unlocking Justice* coherently lays a path to achieve accommodations that adhere to a standard for each case that will come before court administration.

Obviously, there cannot be one rigid formula that would apply to millions of conditions compounded by unique manifestations of afflictions. However, oddly, after managing hundreds of cases representing a range of disabilities that almost defy imagination, one would think accommodations would also demand hundreds of alterations. The beauty in reviewing the volume of accommodations requested and allowed is that most cost the court no money and requested such minor exceptions that with reasonable human kindness, such as taking short breaks, being allowed to personally record legal proceedings to offset memory lapses, extend deadlines, and offer some ability to bring judicial notice to gratuitous lying in the courtroom. It seems strange that a a law has to be invoked. *Unlocking Justice* makes sense of this fact by joining with the American Bar Association and Department of Justice in urging replacement of the basic medical model courts now use for approval or denial of ADA Accommodations to a social model.

References

Herman, J. M. D. (1997). *Trauma and recovery: The aftermath of violence--from domestic abuse to political terror trauma and recovery.* (pp. 240). New York, NY: Basic Books.

Hopper, J., Frewen, P. A., van der Kolk, B. A., & Lanius, R. A. (2007). Neural correlates of re-experiencing, avoidance, and dissociation in ptsd: Symptom dimensions and emotion dysregulation in responses to script-driven trauma imagery. *Journal of Traumatic Stress, 20(5),* 713 - 725.

Introduction

This is the age of the certified ADA advocate stepping up and assisting those with special needs to attain justice. This book starts where an over-stressed litigant's "rope" ends. My previous readers found that my first book, *Overcoming the Devastation of Legal Abuse Syndrome*, educated, healed, and provoked fresh thinking about the justice system in the United States and the special needs of human beings. This new age knows that in addition to those who suffer permanent disabilities, any person, as they age, may temporarily or permanently face a disabling condition.

Loss of an ability must not take with it loss of human dignity and rights to access and equality in a court of law. Within the Americans with Disabilities Act (ADA) – and the newly passed Americans with Disabilities Act Amendments Act (ADAAA) – are provisions for advocates/helpers to assist disabled individuals who are seeking to assert their civil and constitutional rights. This part of Congress' solution for guaranteeing individuals with disabilities participation throughout our public institutions offers great promise to speed assistance and a workable solution to the problems of persons with disabilities (PWDs) getting a fair day in court.

This book and the training that accompanies it will meet the growing need for ADA advocates to be part of any legal team involving litigants with disabilities (LWDs). Advocates involved in their litigation help obtain Americans with Disabilities Act accommodations that level the playing field in various public institutions. Accommodations can be as complicated as providing ramps for wheelchairs or as simple as allowing breaks during litigation. Advocates often help the LWD to heal as well as to be functional during their litigation. Typically, advocates go to court with litigants in a supportive role to assure that the court understands the individual's unique needs for accommodations and to speak for them in cases in which they cannot speak for themselves.

Readers of this book who are suffering from PTSD/LAS will learn to use an eight-step healing journey that empowers them as litigants and feeds their endurance. Advocates are guided to overcome barriers to access, design reasonable and effective accommodations, and to be comfortable in a courtroom assisting in myriad ways that finally open the doors of justice for their LWDs. The courts benefit from their assistance to better stay within ADAAA and HIPAA guidelines for privacy, properly accommodate litigants facilitating the economy and momentum of the court.

Lawyers, health professionals, and aspiring ADA advocates will use this work to meet relicensing requirements elevating readers' ethical compliance with ADA mandates. This book sets a much needed standard of care under the Americans with Disabilities Amendments Act of 2008 for ensuring equal treatment in the judicial system for those with functional impairments. In searching for a standard for equitable treatment for LWDs I found none that consistently assure fair and equal access to the judicial system for them. NO organization, regulatory body, or professional ethical requirements among legal and health professionals assure that persons with impairments receive a fair unbiased experience in the courts. No profession involved in the justice system seems to be fully aware of the need to take a firm stand against the burgeoning health menace that the legal system now represents for litigants especially with invisible disabilities.

Worse, I found litigants underserved, exploited, and discriminated against by the very processes provided to them through the ADA. With advocates supporting proper and conscientious use of the ADA and the new ADAAA passed in 2008, PTSD/LAS can be significantly reduced. This book is an effort to engender improved public health by reducing the risk of the judicial system injuring its users and inadvertently injuring LWDs.

UNLOCKING JUSTICE

THE AMERICANS WITH DISABILITIES ACT AND ITS AMENDMENTS ACT PROTECTING PERSONS WITH DISABILITIES IN COURT:

Domestic Violence • Post Traumatic Stress Disorder • Legal Abuse Syndrome
Autism Spectrum Disorders & Other Functional Impairments

DR. KARIN HUFFER

CHAPTER 1

SPOTLIGHTING CONTEMPORARY LITIGANTS WITH DISABILITIES (LWDs)

Whether you are the judge, the lawyer, or the litigant, the equalizer is the threat of you being struck down and disabled changing everything in your potential, your plans, and even how people look at you and treat you. You have been transformed—needs, priorities, and perspectives, in a wink. The question is—Now that this unimaginable thought has been introduced, how would you demand to be treated as the judge, the lawyer, or the litigant?

The disability rights movement redefined disability as a problem mainly out there in society—not just in our bodies and minds, but in society.

Paul Longmore, Deceased

Beyond Ramps and the Them vs. Us Mentality

Litigation thrusts successful taxpayers into a web. They become entrapped, tangled in legal traditions, power, and protocols. Without preparation, advocacy, and skills LWDs are at risk of succumbing to further disabling PTSD/LAS complicating their cases. Abusive litigation exploits disability stripping away valuables, pride, and power. A new class of nouveau pauvre, newly poor, is being born. The justice gap then relegates them to "low income" status further stigmatizing them. Without the excessive burdens of litigation, the larger percentage of these people used to be and would still be successful career people contributing to the community.

In 2007, the Legal Services Corporation completed a report, *Documenting the Justice Gap in America: The Current Unmet Civil Needs of Low-Income Americans.* The term "low-income" historically has carried a loser stigma attached to it. Low income reflected those who made poor life's choices, had unfortunate experiences, and just didn't measure up. These people cannot afford lawyers. However, my clients become low-income and unrepresented as a result of the exorbitant cost of litigation and do not fit the low-income stereotype. In this work, cases are revealed of mothers who, due to the long arm extension of domestic violence through litigation, are being relegated to low-income status (*The Women's Legal Defense and Education Fund, 2011)*. They are among the newly poor often created by litigation abuses.

As a therapist diagnosing Legal Abuse Syndrome, I look for that thunderstruck moment when coping mechanisms cannot grasp that litigants already struggling to overcome a disability are being injured by their judicial system. Psycho-legal traumatic experiences have usually accumulated over time while the litigant has fought with the best rules and tools available. My clients are not accustomed to asking for or receiving any type of aid. They have been the contributors, the lifeblood of our culture. Legal aid helps some low-income people but does not touch those freshly made poor by their legal system.

For more than twenty years, I treated a hundred plus clients a year. I listened to, diagnosed, coached, and followed a progression through the Family and other Courts with their army of lawyers and court appointed services. All of the services had hopeful goals expressed by descriptions, i.e. "best interests of the child," "reunification," and other therapeutic duties the court had subsumed. The names do not reflect the quality of services my clients receive. These mandated services are slow, expensive, and often range from baffling to toxic.

Gradually, I realized with a sickening knot tightening in my professional gut that a pattern was emerging. The court system was being used as the process to literally create "low-income" people. Shifting the assets was a major legal strategy to weaken the opponent. Such an insight felt like a hairball must feel when a cat is coughing with fierce purpose. My successful middle class clients were being reduced to disability sustenance by involuntary contracts with court appointees, exorbitant legal fees and costs, and/or abusive attorneys who steamrolled them as their disabilities weakened them. I have witnessed preventable ruination of fortunes, careers, parents, businesspeople, because they could not hold their own in the multilevel madhouse that abusive litigation can become when trauma is created or piled upon an existing impairment.

Fig. 1.1 Public Satisfaction with the Court System

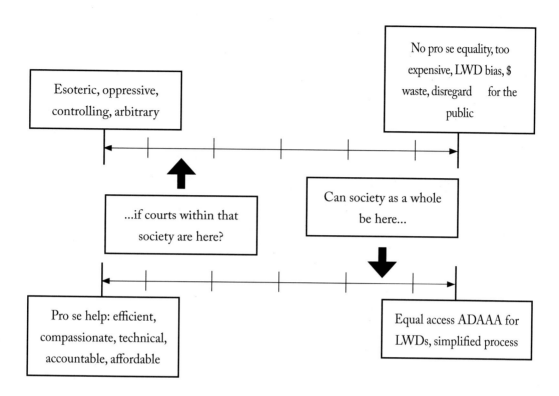

It is critical to use an accurate lexicon if problems are to be solved. Huffer's 8-Steps provides vocabulary to help clients navigate the system while peeling off the layers of emotional trauma, financial ruination, psychiatric injury, physical and immune weakness, and mental confusion. Once I was enlightened as to the human carnage created by abuses of the judicial system, I could not turn back. Needless suffering is unacceptable. Prevention is a major objective and a professional ethical responsibility. Developing methods for my client's self-protection and healing is now a moral obligation. My program provides a continuum of care model for management of individuals who are reacting to shared traumatic events (Macy, 2004).

Right at the time that the Americans with Disabilities Act Amendments Act passed as an unfunded mandate placing a greater burden on the courts to accommodate and serve LWDs, it was greeted by American courts facing their worst financial crisis in decades. In growing numbers LWDs are facing foreclosures, bankruptcies, collections, employment disputes and domestic relations matters. Many LWDs are forced to self-represent due to financial hardship at some point during their litigation putting even more pressure on judges and court personnel. It is a collision of crises that, without conscious effort through advocacy will see PWDs fall through the cracks of justice in spite of the ADAAA. It's a recipe for disaster, says ABA President Stephen N. Zack, and "the potential to lose the rule of law in our country is very real" (Podgers).

David Boies, co-chair of Task Force on Preservation of the Justice System and chairman of Boies, Schiller & Flexner, commented in March, 2011(Podgers), "..., our basic promise of justice is being undercut. Who are we going to tell they won't get justice?" Obviously, LWDs who just recently through the ADAAA have felt hope of equal access to justice have still not established a pattern or momentum of gaining the assistance they need to assure their due process rights are protected. In fact throughout the discussions surrounding the court's budget crisis, LWDs are rarely even mentioned as at risk. Without ADA advocates, no regulators assure fairness. No assessments yielding statistical data or empirical measures of public access to legal proceedings seem to exist. "Assessing the legal landscape for the ordinary citizen who has sporadic contact with the legal profession is a game played mostly in the dark," as Gillian Hadfield, PhD, J.D., economist, and Stanford educated lawyer, writes (129).

Many LWDs not only play in the dark they stay in the dark denied due process rights. It is time to shed light on the darkness ensuring that LWDs are not forced into the justice gap prioritizing budget cutbacks over human service. I am compelled to bring together the best empirical evidence connecting legal and medical research with my observations in order to eliminate the justice gap forced by litigation.

I formed a thesis in my first book that our legal systems were contributing to an epidemic of PTSD and exacerbating the conditions of LWDs. Medical research has offered excellent supportive evidence in spite of the fact that PTSD is hard to pin down to empirical constructs. Nevertheless, the dedicated researchers listed in the references for this book provide ongoing and exciting insights into PTSD and other disabilities. A consistent theme in dealing with stress disorders emphasizes a social model of positively serving all litigants. Attitude costs nothing and goes a long way to assuring fair treatment of LWDs. Federal funding efforts should work to prevent low-income status by making judicial services more efficient and cost effective. Along with requesting federal funds to assist those unable to afford representation, it is time to ask how these people in need of lawyers got to be "low-income." Once the cause of low-income status is better understood, some proactive measures can be put in place by and for the public before entering the judicial system.

Minimizing Traumatic Stress through Proactive Measures— Pre-legal Preparation

Wise preparation and facing the realities of the system can prevent reversal of fortune in a significant number of cases. It is clear to me that the most promising approach in addressing the failure of the judicial system to provide consistently practical and useful services to the LWD public is to develop a process for self-protection, resilience, and healing while simultaneously dealing with litigation challenges and disappointments.

Guidelines for Treating PTSD/LAS

Traditional Verbal Methods

The International Society for Traumatic Stress Studies, ISTSS, has established eighteen guidelines for treating PTSD. Many are not applicable to the type of traumatic stress caused by litigation, but one method with modifications achieves a fit.

Edna B. Foa, PhD is a professor of clinical psychology in psychiatry at the University of Pennsylvania and Director of the Center for the Treatment and Study of Anxiety. She is currently one of the world's leading experts in PTSD. In *Effective Treatments for PTSD: Practice Guidelines from the International Society for Traumatic Stress Studies,* Foa puts forth her concept of Prolonged Exposure Therapy, the most scientifically-tested and proven treatment that has been used to effectively treat victims of all types of trauma. In this treatment, clients are exposed to imagery of their traumatic memories, as well as real-life situations related to the traumatic event in a step-by-step, controllable way. Through these safe exposures, those with PTSD learn to confront the trauma triggering different feelings that lower their anxiety. They are also provided education about PTSD including training in breathing. Currently, exposure therapy uses "virtual reality" programs that allow you to re-enter the setting in which you experienced trauma.

Non Verbal Methods: Treating the Effects of Prolonged Litigation with EMDR

I have added to my treatment menu Dr. Francine Shapiro's, clinical psychologist, Eye Movement Desensitization and Reprocessing (EMDR), a series of guided eye movements that help you process traumatic memories, as a choice in treating PTSD/LAS (Shapiro, 1989, 2001). Deborah L. Korn, PsyD, EMDR facilitator and instructor with the EMDR Institute, points out that PTSD, as defined in the current DSM-IV, which provides a common language and standard criteria for the classification of mental disorders, (1994, Update DSM-V in 2013), "fails to account for the complex symptomatology that emerges following chronic interpersonal traumatization." This complex symptomatology is found in LWDs facing prolonged litigation trauma leading me to diagnose Legal Abuse Syndrome in 1995.

Korn's treatment of adults of childhood abuse is EMDR. As a treatment, it is largely nonverbal. The traumatized person establishes certain base lines and goals and then does a rapid eye-movement exercise. Regular measures are taken against the baselines after each exercise of eye movement or crossing the body's midline in another way. The main task is to cross the midline of the body replicating REM sleep. For the person who is traumatized and therefore unable to use expressive speech due to a traumatic brain reaction to it EMDR has proven to be an effective therapy. Meta analysis of research finds EMDR more efficacious when compared to exposure therapy where the person is taken back to the site of the trauma either in imagination or simulation and then encouraged to express feelings in a safe environment (Bisson, 2007).

Psychotherapy such as cognitive therapy (talk therapy) helps you recognize the ways of thinking (cognitive patterns) that are keeping you stuck in, for example, negative or inaccurate ways of perceiving normal situations. Exposure therapy, safely facing the very thing that you find frightening, so that you can learn to cope with it effectively; and, eye movement desensitization and reprocessing (EMDR) can be tried individually or combined.

The task, therefore, is to develop a treatment program that borrows from Foa's therapy, uses EMDR, but adapts them to peri-trauma (around trauma) instead of focusing on one critical event. Huffer's 8-Steps (H8S) along with using an advocate strengthen the litigant providing support and protection. Litigation conversely forces unsafe and prolonged exposure to a cycle of re-traumatization. Becoming skilled at employing Huffer's 8-Steps prior to hiring an attorney or continuing an involved court experience provides the litigant with the therapeutic components required for controlling the cycle of re-exposure.

More than twenty years of research, peer review, and immersion in the interface of human frailties and the legal system have produced Huffer's 8-Steps. The eight steps were formed and peer reviewed between 1988 and 1995 leading to them being first published in *Overcoming the Devastation of Legal Abuse Syndrome*. They have continued to be perfected for fifteen years since then. *Unlocking Justice* has named the protocols Huffer's 8-Steps in order to identify them as a unique process for treating litigants with disabilities versus other step programs. The variable of litigation introduced into the treatment of PTSD forces conditions that profoundly affect the outcome of therapy and must be treated differently.

Finally, whether you are at a competitive sports event or the court, you must prepare yourself physically and psychologically for the competition. Our research and experience has shown us that eight steps can be helpful in the psychological preparation for the stress of litigation. Huffer's 8-Steps are crucial to making prudent decisions, protecting yourself, and ensuring that your legal case survives to a point of closure.

Author's Notes:

www.lvaallc.com provides an additional survey for litigants with disabilities (LWDs) that contributes to compiling a database to achieve improvements in judicial and attorney service to the public.

References

Bisson, J. I., Ehlers, A., Matthews, R., Pilling, S., Richards, D. & Turner, S. (2007). Psychological treatments for chronic post-traumatic stress disorder: Systematic review and meta-analysis. *British Journal of Psychiatry*, 190, 97–104.

Cohen, S. & Janicki-Deverts, D. (2009). Can we improve our physical health by altering our social networks? *Perspectives in Psychological Science, 4*, 375-378.

Cohen, S. Janicki-Deverts, D., & Miller, G.E. (2007). Psychological stress and disease. *Journal of the American Medical Association, 298*, 1685-1687.

Foa, E.B., Keane, T., Friedman, M. & Cohen, J., (Eds). (2009). *Effective Treatments for PTSD: Practice Guidelines from the International Society for Traumatic Stress Studies.* New York: Guilford Press.

Hadfield, G.K. (2010). Higher Demand, Lower Supply? A Comparative Assessment of the Legal Landscape for Ordinary Americans. *Fordham Urban Law Journal* (2010). Retrieved from http://works.bepress.com/ghadfield/31.

Korn, D. (2009). Emdr and the treatment of complex ptsd: A review. *Journal of EMDR Practice and Research, 3(4)*, 264. doi: 10.1891/1933-3196.3.4.264.

Legal Momentum. (2011). *Single Mothers Since 2000: Falling Farther Down.* Retrieved from http://www.legalmomentum.org/our-work/women-and-poverty/resources--publications/single-mothers-since-2000.html.

Legal Services Corporation. (2009). *Documenting the Justice Gap in America: The Current Unmet Civil Needs of Low-Income Americans.* Retrieved from http://www.lsc.gov/sites/default/files/LSC/pdfs/documenting_the_justice_gap_in_america_2009.pdf.

Macy, R.D. PhD, et al. (2004). Community-Based, Acute Posttraumatic Stress Management: A Description and Evaluation of a Psychosocial-Intervention Continuum. *Harvard Review of Psychiatry, 12(4)*, 218-9.

Podgers, J. (2011, June). Sustaining justice: 10 experts tell how courts can do more with less. *ABA Journal.*

U.S. Census Bureau, *"Table C2. Household Relationship and Living Arrangements of Children Under 18 Years, by Age and Sex 2010,"* Retrieved from http://www.census.gov/apsd/techdoc/cps/cpsmar10.pdf.

Shapiro, F. PhD. (2001). *Eye Movement Desensitization and Reprocessing (EMDR): Basic Principles, Protocols, and Procedures.* (2nd ed.) New York: Guilford Press.

Shapiro F. (1989). Efficacy of the eye movement desensitization procedure: A new treatment for post-traumatic stress disorder. *Journal of Traumatic Stress, 2(2)*, 199-223.

Additional Resources

American Psychiatric Association. (1994). *Diagnostic and statistical manual of mental disorders* (4th ed.). Washington DC: Author.

Foa, E. B. et al. (2010). Development and validation of a child version of the obsessive-compulsive inventory. In *Behavior Research and Therapy, 41(1)* ed., 121-132.

Freeman, J.F., Choate-Summers, M.L., Garcia, A.M., Moore, P.S., Sapyta, J.J., Khanna, M.S., ...Franklin, M.E. (2009). The Pediatric Obsessive-Compulsive Disorder Treatment Study II: rationale, design and methods. *Child and Adolescent Psychiatry and Mental Health, 3(4)*, 1-15. doi:10.1186/1753-2000-3-4.

Freeman, J. F., Summers, M.L., Garcia, A.M., Moore, P.S., Sapyta, J.J., Hajcak, G., ...Simons, R.F. (2008). Increased error-related brain activity in pediatric obsessive-compulsive disorder before and after treatment. *American Journal of Psychiatry, 165(1)*, 116-123.

Huppert, J. D., Strunk, D. R., Ledley, D. R., Davidson, J. R. T., & Foa, E. B. (2007). Generalized social anxiety disorder and avoidant personality disorder: structural analysis and treatment outcome. Anxiety disorder and avoidant personality disorder: Structural analysis and treatment outcome. *Depression and Anxiety, 25(5)*, 441-448. doi: 10.1002/da.20349.

Simon, N.M. (2008). Paroxetine CR augmentation for posttraumatic stress disorder refractory to prolonged exposure therapy. *Journal of Clinical Psychiatry, 69(3)*, 400-405.

Simpson H.B., Zuckoff, A., Page, J. R., Franklin, M. E. & Foa E. B., Adding motivational interviewing to exposure and ritual prevention for obsessive-compulsive disorder: an open pilot trial." *Cognitive Behavior Therapy, 37(1)*, 38-49, 2008.

Simpson, H.B., Cheng, P.E., Huppert, J., Foa, J., Liebowitz, E. MR. (2008). Statistical choices can affect inferences about treatment efficacy: a case study from obsessive-compulsive disorder research. *Journal of Psychiatric Research. 42(8)*, 631-638.

Simpson, H.B., M. Maher, J. R. Page, M. E. Franklin, & E. B. Foa, "Development of a Patient Adherence Scale for Exposure and Response Prevention Therapy." *Behavior Therapy*, 2008.

Ulrich, O., Cahill, S. P., Foa, E. B., & Maercker, A. (2008). Anger and Posttraumatic Stress Disorder symptoms in Crime Victims: A Longitudinal Analysis. *Journal of Consulting and Clinical Psychology. 76(2)*, 208-18.

Website Resources

Detailed Census poverty data for 2010 is available http://www.census.gov/hhes/www/income/income.html

CHAPTER 2

INNOVATIVE ADA ADVOCACY:
LEGAL GAME CHANGER

The public must implement skills i.e. Huffer's 8-Steps for overcoming litigation stress that injures and devastates litigants. Advocates trained in The Americans with Disabilities Act Amendments Act Titles II and III are emerging as a necessary part of the litigation process. Impaired justice seekers need to use the ADAAA to ensure they have equal access to the court in every way.

If one set out by design to devise a system for provoking intrusive post-traumatic symptoms, one could not do better than a court of law.

Judith Herman, M.D.

PTSD Hostage under the Stress of Coercion/Intimidation

Remember being grabbed by a bully on the schoolyard? He would get you from behind locking your arms so you could not get away. Then he would taunt you, embarrass you. He would say nasty things, lies that hurt your feelings. The onlookers had varied reactions, but you had an overwhelming fear that they would believe him. You were taken hostage. You wrested and wiggled, and threatened him with the school rules, anything you could think of but to no avail. He had his way with you and when he let go, you were left feeling powerless to your core. Life changed after that as a result of being taken hostage. Your image was damaged. An ugly seed potentiating hatred was planted in a rough garden of vulnerability.

You needed authority to do its job of fairly enforcing the rules. But, the authorities took little or no interest. They even responded with outrageous and evasive answers that could not deter the bully. The bully's parents were bullies too who threatened to sue the school. Much of the teacher's time was taken trying to keep order while the bully challenged the teacher's power. You feared the bully. The teacher feared administration. Administration feared the parents. The bully feared no one.

Whether or not you were a student with a disability when this occurred, seeds of a psychic injury were planted that day. Boundaries were annihilated and trust wiped out. From then on, you were afraid to run freely. The inner sense of security needed for spontaneity and creativity was eroded. Feelings of being held hostage are etched in your brain to this day. Over the years you saw others, especially students with disabilities, being called names and abused by this same ilk on campus. It was torment dramatized in a major public institution. A few of your true friends tried to comfort you, but it was not enough. Strangely, the observers even seemed to flock toward the bully.

All too often an ADA litigation advocate is similarly witness to a constellation of symptoms so closely aligned with Post Traumatic Stress Disorder that it constitutes a subset. PTSD is commonly characterized as a psychiatric injury that occurs when a person feels jeopardized and there is no place to turn for substantial help (Bremmer, 1995). Legal Abuse Syndrome can be triggered from bureaucracies and official organizations by personnel failing or refusing to provide individuals the honest services their agencies were established to provide and/or being unable to supply the equitable protection an individual may need (Huffer, 1995). Such bureaucratic failures to provide, protect, and assist are becoming increasingly common leaving citizens without fair access or assistance.

When I am called upon to speak, I want the audience to know that our memories of encounters with bullies illustrate exactly what litigants with disabilities experience in our courts of law. This work is not an attack on lawyers, but I do hold those lawyers who do not have the courage to do the right thing in court accountable for a broken justice system. The institutions that allow, profit from, or foster wrongdoing also must be taken to task. This work is designed to guide litigants with disabilities and their advocates including lawyers to work effectively through the process of litigation.

The Americans with Disabilities Act has the potential to provide protection for those with functional impairments. ADA advocates, including lawyers and litigants with disabilities must learn now to use the law to level the playing field they will encounter in court. No one needs to be reminded of the maltreatment of those with disabilities who struggle to survive in our culture. They are ignored, underserved, excluded, ridiculed, exploited, causing them to be at the lower end of the economic spectrum. The Americans with Disabilities Act and civil rights legislation is helping but is far from impacting the culture effectively. Great inequities still exist.

Advocacy is critically needed to drive research and the law into practical application for persons with disabilities especially when they need to or are forced to use their court of law. Self and other advocacy for litigants with special needs are the sentinel purpose of this book.

Certified ADA Advocate
Titles II and III

A new career path is emerging as part of legal and social services in order to carry out the mandates of the Americans with Disabilities Act. Those with disabilities must have the assistance of a knowledgeable and committed person who helps to:

1. Assess their needs as to their functional impairments and within the scope of the ADA Title II design by: accommodations that equalize access to the court.

2. Prepare and submit a report that follows local rules as to diagnosis, history, and impairments aligning with HIPAA and ADAAA mandates of confidentiality.

3. Assure that ADA Accommodations are timely submitted and an administrative response is rendered supporting the litigant's functionality at the time of court proceedings.

4. Attend court with the litigant with disabilities continually monitoring their functionality and intervening at the first sign of symptoms.

5. Monitor accommodations throughout the life of the case making changes and additions as necessary.

6. Protect the dignity and privacy of the litigant with disabilities.

Carefully managed, the ADAAA can substantially reduce the incidence of PTSD/LAS from litigation. Ultimately, it is the litigant's choice whether or not to use the ADAAA. Sadly, fear of discrimination and painful symptoms keep many litigants with disabilities from implementing the ADAAA.[1]

The PTSD/Hostage under the Stress of Litigation

This work is not intended to be a treatise in neuropsychiatry. However, the research from neuropsychiatry clearly supports the observations made herein and is consistent with the assertions made by the expert in court regarding the brain and Post Traumatic Stress Disorder/Legal Abuse Syndrome. The lawyer and ADA sensitive psychologist working together can clarify and overcome symptoms that weaken a legal case.

The various participants in the judicial system thusly are made to understand that the litigant and advocate have a wealth of research backing their requests for equitable accommodations for those with disabilities while they seek justice. This is the point where the ADA advocate draws from research from the medical sciences, neuropsychology, neuroimaging, trauma studies, brain function, and current information on stress and health. Without significant and uniquely tailored accommodations, PTSD litigants cannot effectively function through the litigation process.

---

[1] To better inform readers, in Chapters 2 and in the Empowerment Section of this book, the utilization of the Americans with Disabilities Act will be explained thoroughly with examples and legal options given.

Re-experiencing the underlying traumas triggers symptoms due to brain dysfunction of the frontal-subcortical circuitry and corticothalamic integration. The frontal-subcortical circuitry and corticothalamic integration are the processes necessary to execute personality, prevent apathy, and neuropsychiatric disorders including depression, obsessive-compulsive disorder, and other disorders (Clark, 2003). It feels like the sufferer is working with half of the brain over stimulated and half dormant.

The court needs to be made aware that such disabilities widen the power differential between the court and the litigant multiplying the opportunities for discrimination against the special needs litigant. That is the time that the attorney or advocate must act to obtain ADA accommodations or insist upon legal protection from exploitation of those with disabilities in court. A common abuse causing re-traumatization is to respond to the request for ADA accommodations by accusing the impaired litigant of being incompetent or "insane." Incompetence or "insanity" in court terms threatens the litigant with loss of control of their lives and is a cruel, outdated, and an inaccurate intimidating tactic.

To my knowledge, no current research exists that examines the public health consequences of various bullying techniques commonplace in our courts. Other countries are seriously addressing issues of bullying with severe penalties imposed. The United Kingdom has made great strides against bullying at work, home, in court, and in schools. Japan and Australia are leading with laws against such hostage taking (Harthill, 2008). The American Bar Association's "Survey of Public Perception of the Judicial System" in 1999 indicated in many areas that there were concerns about bias and health. However, the ABA's conclusion was disappointing in that they recommended advertising to improve the perception of the judiciary instead of addressing the concerns of the respondents (ABA, 1999).

PTSD Becomes Legal Abuse Syndrome

My patients repeatedly tell me that the initial betrayal or traumatic assault was only a first step toward their resulting psychic injury. The initial trauma may have been a tough experience, but it was manageable. They could not imagine that, when they turned to the court, pressure and stress would be exacerbated to the point of a disability. If the legal system does not address the problem and continues to cast the litigant into further pain and complications, we are facing a serious but entirely preventable public health catastrophe.

PTSD is commonly characterized as a psychiatric injury that occurs when a person feels simultaneously jeopardized and helpless. When the stakes are high, such as in child custody cases, LAS can be triggered from court appointees who lack sensitivity, experience, proper motivation, and responsibility. Adding to traumatic encounters are enforcement agencies, regulators, and other official resources failing or refusing to provide individuals the services their agencies were established to provide. Traditionally, litigants have had no definition of this condition and no healing protocols available. The advocate now has eight steps in this book for practical assistance when their clients manifest symptoms of PTSD/LAS.

All the while accommodations are being sought, the litigant's adversary usually characterizes the disabled person as "crazy," and at moments, my patients wonder if they are crazy. But, they are not and it is most satisfying when the advocate can assure the litigant, once again a victim, that it is not the victim who is crazy. Further, medical research has established that the demands of the ADAAA to shore up the litigant suffering from disabilities are not only appropriate but also long overdue. The burden is on the court to reasonably accommodate. More on this in Chapter 12, Empowerment. I often testify under oath as an expert witness regarding the accusations of "craziness" of patients, their right to dignity, respect, and a fair day in court. My expert testimony has met forensic standards around the nation. While I face off with expert witnesses possessing fancier dossiers in court, no one can responsibly argue in favor of extreme stress being an acceptable by-product of litigation. No one can successfully or legally argue that those with disabilities should be denied due process of law. No one can defend medically unqualified clerks and lawyers determining the accommodations needed by litigants with disabilities. No one can successfully argue that the rights to parent, manage assets, live independently, and other fundamental rights should be denied a person with a psychic injury. When the adversary shouts "crazy," that is discrimination. There is no evidence that a person who is diagnosed with a severe mental illness cannot successfully parent or live effectively with proper humane support.

Striving for Testimonial and Participatory Equality

What has to be explained to the court administratively and in sworn expert testimony is that symptoms of psychic injuries caused by trauma are not addressable through the usual run of solutions offered during litigation. Litigants with PTSD do not fall into line when ordered to, they can't. Litigation demands that a person is able to think on their feet and speak quickly and effectively after analyzing the message. Trauma attacks the invisible internal connections in our neurophysiologic and psychological systems that make such responses impossible.

Once traumatized, the litigant is afflicted with untimely hesitation. Their physiology is reacting to sensory information involving nerve centers in the brain located right below the cerebral cortex initiating irrelevant responses in the present moment. In fact, their concentration is distracted away from the present moment. The disabled litigant either may not speak at all or speaks out uncontrollably. Their inability to "speak litigation" can be devastating to their courtroom presentation. In such circumstances, the advocate must be able to speak for the litigant (van der Kolk, 2006, 1-17). They resist and dissociate from the very data and processes that could help them most.

The Need for ADA Advocacy

Until human faces and hearts are linked to litigation, the legal process is no more than a stressful war of words, rituals, papers, perceptual tricks, bullying, and prevarication. Once a human being is respected as the very reason for having a justice system in the first place, the litigant can begin to put into effect the mandates of Americans with Disabilities Act of 1990 (ADA), and the newest iteration of the law, the Americans with Disabilities Amendments Act of 2008 (ADAAA). The Act's long description is "An Act to establish a clear and comprehensive prohibition of discrimination on the basis of disability." Designed in part to protect litigants with special needs, this Congressional mandate was intended to insure that all persons, regardless of any disability they may suffer, apparent or non-apparent, are granted equal access to all areas of public and private activities. That means physical access, testimonial access, and participatory access to the courts of law.

Congress Provides for ADA Advocates

A key feature of the law in this regard is Congress' provision for individuals to help and protect PWDs attempting to assert their rights under the ADA. The "advocates" envisioned by Congress and written into the law can work in any reasonable capacity in support of a person with disabilities. This is especially important in litigation where advocates are often the very key to equal access through effectively seeking and affecting courtroom accommodations of various sorts.

The Supreme Court in *Tennessee v. Lane, et al.*, 541 U.S. 509 (2004) pointed out that Congress Constitutionally abrogated the States' Eleventh Amendment immunity, making suits for damages available to individuals who proceed under Title II of the ADA with claims of violations of Due Process of Law. This means that if judges do not adhere to the ADAAA they lose their immunity from being sued. The *Lane* Court found that *"Congress enacted Title II against a backdrop of pervasive unequal treatment of persons with disabilities in the administration of state services and programs, including systematic deprivations of fundamental rights."* [¶ 13] Specifically, *Title II seeks to enforce a variety of basic Constitutional guarantees, including the right of access to the courts, "infringements of which are subject to heightened judicial scrutiny." Id. The Court found that all courts have a duty to accommodate that is perfectly consistent with the well-established due process principle that a state must afford to all individuals a meaningful opportunity to be heard in its courts.* [¶ 14] (LII, 2004). The ADA is designed "to provide a clear and comprehensive national mandate for the elimination of discrimination against individuals with disabilities." [¶ 29] The Supreme Court concluded in Lane, "that Title II, as it applies to the class of cases implicating the fundamental right of access to the courts, constitutes a valid exercise of Congress' authority to enforce the guarantees of the Fourteenth Amendment."

After Lane, public services—the courts—began to accommodate physical disabilities. Focus was on those who needed wheelchair access, devices for hearing for sight impairment, and other such apparent disabilities. It seemed that the courts fell into step. However, in situations where litigants may have mental, psychological or psychiatric impairments, too often public services have been slow and suspicious in their attitudes toward accommodations. They have adopted a medical accommodations model adding layers of bureaucratic burdens to litigants with disabilities as litigants attempt to get reasonable accommodations. Prior to any litigation stress, these litigants are suffering additional stresses by being required to prove up their disabilities and related need for accommodations.

The role of the ADA advocate is essential if the mandates of the ADAAA are to be honored. Unfortunately, while visible disabilities are easily observed and grasped by judges and other legal professionals, the less visible–and often more difficult to comprehend and understand–psychological impairments are more challenging to address with accommodations. However, litigants nonetheless are entitled to reasonable accommodations the same as if they had obvious physical impairments.

The ADAAA is expected to positively impact resistant attitudes toward inclusion of those with functional impairments. Evidence from a 2007 Rutgers University study shows that one third of employers stated that persons with disabilities cannot effectively perform the required job tasks. Or, if they could, the employer feared having to install costly special facilities (UN). In 2010, a survey found that only 35 per cent of working-age persons with disabilities are working. This compares with 78 per cent of those without disabilities (UN). After the passage of the ADAAA, the burden has been shifted to the employer or public or private entity to accommodate without an exhaustive vetting process. The tide has turned for employers, courts, and private organizations serving the public. They must now risk being sued if they don't accommodate.

A critical economic matter often missed is the market that PWDs represent. The National Organization on Disability/Harris Interactive-Survey of Americans with Disabilities, 2004, shows the projected growth of the disability segment of the population in the next 10 years:

- Americans over 50 will increase by 40%.

- Between 2000 and 2030, the numbers of Americans over age 65 will more than double, from 34.8 million to more than 70.3 million.

- Americans 50 and older represent 25% of the population, but control 50% of the nation's buying power and 75% of its assets, representing $150 billion in annual discretionary income, and billions more for necessities like housing and food.

- About 30% of all Americans become disabled prior to retirement age.

- More than 7 out of every 10 Americans will acquire some sort of disability by the time they reach the age of 75.

In 2010, the summary of a follow-up survey states that "the environment for hiring people with disabilities needs a great deal of improvement (Harris, 2010)."

Exponential Negative Ripple Effect
from Non-accommodation of a Growing PWD Population

If PWDs are not accepted and accommodated in litigation, they can become locked into a negative cycle of victimization that they often then unconsciously extend to everybody around them, including friends, family, employer, co-workers, neighbors and advocates who try to engage with them for the sole purpose of conflict resolution. Having lost their ability to sense which individuals are trustworthy in their lives, it is as if their "trust-sense" memory is so greatly impaired as to no longer function.

Neuro-imaging studies of PTSD also help to clarify the underlying neurobiological changes that cause these kinds of complications for those with litigation-related stress disorders during litigation. "You aren't crazy: you're coping" explains trauma expert van der Kolk (2006). And, while you struggle to cope, your opponent proceeds using the court to take the assets, obtain custody of the kids, and dominate and abuse the family as well as legal process right under the judge's nose.

Without advocacy and intervention, such traumatic development can cause damaged litigants to engage in greater and greater conflict in all areas of their lives; and thus, they are seldom free of conflict again. They are resigned to live from an almost-pugilistic standpoint, fists clenched, suffering from increased stress symptoms in a circular pattern of ever-widening dysfunction. The harasser/abuser grabs the moment and is able to claim to all around him or her, "I told you she/he was crazy" and the distorted perception from the victim's "punch-drunk" status would make it appear so. But, the appearance of craziness was preventable and preventing it is the focus of this work.

Unless time is spent using the eight-step counseling protocols, communication between the CADAA and the client can become challenging, even burdensome. Every CADAA and lawyer has had the experience of helping a client prepare for court only to be shocked when the client, who needed to perform as planned, became unexpectedly consumed in flashbacks and shocked the proceedings by cycling through irrelevant (to the task at hand) repetitive statements, pleas, and emotional outbursts. Their interaction ceased to reflect the reality common to others present. They were absorbed in self-preservation of a trauma-driven primitive nature and desperately needed the forum to have empathy and to "get it."

This trauma reaction caused the LWD to dig in blocking out new external stimuli driven to rehash their familiar, polished, grieving narrative. It follows that the advocate and LWD may find themselves seemingly on opposites sides of a situation. The CADAA is informed and apprised of the behavior needed to present the LWD's position. The LWD is psychologically and physiologically stuck in what appears to the court to be an uninformed, unrealistic, and unresponsive stance. The effectiveness of the court and the advocate are neutralized as the LWD, unaware of the climate in the courtroom, takes center stage resuming the trauma narrative. The impact on the outcome of the day's hearing, as I recently witnessed, can be case altering. The judge actually had awarded to the side of the LWD and required only that the litigant pro se respond appropriately. Unfortunately, the symptomatic ranting began as soon as the LWD was called on destroying the amiable atmosphere and along with it all advancement made to that point. Neither the advocate nor the judge was able to calm and explain the positive situation to the LWD. A guardian ad litem was appointed and the litigant lost their strong position.

The courtroom is never a forum in which to project the trauma in raw form. It demands a carefully prepared point of view that may or may not include many highly charged facets of a case. Those are the interests that are sorted out during debriefing. It is all about legal position-- only. Minimizing dialogue and keeping strictly to the point protects the LWD's position. But they must be able to perceive when they are winning. Many invisible disabilities cloud perception when under stress and without skilled counseling, will fall prey to not only their opposition but their own protective psyche. LWDs achieve litigation posture through careful use of Huffer's 8 steps and adhering to the Standard of Care.

Many Conditions Require Communication Assistance

(PTSD for the purpose of this work is the name we associate with Legal Abuse Figure 2.1 Communication)

Especially in cases of autism, stuttering, lisping, dysnomia, aphasia, Semantic Pragmatic Disorder, expressive language disorder, mixed receptive-expressive language disorder or other conditions that can cause a litigant to become either loquacious or silent, their advocate must be able speak their words for them. As a result of the litigant's disorder, the advocate is there to step in to speak, both for the economy of the court and to serve the litigant's special needs while they are suffering physiological disruption of their communication patterns. This type of interpretation is not unlicensed practice of law; however, opposing counsel may use that as an intimidation technique.

In some, I have observed cruel taunting, mocking, and ridicule of a litigant's disabling speech pattern. Broca's Area, the expressive speech pathway in the brain, shows increased cerebral blood flow during stress. This means that when litigants are forced to relive

Figure 2.1 Communication

their personal trauma during litigation, the memory simultaneously activates brain regions that support intense emotions on the one hand and decrease activity of brain structures involved in the inhibition of emotions on the other. Therefore, speech, the skill a litigant depends upon most in court, diminishes. The dual physiological response creates a major disturbance (Hull, 2002), (Lindauer, 2004). The litigant cannot translate the litigation experience into communicable language, as would a normally functional individual. What is a person with disabilities to do alone? There must be assistance and advocacy. Yet, because this disability is virtually "invisible," courts often find it difficult to address the issue with the cheapest and easiest method, an advocate to speak and pay attention to the paperwork submitted to the ADA Access Coordinator.

The dysfunctional litigant's rational mind seems to be able to organize feelings and impulses but has trouble abolishing trauma-related emotions, thoughts, and impulses. Once "litigation language" and the related skills fail, the opponent will seize upon stammering, silence, or off topic words as indicators of a weakness to be exploited. I often observe, in court, excessive objections made by the adversary, snide, insulting and/or pejorative remarks, and introduction of provocative, outrageous false information to further the litigant's suffering and weaken the PTSD litigant's standing in the judge's eyes. While the litigant stutters and struggles the opposition will plant misinformation into the record further traumatizing the litigant and thereby unfairly damaging the disabled litigant's case.

Antonio Damasio, professor of neurology, lays the neurological foundation for human behavior in the context of this diversity of behaviors. Emotions that litigants frequently report, fear, sadness, anger all reduce blood flow in the frontal lobe of the brain (1999). This explains why litigants, especially those with no attorney, have difficulty organizing an effective, timely behavioral response "on their feet" during litigation. Intense emotions are first triggered simply by having to be present in court. They cannot put aside intrusive flashbacks and symptoms that cause distractions and those with impairments certainly cannot choose whether or not they have their disabilities.

Mentally reliving the trauma during legal proceedings simultaneously activates parts of the brain that support intense emotions while diminishing the functions of the central nervous system that controls motor output, regulates physiological arousal, and impedes the ability to communicate in words. Memory fails and intrusive emotions sabotage concentration on the task at hand. Litigants feel incapable of the spontaneous verbal response and interaction required in typical courtroom exchanges. As a result, the litigant with PTSD might be driven to avoid topics. They literally do not hear them. They disconnect when they need to engage. And, at times, they clearly are nonfunctional and are unable to communicate their symptoms and needs in a formal manner accepted by the courts.

The American Psychiatric Association owns, classifies, and compiles criteria for recognizing mental disorders diagnosed by mental health professionals. It is called the Diagnostic and Statistical Manual of Mental Disorders (Corporate Author, 2000). Courts, to forensically validate medical diagnoses, rely upon this manual. First published in 1952, it has been revised five times. Known for inaccuracy and acknowledging that disorders are added and removed with each revision, it is the best effort to bring order and consistency to the classification of behavioral disorders. The basis for profiling such disorders includes the gathering of census, psychiatric institution's statistics, and a manual developed and used by the U.S. Army. It is the best source for diagnostics but has clear limitations.

The new *DSM V* is currently being created and publishing is expected in 2013. Whatever criteria are agreed upon for traumatic stress, it is expected (and hoped) that Complex Post Traumatic Stress Disorder will be included (C-PTSD), (Korn, 2009). This particular type of PTSD results from cumulative trauma and long-term injury rather than one event. My first book used the DSM III and this current book uses the DSM IV while we wait for the publication of the DSM V. While PTSD will remain the formal designation for the constellation of symptoms that can be triggered by litigation, an elastic paradigm needs to be recognized and employed when professionals consider PTSD. Regardless of the designations for trauma victims in the new DSM V, this work will continue to focus on human-on-human trauma that forces an injury resulting in today's profile of Post Traumatic Stress Disorder. Other names can be used to describe the symptoms, Peri Traumatic Stress Disorder, Complex Post Traumatic Stress Disorder, and/or any other designation that deals with trauma sequelae symptoms may even be more exacting of Legal Abuse Syndrome. But, we are aligned with the DSMIV and whatever the name in future editions, the trauma remains the same.

Certain pioneers like Judith Herman, M.D., and Bessel van der Kolk saw early on that the symptoms of PTSD come from trauma in whatever form it presented. After twenty years of research done by me, it is now clear that there is actually no "post" about litigants' trauma. Therefore, a more accurate prefix is "peri-" meaning around or surrounding. Thus, "Peri-Traumatic Stress Disorder" needs to be understood in the context of litigation. Litigants cannot get to a "post" stage while their trauma is being replayed with continuing and ongoing new assaults that become integral parts of the litigation process.

Whether ongoing and cumulative or resulting from a single "big bang," the onset of traumatic symptoms that are then drawn out during litigation becomes even more insidious and devastating than a natural disaster. LAS trauma recycles and extends ongoing abuse for years. When wondering how Legal Abuse Syndrome differs from Post Traumatic Stress Disorder, I use a quick informal test to assess the presence of Legal Abuse Syndrome. Simply ask if the litigant can comfortably get the mail. A second sign of LAS is found in the boxes, baskets, shelves, and stacks of documents that surround the litigant. Legal papers and fear of legal papers displace all signs of enjoyable and normal living.

Courtois and Ford, researchers/editors, list cumulative adversities that either contribute to or worsen trauma (Courtois, 2009). Their recognition that abuse of power, irrationality, disregard of a person's time, expense, and lack of respect for integrity profoundly injures the human psyche and relates directly to the injuries of LAS sufferers. Thus, litigation functions as a potential source of trauma that creates complex PTSD (Stark, 2007) and LAS in and of itself.

To summarize, at the outset, PTSD/LAS sufferer's symptoms cause them to be out of step with litigation procedural requirements. So, a PTSD-afflicted litigant cannot respond in a timely manner to crucial motions or important court orders and needs breaks and special considerations in court. Offsetting the detriment to the disabled are accommodations allowing them extra time or other flexibility within the regular rules of court. Simple human consideration is usually all that is needed. Otherwise, litigants with disabilities fall victim to lawyers' tactics involving disingenuous verbal attacks designed to destroy or undermine the sufferers' credibility and uses of the rules to unbalance the scale of justice.

Family Court Extends to Family Trauma

Complex PTSD or LAS is seeded in children of divorce extending the traumatic effects far into the futures of family members. Family litigation that I have observed has sometimes lasted for decades, consuming the years that should have been dedicated to childhood experiences of the litigants' offspring. Too often, with full power and authority of the court, lawyers harass, vex, delay, and suspend the lives of the targeted spouse and the children. Domestic violence can be extended through the court in cases of coercive control identified by Dr. Evan Stark (2310-14). The children get used to being interrogated, investigated, and intruded upon. Their caregivers are forced to appear in court and they report that they must absorb false accusations. They often lose multiple homes, pets, friends, family, and schools at the hands of court appointed personnel and lose power over normal life activities and decision-making. ADA advocates must keep the sufferer's wellbeing as the center focus during litigation—especially family litigation.

The children involved in divorce actions often appear moody, disrespectful, untrusting, undisciplined, and perceive most adults to be hypocrites. Their energies are not put into their optimal development (van der Kolk, 2004). Instead they are drawn into traumatic symptoms.

Common Symptoms of Complex PTSD among Litigants

- Intrusive thoughts and nightmares/flashbacks seep in through the numbness. Litigants may be physically there but mentally occupied. Children cannot listen or focus.

- There is difficulty concentrating, repetition is a must.

- Memories are painful; flashbacks are unrelenting. Supportive help is needed to help the litigant feel safe.

- The victims will route themselves around reminders and cringe from people, songs, news stories, or events that trigger memories and intense distress. It helps to have a trusted individual accompany and even drive the litigant to court and provide support if they must be exposed to traumatic reminders.

- Ordinary activities require tremendous energy; the victim is mentally, emotionally, and physically exhausted. Litigants need breaks during litigation. They may need continuances simply to rest and shed symptoms.

- The victim frequently trusts no one. The advocate must not allow lack of trust to offend them. It will take time to earn trust.

- The failure and refusal to trust others has reached the point that it has begun to erode the quality of the victim's life. Advocates will find litigants frozen from lack of trust or conversely attempting to micromanage. They sometimes shut down while litigation moves on. It is frustrating for the advocate (and/or legal team) to know what needs to be filed, responded to, and done while having the litigant virtually freeze in the face of his or her own demise.

- He or she feels off-balance. An advocate is a rudder.

- The victim's creativity is blunted.

- Intensity of interest in the world around the victim is dulled. It seems to the advocate that the litigant has lost a sense of gratitude. Thank yous may be few and mixed with criticisms. That is normal for litigants overwhelmed by disability and litigation in the short term.

- A tension/anxiety/depression cycle sets in; the victim may self-medicate with alcohol or drugs. An advocate needs to be firm about self-destructive behaviors. That is when medical professionals may need to be employed. A trusted family doctor is a good place to start. Some mental health professionals commonly called "MHPs," suffer sullied reputations from being court appointed and then appear to have violated ethical standards. Mental health professionals need to be carefully selected according to their reputations of ethical and professional behavior (Neustein, 2005).

- Fear is the main motivator of life's decisions. The victim becomes hyper-reactive, hyper-vigilant, and obsessive. An advocate can help the client deal with OCH – Obsessive Compulsive Hyper-vigilance using the steps in Chapter 10, "Obsession-Compulsive-Hypervigilance."

- Physical changes take place as stressors continue to pound away at those victims who try to stand up for themselves. They should be referred to medical professionals if it appears that somatic conditions are developing as a result of stress (van der Kolk, 1996).

- Eighty-five percent of victims will manifest physical symptoms (AMA, 2009). They should be encouraged to implement a healthy diet and physical regimen to bolster the immune system. It helps for advocates to know local health professionals who are sensitive to litigation stress.

Litigants suffering PTSD/LAS often complain of exhaustion, weight gain or loss, inflammatory conditions, digestion problems, hair loss, insomnia, and worsening of any existing physical condition.

Health problems are invariably complicated by unrelenting stress. There is significant evidence that fat in the diet, cigarette smoking, salt, and lack of exercise have much less to do with coronary heart disease and other stress-related illnesses than do rage, anger, and frustration (Courtois p. 17).

Helping the Justice System Help Itself:
Certified ADA Advocates As Part of the Litigation Team

Litigants with disabilities often need advocates in addition to legal counsel. Advocates manage the extra-legal symptoms freeing the attorney to concentrate on the legal aspects of the case. The role of the advocate is the missing link in the judicial system reforming to provide justice for all people. Advocates take on even a more important role if litigants do not have attorneys. In that event, their role as supportive counselor is greatly enhanced. Advocates serve a unique and critical function in implementing the Americans with Disabilities Act to secure equal access. Opposing counsel will sometimes accuse them of unlicensed practice of law; however, the law is clear that an advocate simply ensuring the functionality of the client is protected under the ADAAA against all harassment, retaliation, false accusations and, when brought to the court's attentions, a stop is generally put to such tactics.

The ADA as amended by the ADAAA 42 U.S.C. § 12101 et. seq. Findings and purposes: *Congress intended that the original Act [ADA] provide a clear and comprehensive national mandate for the elimination of discrimination against individuals with disabilities and provide broad coverage.* 42 U.S.C. 12201(d), continues with the following statement assuring that LWDs have individual choice in managing accommodations that best offset their disabilities. *Nothing in this Act shall be construed to require an individual with a disability to accept an accommodation, aid, service, opportunity, or benefit which such individual chooses not to accept that violates this protective provision.*" In other words, a person must not be forced to accept restrictive accommodations such as residential care rather than accommodations or removal of custody of children from a mother suffering from cancer versus accommodations allowing the PWD the greatest degree of dignity and independence.

Therefore, there is a firm foundation for Certified Americans with Disabilities Act Advocate(s) (CADAA) to ensure that those with limited language proficiency (LLPs) are accurately heard during legal proceedings. Unless the PWD is able to effectively express themselves, they are apt to be over restricted on the one hand or fall through the cracks of justice on the other. The Federal Rules of Civil Procedures (FRCP) also provides support for this argument; Rule 17, "Next Friend" – A next friend is a person who represents *someone who is unable to tend to his or her own interest* – precisely as a CADAA does.

At issue is whether or not an LWD has the right under law to have a CADAA speak on their behalf, in their place, or for them in court when they are symptomatic, unable to respond, articulate grievances, or defend themselves. Prior to the ADAAA, John W. Parry , J.D. and forensic psychologist, & Eric Drogin, JD, PhD, ABPP (Forensic), in 2007, illustrates the limitations of ADA prior to the Amendments Act of 2008 when they wrote on what constituted a person's ability to communicate in court in *Mental Disability Law, Evidence and Testimony: A Comprehensive Reference Manual for Lawyers, Judges and Mental Disability*, still available. Their point of view, at that time, reflects a lack of concern for equal access to a fair hearing and ignorance of various characteristics related to the specific invisible disabilities. "There are no specific tools to measure communication abilities in the context of testimonial capacity per se (Parry, 2010)." They go on to say that such abilities are measured by the witnesses, judge, and jury with little need for expert testimony (197).

So, where does that leave the question of the law regarding a CADAA speaking on behalf of a disabled person in court? Today, litigants with diagnosed PTSD are protected under the law, but routinely face the harsh reality that "the law often insists on definitive black and white standards, levels of certainty, and thresholds (Parry, 2008)." It is a slippery slope from this black and white version to the interpreting of the deliberately vague ADAAA. In Parry's 2008 opinion, "The ADA Amendments Act of 2008: Analysis and Commentary," authors John W. Parry and Amy L. Allbright write, "The amendments strongly encourage the regulatory agencies and the courts to interpret the disability definition in a manner that will benefit as many people with disabilities as possible. For these accomplishments, Congress should be applauded (Parry, 2008)." As an advocate and forensic specialist, the court, the ADA Coordinators, lawyers, the judges, and the LWD jockey to read into this act what suits their interests. It is a tour de force as whatever happens—is allowed in court— sets precedent for the LWDs of the future. Ideally, attorneys and judges will see that unnecessary hardships can be eliminated through small non-threatening accommodations. CADAAs, without a license to practice law, intend only to help LWDs suffering from limited language proficiency due to brain reaction to their trauma or disability.

An ADA advocate is someone who will serve the litigant in the worst of times and take time to know the litigant in the context of the ADA protections available. The advocate chosen can be a trusted friend, a family member, or a professionally trained and certified advocate who can ensure that the litigant with a disability has access to needed accommodations. A good reason to select a certified advocate rests in the fact that the litigant with a disability must be confident that the advocate is a specialist in their position and they are willing to protect the litigant against intimidation and denial of the litigant's right to due process of law. This effort can be a daunting challenge demanding the education of many clerks, lawyers, and judges to arrange requested accommodations.

Passed in 1990, the ADA is a relatively new law. Therefore, it is mostly an unfunded mandate. Training has been spotty at best among judicial personnel. Thus, implementation has been slow. No one can depend on a particular court to be prepared to properly accommodate an LWD. Often the court personnel must be informed of ADAAA requirements, rules, policies, and procedures as a matter of course. If the advocate is not educated as to the law and sure of him or herself while staying firm with the court, the advocate or the litigant can be bluffed or misdirected and lose access to the court. Trained advocates may be hired on an as-needed basis or retained for a long-term relationship.

Throughout this book I discuss the model I have developed for the training of advocates. The ADA advocate performs a many faceted job involving supportive counseling and liaison work, court assistance, as well as creative design and arrangement of appropriate accommodations. Therefore, this book discusses specific considerations clarifying the services a typical advocate usually performs. As litigants' needs vary, an advocate must be flexible and familiar with how a litigant's disability may manifest within the judicial setting. This understanding is crucial to building and maintaining a successful relationship that works for both the advocate and the client.

Litigants suffering from PTSD/LAS often have their "legal arms" held behind their backs by opposing counsel or the court causing them to feel powerless and exacerbating their hostage mindset (Herman, 1997). The litigant needs supportive help and insight as to this power differential. The court has the power to compensate financial or emotional losses, impose sanctions, set the parameters of child custody, and all matters related to livelihood and wellbeing. Often ADA advocates encounter clients at all levels of the litigation process who are already feeling betrayed by lawyers, regulators, and other professional pillars of the community.

Most importantly, these circumstances require that the advocate be patient and possess knowledge as to the trauma that lends toward troubling behaviors. The advocate often enters the case just as the litigant's psyche may be taking a detour. In such moments, the litigant may feel thunderstruck and be undergoing physiological changes and intense feelings of helplessness. The litigant's ability to cope has been overwhelmed. They feel stark fear unleashed by cumulative psychological injuries and losses. Over time, symptoms often worsen. The advocate will be called upon to provide resources for "legal first-aid," but it may take more than advocacy if the litigation is protracted and there is no on-going relief for the litigant. In extreme circumstances, the advocate needs to be able to see the signs that indicate a referral to medical or mental health professional may be necessary.

Advocates witness first hand times of emotional meltdown of litigants with disabilities. Human beings rely on the justice system to function fairly and equitably allowing them a reasonable sense of safety against oppression and anarchy. Without that healthy sense of safety, psychological mechanisms of denial kick in to protect the litigant from the terror of their vulnerability that to them feels like impending doom. When litigants with PTSD/LAS dissociate from reality, they shun the present moment, have trouble listening, and often cannot speak or communicate effectively. Flash back just for a moment to the schoolyard, how many times have you heard that a student just "won't listen." Understanding the dynamics of the schoolyard can give you a direct parallel to understand what happens in litigation. Wherever the rules against predatory behavior and bullying are not enforced, victims are left in the wake. This normal reaction to extreme stress can cost a litigant dearly in court. Their freeze and/or flight reactions primitively protect them while authority does them in often inadvertently.

Moving parallel with the litigant's denial, is the reintroduction in court of trauma that compounds and freshens the wound sometimes for years on end. For anyone, the typical normal reaction to such pain is avoidance, inability to listen, amnesic moments, and being momentarily dumbstruck during litigation. It is a cycle that washes litigants out of the legal system especially those with disabilities such as PTSD.

Advocates Become the Interpreter Communicating for the LWD

Many of the assaults during litigation are verbal conflicts and difficult for the court to sort out. The advocate is in the best position to communicate to the court the accommodations that will limit emotional abuse during litigation. They can point out to the court that verbally abusive behavior is "psychic on psychic abuse" in any context (Gillin, 2007). Whether on a playground, on the job, or in a courtroom, cruel words and body language are intimidating and injurious–particularly to individuals who believe they are at a disadvantage. Without assistance, there is a piling on of one frustration after another that multiplies the sufferer's stress and exacerbates the PTSD/LAS.[2]

Advocates and litigants can learn to note pertinent symptoms and to use the core of this book, Huffer's 8-Steps that I developed in 1995, to allay them. This book includes additional current research further supporting effective identification and treatment strategies for PTSD/LAS. The steps remain intact and have been updated and perfected reflecting my experiences with patients and the impact of the ADA in court over the past fifteen years. The eight chapters explaining the steps now include samples of how clients can benefit from recognition of their symptoms, use specific steps to reduce their vulnerability, and with some, opt to use an advocate. Having this insight into a disabled litigant's symptoms is crucial when adapting the Huffer's 8-Steps to strengthening self. Nothing is easy or instant. For advocates, the steps tend to be cumulative in helping clients and some steps may need to be repeated several times.

Huffer's Log

Huffer's Log recounts ongoing and past cases (with consideration for legal protection) chosen for their application of a particular step. The lives cited reflect various degrees of use and success. The logs outline the event(s) that lead to the need for legal and therapeutic intervention. As the protection of the ADAAA and implementation of Huffer's 8-Step protocol frame my work, the cases cited are to such a degree of psychic trauma as to warrant its, ADAAA, application. My cart, my heart, overflows with requests for help with unending stories of mind-bending personal tragedies coming out of the court system. The logs help us to analyze where we need to go with the ADAAA and my protocols just to provide the level of protection required to function in court. Civilizing our judicial system and accommodating its users are my goals.

---

[2]Using a method of Data Analysis for informing the judge of the difference between adversarial issues of the case and pointing out abusive verbal attacks on a litigant with disabilities an ADA Advocate can address these issues.

Case Example of Using an Advocate

The following true account exemplifies why unrepresented litigants benefit from the ADA accommodation permitting the use of an advocate:

Libby, who chose to employ an advocate, cycled through stages of going to bed and staying in a fetal position for days on end. When she got up, she was effective, smart, and focused. Although she fell behind in the legal process, she could get caught up. These were the good days to prepare for her lawsuit. Then, Libby's adversary would serve papers that impacted Libby like a sledgehammer to her head. She would emotionally reel and soon be back in the fetal position. Without her advocate to continue the required actions of her case as her liaison, Libby's case would have died of attrition or been dismissed by the court. She would have been denied due process of law and denied her 14th amendment right to equal treatment under the law. As with many advocates, Libby's held a Power of Attorney to act in her behalf if needed.

While Libby suffers with PTSD, her ex-husband, her abuser/ adversary, keeps filing punitive actions and using the court to remind her of the domestic violence that caused the divorce and legal action in the first place. Of the two, she has the strongest case; however, she loses spirit and initiative when she is symptomatic. Just seeing her abuser in court makes her unable to concentrate, to speak, or to remember. Her brain floods with the terrible things that he said to her since he decided to "dump her" like trash and deprive her of all assets including contact with their children. She has no lawyer because the cost of keeping lawyers waiting during PTSD symptoms becomes prohibitively expensive as a practical matter. Several have quit on her when she was symptomatic.

Libby's advocate must help her work slowly through the steps outlined in this book to reduce her symptoms and litigate more effectively and consistently. But, such healing takes time in the face of her adversary's schemes and perceived competency in court. Because her adversary does not suffer from her symptoms but causes them, he maintains his unfair advantage.

Author's Notes:

When the word "you" is used below, it is assumed the litigant will have the assistance of an advocate.

Filtering through the voluminous material on the ADA, www.lvaallc.com will maintain a resource section listing the most pertinent material for ADA advocates under Titles II and III for invisible disabilities.

The following legal tips put the burden on the litigant to study and know their cases. From the outset, those who are traumatized are placed at a disadvantage because these rules, laws, and memories will in many instances block the litigant's ability to be effective in litigation. Attorneys are not schooled to handle disabilities. The pressure on lawyers and hourly fees defy the practicality of lawyers being the advocate used to sort out the seminal issues in the case. They get impatient from client's symptoms coupled with clients running out of money before they get to court.

Once you are involved in litigation, whether you are suing or being sued, you cannot assume your lawyer will simply take care of the matter without any participation from you. And if you are proceeding without a lawyer, you need to be even more vigilant. In fact, either way, you will need to remain intimately involved for the duration of your case. In essence, it's a simple matter of mathematics: Your judge may have a few hundred cases on his or her docket; your lawyer will be working on a few dozen cases at any given time; but for you, your case is (or should be) the center of your attention and the focus of 100% of your litigation efforts.

If so, your work is cut out for you. As quickly as possible, you should gather all of the "intelligence information" about your case and attempt to understand the statutes and rules that govern your case. Some of these tasks include:

1. Look up the judge on the internet to determine his or her background generally, what he or she did as an attorney, and what appeals he or she may have been involved in. Find other litigants who have had the same judge and get their impressions of the judge's performance, biases, and other characteristics and experience.

2. Look up the opposing attorney on the state bar website and perform internet searches to determine his or her background generally, his or her experience and special experience as an attorney, what cases similar to yours he or she may have been involved in, and what appeals he or she has participated in. Ask the clerks you encounter if they know anything about the opposing lawyer that may be of interest to you. Their impressions may give you a hint as to what type of adversary you have.

3. Visit your local law library (at the courthouse or a local law school) and ask the librarian to assist you in finding following kinds of resources:

   a. The statute or statutes that govern the lawsuit in which you are involved;

   b. The rules of civil procedure for the state in which you live;

   c. The "local rules" of court for the particular court in which your case will be tried;

   d. Any "civil forms" manuals that may be appropriate for the case in which you are involved;

   e. The "civil trial rules" for your state;

   f. The "rules of civil evidence" for your state;

   g. Any reference books for "causes of action pleadings manuals" that are appropriate for the case in which you are involved; and,

   h. Any other references the librarian suggests that might be of help in understanding the litigation process or preparing materials for your case.

4. Look on the internet for ADAAA materials applicable to your state AND the particular court in which you are involved. Look particularly for local and state resources that will

help you in obtaining ADAAA accommodations. You should be able to find the persons responsible for properly implementing the ADAAA at the state level, and the persons that are locally responsible for providing ADAAA accommodations for the court in which your case will be tried.

5.   Make a list of the accommodations you believe you will need to have a fair and equitable experience in the court to which your case as been assigned.

For an example of the types of resources that are available to you on the internet, see the California ADAAA site: http://www.disabilityaccessinfo.ca.gov/goverment.htm There should be a similar site for your state's resources as well (Goldblatt)©.

Remember, this is neither an exercise in "literature collection" nor a pointless effort. The statutes, rules, and requirements you are reading about will be governing your life for the foreseeable future–maybe for years. So the more you know about them and the better you understand their meanings, the more likely you will be to prevail in court–or at least avoid having the opposing attorney pull a fast one that you find out about only after it's too late to do anything about it (Goldblatt)©.

Find the materials and either copy them at the library or buy them through a local bookstore or off the internet. Then READ them carefully and thoroughly. It may be tough going at first, but if you keep at it, you'll learn to "speak litigation" as a first step in protecting yourself from the dangers and frustrations of litigation. The more diligently you pursue the knowledge, the more likely you are to prevail. So stay with it (Goldblatt)©.

References

The American Bar Association. (1998). *The American Bar*. Retrieved January 24, 2000 From http://www.abanow.org

American Psychiatric Association (2000). Diagnostic and Statistical Manual of Mental Disorders. (DSM-IV-TR).

Americans with Disabilities Act Amendments Act of 2008, 42 U.S.C. §§ 12101 *et seq.*

Bremner, J. D. et al. (1995). MRI-based measurement of hippocampal volume in patients with combat-related posttraumatic stress disorder. *Am. J. Psychiatry, 152(7)*, 973-981.

Clark, R. et al. (2003). Cerebral function in posttraumatic stress disorder during verbal working memory upgrading: a positron emission tomography study. *Journal of Biological Psychiatry, 53*, 474-481.

Courtois, C., & Ford, J. (eds.). (2009). *Treating Complex Traumatic Stress Disorders: An Evidence-Based Guide*, 16, 90. NY. Guilford Press.

Damasio, A. (1999). *The Feeling of What Happens: Body and Emotion in the Making of Consciousness.* (pp. 35-7). New York: Harcourt Brace.

Gillin, M., & Associates. (2007, Spring). Workplace Injuries. (pp. 1). Pennsylvania Legal Update. Retrieved from gillinandassociates.lawoffice.com/newsletter.htm.

Harris Interactive (2010). Survey of Employment of Americans with Disabilities. Kessler Foundation/NOD. Fieldwork: March-April, 2010.

Harthill, S. (2010). The Need for a Revitalized Regulatory Scheme to Address Workplace Bullying in the United States: Harnessing the Federal Occupational Safety and Health Act. *University of Cincinnati Law Review, 78.4*, 1250-1306.

Health Insurance Portability and Accountability Act of 1996 (HIPAA), 42 U.S.C. § 300gg *et seq.*

Herman, J. L. (1997). *Trauma and Recovery.* (pp. 74-95). New York: Basic Books.

Huffer, K. PhD. (1995). *Overcoming the Devastation of Legal Abuse Syndrome.* US: Fulkort Press.

Hull, A. M. (2002). Neuro-Imaging Findings in Post-Traumatic Stress Disorder. *British Journal of Psychiatry, 181*, 102-10.

Katz, E., & DeRose, R. (2011, January). A Call to Action: The 2010 Survey of Employment of Americans With Disabilities. *J Spinal Cord Med. 34(1)*, 4–5. doi: 10.1179/107902610X12 931186126969.

Korn, D. (2009). EMDR and the Treatment of Complex PTSD: A Review. *Journal of EMDR Practice and Research, 3(4)*, 264. doi: 10.1891/1933-3196.3.4.264.

Lindauer, R. et al. (2004). Cerebral Blood Flow Changes During Script Driven Imagery in Police Officers with Posttraumatic Stress Disorder. *Biological Psychiatry, 56(11)*, 853-61.

Neustein, A. & Lesher, M. (2005). *From Madness to Mutiny: Why Mothers are Running from the Family Courts—And What Can Be Done About It.* (pp. 225-35). Boston, MA: Northeastern University Press.

Parry, J. & Allbright, A.L. (2008). *The ADA Amendment Act of 2008: Analysis and Commentary.* Publisher: ABA.

Parry, J. & Drogin, E. (2010). *Mental Disability Law, Evidence and Testimony: A Comprehensive Reference Manual for Lawyers, Judges and Mental Disability.* Publisher: ABA, 197.

Pennsylvania Legal Update. (2007, Spring) Available through the Pennsylvania Workers Compensation Updates.

Stark, E. (2007). *Coercive Control: How Men Entrap Women in Personal Life.* NY: Oxford University Press, 2310-14.

Tennessee v. Lane, 541 U.S. 509 (2004).

United Nations Enable (2007). Disability and Employment. Retrieved from http://www.un.org/ disabilities/default.asp?id=255.

United Nations Enable (2010). Fact Sheet on Persons with Disabilities: Overview. Retrieved from www.un.org/disabilities/documents/toolaction/pwdfs.pdf.

van der Kolk, B. A. (2006). Clinical Implications of Neuroscience Research in PTSD. *Academy of Sciences*. 1-17. doi:10.1196/annals.1364.022.

van der Kolk, B. A. (2004, Jan/Feb). In the Eye of the Storm. *The Psychotherapy Networker, 45, 66.*

van der Kolk, B. A., McFarlane, A., & Wallerstein, L. (Eds.). (1996). *Traumatic Stress: The Effects of Overwhelming Experience on Mind, Body, and Society.* (pp. 220-241). New York: Guilford Press.

CHAPTER 3

MEETING ETHICAL DEMANDS OF THE ADAAA

There is an intended ethical and administrative mandate for directing persons with disabilities toward equal access to the court. We are in an age with vast reasonable resources for accommodating court users. Litigants can appear by telephone, Skype, or other means relieving the qualifying burden. Those with disfigurement and invisible disabilities should no longer be subjected to additional burdens, ridicule, and inadvertent exploitation of their disabilities directly denying their participatory and testimonial access to the proceedings. A new social model providing a shift that automatically responds to the reasonable functional needs of every person in all public services must be adopted and enforced. Certified ADA Advocates (CADAA) provide the services that assure compliance with the intended ethical administrative requirements.

Any Civilized Culture Must Address the Causes of Human Suffering.

Alexander McFarlane, 2004

Overview

I developed in my capacity as Associate Professor of Counseling and Forensic Psychology, two courses. One trains and certifies ADA advocates. Advocates can then train on a higher tier to become Certified Forensic Disability Specialists. One services the client during litigation and the Forensic Disability Specialists is an analyst and leader in the effort to improve delivery of service at the policy level. *Unlocking Justice*, in an expanded form, serves as the basic training manual for these courses. Advocates fill a much needed gap in delivering the accommodations necessary for equal access to the courts. Many times advocates find that the administrative process mandated to be set up in each court for arranging accommodations for litigation is not apparent or user friendly without advocacy. Worse, attorneys sometimes advise their clients against requesting such accommodations out of fear of judicial discrimination.

Advocates especially need to intervene when judges allow ridicule under the pretext of "zealous representation" assisting the opposition to declare "open season" on the litigant suffering from disabilities. Opposing counsel then misleads the court with falsehoods viciously attacking the disabled litigant. The worst of them attempt to intimidate and attack those who help the disabled as well. They try to intimidate me by threatening to bring actions of practicing "law without a license." They depose the disabled litigant's lawyers steadily encroaching on privileged territory undermining the lawyer-client relationship. Fortunately, the ADA laws have strong protections for advocates as well as the disabled. These legal protections allow ADA advocates to tackle these injustices head on.

When the ADAAA and its former related laws were passed, the role of the advocate was left to broad interpretation, but that is not the case today when it comes to protection of those who advocate for persons with disabilities. The law is crisp and clear about protecting ADAAA advocates from harassment, intimidation, or any attempt to interfere with their advocating for those with special needs.

Congress saw fit to pass federal law, 42 U.S.C. 12203 *et.seq*. protecting advocates against any and all retaliation, coercion, threats and intimidation, specifically stating, "It shall be unlawful to coerce, intimidate, threaten, or interfere with any individual in the exercise or enjoyment of, or on account of his or her having exercised or enjoyed, or on account of his or her having aided or encouraged any other individual in the exercise or enjoyment of, any right granted or protected by this chapter." Further, "No litigant is to be forced to accept an accommodation preventing the advocate or attorney-in-fact from acting fully and completely in the best interest of the litigant pursuant to 42 U.S.C. 12201."

There is sometimes discomfort and awkwardness encountered when the ADA advocate attempts to help the litigant get their accommodations. This is reflective of the newness of the law in that many courts are unfamiliar with accommodating invisible disabilities. If official forms exist for applying for accommodations, they are usually inadequate. Wheelchairs, magnifiers, and accommodations for hearing impaired are listed, but no other type of disability is usually contemplated. Commonly, many litigants with disabilities cannot even get through the application procedure without the assistance of an advocate.

CADAA act under the ADAAA similarly to special education teachers simply carrying out the law for the intended recipient. Before the ADA and other federal laws designed to protect them, children who suffered from disabilities were not accommodated in schools. They were humiliated by being symbolically put on a stool in the corner of the classroom excluded from class interaction and made to wear a dunce cap. Unfortunately, today's litigants, who suffer from disabilities and especially when they have no attorney, are vulnerable to the same types of discrimination, exploitation, humiliation, taunting, and bullying. In terms of systemic cruelty to litigants, the courts seem to have a blind spot and treat the pro se and/or disabled litigants with the same "dunce" status that damaged students not so many years ago.

Ridicule and cruel words have been progressively discouraged in society since the civil rights movement. However, the courtroom still allows shocking and false accusations. From this perspective, I determined that the strengths of the individual were my focal point and that a social model of treating individuals fairly matter most. The social model is long overdue in our courts of law allowing reasonable accommodations to all people to assure a fair day in court. The medical model presently used is not working and is discriminatory. Fostering the transition from medical to social models is a major purpose of this work.

The rise of the civil rights movement awakened consciousness as to the many guaranteed rights denied various segments of society. Martin Luther King opened a door through which excluded groups other than Black Americans are still marching. The disability rights movement is but one. This civil rights awakening brought to new light a long history of denial of rights faced by individuals with disabilities. Their worst difficulties are not caused so much by their impairments but rather by the social treatment they encounter.

Early on, supporters of the ADA envisioned more of a social model rather than medical model where the burden was on society to fairly include those with disabilities in broad terms. In fact, that was Congress's intention in passing the original Americans with Disabilities Act. During the Reagan years, impediments to individuals being independent and economically self-sufficient took center stage. It was a push away from Government benefits and toward self-support and independent living.

The social model fits this thrust as well because it supports all human beings regardless of functional impairment emphasizing their strengths. The first drafts of the ADA clearly emphasized prohibiting discrimination on the basis of disability. However, unforeseen was that by medically separating out a class of citizens they would eventually have to "prove" their disability in order to avoid discrimination in public services. All precedent to 1990 supports that disability is a socially constructed phenomenon as diverse as the more than 43,000,000 Americans who suffer from some impairment. Broad and accepting parameters were put forth. The objective is self-sufficiency.

It was against this backdrop that the Americans with Disabilities Amendments Act was passed in 2008 and went into full effect on January 1, 2009. The purpose of this Act was to override four cases wherein the Supreme Court had narrowed the scope of what qualified as a disabling condition. Congress reinstated a broad scope of protection to be available under the ADA, rejecting Supreme Court decisions forcing the Equal Employment Opportunity Commission to revise its regulations and redefine the terms "substantially limits" and "significantly restricted."

Those with disabilities cannot be expected to overcome extra barriers as they seek their civil rights under the ADAAA. Professionals who serve persons with disabilities and judicial personnel have ethical and moral duties to help provide relief for a disabled litigant. That means educating such litigants about their opportunities under ADAAA and assisting them through the process for obtaining their accommodations. Unfortunately, most do not. This creates a profound need for advocates willing to take on this job.

With the ADAAA in full force as of January 1, 2009, the courts now have a legal obligation to provide all litigants with equal accommodations that ensure full access to the justice system. This chapter explains the basic law and discusses how it can be implemented in litigation. Simplified with emphasis on practical "how to" knowledge, academic legal literature on disability is synthesized to focus on the reality of the litigant with a disability intersecting with the legal system. The very habits and customs of the litigation process are examined from the perspective of the many times unrepresented citizens with disabilities need to use their judicial system.

The ADA advocate is aware of the ADAAA and its implications in providing a feasible environment and set of procedures that level the playing field for the litigant. Modes of persuasion and power used during litigation have too often evolved into mean exploitation of disabilities during legal actions. It seems that the invisible disabilities have been neglected in the working body of legal knowledge about disability and the ADA. The realities of implementing the ADAAA to ensure inclusion and equality for invisible disabilities are explored below.

Unbending Ethical Obligations under the Americans with Disabilities Act (ADA), Titles II and III and the Americans with Disabilities Act Amendments Act of 2008 (ADAAA)

Certified ADA advocates have become indispensable to the ADA Accommodations process. They assist attorneys and clients in meeting ethical and legal requirements imposed by the ADAAA. Advocates must overcome the faulty thinking that litigants with disabilities both demand equal rights and special services as though the two are not interdependent. The seismic paradigm shift needed here is that it is the special services or accommodations in procedure that provide equal rights. It is not an inconsistency. Obtaining their requested ADAAA accommodations is necessary for equal access to the legal system.

ADA advocates, as a matter of their work, educate while they execute the process necessary to establish effective accommodations for the litigant. It is not uncommon for advocates to be greeted by barriers in the form of biases that are deeply entrenched with roots going well back into Western history. Certain religious views are still influencing the treatment of some disabled individuals. Disabilities have been and are still, in some circles, attributed to moral failings. Those who have disabilities suffer from societal attitudes as primitive as believing they are sinners paying for their sinful ways through their impairments. Litigants have difficulty enough without the extra job of formally requesting accommodations in today's inconsistent system. Advocacy makes the difference. The ultimate advocacy will be the social model.

The ADA is divided into five sections. Title II is the most important for the purposes of this work since it encompasses all courts. Title II addresses access to public services for all disabilities whether apparent or not. It provides that "no qualified individual with a disability shall, by reason of such disability be excluded from participation in or be denied the benefits of the services, programs, or activities of a public entity, or be subject to discrimination by any such entity." But, while disabled people have a right to participate in all services offered by the courts, accessing those rights and overcoming obstacles is a rocky road for litigants with special needs.

Limitations of the Medical Model for Qualifying Accommodations

There are numerous flaws in the Medical Model for qualifying accommodations. The ADA Coordinator appointed at the trial court level often determines whether or not accommodations are allowed usually using a Medical Model. This model conceptualizes disabilities in medical terms. Individuals with disabilities are viewed as having medical "problems" that can be diagnosed, treated, and managed by medical practitioners. It is interesting that those without medical credentials, law clerks, judges, lawyers, and other legal personnel, are assigned a duty outside of their areas of expertise. These unqualified determiners react within an inconsistent range from disgust, impatience, and disdain to pity, forced treatment, and violations of privacy rights. But, sometimes they sincerely, willingly, and kindly accommodate disabilities during litigation. It is an uncertain obstacle course for the person with disabilities that adds a burden of anxiety and extra work for the litigant already impaired and seeking relief. Andy Imparato CEO states that "the bigger problem is that most DC based disability organization are not controlled by disabled people and often lack the insight that comes from first person experience (Imparato, 2011).

Example of Barriers to Access with Current Medical Model

Georgia, a pretty blond lady with a generous heart, suffered from multiple diagnoses. Her psychiatrist wrote a letter instructing the judge to assist her when she became symptomatic during litigation from bipolar disorder, depression, and anxiety all exacerbated by litigation. Yet, not one person among legal professionals (judge, bailiffs, or clerks) sent her to the ADA Coordinator or even explained how to get there. Her church pastor even came to court pleading for help for her to no avail. The rule in Georgia's court was (and still is), "If you don't find out and inform the court of the rule, you will stay ignorant of the procedure regardless of the waste of court resources, denial of due process of law, and preventable pain."

In 2002, the American Bar Association House of Delegates passed a resolution urging all courts to make their services accessible. They included "all impairments" whether obvious or invisible (Hurder, 772). Therefore, the Congress, the American Bar Association, and the United States Department of Justice all formally stand behind equal accessibility to court services.

The first step is obviously providing clear, published, and understandable information educating persons with special needs regarding what accommodations are available and how to obtain them. Advocates are indispensable in this role. They can help explain and interpret the rules and help the litigant to determine what accommodations they may need to have a level playing field. This assistance allows disabled litigants to make informed decisions about using such accommodations or not. The advocate is the key liaison responsible to see that the courts respect litigants' rights.

Social Model for Qualifying Disabilities for Approval of Accommodations

Courts are obligated to provide reasonable modifications in policies, practices, and procedures that would otherwise deny a person with a disability equal access to services, unless the modification would fundamentally alter the services provided. There is a movement afoot to implement the "Social Model," supported by the American Bar Association and the United States Department of Justice, to simply integrate humane processes, sensitive treatment, and reasonable alterations for all persons as a matter of public service. Accessible physical facilities already are in the spotlight and being addressed. Massachusetts Supreme Court in 2010 ruled that invisible disabilities must be accommodated as well. Participatory and testimonial access is now being recognized.

The Social Model acknowledges that at any moment a person can be rendered disabled especially in an aging population. A social model is much more in step with the ADAAA (Peyton, 2009). There is no question after the passage of ADAAA of 2008 that persons with disabilities are to be respectfully included, accommodated, supported, and accepted in the mainstream as much as humanly possible as a matter public policy.

Separating persons with disabilities should be restricted to only those cases where the integration into the whole is impossible. Persons with disabilities cannot be required to participate in separate services, or punished for their disability. Under the law, their adversary is not to have knowledge of private medical information and certainly cannot challenge the existence of an impairment or litigate the existence of that impairment in open court. Further, exploitation cannot be used as a means to gain advantage in the case. No court personnel are to ask about the disability. They may only discuss needed accommodations in the light of the need for them. Courts may not charge for accommodations but may be billed for reasonable accommodations. Specific provisions of the ADA are outlined below in response to some frequently asked questions. Although the law provides that accommodations are provided at the expense of court funding, we have never had an accommodation approved where expense had to be borne by the court except for the physical accommodations referenced above.

Questions Regarding ADAAA Title II and Title III

The judicial system is a public service guaranteeing equal access to persons with disabilities. The lawyers and other private entities that serve the public, integral to litigation, are covered under Title III, private entities serving the public, and bound by the same duty to provide equal services for special needs litigants.

What Is a "Disability" under This Law?

The term disability is defined in ADAAA as:

1. a physical or mental impairment that substantially limits one or more of the major life activities of such individual,

2. a record of such an impairment, or

3. being regarded as having such an impairment, 42 USC §12101(2).

Will invoking the ADA Protect Me or Hurt Me in Court?

ADAAA provides that "no qualified individual with a disability shall, by reason of such disability, be excluded from participation in or be denied the benefits of the services, programs, or activities of a public entity, or be subjected to discrimination by any such entity" 42 U.S.C. §12132.

What Is Meant by "Qualified Individual with a Disability"?

An individual with a disability, visible or invisible, who, without reasonable modifications to rules, policies, or practices, the removal of architectural, communication, or transportation barriers, or the provision of auxiliary aids and services, meets the essential eligibility requirements for the receipt of services or the participation in programs or activities provided by a public entity, 42 U.S.C. §12131(2).

What Is a Public Entity?

The law defines a public entity as:

4. any state or local government

5. any department, agency, special purpose district, or other instrumentality of a State or States or local government. The term "State" means each of the several States, the District of Columbia, the Commonwealth of Puerto Rico, Guam, American Samoa, the Virgin Islands, the Trust Territory of the Pacific Islands, and the Commonwealth of the Northern Mariana Islands, 42 U.S.C. §12101(3).

Is My State or Its Employees Immune from a Lawsuit?

No, the United States Supreme Court made it clear in *Tennessee v. Lane*, 541 US 509 (2004), that:

"A State shall not be immune under the Eleventh Amendment to the Constitution of the United States from an action in federal or State court of competent jurisdiction for a violation of this chapter. In any action against a State for a violation of the requirements of this chapter, remedies (including remedies both at law and in equity) are available for such a violation to the same extent as such remedies are available for such a violation in an action against any public or private entity other than a State, 42 U.S.C. §12202."

What if I Am Discriminated Against?

You can contact a lawyer or you can file a complaint by using the Department of Justice Title II Complaint Form, OMB No. 1190-0009 with the U.S. Department of Justice, Civil Rights Division, and Disability Rights Section. The ADAAA identifies the remedial provisions and procedures for discrimination:

"The remedies, procedures, and rights set forth in 29 U.S.C. 794(a) shall be the remedies, procedures, and rights the ADA provides to any person alleging discrimination on the basis of disability, 42 U.S.C. §12133."

Title 29 U.S.C. §794(a) provides that:

"The remedies, procedures, and rights set forth in section 717 of the Civil Rights Act of 1964 (42 U.S.C. 2000e–16), including the application of sections 706 (f) through 706 (k) (42 U.S.C. 2000e–5 (f) through (k), shall be available, with respect to any complaint under section 791 of this title, to any employee or applicant for employment aggrieved by the final disposition of such complaint, or by the failure to take final action on such complaint."

In fashioning an equitable or affirmative action remedy under this section, a court may take into account the reasonableness of the cost of any necessary workplace accommodation, and the availability of alternatives or other appropriate relief in order to achieve an equitable and appropriate remedy. (Our clients often use employment examples or law applying it to litigation and the courts because it reflects substantial testing of the ADA laws.)

The remedies, procedures, and rights set forth in Title VI of the Civil Rights Act of 1964 [42 U.S.C. 2000d *et seq.*] are also available to any person aggrieved by any act or failure to act by any recipient of federal assistance or federal provider of such assistance under section 794 of the title.

In any action or proceeding to enforce or charge a violation of a provision of this subchapter, the court, in its discretion, may allow the prevailing party, other than the United States, a reasonable attorney's fee as part of the costs.

Will the Court Use my Complaint Against Me?

The ADA has its own built in protection against retaliation. Section 42 U.S.C. § 12203 states specifically that:

1. Retaliation - No person shall discriminate against any individual because such individual has opposed any act or practice made unlawful by this chapter or because such individual made a charge, testified, assisted, or participated in any manner in an investigation, proceeding, or hearing under this chapter.

2. Interference, coercion, or intimidation - It shall be unlawful to coerce, intimidate, threaten, or interfere with any individual in the exercise or enjoyment of, or on account of his or her having exercised or enjoyed, or on account of having aided or encouraged any other individual in the exercise or enjoyment of, any right granted or protected by this chapter.

3. Remedies and procedures - The remedies and procedures available under sections 12117, 12133, and 12188 of this title shall be available to aggrieved persons for violations of subsections (a) and (b) of this section, with respect to subchapter I, subchapter II and subchapter III of this chapter, respectively.[3]

Huffer's Log

Examples of Advocate Observations and Interventions

Cues indicating inability to concentrate, remember, speak, and generally lose functionality in the court can be extremely subtle. I watch the client to ensure breathing is regular, no new signs of extreme stress i.e. fist clenching, dry mouth, glazed eyes are present. If I observe these changes in the client, I call for a break and immediately address their level of functionality. The advocate's goal is to prevent symptoms that interfere with effective litigation. The advocate must be a diligent observer and listener to pick up on the cues timely.

One disabled litigant, Mary, regularly became symptomatic in court. She cried out sobbing. She begged for the hearing to end. She could not concentrate or stop talking. Once she got an ADA advocate, her ADA advocate, knowing she had ADHD and PTSD, obtained her ADA accommodations, stayed by her side, brought her strong coffee during breaks which extended the effects of her medication, and kept the judge cued as to when breaks were needed. The advocate protected Mary's functionality by seeing that her accommodations were in place and enforced.

The advocate also halted distracting and insulting comments to and about Mary from the adversary during the litigation. The advocate kept documents indexed and ready for Mary to use in her courtroom presentation. As a result, instead of crying, sobbing, vomiting, and losing concentration in the courtroom, as she had in the past, Mary was able to complete the day's litigation successfully. She finally had access. Prior to

---

[3] Contact information for the Department of Justice is available in Appendix B in the back of this book.

this court date, the judge was impatient and punitive with this woman who did not use courtroom decorum. ADA accommodations ended her status as dunce in the eyes of the court.

Use of this law is a personal choice of many who suffer from functional impairments. It is a powerful tool for litigants shoring up their performances. It defines for the court what the litigant's particular impairment requires for functionality. The client's psyche and medical condition is removed from the realm of the adversary who usually attempts to define the impairment in terms that discriminate and damage the person with the disability. Importantly, the ADAAA provides confidentiality preventing the psychology or disability of the impaired person to be fodder for distortion in public argument. In my experience, it has strengthened the disabled litigant's case when used properly.

Author's Notes:

Learning to use case law and legal authorities is no easy task. Yet, it is an absolutely necessary skill, because of the way the litigation game is played. Make no mistake. It is never enough to take an article about "what a case says" from the internet, or a magazine, or another secondary source, and expect a judge to accept it as authority to support the point you are trying to make. More important still: the case has to say what you say it does – and be directly related to the point you are trying to make. The initial thing to understand about basic legal research is that there are two categories of case law opinions: published and unpublished. Published opinions can be cited as "authority" that the court (theoretically, at least) is required to follow: unpublished opinions cannot be cited. This is an important distinction for two reasons: First, published opinions support your argument or rebut your opponent's argument. Second, you can use an unpublished opinion as "persuasive" authority, not "precedential" authority, and you can attack your opponent's use of unpublished cases and destroy his or her position if you know the difference and can identify a contradicting published case.

Next, it should be your strict policy to check each and every citation your opponent uses in any submission to the court to make sure that those citations contain the information (and authority) your opponent claims they do. Many lawyers (and *pro se* opponents) frequently cite cases that are not "on point" (or "inapposite" in "litigation speak"). Your ability to point out that an opponent's case does not say what he or she claims it does immediately tarnishes his or her credibility before the court while it enhances yours. Once you catch an opposing counsel or party using inapposite cases, you can bet it's a habit that will play out in your favor. So do the extra work and catch them at it every time you can.

The most common mistake most new litigants make (whether they have disabilities or not) is to assume they understand what they are reading when they are doing legal research. In some ways, you will be mastering a "new language." In legal writing, a given word can have its commonly understood meaning, it's meaning as defined in a legal dictionary, or it's meaning as defined in a statute or regulation. Sometimes all three are the same; oftentimes they are not. So make sure you understand that what you think you are reading needs to be verified in the source it comes from. If it's from a quotation of a statute's language, go read the statute. If it is not, check the legal dictionary definition, then the commonly understood definition.

Similarly, certain rules or legal concepts may vary depending on the kind of statute or authority that they come from. In one "code" (compilation of statutes, such as the Business and Professional Code, or the Real Estate Code, etc.) a word or concept may work one way, while it has a different effect under the authority of a different code. So make sure the statement you're making, or the concept you're explaining, is based on the proper authority from the proper code. Otherwise, you'll be more than embarrassed, you'll lose the point (and maybe the case).

Remember, if your adversary is opposing counsel, he or she has been to law school for three years and does for a living what you're trying to do. Effectively, you have the equivalent of three minutes experience and no training whatsoever. So be prepared to roll up your sleeves and play some serious catch up. If you can afford to hire a lawyer, make sure you find one that is willing to allow you to participate fully and learn as much as you can as you go along. If you can't afford a lawyer, find a legal secretary or a paralegal with good skills and a lot of experience to help you as much as you can afford. Otherwise, go to the local law library and be as courteous and polite as you can be to the librarian. If you're lucky (and pleasant, and ASK for help instead of demanding it), he or she is likely to be an important resource for you to get your case together.

The most important thing you have to remember about the application of the ADAAA is that the organizations administering it are required to provide you equal "access" to the facilities you require. They are NOT required to provide you with equal "justice." That means that once you are in court – and on a reasonably level playing field – you still have to make your case to the judge, or have a support team that can assist you in doing it or do it for you.

If you're proceeding *pro se,* you're standing in the shoes of a lawyer in the eyes of the court. Therefore, you have to know and follow the rules we talked about in the last chapter, and be able to use the authoritative resources of the legal system – statutes, regulations, case law, and legal treatises– discussed in this one to support your theory of why the judge (or jury) should rule for you instead of your adversary.

In one Supreme Court case on the issue, *School Board v. Arline,* 480 U.S. 273 (1987) the Court, per Justice Brennan, provides a broad interpretation of disability, finding that the Rehabilitation Act's definition could apply to a non-traditional disability such as a contagious disease.

Court personnel may not be up to date on the ADAAA of 2009. Originally, the court stood in the position of deciding whether or not the disability should be accommodated and often stringently vetted the litigant adding a discriminatory burden for litigants with disabilities. Examples, *Thornhill v. Marsh*, 866 F.2d 1182 (9th Cir. 1989) holds an individual may be both "handicapped" and "otherwise qualified" for the purposes of the Rehabilitation Act; and, *Katz v. City Metal Co.*, 87 F.3d 26 (1st Cir. 1996) holds that determining whether an individual is disabled must be made on an individual bases and is a question for the jury.

That attitude can no longer hold since the passage of the ADAAA.

Overridden by ADAAA of 2008, *Holihan v. Lucky Stores, Inc.*, 87 F.3d 362 (9th Cir. 1996) holds that a disability includes "being regarded as having a substantial limiting impairment." The litigant must simply report the basic functional impairments and needed accommodations. If they are reasonable, accommodations are to be granted. Examples are: Steven S. Locke, The Incredible Shrinking Protected Class: Redefining the Scope of Disability under the Americans with Disabilities Act, 68 U. Colo. L. Rev. 107 (1997); Arlene B. Mayerson, Restoring Regard for the "Regarded As" Prong: Giving Effect to Congressional Intent, 42 Vill. L. Rev. 587 (1997); Wendy Wilkinson, Judicially Crafted Barriers to Bringing Suit under the Americans with Disabilities Act, 38 S. Tex. L. Rev. 907 (1997). These attitudes led to the need for the ADAAA of 2008, implemented 2009.

Anita Silvers, Double Consciousness, Triple Difference: Disability, Race, Gender, and the Politics of Recognition, in Disability, Divers-Ability and Legal Change, 85 (Melinda Jones & Lee Ann Basser Marks eds. 1999). Anita Silvers, Formal Justice, in Disability, Difference, Discrimination: Perspectives on Justice in Bioethics and Public Policy, 13, 75 (Anita Silvers, et at eds., 1998). The social model of disability transforms the notion of 'handicapping condition' from a state of a minority of people, which disadvantages them in society, to a state of society, which disadvantages a minority of people. The social model traces the source of this minority's disadvantage to a hostile environment and treats the dysfunction attendant on (certain kinds of) impairment as artificial and remediable, not natural and immutable. *Id.* See also Richard K. Scotch, Models of Disability and the Americans with Disabilities Act, 21 Berkeley J. Emp. & Lab. L. 213 (2000).

Robert, L Jr. (1997) *"Substantially Limited" Protection from Disability Discrimination: The Special Treatment Model and Misconstructions of the Definition of Disability.* Vill. L. Rev., 42(2): 409 - 585. Burgdorf, Robert quoted ("A person may perform some mental or physical function in a way that falls short of most other people, but the limitations imposed upon that individual frequently result as much from the social context as from the impaired function itself.") A 1976 analysis of the definitions of disability and discrimination in Section 504 showing how the phrases "otherwise qualified" and "solely on the basis of a disability" produced problems. The "otherwise qualified" part of the definition means that a person with a disability who can do the job without a reasonable accommodation, but when the regulations were written, they specifically said that the "otherwise" would be disregarded.

These definitions led to problems in the courts. The ADA definition tries but does not escape these problems. Basically it is because the courts treat people with disabilities as being in a special class, but both statutes were written so that people with disabilities would be treated in an equal way (sometimes with adjustments which non-disabled people routinely receive).

49 U.S.C. §1301 (1994 & Supp. IV 1998), amended by General Aviation Revitalization Act of 1994, 49 U.S.C. § 40101 (1994 & Supp. IV 1998). Silvers cites the 1986 Air Carriers Act as legislation related to the ADA, which "offers added insight into the discrimination against disability that must be arrested if the disabled are to increase their social participation." Anita Silvers, *Disability Rights, in Encyclopedia of Applied Ethics* 781, 790 (Ruth Chadwick ed. 1998). See also Silvers, *supra* note 49, at 125.

Southeastern Cmty. Coll. v. Davis, 442 U.S. 397 (1979). Davis involved section 504 of the Rehabilitation Act of 1973 wherein Justice Powell wrote an opinion for a unanimous Court frequently using the language of affirmative conduct and affirmative action. He used this language in discussing the question of whether Southeastern was required under section 504 to modify their program to permit participation by the plaintiff and disabled people generally. Justice Powell stated, "situations may arise where a refusal to modify an existing program might become unreasonable and discriminatory. Identification of those instances where a refusal to accommodate the needs of a disabled person amounts to discrimination against the handicapped continues to be an important responsibility of HEW." *Davis*, 442 U.S. at 412-13 (Goldblatt)©.

References

Americans with Disabilities Act Amendments Act of 2008, 42 U.S.C. §§ 12101 *et seq.*

Brandwein, P. & Scotch, R. K. (2008). ADA Amendments Act of 2008, *Ohio State Law Journal Pub. L.* 110-325.

Burgdorf, R. L. Jr. (1997) "Substantially Limited" Protection from Disability Discrimination: The Special Treatment Model and Misconstructions of the Definition of Disability. *Villanova Law Review, 42(2)*: 409-585.

Chadwick, Ruth ed. (1998). *Disability Rights, The Encyclopedia of Applied Ethics.* San Diego: Academic Press, Inc. I (781), 790.

Erwin, M. (2011, July 4). Andy Imparato: Making a Difference from the Inside. Independence Today.

Evans, J. (2004, Fall). Why the Medical Model Needs Disability Studies (and vice-versa): A Perspective from Rehabilitation Psychology. *Disability Studies Quarterly, 24(4).*

Hurder, A. J. (2002, September/October) ABA Urges Equal Access to Courts for Individuals with Disabilities. *Mental and Physical Disability Law Review (MPDLR), 26(5)*, 772.

Imparato, A. J. (2005, May/June). *Addressing Mental Illness in the Legal Workplace, Diversity & the Bar,* 60-63.

In re: Ruby McDonough, 457 Mass. 512. 2010.

Jones, M. & Basser Marks, L. A. (eds.). (1999). *Disability, Divers-Ability and Legal Change.* The Hague: Kluwer Law International.

Lucas, C.A. (2009, May 27) Center for Rights of Parents with Disabilities Colorado Cross-Disability Coalition. Webinar, Course ID#: 07782. Retrieved from http://www.ada.gov/.

Peyton, L. Legal Clinic for the Disabled, (2009) ABA/DOJ Webinar.

Scotch, R. K. (2000). Symposium Article: Models of Disability and the Americans with Disabilities Act, *Berkeley Journal of Employment and Labor Law, 21(213).*

Silvers, A. (1999). Double Consciousness, Triple Difference: Disability, Race, Gender and the Politics of Recognition. The Hague (UK): Martinus Nijhoff.

Southeastern Community College v Davis, 442 U. S. 397, 78-711 (1979).

Tennessee v. Lane, 541 U.S. 509 (2004).

CHAPTER 4
STANDARD OF CARE UNDER RUBRIC ADAAA

We cannot mess with each other in the wake of trauma. When people do terrible things to each other, it is very different from accident trauma.

van der Kolk

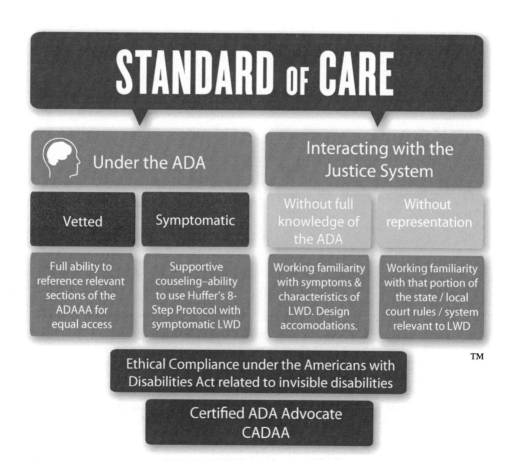

CADAA Rely on the Rubric
When Setting the Standard of Care

The job of ADA advocate can appear to be impossibly broad and burdensome. However, rather than being all things to all clients, the advocate guides the client in the direction of each of the five focus areas falling under the Certified ADA advocate rubric. The goal is always to enhance the independence of the client so the advocate can step back remaining in a supportive role whenever possible. The entire intent of the ADA is to offer the least restrictive and intrusive accommodations. Advocates must not encourage dependence but rather lead and support the client in each of the five focus areas toward success and self sufficiency.

The role of certified ADAAA advocate is a link to successfully implementing the mandates by unique training and skills that will smooth out the wrinkles bringing the strengths of the person with disabilities to the forefront. All give a little and in the middle there is great reward and protection for all parties. The key to unlocking justice and setting a positive path for humane courts of the future lies in the trained advocate who anticipates and prevents problems.

An effort to creatively develop ways to use the legally mandated role of ADA advocates to their maximum effect under the law involves recruiting and training a national pool of individuals who are personally dedicated to helping disabled litigants obtain and protect their rights in courts throughout the United States. Our organization through an accredited university certifies individuals as having a basic level of skills and knowledge to be of genuine assistance to the disabled litigants they are trained to help. They are invaluable to attorneys who open their minds to this strategy and their participation saves the court a great deal of time and resources.

Through our research and experience the role of the ADA advocate has emerged as absolutely critical to those with disabilities being functional in court and the need for services continues to expand. The result has been recognition that affordable professionals, who are specifically trained both in the laws that are in place to protect the disabled and the litigation process itself, can often help clarify issues, provide or obtain supportive services, and assist with case organization and management saving the client thousands of dollars. As we have progressed, we have seen a general positive impact in every facet of litigation. When advocates are able to work effectively, the system works better, the law works as intended, legal consumers are more satisfied, and judicial personnel are much less frustrated especially by pro se litigants.

Defining the Role of the CADAA

Neither the word nor the role of "advocate" is defined in the ADA statutes. This leaves us then to the standard dictionary that defines the word as: 1) to speak or write in favor of; support or urge by argument; recommend publicly, 2) a person who speaks or writes in support or defense of a person, cause, etc., 3) a person who pleads for or in behalf of another; and/or 4) a person who pleads the cause of another in a court of law. In practical terms, however, the advocate's role may be broader than that. According to the ADA, the advocate may oppose any act or practice made unlawful by the

ADA, charge, testify, assist or participate in investigation, participate in proceedings and hearings, and/or aid any individual in the exercise or enjoyment of his or her rights granted or protected by the ADA (ADAAA, 2008).

At any time, the advocate may be functioning as clerk, draftsperson, legal assistant, paralegal, attorney-in-fact, litigation manager, next-friend or *ad litem*, confidant, representative, spokesperson, interpreter, consultant, or in any other capacity necessary to assist the client in gaining, protecting, or expanding his or her rights as granted by the ADA. When applied directly to litigation, the advocate may act as follower or leader, depending upon the skills and experience of the client and those of the advocate. Some clients may need only superficial support and assistance; others may need substantial support, guidance and counsel. It is important to choose an advocate who has the mix of skills and experience that can best compliment those of the client to form an effective litigation team. The engagement of an advocate is a critical prerequisite for litigation.

Preliminary Menu of Goals and Tasks:

- ensure equal access to the litigation process;

- foster the highest level of functional effectiveness for the litigant during legal proceedings;

- enhance the independence of the client;

- navigate the bureaucracy to mitigate and/or overcome obstructions that threaten to prevent the disabled person's equal participation;

- act as liaison/filter/translator when communication is traumatic for the client, i.e. domestic violence cases requiring communication with abusive spouse;

- ensure boundaries are maintained to prevent intimidation or exploitation of the litigant;

- help to establish safe emotional boundaries during court for the client while adhering to the rules of the litigation process (The judge will sometimes ask that the advocate perform tasks helpful to the court, i.e. help smooth out problems with service of documents or other procedural matters);

- assist getting witnesses in and out of the courtroom in a timely and orderly fashion;

- expect the unexpected. Be prepared to assist in a broad spectrum of issues that will pertain to the client's accessibility and assist to maintain a fair legal process keeping advocates role under the ADAAA;

- attend court to assist the litigant and attorney;

- design and request accommodations;

- hold a power of attorney for legal, medical, and/or other purposes as narrow or broad as is needed;

- provide supportive counseling using Huffer's 8-Steps as a guide keeping the momentum of the case moving supporting the litigant to be comfortable and functional;

- act as liaison keeping in contact with the appropriate ADA administrative office, the judge's staff, and opposing attorneys;

- prepare for courtroom requirements such as planning the litigant's table arrangements, preparing the client for the next hearing, meeting with opposing staff, or designing cues and working out a system of cuing the judge when an accommodation is required;

- provide or arrange for notary public services to facilitate proper and timely document filing and swearing in if testimony is provided long distance;

- help to index and maintaining files in proper order in court;

- supporting client to find target research helpful to the case;

- refer the client to medical and legal resources as needed;

- evaluate the appropriateness of mediation;

- establish client's weaknesses and strengths to rule out malingering;

- testify as an expert witness if qualified.

For the purposes of this work, access to legal proceedings means *full*:

- emotional ability to participate,

- cognitive and mental capability with concentration,

- ability to communicate, verbalize, and form concepts,

- ability to get into the courtroom, physically maintain a posture conducive to participation in the process maintaining reasonable physical and mental health throughout the process,

- knowledge of the rules that are to be followed by all participants in the process,

- ability to fund the case to its completion,

- confidence in tenets of honest services, good faith, fair and ethical dealing, and goodwill, free from oppression by an adversary with more money, more power, and/or corrupt motives.

Tools for CADAA

Basic Functionality Screening before Designing ADA Accommodations

The advocate conducts Basic Functionality Screening. Advocates generally start with a structured interview similar to the example below:

1. Describe any mobility impairments you have that cause or are causing difficulty

_____Climbing stairs

_____Opening doors

_____Using restrooms

_____Sitting long periods

_____Other _____

2. Identify and discuss any functional impairments that you may have that can affect your competence during the stress of litigation:

_____Concentration

_____Hearing

_____Receiving information

_____Seeking information (discovery)

_____Expressing needs

_____Understanding rapid speech

_____Remembering – schedules, facts, and/or instructions

_____Screening out external stimuli/maintaining focus

_____Stamina

_____Evaluating data and making decisions quickly

_____Verbalizing thoughts forming concepts

_____Other

3. Next, the advocate and the client assess areas that contribute to heightened anxiety and stress that can affect the litigation. Level of anxiety scale 1 – 10 (10 = highest)

_____Getting mail

_____Being subpoenaed

_____Traveling to court

_____Receiving information from my attorney

_____Receiving information from the opposing attorney

_____Receiving bills and paying legal fees and costs

_____Transcript availability

_____Intimidation surrounding litigation

_____Maintaining responsibilities while in litigation

_____Deep sense of man's inhumanity to man

_____Trust in judge's neutrality

_____Trust in attorneys' ethics

_____Availability and procedure for securing needed witnesses

_____Confidence that due process is assured

_____Waste of money, time, assets demanded by litigation

_____ Loss of quality of life

_____Status of health

_____Status of friends and family-support system

_____Ridicule, humiliation, slander, libel

Any anxiety issues rated over 5 by the client need to be considered as needing accommodations or other intervention. For example, if intimidation is a concern, the advocate may suggest that the litigant seek an accommodation that he or she ask to appear from a separate sequestration room or area. Sometimes accommodations can successfully address the anxiety issues while in some instances disabled litigants need counseling attention. Some of the anxieties can be accommodated in court and others are beyond the scope of litigation such as loss of quality of life, status of health, friends, and family.

4. After completing the anxiety assessment, the advocate will routinely introduce the self-help skills for assisting with symptoms of Legal Abuse Syndrome.

The client is introduced to Huffer's 8-Steps, a process that is preparation for effective performance and general survival during litigation. Too often, disabled litigants initiate litigation prematurely and are consequently unprepared for the realities and rigors of the litigation process. Throughout Huffer's 8-Steps process, the litigant is encouraged to use each of the steps for healing and preparation. Jumping into litigation too soon can doom the litigant's chance for going the distance and winning. Consider the following example: If you have ever had to drive a car that sat out in winter weather, you know how imperative it is to scrape off or de-ice the windshield and back window before your journey can begin. If you jumped into the car and took off, you found it extremely difficult to reach your destination and, for sure, you were without proper visibility and safety. Jumping into a lawsuit is just as dangerous. Unless you know where you are going, where you want to end up, and what the costs, distances, and health and comfort requirements are going to be, you are vulnerable to a host of threats and just as unlikely to "get there."

Now think of putting the iced up automobile onto a racetrack where a competitor wants to run you off the track and the rules are inconsistently enforced. That scenario is even more akin to what you may experience in litigation. Just as in racing you need a crew to support your efforts, a team with different organizational and technical skills and expertise, an array of tools to support your efforts at every turn, and the money to make sure you can remain competitive over the long haul. You need all that–and more–when you decide to litigate.

Vetting the LWD

Historically, the validity of PTSD in litigation is sometimes challenged as being "PTSD for profit" in the court. For us, it has been rather simple to ascertain the sincerity of clients. Those who will courageously endure the rigors of the eight protocols in treating Legal Abuse Syndrome are not likely to be malingerers. The fakers who seek a false diagnosis for profit frequently want us to provide a quick report and resist working through their painful psychological issues to a point of recovery. The client's case history will also give clues as to his or her seriousness and credibility.

We generally attempt to rule out malingering before advocating for any client. To do so, we've developed some procedures to determine whether the likelihood is more or less certain. By using the following list of questions. An advocate can determine the relative credibility of an individual claiming to be deserving of ADA protection:

- Does the individual have a poor work record?

- Were the individual's prior "incapacitating" injuries questionable?

- Is there a discrepancy between the individual's participation in work and recreation?

- Does the person experience unvarying, repetitive dreams?

- Does the person exhibit antisocial personality traits?

- Does the person describe over-idealized life prior to the trauma?

- Is the person evasive about relevant issues?

- Is the person inconsistent in his or her symptom presentation?

- Is the person too accurate and does he or she exhibit perfect consistency in reporting symptoms. (True memory always varies somewhat.)

By completing this process, the advocate can assure the court that the client has been vetted and their behavior is not consistent with malingering or deceiving the court in any way.

Administrative Responsibilities of the CADAA

Negotiate Terms for a Workable Agreement

Advocates' responsibilities usually start with designing and filing for accommodations followed by being in court sitting next to the client as an advocate. Thereafter, the needs may grow exponentially as a case continues. It is important to have a clear agreement and understanding with limitations from the outset and provisions for altering the agreement if circumstances change and an adjustment of the relationship is needed. ADA advocates are usually paid through an arrangement worked out between the litigant and the advocate. The fee arrangement must be satisfactory to both client and advocate.

The ADAAA law mandates that the cost of the accommodations is absorbed by the public entity. However, in our experience, accommodations will be denied if there is cost. Therefore, to be pragmatic and ease the burden on the client, advocates attempt to work out accommodations that do not create cost for the court.

Because advocates may act in a broad range of services depending upon the particular facts of the case or assignment, the agreement between the client and advocate must be clear and detailed as to what services will be performed, where, and how those services will be performed, how they will be paid for, and what expenses may be billed in addition to the advocate's services. The financial arrangements made need to account for contingencies to ensure that the litigant is never left in the lurch and the advocate is paid on a regular and on-going basis, just as any other professional. Advocates may be more cost-effective than attorneys and other licensed professionals depending on the levels of their particular skills. Properly used, an advocate with litigation experience and other skills that allow him or her to become your litigation manager can reduce the requirements for and activities of attorneys and their paraprofessionals leaving them to focus efforts and resources on the issues that demand legal expertise.

Invisible disabilities especially psychological and psychiatric injuries require accommodations less expensive to address than physical disabilities. No equipment has to be provided or ramps or architectural alterations are needed. Accommodating the invisible disability is more a matter of human consideration and awareness than remodeling physical facilities. The advocate provides education as to management of the litigant's disability. Efficiency in this design rests on the willingness of the court personnel to learn, get past old habits, and adhere to the mandated alterations.

The litigant is usually the least able to impart this information effectively. Here is where advocates are cost effective saving the advocate effort and heartache as well as fees in additional legal expenses and inefficient efforts to just arrange a level playing field. At the end of the day, the ADA advocate saves the client untold amounts of money and discomfort while he or she serves the economy of the court and assists all professionals in optimizing their services.

Guide to Conduct in the Courtroom

The courtroom is choreographed, intellectual combat. As with any such contest, the client must first learn the rules. Then, they must follow them and insist that the opponent does the same. Depending upon who initiated the proceeding, one litigant will present his or her side first. The opponent will respond and the first litigant will have a chance to reply. If the litigants are represented by attorneys, their attorneys will make the presentations. Otherwise, the clients will be expected to do it or have their advocate speak for them if they are unable to do it (Gov.com).

The visual impression you make in the courtroom can be an important part of your strategy. You are not dressing to express your personality but to convey an impression to the judge and/or jury of the seriousness of your intention to assure equal access for your client. Therefore, you should dress in a professional, businesslike manner that shows you are serious, prepared, and organized. Do not let the courtroom intimidate you. You belong there doing a critically important job per federal law.

During the proceeding you must be alert to precisely what is being said and the implications of the argument being made. It is important to develop the skills and knowledge to be able to assure your client is able to keep track of the facts being presented, evaluate how they may relate to the law governing the question at hand, and observe the judge's reaction to those facts presented and the arguments being made. You are present as a second set of eyes and ears. You've proven your worth when the client turns to you and says, "What'd he say?" and you can repeat the exchange and help decide on and efficiently take whatever supportive action is required.

Request ADAAA Accommodations

Many courts have an official form designed for persons with disabilities to request reasonable accommodations. However, the forms provided to apply for the Americans with Disabilities Act (ADA) Title II accommodations often pertain to accommodations for obvious physical disabilities but are usually sorely lacking in addressing the needs of persons with PTSD and other "invisible" psychological or psychiatric disabilities. Every court is different. Some court personnel will have knowledge of the ADA and how to accommodate some types of disabilities, but others may have no clerk, no specified department, and no place to file a request for accommodations. The very act of getting the accommodations written and filed timely in the designated office can be challenging and even prohibitive for the LWD without the assistance of an advocate or someone knowledgeable in the workings of that particular court. We have commonly had clients who have been rudely treated, ignored, or simply had their requests handed over to the judge who is just as ignorant of the ADA mandate as the other court functionaries that serve him or her.

Some judges add injury to insult by bringing the request for accommodations out in open court exposing private—and, by law, confidential information to the adversaries. Under ADA rules, only publicly filed information is to be shared with an adversary. HIPAA and ADAAA protections provide that accommodating disabilities is a strictly private matter between the ADA administrative office, the judge, and the litigant. Accommodating disabilities is an administrative/ministerial matter that is not within the purview of judicial discretion (US Dpt.Labor, 2010-11). Therefore, immunity does not protect judicial personnel if they err in their administrative duties. In other words, the judge's immunity is set aside regarding these administrative duties.

After assessment of the LWD then using the client's mind's eye, mentally walk through the reality of court for that person. How do they feel in court? What do they do? What do they wish they could do? What distracts them and diminishes their performance? Using imagination and creativity, what alterations of procedures, what devices, what changes would offset their impairments and help them to effectively manage their cases? Then review the following as just a menu of options that have been used successfully by LWDs.

1. A digitalized audio or visual recorder to run during legal proceedings due to PTSD amnesia and inability to concentrate should be in the litigant's possession at all times. The recorder must be accessible by the litigant. A litigant often needs to instantly replay and have an immediate record. PTSD litigants cannot wait for transcripts that are often inadequate. Transcripts fail to deliver intonation, speed of speech, facial expressions, gestures, innuendo that are critical to the litigant's reactions. Furthermore, transcripts can be tampered with or altered. Many intimidating actions take place in a legal setting using words that in a transcript appear to be appropriate and neutral. However, the manner in which the words are delivered may carry a threat or manipulation that can trigger PTSD symptoms. Real time transcripts are not a substitute for recordings. The recorder must not be confiscated by security, even momentarily.

2. Presence of a psychiatric service dog trained specifically for PTSD and anxiety disorders may need to accompany the litigant to court.

3. A litigant must not be kept waiting long periods of time in the courthouse before a hearing. An LWD must have an opportunity to go to a restful environment and be notified when it is time for the hearing. There are lounges for lawyers; there must be lounges for those with PTSD who must wait. The waiting area must be separated from the adversary.

4. Breaks when needed during proceedings are customary. If flashbacks are triggered by the testimony, the litigant will need a break to recover and refocus.

5. Plain English, slowly spoken, is necessary during proceedings. Verbal functioning is often impaired by PTSD and must have no further complications from "litigation language." Much traditional legal language is Latin, a dead language that is not useful and reflects an exclusive appearance that shuns and often confuses *pro se* litigants.

6. Equal access to discovery and all rules of court need to be followed especially for PTSD self-represented litigants.

7. Litigants with PTSD may need extended deadlines for legal filings if they are symptomatic.

PTSD imposes an additional burden in working through traumatic memory and physiological symptoms that must be aided by flexibility in the court's handling of filing deadlines.

8. Domestic violence victims must never be questioned by or placed under the authority of their abuser. They need separate entrances and to sit out of the presence of the abuser or even to appear telephonically or by Skype and such video services. They need to feel safe. Bailiffs may need to walk them into the courthouse and back to their transportation. Correction of misinformation that attacks character and is designed to outrage and interfere with concentration of the PTSD litigant must be immediate. Lies and misinformation are often used as tactics to create severe stress in PTSD litigants. This accommodation will be thoroughly discussed throughout this book and is a major focus in the Empowerment Chapter. Misinformation creates a type of fundamental attribution error more recently called correspondence bias that prevents the judge from making a fair decision (Gilbert, 1995). A form exists to submit for this accommodation to be triggered.

9. Unintentionally, the ADAAA creates another barrier to be overcome by litigants suffering from disabilities by creating a process to qualify for accommodations. Advocates assist in filing for and securing accommodations but too often find that the process is arbitrary, disorganized, and results in unintentional denial of access and due process for the disabled litigant unless immediately confronted. Ironically, in such instances, disabled litigants can be frustrated and defeated while attempting to file the first court document designed specifically to assist them in gaining equal access to the judicial system.

Thus, specific, high-level communications skills are needed because court functionaries' sheer incompetence or unfamiliarity with ADA law too often contributes to this tragic denial of due process and addition of traumatic stress. Simple persistent communication can avert the occurrence or worsening of LAS. Some clients with PTSD are veterans freshly back from active military service. Many are citizens who enter the courts naively believing their rights to a fair hearing will be automatically protected. Instead, in the heat of battle, their rights are denied, their disabilities exploited, and they sustain life-altering losses unfairly.

Next, the CADAA does a visual check of the LWD as a mental dress rehearsal for court. How is the LWD dressed? One LWD wore very low cut blouses and tight pants to court. She toted overfilled file folders and wobbled on her high heels. With her blond windblown hair, her image played into the disorganized, irresponsible, neglectful mother that the opposition attempted to put forth to the court. She needed to alter her image as the judge looked from the bench and ensure that it was incongruous with the opposition's words of attack.

Non-administrative Responsibilities of the CADAA:
Coach, Counsel, and Advise the Client After Accommodations Are Designed

Antonin Scalia, United States Supreme Court Justice and Bryan Garner wrote in their book, *Making your Case: The Art of Persuading Judges*, that the job of the litigant and the litigant's attorney if represented, is to become salespeople (2008). It is their job to sell the Judge on their case. Therefore, the disabled litigant must be aware of their accommodations and be able to communicate through posturing and perception as well as words. It helps to videotape the proceedings for review, critique, and determination of initial accommodations or a need for a new or modification of an existing accommodation keeping the following in mind:

1. Grooming and dress—should be like the attorneys.

2. Verbal and physical responses to the hearing—Role play: Advocates and all LWDs need to mentally walk through mock litigation scenarios helping them to see in their mind's eyes how they can actually appear and function in court under stress.

3. Following either the advocate's witnessing of the client's courtroom persona or a videotape of, responses to the following questions and observations add further information necessary to the choice and design of accommodations:

- Ask the litigant what background emotions are perceivable when they are under stress in court.

- Determine what feelings drive the litigant's performance in the courtroom.

- Look closely at the physical layout around the litigant and the appearance and functionality of the litigant's table to determine how files should be organized and how they can best be accessed.

- Notice, when the litigant speaks, what tone of voice is normally used, and what does it communicate. Encourage him or her to speak in a voice tone that is warm, firm, and factual and to practice that tone in role-playing settings.

- Ask the litigant what symptoms of PTSD they suffer and if there is evidence of symptoms of other hidden disabilities.

- Determine if the litigant cries, sounds angry, quivers and shakes, vomits, and/or loses hearing or speech functions at critical moments.

- Notice if the litigant's facial expression is as poker-faced as possible under most circumstances.

Advocates need to explore creative ways that the court can alter its procedures to provide the litigant with improved and equal access. They should determine whether the litigant is able to interact, concentrate, speak, and differentiate between the adversary's "bait" used to exploit the disabled litigant's symptoms as contrasted with directly addressing allegations or accusations that merit a response. They should also determine how well the litigant remembers important statements when he or she is under stress.

If the litigant cannot cognitively function and effectively communicate under stress there is no access to the court even if the litigant looks absolutely normal during litigation. This is the major point to be addressed. Cognition and speech are necessary to presenting and defending a case in a court of law. Many litigants with invisible disabilities are functionally impaired with regard to their abilities to communicate during litigation.

Author's Notes:

Judicial Immunity from Lawsuits

The Supreme Court has held that judges can be held liable for damages in suits where actions, which are administrative in nature, are challenged. Given this abrogation of state immunity under the ADA, claims can be brought against a state judge in his/her individual or official capacity under the ADA without regard to the doctrine of judicial immunity. Ordinarily, judges enjoy immunity from damage suits from virtually any action they take in their capacity as a judge that requires the exercise of judicial discretion. See *Stump v. Sparkman*, 435 U.S. 349, 356 (1978). The United States Supreme Court in *Forrester v. White*, 484 U.S. 219, 224-225 (1988) refused to attach judicial immunity to a judge's decision to fire a court employee, because the act was not "judicial" in nature. The Court held that truly judicial acts must be distinguished from the administrative, legislative or executive functions that judges may occasionally be assigned to perform. According to the Supreme Court, it is the nature of the function performed—adjudication—rather than the identity of the actor who performed it—a judge—that determines whether absolute immunity attaches to the act. Any time an action taken by a judge is not an adjudication between parties, it is less likely that the act [will be found to be] a judicial one. *Cameron v. Seitz*, 38 F.3d 264, 271 (6th Cir. 1994). (*Badillo v Garcia*, USA Amicus Curiae).

Many references will be online resources due to the newness of this information. The passage of the ADAAA was just accomplished in 2008 going into effect in 2009. The most pertinent up-to-date material must be accessed online.

It is clear that the ADA was meant by Congress for all persons to have equal and fair access to the courts as well as other public accommodations. ADA advocates can read the voluminous, original ADA Act by accessing http://www.sba.gov/ada/adaact.txt, paying special attention to Title II of the Act where the public service of the judicial system and intentions regarding invisible disabilities are covered.

What Are Ministerial Acts?

A ministerial act has been defined as one that a public officer is required to perform under a given state of facts, in a prescribed manner, in obedience to the mandate of legal authority. An act is ministerial if it does not involve the exercise of any discretion. If there is any discretion or judicial determination attendant to the act, it is not ministerial, nor is it a ministerial act if the trial court must weigh conflicting claims or collateral matters which require legal resolution. The law must spell out the duty to be performed with such certainty that nothing is left to the exercise of discretion or judgment. We have also described the ministerial act requirement as a requirement that the litigant has a clear right to the relief sought. The act must be positively commanded and so plainly prescribed under the law as to be free from doubt.

Accommodating disabilities is an administrative/ministerial matter that is not a matter of sole judicial discretion. Therefore, immunity does not protect judicial personnel from erring in their administrative duties in other words, the judge's immunity is set aside regarding administrative duties as was found with Judge Berrios: *Judge Berríos is not Immune from Suit.*

Given the abrogation of state immunity by the ADA, claims can be brought against a state judge in his/her individual or official capacity under the ADA but for the doctrine of judicial immunity. It has been established that this doctrine generally affords judges immunity from damage suits. *See Stump v. Sparkman*, 435 U.S. 349, 356 (1978). However, the Supreme Court has held that judges can be held liable for damages[5] in suits where actions, which are administrative in nature, are challenged. *See Forrester v. White*, 484 U.S. 219, 224-225 (1988).

References

The American Bar Association. (1998). *The American Bar*. Retrieved January 24, 2000 From http://www.abanow.org

Americans with Disabilities Act Amendments Act of 2008, 42 U.S.C. §§ 12101 *et seq.*

Gilbert, D, T. & Malone, P. S. (1995). The Correspondence Bias. *Psychological Bulletin 117*, 21-38.

Gov.com. Rule 5072-1Courtroom Decorum. Retrieved from www.flmb.uscourts.gov/localrules/documents/rule5072-1.pdf.

Health Insurance Portability and Accountability Act of 1996 (HIPAA), 42 U.S.C. § 300gg *et seq.*

Scalia, A. & Garner, B. (2008). *Making your Case: The Art of Persuading Judges.* (pp. 1-5) NY: Thomson/West.

U.S. Department of Labor (2010-2011). Occupational Outlook Handbook, Judges, Magistrates, and Other Judicial Workers. *Bureau of Labor Statistics.* www.bls.gov/OCO.

http://hrdailyadvisor.blr.com/

CHAPTER 5

CHALLENGES TO IMPLEMENTING THE LETTER AND INTENT OF ADAAA

Millions of dollars are spent on architectural reconfiguration altering parking spaces, walkways, buildings, and bathrooms to accommodate those with disabilities. However, the most important access is afforded by ADA administrative staff putting forth attitudes of acceptance, flexibility, inclusion, and service. The job has just begun with filing the request for ADA accommodations. The advocates and LWDs typically encounter myriad challenges as they work to keep the client adequately accommodated throughout the litigation.

An error does not become truth by reason of multiplied propagation, nor does truth become error because nobody will see it.

Mahatma Gandhi

CADAAs Pick Up the Slack in a System with No Organized Intake Process for LWDs

Advocates are invaluable in overcoming the obstacles to fair hearings for litigants with disabilities. Usually, the first obstacle is finding the ADA contact person for the court who usually serves in the role of "ADA Coordinator." Once that person is located, then the proper forms must be identified, filled out, and submitted to the Coordinator. Such forms are usually found either preprinted by the particular state or, in some cases, by the individual court. Ordinarily, an internet search can be used to locate them and the directions for filling them out.

Once the forms are completed (usually with attachments), they can be filed personally or often can be mailed into the ADA administrator's office. If you choose to file your papers by mail, be sure your envelope is posted with a tracking capability or return receipt, a green card proving delivery and acceptance is returned to the litigant. If possible, you should plan to give at least five days notice prior to the court date. In addition, you should pay close attention to the following issues:

1. Insist that the ADA Coordinator respond timely in writing. If the accommodations are accepted, then planning can begin. If they are partially accepted, there is time for negotiation and substitutions to be worked out. If they are denied, then the litigant can (and should) file a grievance or appeal.

2. Never assume that the clerk is correct regarding any information you are given—particularly in regard to ADA issues. Many judges and clerks do not know the ADAAA law and will advise the litigant out of habit that they must file a motion, serve the other side, and have their accommodations heard in the court with the adversary present. That is simply NOT true. A motion before the court is NEVER mentioned in the ADA or ADAAA.

In one case in our experience, an actual court transcript dramatizes how an opposing counsel violated the ADAAA and HIPAA privacy laws and a judge either did not know the law or chose to allow opposing counsel to violate it. (Note the disrespectful and demanding tone of opposing counsel.)

> OPPOSING COUNSEL with a distinct tone of disdain: *I need hospital and doctors' records, not Ms. Huffer or whatever her name is. I need the doctors' records immediately. Okay?*
>
> THE COURT: *I just wanted to know what my timeframe was. I just want it to say that she was suffering.*
>
> OPPOSING COUNSEL: *What you said was doctors' notes. We haven't seen a single doctor's note. In fact, you were adamant at the last hearing.*
>
> THE COURT: *Do you have a doctor's note or anything?*
>
> OPPOSING COUNSEL: *And the order says, 'Doctors' notes.'*
>
> THE COURT: *Do you have anything to tell me about her prognosis?*
>
> DISABLED LITIGANT'S LAWYER: *She has appointments scheduled this week.*
>
> THE COURT: *Why didn't you just get a note or something?*

3. If medical information is requested by the ADA Administrative office, it must be limited to basic diagnosis and courtesy information for the ADA Administrator's and judge's eyes only in the context of accommodations. Such information is protected, private information and to be kept under the stewardship of the ADA Administrative office. When we prepare a report and requests for accommodations, we encourage the patient to give a little more information to the judge than is legally required to aide the judge in being sensitive to their needs BUT NEVER TO THE ADVERSARY. It is a courtesy for the judge and ADA Administrative Office only.

4. Obtaining accommodations is a dynamic process that has no end once it is put into motion. Needs for accommodations can—and often do—change over time. Good working communication and observation are the keys.

5. The litigant always has the right to refuse an accommodation.

6. If the court requests medical information, it must be directly related to the specific accommodation. The adversary cannot fish through the disabled litigant's medical information to use any of it against the disabled person in a biased way.

Protecting medical privacy requires a degree of pluck on the part of the disabled litigant, but choosing to use the ADAAA as a federal mandate requires the courts to privately accommodate litigants. When a disability is in the litigation picture, the first step is to protect the litigant under this law demanding confidentiality regarding their accommodations. A functional impairment is never to be used against a litigant in a court of law. Advocates face a challenging dynamic process once the initial bureaucratic work of gaining accommodations is done. Advocates and litigants must work diligently to protect privacy while monitoring the accommodations seeing they are up to date and pertinent.

CADAAs Effectively Communicate the Demands and Protections of the Mandate

Every judicial service needs clear signs posted, online pop ups, and geographical directions that make requesting accommodations easy to complete. The guidelines need to be visual, auditory, and in Braille. The actions of court personnel need to reflect acceptance, imagination, and compliance with the intent, spirit, and letter of the law. Communication is the first order of business and, rather than warning of UPL if non lawyers interpret for those who cannot speak for themselves, they need to be welcomed as assistive to the duty of the court.

Requesting and monitoring accommodations is a communication issue that sometimes requires negotiation with judicial and administrative staff. However, the ADAAA, being a federally mandated ministerial/administrative duty, requires that most reasonable accommodations be honored. It takes persistence and reminding the court staff that the law mandates accommodations sometimes even for those just "regarded as having a disability" as well as those who are not symptomatic because they are on medication, wear corrective devices, or have been otherwise successfully treated for their impairments. You should remember that ADA accommodations are a federal civil right that cannot lawfully be refused.

Dispelling the LWD's Fear of Discrimination from Using the ADAAA

Regardless of the fact that The Americans with Disabilities Act is a powerful law that provides a person requiring special accommodations equal access to litigation, we frequently encounter a strange misguided response from certain lawyers when our patients and clients need to use the ADA. Some lawyers have advised clients not to use the ADA because, if they admit to their disability, they will be discriminated against in the court by the judge for being disabled. So, let's get this straight. Certain legal advisers or officers of the court are saying, "Don't tell the truth." "Don't use the powerful law that Congress intends for you to use under the Federal Civil Rights umbrella or you will have your Federal Civil Rights violated by the judge, who is bound by canons of judicial ethics and federal and state laws to protect your civil rights in the court." This is deeply flawed reasoning in the context of judicial behavior and needs to be addressed wherever it is encountered.

The second most often misguided instruction given to those with special needs by lawyers, judges and clerks is that in order to gain accommodations in the courtroom, the litigant must file a motion serving the adversary and hold hearings on the disability and whether or not accommodations should be granted. Such an act places private medical information in public files in violation of HIPAA and ADAAA confidentiality further traumatizing the litigant. Inadvertently, a biased burden is put on the litigant with disabilities by threatening to throw the confidential request for accommodations into the adversarial arena. This defies the intent and purpose of the ADA and the ADAAA. Most states have embraced the concept, but some judges and attorneys lag far behind in updating their practices to be in step with their states' positions, which are properly aligned with the ADA and ADAAA.

Stop here. The destruction of a case has already begun if there is a tendency to run scared and begin lying to cover the disability. The absurdity of omitting important information for fear that the judge will behave like a despot and discriminate against the litigant for having a disability speaks for itself. That very issue must be brought out in court and clarified.

The first rule needs to be just the opposite. That is, use the law truthfully as it properly applies to the litigant's needs. A functional impairment will worsen in court simply due to the stress of litigation. To deny ADAAA accommodations is like sending a child with special needs to school and expecting him or her to function normally in a regular classroom. Exploitation can hardly be avoided in a "win/lose" adversarial process. In fact, what is defended as "zealous representation" too often crosses the line discriminating through misinformation, lies, and mischaracterization of the adversary. This risks that the case will take on a life of its own and suddenly the facts of the litigant's case are at risk of being replaced by the adversary's interests. It is often very hard to refocus the case after losing ground to such a tactical detour. The advocate must keep the focus on the ADA accommodations ensuring equal footing during every minute of the litigation.

Controlling the Fallout
from Fundamental Attribution Error/Correspondence Bias

Scope, perspective, what do you see? I see a very angry litigant. I hear a babbling litigant. I see a litigant's rolling eyes and offensive, unattractive facial expressions. I see a distressed person not participating, unprepared, not speaking, crying. How did you feel about the person when you witnessed their unusual behavior? A court participant is expected, no demanded to behave in a precise decorum. We perceive what is in front of us and, as we reach for a reaction: disgust, disinterest, embarrassment, dislike, distrust, we are also characterizing the individual setting them up for how they deserve to be treated. If we were to assume that their unusual behavior is due to internal personality factors and if we were to underestimate the role of situational factors, we would be making a "fundamental attribution error." The situational causes of the litigant's behavior are less salient to us and may be unknown, unappreciated (Heider, 1983; Ross, 1977; Fiske, 1991; Jones, 1979, 1990). It is here in "the situation," the court of law, the adversarial relationship of the litigants, lawyers, and judges, that we begin.

Fritz Heider, (1896–1988), created the balance theory and the attribution theory. He looked at how people's perception of others is formed, whether personal or as a group, and he found them to have the same rules. When, whether personal or as a group, we attempt to explain the behavior of others or attribute reasons for that behavior, biases sometimes lead to errors in our reasoning. The behavior could be the result of personality traits or attitudes, for example. On the other hand, the behavior could be a result of their situation or of peer pressure, for instance. Heider argued that people tend to overweigh internal causes over external causes, later known as the fundamental attribution error. Heider's rule of "psychological balance" says positive and negative opinions need to be represented. The positive and negative opinions minimize simultaneous and conflicting feelings, thoughts, and/or emotions about the person. They decide on our degree of attraction or aversion. The positive and negative opinions maximize a simple and straightforward instinctual reaction to the person (1983). Heider's attribution theory was later known as "correspondence bias" (Fiske & Taylor, 1991; Jones, 1979, 1990).

Years ago research proved we do not hesitate to be judge and jury when given even a single snapshot of an individual's behavior. As a psychiatric therapist and ADA advocate and expert witness, the fundamental attribution error when applied to the invisibly disabled contributes significantly to spike symptoms associated with their disability and verifiable chemical changes in the brain resulting in a negative impression on the court and decreased ability to influence. These psychic injuries caused in court compound, calcify, and return intact for the next court date if the individual does not seek therapy.

Visualize the same litigant with or without legal representation and having a diagnosed invisible condition (PTSD, Legal Abuse Syndrome, autism, depression, etc.) trying to keep track of their proceedings. They dread, strategize, anticipate, and prepare their case for each court date. Finally, the confrontation begins. Legalese, complicated, quick, tricky, Latin, flares out from opposing counsel, Bouncing Betty's destroying the defense used to control ticks, grimaces, temper, concentration, and emotions. As accusations and lies are launched and land on to the record, symptoms of the invisible condition can no longer be contained and are expressed uncontrollably.

Attribution theorists have identified a number of common errors in understanding the causes of behaviors. Most prominent among them is the "fundamental attribution error" or the "correspondence bias" (Humphrey, 1985; Jones & Harris, 1967;), which refers to the general failure to recognize the power of the situation to influence behavior. In other words, in perceiving the cause of others' behavior and explaining to ourselves why they behave the way they do (and say the things they do), we tend to be "personality" psychologists. We assume that people behave and say things in the manner they do because of the kinds of people they are, rather than their situations. In the chapter on Empowerment, you will be given tools to address the phenomenon of fundamental attribution error in court.

ADA advocates and LWDs encounter various biases. Judith Herman, M.D., Harvard Professor, researcher, and author on Post-Traumatic Stress Disorder, observes that efforts to seek justice often further traumatize the sufferer (1997). The legal system is a formalized hostile environment that plunges litigants into battle. Strategies using argument and psychological attack are some of the weapons.

Herman asserts that there is legal bias and institutional discrimination against women. *Unlocking Justice* adds persons with disabilities to that list. It is significant when any group of people are marginalized because they are women, or disabled, or of a certain race or ethnicity. No one can argue with Dr. Herman that women are still disadvantaged by physical and social environments that have evolved for the advantage of men (69). An example is that the workplace considers pregnancy as an issue for women but not men in terms of being a disability impacting work (Francis, 2000).

Herman's opinion is that the legal system is designed to protect men from the superior power of the state but not to protect women from the superior power of men. Similarly, the weakened or disabled are not protected from polarization that divides the court insiders from the justice seekers. The rights of the accused are often protected over the rights of victims (65). The rights of the wealthy and powerful including corporations are protected over the rights of the individual litigant, especially one with meager resources or without an attorney (ABA Survey, 1999).

It does not matter what bias may come into play. The advocate must stay focused on the fact that all persons are entitled to equal access to the court in which they are required to litigate. For instance, one man, with organic brain diagnosis cannot speak. He has garnered the support of a friend who is mentally challenged and tries to be his advocate. The mentally challenged advocate cannot drive a car so must take the bus and walk long distances to get paperwork to the court and attempt to get help for his friend and client. The disabled litigant had property taken from him by a swindler who saw an opportunity to grab an apartment building owned by the disabled man. This rightful apartment building owner has long ago run out of money for attorneys because the swindler's lawyers made the litigation prohibitively expensive for the disabled litigant. We prepared the victim's request for accommodations that included having an interpreter. Because he is not able to address the court without someone to speak for him, he is being severely discriminated against. The ADA Administrator refuses to return my phone calls promptly anymore, claiming to be "weary" of the case. It gets shuffled around to clerk after clerk violating his right to privacy. The very act of obtaining accommodations has become a significant burden added to the litigation that is denying the disabled litigant due process of law. In such circumstances, the process for requesting accommodations itself discriminates.

In another case, we have a person so depressed he almost has no voice. Once a successful businessman, he has assets in real estate and other investments. He married a young Asian woman–who turned out to have previously been a man, but he met her after transsexual surgery. She fraudulently married him for economic and immigration advantages. When he contacted us, he was devastated and trying to protect his holdings from this obvious fraud. He needed help to get moneys that were being illegally controlled by his ex-wife. Barely audible he whispered and broke down crying before the judge saying he needed help in open court. A public guardian was appointed.

A woman from the public guardian's office awakened him one morning. She was at the door with a locksmith changing his locks to put him out of his house. When he said, "I thought you were supposed to help me." Her response was, "We took guardianship of your property but not you." When he got to me for help, thirty thousand dollars had been released by his ex-wife after a questionable check scheme was revealed.

However, the thirty thousand dollars was kept in an account at the guardian's office and used for an appointed attorney who collected against the account. The attorney met with the victim but provided no substantial help. We contacted his sister out of state and asked her to come and help him. She did. One person in the guardian's office cooperated with his sister coming into his case and becoming his guardian. He has now moved out of state with his sister and she controls his assets. He is no longer terrified that he will be homeless and destitute.

The apartment building owner will need ongoing advocacy and action to force the local ADA administrative office to do its job, relieving and supporting the person with disabilities. The second victim's problems were largely resolved with a timely phone call to his sister. An advocate needs to be committed to a single goal to flexibly do whatever can be done to help the person with a disability obtain fair and equitable treatment from the court. Discrimination is habit in some jurisdictions and must be confronted each time and to the level it is encountered. In the first case the advocate is needed to organize, speak for, and manage the entire case.

Conversely, the other simply required locating family support. The work of an advocate may cover a broad range of client needs. Some clients will need assistance for years. Others can be assisted in a short term where it is possible to create support networks from family or friends. That is not usual. Most often advocacy work is challenging calling upon the advocate's ability to sort through the litigant's legal demands and solve ongoing problems creatively, while bolstering the litigant with whatever psychological support may be required. Litigants vary in their ability to manage the legal requirements and to sustain behavioral balance during litigation. Some clients will fall into re-victimization and some will be motivated by fear to the point that they defy what the advocate considers good judgment. Yet, the advocate must maintain reasonable distance respecting that the case belongs to the litigant and their role is limited to simply seeing that the litigant is afforded their right to a fair hearing and a level playing field.

Communication Challenges for Advocates

Inferences and assumptions come from each individual's past experiences. The sum total of these experiences create an orientation toward life that will be projected onto others. Past trauma will sometimes emerge while an advocate is working with an LWD. Advocates need to be aware of their own emotional protective filters sometimes causing a type of "tuning out." If the information shared or the experiences witnessed threaten the advocate's feelings of safety, he or she may try to divert the data or simply not hear it at all (Kolassa, 2007). Any person is capable of such denial. Painful data is unconsciously tempting to deny.

Advocates and lawyers can be shaken by the terrifying stories their litigants progressively uncover. It is also possible for friends or family to not hear the victim, due to their protective psychological filters shielding them from vicarious pain. The victim is left feeling rejected and alone. However, when the advocate is experienced and not afraid to deal with the realities of the case, the litigant will likely feel empowered to open the door to communication necessary for a fair day in court. Implementing ADA accommodations can virtually crack the code for the litigant to accomplish this by making the legal process less threatening. Advocates may well need to meet with the LWD in short sessions and be cognizant of dealing with their own emotions as well as their client's.

The advocate also helps to communicate with the lawyer. Effective communication with the lawyer can yield a powerful ally. Emotional, disorganized communication can devastate the case and discourage lawyers from becoming involved. This may present a dilemma for an advocate. The forces surrounding the lawyer/client relationship can be contradictory. The litigant needs affordable, aggressive protection. The attorney needs income, to abide by the bar requirements, attend to the local politics of law practice before judges they will see again and again and to take cases they feel can be successfully managed.

Advocates entering a case after an attorney is worn and confused by progressive symptoms requires great tact and sensitivity to both parties. Sometimes attorneys request that I talk with the client and insist they settle or take the attorney's advice. That is not the advocate's job. However, it is their job, as liaison, to communicate to the client the level of frustration the attorney is feeling and to the attorney the symptoms that are creating the problem and how the advocate possesses the skills to intervene and improve the working relationship.

Making Communication Feel Safe

An advocate must keep the following precepts in mind:

- Do not mirror behavior; reflect in paraphrase what you hear.

- Don't be objective, logical, and sensible trying to convince when the litigant is emotional.

- Don't play devil's advocate.

- Don't teach. Make options available.

- Don't analyze the litigant.

Absolutely What Not to Do or Say to an LWD

1. "You must forgive and forget."Maybe a victim will forgive in his or her own time; but, he or she will never forget.

2. "It's only money."Money reflects the victim's status, feelings of worth, security, earned lifestyle and taste Every item is a part of the inner person.

3. "There are two sides to every story."When a crime is committed or an egregious act, there may be two sides, but one side can be dead wrong. The victim is not responsible for both sides, only a healthy resolution of his or her side.

4. "I know just how you feel.""I care how you feel," is better.

5. "I believe you.""I believe in you," is better.

6. "You still have your health/kids/family."Comparing children, family and health as opposed to material goods is irrelevant. One does not relate to the other in emotional terms. The mourner does not have to bargain, "Take my money, just don't let my kids get sick, take them away or let them die."The victim does not need to subordinate loss of property in his or her emotional experience. He or she is entitled to all of it.

7. "You're young, you can start over."A crime is a crime no matter what the victim's age. Abuse is abuse no matter what the victim's age. Youth does not forgive wrongdoing or cure trauma.

8. "It's not as bad as it seems." Imagine how lonely a victim feels to know how bad it is and to have the other person unwilling to see it. It may be every bit as bad as it seems and it might even get worse from there.

9. "Crying isn't going to help anything."We don't cry to help things. We cry because nothing helps. It is the natural response. If the victim doesn't cry and grieve, he or she will become depressed. Depression lasts longer than mourning.

10. "You're not alone."We are all in this alone. A better response is, "I'm beside you." The experience is the victim's alone.

11. Regarding crimes of the heart, "I know he/she really loves you." Love is not a reliable indicator of healthy relationships. Let's settle for being treated well and not being deceived or abused.

12. "You should have..." These are efforts for the listener to feel better by finding what the victim did wrong. These responses cause further guilt in the victim. The victim did not cause the crime or the abuse.

13. "Why didn't you. . ." No one needs any criticism, ever. The victim has endlessly replayed the incident and knows every option he or she "should" have taken.

14. "There are starving people ..." "It could have been worse." The better anything gets, the more one misses it when it's gone. Others' misfortunes are not comforting, only more distressing.

15. "Put it behind you." You are obsessed." The sufferer cannot "not be" obsessed. Obsession is a healthy reaction to trying to get one's life back under control. Society has been helped by obsessions of offended people. Look at what MADD (Mothers Against Drunk Driving) has done for highway safety.

16. "He'll get his someday." "What goes around comes around." Maybe so, but it never comes around fast enough. Some spiritual and religious beliefs can be comforting if the victim truly believes. When trust has been shattered, it is as hard to trust a just God as it is life sometimes.

17. "That's just how the system works." "It's the best system in the world." This condones outrage. We're not comparing lousy systems. This one happens to owe us as taxpayers an honest response to crime that punishes wrong and rewards right.

18. "It's only business." This assumes ethics and morals aren't to be expected in business dealings. Greed and power are accepted as revered ruling forces. That is unacceptable to most people.

19. "Don't cry over spilled milk." "Spilled milk" is a loss. There is no more appropriate time to cry than when one has experienced a loss.

20. "There is nothing you can do about it. You can't fight the courts." You must do what your sense of responsibility dictates. Some stakes are too high to abandon.

21. "You can't behave that way in court. Instead, acknowledge what the LWD just experienced that caused the undesired behavior. Then address the behavior in terms of what it will take to accomplish the goals, addressing any manipulation from the opposition and how the LWD's undesired behavior could work against them.

Suggested Internet Resources:

- www.bazelon.org - This is an excellent site for disability advocacy. They offer amicus curiae to support legal actions as well as new information on disability law.

- http://www.giftfromwithin.org/html/counting.html

- www.traumacenter.org - Elegant research in trauma and traumatic stress is available on this site.

- (Health Care Financing Administration, 1999).

- http://www.cms.hhs.gov/medicaid/default.asp?

- http://www.ismho.org A non-profit organization formed in 1997 to promote the understanding, use and development of online communication, information and technology for the international mental health community.

- Long, M.D. Essentials for Litigating Post Traumatic Stress Disorder (PTSD) Claims:

- http://www.va.gov/

- The National Institute for Clinical Excellence (NICE) makes national recommendations on best practice in medical treatment and care, with the aim of ensuring an equal and effective service across the NHS in England and Wales.

References

Americans with Disabilities Act Amendments Act of 2008, 42 U.S.C. §§ 12101 *et seq.*

Citizens United v. Federal Election Commission, 558 U.S. 08-205 (2010).

Fiske, S., & Taylor, S. (1991). *Social Cognition*. New York: McGraw-Hill.

Francis, L. P., & Silvers, A. (2000). *Americans with disabilities: exploring implications of the law for individuals and institutions.* (pp. 131-132, 335-336, 109, 126, 141, 333. New York, NY: Routledge.

Health Insurance Portability and Accountability Act of 1996 (HIPAA), 42 U.S.C. § 300gg *et seq.*

Heider, F. (1983). *The psychology of interpersonal relations.* Portland, OR: Psychology Press.

Herman, J. L. (1997). *Trauma and Recovery.* (pp. 176). New York: Basic Books.

Huffer/Alexander Survey (2007). Appendix.

Humphrey, R. (1985). How work roles influence perception: Structural cognitive processes and organizational behavior. *American Sociological Review, 50(2)*, 242–252.

Jones, E. E. (1990). *Interpersonal perception.* New York, NY: Macmillan.

Jones, E. E. (1979). The rocky road from acts to dispositions. *American Psychologist, 34*, 107—117.

Jones, E. E., & Harris, V. A. (1967). The attribution of attitudes. *Journal of Experimental Social Psychology, 3*, 1-24.

Kinchin, D. (2001) Post Traumatic Stress Disorder: the invisible injury. (pp. 157). United Kingdom: Success Unlimited.

Kolassa, I., et al. (2007). Altered oscillatory brain dynamics after repeated traumatic stress. *(BioMedCentral) BMC Psychiatry, 7*, 56. doi:10.1186/1471-244X-7-56.

Ross, L., Greene, D., & House, P. (1977). The false consensus effect: An egocentric bias in social perception and attribution processes. *Journal of Experimental Social Psychology, 13(3)*, 279-301.

Ross, L. (1977). The intuitive psychologist and his shortcomings: Distortions in the attribution process. *Advances in Experimental Social Psychology, 10*, 173-220.

Social Security Disability (2008, September). Blue Book. Section 12.00: Mental Disorders – Adult Evaluation. Retrieved from www.socialsecurity.gov.

U.S. Department of Labor (2010-2011). Occupational Outlook Handbook, Judges, Magistrates, and Other Judicial Workers. *Bureau of Labor Statistics*. www.bls.gov/OCO.

CHAPTER 6

RESEARCH IDENTIFIES LWD AND DETECTS TWO CRUCIAL CADAA INTERVENTIONS `ADA`

1. Assist the LWD with the bureaucracy involved in obtaining reasonable accommodations or the LWD may give up out of frustration.

2. Continue to monitor and update the original accommodations request as needs and circumstances change.

When you have gone so far that you can't manage one more step, then you have gone just half the distance you are capable of

Greenland Proverb

Low Tolerance for Inconvenience can Defeat LWDs

When a disability is not noticed or is ignored and inconvenience is put before them, many give up in despair. The CADAA offsets the symptoms effectuating their performance and helping them to go the distance. The common complaints listed below demonstrate how low tolerance in LWDs can discourage them from using their courts while the improper behaviors that devastate an LWD are hardly recognizable to judicial personnel or the general public.

1. Quiet personal biases by professionals and court personnel against those who are unattractive, different, needy, awkward, or easily upset.

2. The ADA Access Coordinators are often loathe to stand firm against the demand of a judge to formally approve or deny accommodation. So, at the clerk level, there may be severe violations of the intended confidential administrative process.

3. Sometimes security at the courthouse door is not advised of approved accommodations that certain people will need. Therefore, security may step in andremove accommodations

(i.e. a tape recorder) without direction, sensitivity, or knowledge. It can cause the LWD to become symptomatic and unable to function in court.

4. Judges are typically not administrators; therefore, they technically are not given the role of determining which accommodations are approved or denied. The role of arranging accommodations is a ministerial/administrative function (US Department of Labor, 2010-11).

When judges encroach on the administrative territory, their actions can even abrogate the 11th amendment that allows judges immunity. Opposing counsel will often demand access to the confidential information included in the ADAAA request for accommodations. The judge will then mistakenly consider the information ex parte communication and open the entire file to the public court and the opposition. At this point, most informed litigants or their attorneys file for disqualification of the judge as well as a grievance for ADAAA accommodations and protection to the appropriate oversight body.

CADAA Monitors and Updates Accommodations

When ADHD, autistic, Asperger Syndrome, OCD, Dyslexia, and Dyspraxia, to name a few (SSA, 2008), are introduced into the court system as litigants under the ADAAA, pro se or not, the protection of their rights requires additional consideration. By the very nature and management needs of the condition (i.e. ADHD, ASD) their early school attendance, time on task in class, learning objectives and outcomes have altered the foundation of their basic education. Therefore, basic orientation and education level varies for an LWD from that of an individual with no condition from the outset. If there were interruptions in the learning process and necessary skills were never mastered, the resulting level of proficiency would not meet the rigors of comprehension, speech, and writing proficiency demanded by the court. In these cases, a certified ADA advocate's presence to address the physical and emotional needs of the client, collect and follow court requests and directions timely, for example, is a mandatory accommodation. Ideally, I suggest an attorney and advocate work together.

The accommodations for this LWD population require not only the presence of an advocate but expanded authority to act at times on behalf of the litigant. However, a direct affront is found when the opposition challenges:

1. The validity of the disability,

2. The confidentiality of the medical information, or

3. Threaten to discriminate by denying the litigant with disabilities equal rights to intellectual support, parenting, property, opportunity, and attempt to quash the revelation of the disability and the protections afforded by the ADAAA.

The opposition often claims the litigant is asking for special treatment. They will demand medical records when they are not entitled to private medical information and ask that psychological evaluations be ordered by the court to open the information to them. In violation of HIPAA intentions, they want to fish in the brain of the litigant.

Huffer/Alexander Longitudinal Study Exposes Public Health Risk to Legal Consumers

A ten-year longitudinal study, "Survey of Court Litigation Participants Measuring Perceived Legal Abuses and Public Health Risks," was conducted between 1997 and 2007. It targeted the understudied population of those who seek justice and are dissatisfied with the court system. The objective was to determine the nature and validity of those dissatisfactions as well as noting the health consequences of being a dissatisfied litigant. The exciting part of this study robustly confirmed that litigation can cause or exacerbate PTSD. That means that Legal Abuse Syndrome as a secondary condition was affirmed by this survey. Why is that good news? Because the implication, then, is that such PTSD is preventable and is not to be considered a "mental illness" but an "injury," a clarification already established in the United Kingdom (Kinchin p.157). Litigant/respondents most often attributed their Legal Abuse Syndrome to being a complication of an existing condition or creation of an injury occurring during their litigation. Their conditions were medically validated dispelling the myth that dissatisfied litigants are just sour grapes. Listed below are the experiences that exceeded LWD's tolerance creating the injury:

1. They suffered due to prolonged, unsafe, and stressful exposure to horrific memories required by protracted litigation.

2. The litigant sought protection from the court and an end to contact with the perpetrator but, instead, received no effective protection from court or speedy justice.

3. They felt denied ethical behaviors from legal professionals affecting basic trust.

4. Economic depletion was caused by years of delays and obstruction of their evidence.

5. Critical issues worsened, such as child abuse while they awaited outcomes that amounted to years of additional stress and anxiety.

The respondents in the Huffer/Alexander Survey clearly dramatized that, unlike violent crime, deceptive assaults and loss of trust in protective systems quietly wound that very sacred, inner place which is the essence of self. Although the attack is clandestine and often clouded in pretext, it is more brutal than violent physical or verbal assault. Profound changes take place in the victim's life; yet, they can go completely unnoticed. The victim becomes isolated. He or she may rise every day, go to work, come home, appear at family functions, and look relatively normal; however, it is as if layers of cellophane wrap have enveloped the victims in a cocoon of numbness. The entire element of trust shifts within the victim.

The survey identifies ten most common invisible disabling conditions: Post Traumatic Stress Disorder (PTSD), Traumatic Brain Injury (TBI), depression, anxiety disorders, Bi Polar Disorder, Attention Deficit Hyperactive Disorder (ADHD), Autism Spectrum Disorders (ASD), mood disorders, and schizophrenia. Suicide ideation, is a frequent occurence but not considered a disability.

Even though ADA advocacy is a tough job, it is the key to bridging those with disabilities into full functioning in the court. Certainly, our ability to prevent victimization depends on our willingness to confront its existence. So, an open and accepting environment created for the litigant with disabilities goes beyond following the law. It means making it bearable to face the reality of their next court date. Advocates need to be appreciated as a very special group of individuals who assume an unwieldy responsibility with no clear guidelines. We do see wins. We see great human tragedy and suffering and we see opportunity to help fix a very broken system. Such is the world and honor of advocacy in the trenches.

Huffer's Log

Huffers' Log contains cases that demonstrate how, oddly, the first violator may not be the worst violator. LWDs may suffer more from criminal court, civil court, family and/or bankruptcy court than from the initial criminal attack or conflict. Legal abuses abound in all courts. There is no single entity that comprises "the court" or "the system." The judicial system is fraught with abuses clouding denial of honest services promulgating injustices, and health risks (Huffer/Alexander, 2007). However it is not them and us, we are the system. And we have to firmly implement any law that helps to bring justice for those with special needs.

How the advocate participates and the extent of that participation currently varies widely from case to case, court to court, county to county, and state to state. So far, there is not enough case law or experience by the courts to have established consistent standards governing the role and parameters of participation of advocates. An advocate's actions are generally dictated by the facts and circumstances of the particular case on which he or she is working. It is unlikely that such standards will be forthcoming anytime soon without strong public demand.

One day it will be recognized that the ADA advocate was a missing link that allowed the judicial system to become toxic to the point of crisis for litigants with disabilities. We all know that there are some greedy bastards with dirty power motives that have stolen from, hurt, and killed humans for profit from the beginning of time. Some of these are lawyers who infiltrate the justice system abusing their power. Unfortunately, zealous representation has provided a cloud cover under which denial of access to court for LWDs has become a cruel type of business-as- usual. However, the exploitation and shunning of the LWDs is now prohibited by the ADAAA. The missing link, the ADA advocate, is actively reversing exploitation. Further, their assistance clearly demonstrates that ADA advocates belong as part of every litigation team.

References

Americans with Disabilities Act Amendments Act of 2008, 42 U.S.C. §§ 12101 *et seq.*

Health Insurance Portability and Accountability Act of 1996 (HIPAA), 42 U.S.C. § 300gg *et seq.*

Huffer/Alexander Survey (2007). Appendix.

Kinchin, D. (2001) Post Traumatic Stress Disorder: the invisible injury. (pp. 157). United Kingdom: Success Unlimited.

Social Security Disability (2008, September). Blue Book. Section 12.00: Mental Disorders – Adult Evaluation. Retrieved from www.socialsecurity.gov.

U.S. Department of Labor (2010-2011). Occupational Outlook Handbook, Judges, Magistrates, and Other Judicial Workers. Bureau of Labor Statistics. www.bls.gov/OCO.

http://hrdailyadvisor.blr.com/

The Official Website of the Commonwealth of Massachusetts. "Rules of the Board of Bar Overseers" Section 3.60 Reopening by Hearing Committee or Panel. At any time prior to the filing of its report a hearing committee, hearing panel, or special hearing officer may reopen the proceeding sua sponte to receive further evidence there is reason to believe that facts or law require, or that the public interest requires, the reopening of such proceeding.

Resources

- The National Institute for Clinical Excellence (NICE) makes national recommendations on best practice in medical treatment and care, with the aim of ensuring an equal and effective service across the NHS in England and Wales.

- The Official Website of the Commonwealth of Massachusetts. "Rules of the Board of Bar Overseers."

- Section 3.60 Reopening by Hearing Committee or Panel.

- At any time prior to the filing of its report a hearing committee, hearing panel, or special hearing officer may reopen the proceeding sua sponte to receive further evidence there is reason to believe that facts or law require, or that the public interest requires, the reopening of such proceeding.

HUFFERS 8-STEP PROTOCOL

1. REFRAMING
2. DEBRIEFING
3. GRIEVING
4. DESHAMING
5. REGAINING CONTROL, OBSESSIVE-COMPULSIVE, HYPER-VIGILIANCE
6. BLAMING
7. EMPOWERMENT
8. RECOVERY

Chapter 7 demystifies disabilities and the erratic symptoms they represent for administration. First, it introduces by name only the list of counseling protocols called Huffer's Eight Steps. Chapters 8 through 15 will teach each counseling protocol in detail. Huffer's Eight Steps are the mental health tools that make working with persons with invisible disabilities manageable.

Once symptoms of the invisible disabilities are identified, counseling steps assist to offset those symptoms that interfere with performance. Help can be personal (e.g. person with disabilities driven to court, assisted in organizing documents). Some require formal accommodations. Alterations of the way things are usually done (e.g. breaks for medication management during the stress of litigation, separation of legal from personal issues, assistive advocacy during legal proceedings) or any other reasonable bending of procedure to ensure equal access per the ADAAA.

If formal accommodations are required, the burden shifts from Huffer's Eight Steps to the entity providing the public or private service. In cases of invisible disabilities, the task of accommodating can be challenging. The plethora of possible accommodations and endless disabling conditions overwhelm systems attempting to abide by the ADAAA while maintaining their budget and usual procedures.

The method offered in Chapter 7 lays the groundwork for breaking the issue down into three steps that facilitate the approval of requested accommodations. It simplifies the task examining requested ADAAA accommodations with flexibility using three components: 1) basic information about the disability provided to familiarize ADA administration as to symptoms and needs; 2) developing a model grouping some commonly encountered disabilities that tend to respond to similar application of the eight protocols and accommodations; and 3) design reasonable and effective ADA accommodations always keeping the door open for needed changes. Sometimes ADA administration negotiates with the litigant and/or advocate to assure the best service has been provided. Judges also may negotiate as to accommodations but are not advised to approve or deny.

Chapters 8 – 15 provide detailed descriptions, case examples, and research evidence for each of Huffer's Eight Steps. There is repetition of certain foundational principles in the chapters to promote the independent use of each chapter while maintaining a progression toward an effective advocacy model that prevents re-traumatization from the systems of care.

Using and improving on this process including a mental health component with a positive attitude toward ADA accommodations will contribute to guidelines that over time will grow into a social model. View chapters 8 through 15 through the lens of Chapter 7 aiming at cost effective, sensitive, top-notch service for litigants with disabilities.

CHAPTER 7

ACCOMMODATING OBSCURE DISABILITIES IN COURT

Invisible disabilities are fraught with communication errors resulting in severe discrimination for LWDs. Simply misreading the gestures, words, protocols in the courtroom can wipe out equal access. Each disability presents unique but solvable communication challenges.

DA
H8S

"WE WILL NOW STAND AND SING THE NEXT SONG ON THE OVERHEAD PROJECTOR"

Three-Step Process for Designing Specific Accommodations: 1-Information, 2-Application of Huffer's 8-Steps, and 3-Accommodatons

All criminal and civil justice personnel must develop clear and consistent communication methods that assure equal access for all persons with functional impairments. ADAAA advocates are the conduit to see that accommodations break new ground in an old justice system that functions like an expensive mill treading the same ground for decades on end. Communication technology is fresh saving the infirm the burden of physically appearing in court. New laws have unlocked doors for those with disabilities to get the aids and needed alterations. All it takes now is training and advocacy to finally realize due process of law and rid the judiciary of habits that wound up being biased and unfair.

Advocates will perform on a spectrum of assistance. If the advocate is a mental health professional the assistance will usually include diagnosis and accommodations design. If the advocate is not trained in a medical or health specialty or law, they will simply be the liaison between the ADA administrative office and the specialist. Most advocates will be able to use Huffer's 8-Steps as a coaching device during litigation. Special pointers for advocating for those with the following disorders will be discussed in three phases: A) Information for advocates and education of courts, B) Using Huffer's 8-Steps, and C) Accommodations.

PTSD, TBI, Anxiety Disorders, Depression

A. Information for Advocates and Education of Courts Today

Science is progressing to the point that illustrating the specific functional impairments is finally possible. The task of clarifying them for ADAAA administration in each court is greatly enhanced (SSA, 2001; APA, 2000).

1. A critical symptom of all of the above disorders is dissociation. It is a tuning out when the current incoming experience cannot be tolerated. It is a major symptom that blocks communication during litigation. We now have scans that show dissociation actually happening in the brain. Dissociation is a usual occurrence either occurring along with or following traumatic stress. During dissociation, a person's mind and memory flee from the moment in order to protect the person from an unbearable communication that exceeds their tolerance. Herman warns that the patient's intrusive symptoms must be monitored carefully so that the uncovered work remains bearable (Herman, 1997). When litigants dissociate, the ADAAA advocate must interpret for them in court.

2. We know now that many more people than those who speak foreign languages need interpreters in court. Attorneys, judges, and criminal justice personnel easily misinterpret the avoidant and numbing characteristics of these conditions as evidence of guilt, wrongdoing, indifference, lack of remorse, or disrespect. Lawyers and judicial workers are not equipped to manage litigants with these kinds of disabilities because it takes more than a legal education to properly interpret for those who suffer from the above impairments.

3. An event that causes PTSD triggers the left frontal cortex of the brain to shut down creating more disorders. Depression and anxiety are common features of Post Traumatic Stress Disorder.

4. TBI is becoming more common as service people return from deployment. TBI is usually enmeshed with PTSD, depression, and anxiety. Therefore it has to be

recognized that these conditions affect Broca's area, the center of speech. Litigants with these variations of disorders cannot stay active in a communication exchange in court while traumatic memories intrude. When people relive their traumatic experiences, the frontal lobes become impaired and, as a result, the litigant has trouble thinking and speaking. They no longer are capable of communicating within themselves or to others precisely what's going on. Without an advocate, this is a moment wherein they are silenced and denied due process of law.

5. Attorneys, unable to understand, make decisions for them i.e. encourage them to sign documents. They bend under pressure from the judge. Clients often regret these actions. They might accuse the lawyer of selling them out or malpractice. The lawyer was simply at wits end with the case.

6. Under the stewardship of advocacy, van der Kolk suggests, communication is clear and the client is better served (Wylie, 2004).

B. Application of Huffer's 8-Steps to Specific Disabilities

Huffer's 8-Steps are specifically created and laid out with a major focus on PTSD and above-mentioned disorders. Coaching and supportive counseling using the protocols and guides as they are directed in Unlocking Justice are recommended.

C. Accommodations Recommended:

1. Clarification/correction of misinformation is tricky but a key accommodation for these disorders. Symptoms are easy for judges and juries to misread risking fundamental attribution error/correspondence bias. Use of the simple date analysis form (Appendix A) tends to prevent adjudication error. Bringing perception in line with facts assists both the client and court. It prevents unneeded appeals, reopening of cases, and saves the client the pain and expense of undoing error post adjudication. While the misinformation is assaulting the litigant in court, the client has the task of writing or, if unable to write, quietly recording into their tape recorder the specific misinformation that is put forth. Then, after the hearing or at an appropriate time, the data is put together with proper evidence and provided to the trier of fact for correction on the record. This substitutes for untoward outbursts in court.

2. Video or audio recorder–personally provided, held and controlled by the litigant.

3. Ability to request breaks in the proceedings as needed.

4. Request that plain language spoken, no legalese.

Autism (ASDs), the CADAA's Quirky Client

A. Information for Advocates and Education of Courts. There is no disorder more challenging for criminal and civil court than autism. Courts are blindsided by ASDs. (Taylor, 2009).

1. Those with ASDs must never be without an ADAAA advocate when involved with criminal or civil court (North, 2007). Current research indicates that people with autism spectrum disorders and other developmental disabilities will have up to seven times more contact with law enforcement during their lifetimes than members of the general population (Curry, 1993).

2. Persons with ASD often get into trouble without even realizing they are in trouble.

3. Those with autism are prone to sensory overload causing them to react impulsively.

4. Sometimes they can't stand how they feel while surrounded by others who cannot perceive their discomfort.

5. They have poor social awareness and miss the messages in nuances and nonverbal communication. They do not understand usual verbal interchange.

6. Often if they have committed an offense they did not mean to and did not understand it was wrong. They can be accused of stalking, harassment, making threatening gestures, inappropriate sexual advances, inappropriate laughing or loud voice tone, insensitivity and be completely oblivious to their own behavior.

7. They are fraught with social misunderstandings that bring negative responses from authority figures. They are often punished without ever grasping the reality of the behavior linked to the consequence of their behavior. The advocate in a safe environment needs to explain how the symptoms created the misperception and then they work out prompts to guiding the client's behavior in the courtroom.

8. Autism is part of a group of disorders called autism spectrum disorders(ASDs). They are considered pervasive developmental disorders affecting neurological pathways in the brain. These diagnoses are increasing at an alarming rate around the world. Therefore, statistics are nearly impossible to pin down and estimates range between one in sixty children, to one in ninety births will result in an autism spectrum disorder. ASDs range in severity, with autism being the most debilitating form while other disorders, such as Asperger Syndrome, produce milder symptoms.

9. Complications in litigation result for many reasons beginning with the autistic litigant having difficulty dealing with interruptions in their routine and being labile, their emotions swinging widely and quickly.

10. Fear and anxiety can be sudden discomforts throughout their litigation.

11. Because these adults do not behave predictably and look very normal, the first response to them is often displaced anger from judicial personnel. ASDs can fairly easily arouse the ire of bosses and be unfairly terminated from employment rather than accommodated.

12. Autistic adults in the courtroom innocently challenge all rules, regulations, habits, traditions, and usual protocols. When problems arise, their communication deficits set in only making matters worse (Taylor, 2009). Hints that are dropped to guide behavior are beyond their grasp. To the onlooker, this can look like quiet defiance.

13. They often do not make eye contact causing them to look guilty when they are interrogated by law enforcement or interviewed.

14. They will erratically change the subject in the middle of a conference or while being questioned creating an appearance of being sarcastic or evasive to an investigator, attorney, or judge. They will try to control the topic when they are anxious appearing to disrespect the questioner.

15. The person with Asperger Syndrome will laugh, grimace, and make movements that are reflex actions. It is critical for advocates to explain this to the court assuring that they are not punished for false appearances of disrespect.

16. Standard interrogation techniques fail if they utilize dishonesty, deceit, or try to lead the conversation toward a predetermined goal. They also fail if the interrogator pushes too hard or becomes too intense or threatening.

17. Persons with Asperger Syndrome become overly influenced by a friendly interrogator or authority figure. They often feel isolated and live with a lonely void in their souls triggering a search for friends sometimes in all the wrong places. In that search, they are easily led into saying whatever the "new friend" wants to hear. Especially, persons with high functioning autism such as Asperger Syndrome will produce misleading statements, confusion and/or false confessions under pressure in hopes of being included. This creates a dilemma for lawyers, prosecutors, judges, and other personnel attempting to help or sort out the consequence or justice. ASD's have no clue that their behavior is making them look guilty, uncaring, rude, and sarcastic. They wear the justice system down until even their own counsel can doubt them.

B. Huffer's 8-Steps Applied to Specific Disabilities

1. ASDs litigants will surprise the advocate at times because they are often very bright and will catch onto certain of the steps quickly. The ASD must lead in choosing the steps. Never force but offer the process.

2. Protection and safety are the main goals with the ASDs. Therefore, beginning with

Empowerment, Step 7, is usually a practical tactic. Prepare for court by practicing and familiarizing the litigant with every aspect of the courtroom and the process.

3. When Debriefing, Step 2, it is important to verify the information and be sure the ASD litigant is not saying what they think you want them to say. Linking up the losses, feelings and occurrences are a good cognitive-behavioral exercise for ASDs. ADA Advocates must even be with the LWD during sworn testimony to ensure that the answer is not a rote response or an attempt to say what the questioner wants.

4. Utilize the individual's strong rote memory skills and then keep working the abstract meaning into the processes. Blaming, Step 6, OCH, Step 5, and Grieving, Step 3, will be first attached to the words that remind the litigant of what to do when they feel angry, anxious, or sad. After they recite the words, then expressing their feelings will better fit the words.

C. Accommodations Recommended:

At every part of the autism spectrum litigants or the accused must have ADAAA advocacy by their side. Even litigants with Asperger Syndrome will have language, but the placement and style of that language cannot be trusted.

1. Communication must be short, direct, and concrete.

2. Always double check and take nothing on face value. ASDs learn early on that in order to get out of a tense situation, because their communications skills fail, they just blindly agree with the authority. They quickly learn that by agreeing and saying yes, they are usually out of trouble. Always check affirmative responses with patience providing safety from impulsive or naïve communication.

3. Use simple, direct instructions said several ways. They want to please so disparaging remarks and punitive actions create disabling anxiety. They will be inconsistent; so, answering one question well does not mean they will be able to do the same on the next question.

4. Work out a Power of Attorney for medical decisions and a Living Will with someone the litigant trusts for medical purposes if possible. Since symptoms can be misread, there have been times when ASD litigants have been incarcerated and placed on antipsychotic medication. The result is disastrous. The persons on the antipsychotic in these instances were brought into court completely drugged and unable to protect themselves. These abuses are often avoided if it is clear that there is a POA in place and proper medical supervision.

5. Avoid legalese and rapid speech.

6. Involve persons who the individual knows and trusts.

7. Never isolate persons with ASD.

8. Prepare them for what is coming next.

9. Advocacy in criminal court requires training of personnel and close observation.

   a. If your client with autism is ever taken into custody, alert jail authorities. This person may be at risk in the general jail population. For short-term custody, consider segregation, monitoring, and a professional medical and developmental evaluation. Incarceration for a person with autism will be fraught with risk for the person and anyone in contact with him or her. The ASD's direct manner, offbeat behaviors, and characteristics may be read by other inmates as an invitation to exploit and control.

   b. Corrections professionals may misinterpret their behavior as rude or incorrigible.

   c. Good behavior privileges will be sometimes easy and quickly granted and at other times hard to earn.

   d. Correctional professionals who work with the incarcerated ASD population will benefit greatly from comprehensive training, at the least a good briefing and access to ongoing assistance from a professional who is familiar with autism (Taylor, 2009).

Mood Disorders

A. Information for Advocates and Education of Courts

Coaching and supportive counseling for mood disorders are usually easier than other diagnoses. The mood disorders include major depressive disorder, dysthymic disorder, and bipolar disorder.

1. There are approximately 21 million American adults or about 10 percent of the U.S. population age 18 and older expected to have a mood disorder each year (U.S. Census Bureau, 2005; Kessler , 2005).

2. Major depressive disorder is the leading cause of disability in the U.S. for ages 15-44 (WHO). Major depressive disorder or depression is called the common cold of mental illness in America (U.S. Census Bureau, 2005; Kessler, 2005).

3. Dysthymia is a chronic, mild depression that must persist for at least two years in adults (one year in children) to meet criteria for the diagnosis. It is seen less often than depression and seems like these litigants seem to just live life on "medium low." More than 3 million adults suffer from Dysthymia in any given year. These people will make lawyers and helpers impatient because they are slow to respond

and never seem happy about anything.

4. Bipolar disorder affects approximately 6 million American adults–about 3 percent of the population (U.S. Census Bureau, 2005). The cause of this malady is unknown, but it is one of the worst to deal with in litigation. Also known as manic depression this impairment is characterized by mood swings. So, one day the litigant might be on a roll that can last for weeks with high productivity, little rest, and optimism. Sometimes they are compelled toward activities that are not legally advised nor does it work in their best interest (Angst, 2010).

B. Using Huffer's 8-Steps to Specific Disabilities

1. Debriefing, Step 2, will be the skill that reveals the depth of the depression.

2. It is often helpful to start with Reframing, Step 1, and then go to Empowerment, Step 7.

3. By Debriefing after Empowerment the reminders of the trauma may not be as intense as if Debriefing follows Reframing.

4. After Empowerment, it may be possible to get to the Debriefing constructively.

5. Deshaming, Step 4, is a good next step followed by OCH, Step 5, and Blaming, Step 6.

6. Grieving, Step 3, might be one of the last steps for a person in depression. The key is the degree of productivity that results from the steps. Some may have to be repeated in time. Introduce the steps as therapeutic activities and never academic requirements. They are tools to be used as much as they can be helpful.

C. Accommodations Recommended

Coaching and counseling bipolar litigants toggles between the Grieving, Reframing protocol and OCH skills helping to curb stress triggering bipolar symptoms.

1. When not depressed, it is good to get through as many of the skills as possible. However, take note if the litigant is able to concentrate. Sometimes when the litigant is on an upswing, they sacrifice some level of concentration.

2. External and environmental factors are important to control through accommodations. Sudden changes even seasonal changes can affect those with bipolar. It may benefit the litigant to schedule a trial during certain times of the year if possible.

3. Sleep is very important and may be a key to keeping symptoms under control.

4. Medications and substances of all kinds are associated with triggering manic episodes. Proper medication is very helpful in most cases. Medication management is in order.

D. For these disorders, a prescription of anti depressant medication, lithium, other psychotropic drugs can often make the difference in the litigant being able to endure litigation or not (Beynon, 2008). If the litigant seems to live with a feeling of an empty void, feel as if they have low energy, are hard to motivate, find themselves tearful most of the time, and feeling without hope, it is good to refer them to a professional and consider medication at least in the short term.

Suicide

A. Information for Advocates and Education of Courts

1. Suicide is not considered a disability that qualifies under the ADAAA. However, more than 90 percent of people who commit suicide have a diagnosable mental disorder according to the National Institute of Mental Health (NIMH). The underlying diagnosis must be used in the request for accommodations in a court of law.

2. If the litigant is talking about suicide, check to see if it is a wish to die or is a trauma reaction, "I can't stand to be here anymore." If there is a plan to kill themselves and they seem to want to die, you must get emergency help. If it is a trauma reaction, an assessment by a professional is in order, but you have many tools to help.

B. Using Huffer's 8-Steps to Specific Disabilities

1. Reframing must focus on helping the person at the end of his or her rope learn to validate themselves and not allow others to invalidate them. Reframing is a personal validating experience.

2. Empowerment needs to be creative. This person feels there is nothing left they can do in the face of power going against them. There is empowerment in having an advocate willing to listen and think of the next task to be done. Logic doesn't work to talk someone back into being able to bear life. Listening and from what is heard directions usually emerge.

3. Blaming can help shift anger from going inward to be properly placed. Then, blaming actions follow. Always keep mitigation actions in mind as well.

4. Deshaming is a critical skill for those with suicidal feelings. Shame and guilt are usually at the core of self-destructive feelings. Review Chapter 9 comparing PCs and CCs helping the litigant to see how they have become compromised and then work to shed the guilt and find how to avoid those vulnerabilities in the future.

C. Accommodations Recommended

To qualify you will likely need to get a diagnosis of the underlying issue for the paperwork when requesting ADAAA accommodations. Again, suicide is not considered a disability in and of itself.

Schizophrenia

A.   Information for advocate and the Education of Courts

Schizophrenia is quite rare. The cases I have worked on have been under psychiatric care and fighting for custody or visitation with their children.

1. Their spouse has attempted to use their mental illness against them.

2. Medically managed schizophrenia does not interfere with a person's ability to be a good parent.

3. Men and women both are diagnosed with schizophrenia at equal rates.

4. This impairment is seen in about 1 per cent of the population (NIMH).

B.   Using Huffer's 8-Steps to Specific Disabilities

Coaching and supportive counseling requires keeping stress down as much as possible. These people are sensitive and responsive to Huffer's 8-Steps as they are laid out, but they especially need encouragement.

C.   Accommodations Recommended

It is important to have proper accommodations and to help these parents.

1. I have noticed in court that they will develop a pallor and clamminess that is visible when they are becoming symptomatic and the strain of the process is exceeding their tolerance.

2. They need to know that they will not be abandoned.

3. Advocacy is critical for this diagnosis.

Attention Deficit Hyperactivity Disorder (ADHD)

A.   Information for Advocates and Education of the Courts

1. For ADHD, autism, and TBI, the narrow requirements of communicating with the court are often prohibitive completely denying persons with these disabilities access to the court.

2. The court may only accept written complaints or motions and not allow oral presentations to substitute when needed.

3. ADHD, TBI, and autism create language barriers as severe as if the LWD spoke a foreign language. The court immediately provides an interpreter for foreign languages, but for those who cannot speak, think, and hear due to neurological

deficits, there is no communication assistance provided by the court. It falls upon the ADAAA advocate to request in a meaningful way the accommodations that will offset these deficits and must have assistance in preparing documents as well as speaking under stress.

4. ADHD is not really a deficit of attention but an enrichment and inability to screen out stimuli and focus. Court is overwhelming for those with ADHD who cannot defend themselves in a court of law. Medication is often helpful for ADHD and with careful dosage can facilitate a litigant getting through the full day of court effectively.

B. Using Huffer's 8-Steps to Specific Disabilities

1. Preparation is crucial as is the presence of a trained ADAAA advocate.

2. Careful observation and selection of the specific step needs to be flexible. Sometimes the advocate will use all or just part of a step with ADHD.

3. These are often bright people who cannot focus but can get through the steps and with the advocate's help get organized and be good litigants.

4. Start with the litigant's tendency toward denial and then work through all of the eight steps. The trenches of litigation hold scary realizations.

C. Accommodations Recommended

Many times these are people whose learning disabilities have interfered with their ability to be proficient speakers and writers. Even though they are bright, they cannot perform at a level that protects them in court. Again, if there were interruptions in the learning process and necessary skills were never mastered, the resulting level of proficiency would not meet the rigors of comprehension, speech, and writing proficiency the court.

References

American Psychiatric Association. (1994). *Diagnostic and statistical manual of mental disorders* (4th ed.). Washington DC: Author.

Angst, J. *et al.* (2010, October). Major depressive disorder with subthreshold bipolarity in the National Comorbidity Survey Replication. *Am. J. Psychiatry 167(10)*, 1194-201.

Beynon, S., Soares-Weiser, K., Woolacott, N., & Duffy, S. (2008). Psychosocial interventions for the prevention of relapse in bipolar disorder: systematic review of controlled trials. *The British Journal of Psychiatry, 192:* 5-11.

Census Bureau Release Date: June 9, 2005. http://www.census.gov/popest/national/asrh/.

Curry, K., Posluszny, M., & Kraska, S. (1993). *Training Criminal Justice Personnel to Recognize Offenders with Disabilities.* Washington, DC: Office of Special Education and Rehabilitative Services News In Print.

Herman, J. L. (1997). *Trauma and Recovery*. (pp. 176). New York: Basic Books.

Judge, T.K., Mesibov, G., & Debbaudt, D. (2009, Summer). *Autism in the Criminal Justice System*. The North Carolina State Bar Journal.

Kessler, R.C., Chiu, W.T., Demler, O., & Walters, E.E. (2005, June). Prevalence, severity, and co morbidity of twelve-month DSM-IV disorders in the National Co morbidity Survey Replication. *Archives of General Psychiatry*, 62(6): 617-27.

National Institute of Mental Health (NIMH). www.nimh.nih.gov.

North, A.S., Russell, A.J., & Gudjonsson, G. H. (2007). High functioning autism spectrum disorders: an investigation of psychological vulnerabilities during interrogative interview. *Institute of Psychiatry*, Kings College, London, UK.

Social Security Disability (2008, September). Blue Book. Section 12.00: Mental Disorders – Adult Evaluation. Retrieved from www.socialsecurity.gov.

U.S. Census Bureau. (2005). *European Archives of Psychiatry and Clinical Neuroscience*. Retrieved from http://www.census.gov/population/www/projections/projectionsagesex.html.

World Health Organization. (2004). The global burden of disease: 2004 update. Table A2. Geneva: Switzerland. Retrieved from http://www.who.int/healthinfo/global_burden_disease/GBD_report_2004update_coverTOC.pdf.

Wylie, M. S. (2004). Bessel Van der Kolk Wants to Transform the Treatment of Trauma. *Psychotherapy Networker, 28(1)*: 30-41.

www.victimsofthesystem.org.

CHAPTER 8

REFRAMING: HUFFER'S STEP-1
THE ART OF AFFECT REGULATION

Reframing is the staple skill that repairs and relieves emotional trauma. It is important to cycle through the three-step process often especially when the trauma is purposefully inflicted by another person.

DA
H8S

Figure 8.1 Cyclical use of the skill

"When I use a word," Humpty Dumpty said in rather a scornful tone,

"It means just what I choose it to mean — neither more nor less."

"The question is," said Alice, "whether you can make

words mean so many different things."

(*Through the Looking Glass,* Chapter 6)

Reframing the Internalization of False Accusations

Invalidating remarks, false accusations, libel, slander, and losing when the litigant knows they should have won by all reason plucks away at the LWD's delicate protective frame—like an eggshell crashing to the floor they feel bare and in pieces. While continuing to be attacked, litigants are left injured, and exposed with a painful heart assessing the damage. Raw vulnerability is exposed. As the pieces are picked up, a three-step process mends and reframes self-perception inoculating the litigant against damage from further psychic attacks. The three-step process is called Reframing.

An essence frames a human being. It creates an invisible boundary that extends an impression of the person. It is energy comprised of esteem, pride, competency, and emotional make up. It forms the framework that supports a person while they interact with others. Today's adversarial litigation attacks that framed essence while it is projecting the very self.

Committing to a short reframing ritual can become a mental exercise that wards off repeated invalidation, character assassination, misperception, and stress from using the judicial system. Domestic violence is a major mental health risk factor putting domestic violence victims who seek help from the legal system in double jeopardy. It builds to triple jeopardy if they are an abused immigrant spouse who is not literate in English and the American culture.

Each assault requires reframing or the damage accumulates. The cumulative effects of negative personal appraisals can leave a person feeling that they have no place to turn except to curl up in a fetal position for a time. I often observe this "fetal cycle" as part of the litigation process for those with PTSD/LAS. The checklist below samples feelings that signal a need for the reframing exercise.

Legal Abuse Syndrome Reframe Checklist.

Rate the intensity and frequency of the following emotional reactions/responses to the traumatic incidents you experience. Use 1 for sometimes, 2 for most of the time, and 3 for profoundly felt and interfering with normal activity.

1._____ trapped

2._____ creativity hampered

3._____ wiped out

4._____ anxious about future

5._____ stressed out

6._____ troubled

7._____ crushed

8._____ guilty

9._____ mistrust people

10._____ worthless

11._____ withdrawn

12._____ punished

13._____ unhappy

14._____ weary

15._____ stupid

16._____ at loose ends

17._____ life is irrational

18._____ the system doesn't work

19._____ outraged

20._____ why?

21._____ why me?

22._____ inadequate

23._____ resentful

24._____ rejected

25._____ abandoned

26._____ angry

27._____ depressed

28._____ numb

29._____ isolated

30._____ exhausted

31._____ unenthusiastic

32._____ defensive

33._____ embarrassed

34._____ afraid

35._____ resigned

36._____ disappointed

37._____ cyclical, in a rut

38._____ abusing alcohol or drugs

39._____ compulsive/overeating or starving

40._____ leaning on prescription drugs

41._____ workaholic/keeps busy

42._____ TV and couch become preferred companions

43._____ insomnia/worried about sleeping

44._____ physical symptoms attributed to stress

45._____ daydreaming/mentally escaping

46._____ intellectualizing/rigid/formal/clinical

47._____ avoids closeness with people/intimacy

48._____ others say you harp on your situation

For advocates it helps to encourage litigants to learn this list. After the initial interviews with the litigant, advocates know that naming a feeling is the first step to controlling it. The above list provides a good start for vocabulary needed to identify issues ripe for reframing.

Now, reframe those that rated a 3 or that felt intense according to the following exercises:

Reframing Exercise

First, look at the feeling or symptom. Secondly, put it in a self-appraising statement, i.e., if "physical symptoms" is checked with a 3, the self-appraising statement might be, "I'm too sick to go to court." Or, if you checked "defensive," "I must have done something wrong or be wrong." If you are defensive then an attitude of "don't blame me" emerges taking you off course. These sentences guide you through the three-step process. Third, prepare the statements to reframe according to examples provided below. Try to state the initial perception in as specific feeling terms as you can. This exercise is about self-appraisal, self-evaluation due to your experiences. Key into that self-appraising emotion:

1. List perceptions to be reframed.

2. Write out the reframed perception.

3. Acknowledge wisdom gained from the experience.

"As a result of this experience, I will never _____ again."

"Because this happened, I'm becoming a person who _____."

These are two examples of concluding sentences, but there can be many more. The examples below can be customized. The examples below are merely guides (Flanigan, 1992).

Example 1.

1. Initial perception.

"I was a fool."

2. Reframed.

"I'm a trustworthy person; I believed that others were largely trustworthy too."

3. Wisdom gained.

"Because this happened, I'm becoming a person who checks out everything in a business deal. I leave nothing to the other person's word without verification. I feel sad that I can't trust others, but I choose not to take unnecessary risks."

Example 2.

1. Initial perception.

"I'm so ashamed. How can I face my (wife) (family) (colleagues)?"

2. Reframed.

"I refuse to bear the shame that belongs on the criminal or the person who abused power and violated the moral code."

3. Wisdom gained.

"As a result of this experience, I'm becoming aware that I tend to suffer from inappropriate shame. Because this happened, I will blame the wrong-doer more and myself less in the future."

Example 3.

1. Initial perception.

"I should have seen it coming. How could I have been so stupid?"

2. Reframed.

"I was not responsible to be paranoid or omniscient. I'm an intelligent person who did not suspect wrongdoing."

3. Wisdom gained.

"Intelligence, contracts, or the law does not protect us from con artists. In the future, I'll listen to my intuition and investigate thoroughly when I suspect power moves."

Example 4.

1. Initial perception.

"I couldn't take it if I ever got betrayed again. I couldn't stand it."

2. Reframed.

"All decent people are vulnerable to betrayal. It would hurt to be deceived again, but to not take judicious risk is to be dead."

3. Wisdom gained.

"In the future, I'm going to depend less on others for my feeling of being complete."

Example 5.

1. Initial perception.

"I should have protected my property better and it would not have been stolen. I guess I asked for it."

2. Reframed.

"The criminal was dead wrong for coming into my space and stealing my property. I will prosecute to the fullest extent of the law."

3. Wisdom gained.

"As a result of his experience, I will install more locks and an alarm system."

Example 6.

1. Initial perception.

"The criminal was sure smarter than I was. He knew how to manipulate the system."

2. Reframed.

"I spend my time and energy contributing to society. It is hard to anticipate the actions of someone who spends his time and energy intending to abuse and do harm. The system was used inappropriately."

3. Wisdom gained.

"I cannot depend on the system to protect me. I must use every avenue that a citizen can muster to force reform."

Example 7.

1. Initial perception.

"Being good bought me nothing. There is no justice."

2. Reframed.

"I'm a person with fine values who strives for excellence. I still value living a just life in this unjust world and will do so in my personal life."

3. Wisdom gained.

"Goodness, decency, and excellence don't buy clout. When I must have clout, I'll not expect my fine reputation to buy it. The power-centered attorney I may need to hire for court clout does not have to suit my standard of decency or have my personal respect. . . a tough decision."

Example 8.

1. Initial perception.

"I'm fighting a huge bank. What chance do I have against their power?"

2. Reframed.

"Corporations abuse power by their very structure and focus on a bottom line. I'm a moral person, who doesn't choose to use trickery or under handed tactics in my dealings. I'm at a distinct disadvantage against these people in the courts."

3. Wisdom gained.

"There is a foundation that supports the corporate bottom line. That foundation is composed of consumers. I will take on my role as a citizen. I will turn off advertising designed to manipulate me. I will work to reduce the unfettered power of corporations pitted against citizens in our courts."

Example 9.

1. Initial Perception

"I have paid more than $100,000 in legal fees and have nothing to show for it. The money was used to review paperwork, get transcripts, and make appearances that more neutralized my case than fought for me. I have no way to turn. I can't do this by myself."

2. Reframed

"It is my court. If I back away, I am allowing a small group of 'insiders' to take my judicial system converting it for their own personal gain. The law can't be so difficult that taken one step at a time I cannot go back without an attorney."

3. Wisdom gained and needing to be gained.

"I cannot let my taxpayer funded path to civilized justice be treated as an exclusive club. It will not be easy, but I will gather resources to strengthen me, prepare realistically to face whatever efforts are mustered to discourage me and refuse to give up." The Huffer's 8-Steps and an advocate will be my bridges to a fair day in court.

Example 10.

1. Initial Perception

"I cannot cope with the lies and inhumanity I encountered in court. I am a victim with Legal Abuse Syndrome."

2. Reframed

"Psycho physiological effects of traumatic stress are not weaknesses to be exploited by the court or toys to be played with. I respect my health, my emotional state, and my right to protect my memory, my hormonal system, and my physical health. I cannot let the system induce further injury in me."

3. Wisdom gained

"I must use the Americans with Disabilities Act to properly manage litigation. Inducing a disability, discriminating against me because of the disability partially or wholly precipitated by the judicial system, or exploiting my disability is not lawful or acceptable. I must demand my civil rights. I will be a survivor."

Example 11.

1. Initial Perception

"I can't fight City Hall."

2. Reframed

"I own the court system as a taxpayer and a citizen and have a responsibility to see that it functions as it should. Justice is a real human need I must meet my own needs."

3. Wisdom Gained

"When my intuition tells me to act, I must listen to that over other advice. I can do something even if it feels inadequate. However, that something might just be the tipping point."

Reframing PTSD from Domestic Violence

When instruments of authority are no longer useful and are in fact causing a public health crisis, it is time they are replaced with effective services. The most difficult cases involve domestic violence. Advocates recognize and must force the courts to see that domestic violence is inextricably tied to PTSD/LAS. Those with PTSD/LAS are often disabled only due to their intersections with persons or events that initially created their psychological damage. If the person had not married the abusive, coercive spouse, that party would not be injured. In domestic violence/PTSD cases, courts need to understand that abuse is the precipitator of the impairment. It cannot be dismissed as "all in the past" and be disregarded. In such circumstances, every custody or psychological evaluation must reflect the domestic violence and be understood by the court, or the evaluation is invalid.

If the party had never been victimized by crime, deceit, or betrayal, he or she would not be injured. PTSD/LAS is a normal reaction to an abusive circumstance reflecting power differential. The American Bar Association reports that there is a 50/50 chance any person will wind up in court this year. When IT happens to you, the subpoena arrives or you know that you must file for divorce or file a lawsuit, you embark on a legal path and risk further stress related trauma. The court also needs to recognize that they bear a responsibility to prevent psychic injuries caused or worsened by abuse and protect each individual from having to splay their injured innards out to court personnel or other participants in the litigation. To do so by allowing the adversary to invoke psychological evaluations sets the victim up to be picked apart as nothing more than adversarial carrion.

In the court, the opposing side tries to twist the perception of that litigant like a pretzel. The litigant needs to reframe and refuse to take the bait and be twisted. Litigants protect their access to the court only if they prevent their opposition from "pretzelizing" them. Part of the solution is to learn how to regularly reframe when needed. If the adversary is provoking the litigant, it is the right time to not take the bait but to gain insights that empower, reduce anxiety, and affirm a positive sense of self.

Alongside the abusers and predators are decent people who won't tolerate or adopt actions that contradict their values in their responses. Some may stray for a time, but the reframe endures that aligns with the victim's moral conscience reaching out directly for what they need. The human conscience is a powerful force. While the advocacy mission is huge, in every powerful unwieldy system there are humans driven by conscience that can be sought out that will quietly help. They are insiders who know the right thing needs to be done and while they won't risk their jobs to do it, they will be quietly helping those who have the same values. These are the seemingly small relationships, favors, connections set up by ADA advocates that prove to be the tipping points for winning in many cases.

Advocacy Overdue in Cases of Mental Illness or Injury and Domestic Violence: A Strong Case for the Social Model for Accommodating Litigants

If a litigant suffers from an identifiable mental illness or injury, the abuser, in order to dominate the abused person, may use their condition against them. Mental illness or injury is frequently drawn upon to discredit the litigant in court. The abuser may call the victim "crazy," attempt to take over management of his or her medication, and often will do things to make the victim feel embarrassed or fearful. Reframing is more difficult and requires more coaching in these situations.

DA

H8S

A person may not have entered a marriage with a mental illness or injury; however, it does not take long under abusive conditions to induce a psychic injury from the abuse. Psychic injury can be added to an existing mental illness as well. Thus, it opens a door for the abuser to work to gain social support through bias that runs rampant throughout our society against those considered mentally ill or injured. The abuser will do the talking to medical personnel, take over finances, and relegate the victim to substandard dependency. They then assume control of all facets of the relationship becoming the sole decision-maker, wielding the power in the family.

Escape becomes difficult, if not impossible. Once the abuser has garnered community support, or even sympathy, and assumed control over all assets, the victim's alternatives are diminished. Sometimes abusers go so far as to put their victims under legal guardianship. They request psychological evaluations and then attempt to discredit the victim with the very psychological symptoms they have induced. Litigants cannot speak for themselves to sort this out in the context of litigation.

Therefore, while the litigant self-helps through the Reframing procedure, the advocate educates the court regarding the litigant's right to protection and confidentiality under ADA, ADAAA, and HIPAA. The court is given information as to functional impairments and needed accommodations only. The court must not allow the adversary to fish in the brain of the abused gratuitously.

Some judges will resist this and claim it is ex parte communication. The answer is to provide the judge with the wording of the ADAAA and emphasize that it is an administrative mandate apart from the issues in the case. It is important for the ADA advocate to have contacted the ADA Coordinator and educated that office as well if necessary. Administrative tasks are imperative and do not fall under the judge's discretionary powers.

As discussed earlier, the future trend is to tailor requests for ADA accommodations in court according to a Social Model, getting away from the inadequate Medical Model often used today. In other words, the only time the litigant has to prove a diagnosis and give specific details about their mental and physical condition is if they apply for financial disability benefits. Another is if they want damages from the other party for the existence of the condition. Then, it becomes an adversarial issue. For all other purposes, the details of the impairment can, by law, be kept confidential.

In alignment with the ADA Title II and the ADAAA passed in 2008, courts, employers, schools, and pubic services are required to serve the range of real people as they present and not assume everybody is physically and emotionally fit. These public services, agencies, and organizations can and should estimate and plan for the fact that a certain percentage of the population will need wheelchair access, Braille, magnification, and other accommodations when using public services. Non-apparent disabilities are equally included in the mandate put forth by the American Bar Association's Resolution of 2002 that was only reinforced by the ADAAA of 2008 (Hurder, 2002).

Accommodating the non-apparent disabilities brings humanizing and healing forces into the adversarial culture of the judicial system. They are the least expensive of all accommodations. At the basis of accommodations for PTSD/LAS is simple human on human respect and kindness… while following the disability laws. The advocate can make a good case furthering this cause. Once accepted, the courts quickly see the advantage of accommodating those with disabilities. Judges come to rely on the advocate to keep the case momentum moving. At this point, the court has reframed itself.

CADAAs Promote Legal System Reframe by Adherence to ADA Mandates

Advocates' efforts to promote etiquette and the Social Model by directly educating court personnel can be crucial. They are on the front line educating legal functionaries about The Social Model with the following points:

- It relieves the court from making errors regarding HIPAA and ADAAA.
- It assists in preventing inadvertent discrimination.
- The Medical Model places court personnel in the awkward position of being the exclusive but medically unqualified arbiter of disability for individuals.
- ADA Coordinators are commonly clerks or attorneys who are not medically qualified to decide who is and who is not "disabled." They can't be comfortable or effective in the role.

Expected Progressions from Reframing, Step 1

- Takes the Litigant from Victim to Veteran/Survivor

- Litigant Goes from Vulnerable to Savvy

- Litigants Come from Retreat to Reaching Out

- Litigants Reframe from Numb to Receptive to New Ideas and to Relationships

- Reframing Releases Litigants from Hostage Stance

Reframing Re-educates and Prepares LWDs for Self-validation

Litigants need to set a system of reframing in place at the outset by using the Reframing steps. In and out of court, reframing can help the sufferer and others gain new insight. Otherwise, they are victimized by the litigation process. When negative attacks occur, the reframed litigant responds from a position of strength, for example:

1. "Your Honor has heard efforts to invalidate my sanity, my parenthood, my business acumen, my ... placed on the record. Regardless of those false assertions ..."

2. "I am a strong, capable, loving, trustworthy individual and will not take the court's time to defend against wild accusations."

3. "I will be filing a data analysis form correcting mischaracterizations and inaccuracies for correction of the court record. Evidence will be attached."

LWDs from Victim to Veteran/Survivor

Reframing brings noticeable and liberating changes to sufferers. No longer will the litigant be defined by the traumatic experience. When the sufferer reframes the self-image from "I was the victim of..." to "I am a veteran and a successful survivor of a clear wrongdoing," wrongdoing is no longer internalized. Likewise, the horror story will not be the central topic (or the avoided topic) of conversation. A newly emerged self, centered on strength, will be more easily presented. A more realistic perspective replaces the obsessive struggle of the hostage. Dagi (case cited below) was able to use reframing as well as any client I have served. She has basic ego strength and values from her upbringing that support her efforts now.

LWDs from Grieving Loss to Free and Ready to Fill the Void

A sense of loss reframes into a feeling of ready to fill the void. Litigants seldom choose to lose their beliefs or belongings. Once they are gone, wisdom should guide their replacements. The sufferer needs to be purged and absolved of old responsibilities, naiveté, and past lifestyle. There is an Oriental expression that in every loss there is a gain and in every gain, a loss. The gain is always emphasized during reframing exercises.

From the sufferer's losses, the object is to list the gains. This does not mean "a look on the bright side" approach: it is the maximizing of the strengths required for recovery. Neither does it minimize the wrong that was done nor the magnitude of losses. Extracting gain from loss is a vital habit that survivors must learn to use to force benefit from suffering. Once mastered, this technique greatly enhances recovery.

LWDs Go from Vulnerable to Savvy

Reframing directly confronts the loss of confidence that paralyzes the sufferer's dreams. It takes the sweeping, immobilizing perceptions that follow profound trauma and carefully pinpoints the vulnerability that made the victim a target. Reframing then leads to a recognition that begins the healing; a sort of psychological scar tissue is formed that slowly allows the resuscitation of desires and dreams. Risk is easier when the litigant "knows the score."

LWDs Come from Retreat to Reaching Out

A woman in her late thirty's reached out to me at a conference after being in a forced retreat for two years. Katy was shocked to discover four years earlier that her son we being sexually abused by both his father and grandfather. She was further stunned and began the end of her marriage when she discovers sexual abuse of children was a family tradition. When Katy reported it to the court and tried to get supervised visitation for the father with no visitation for the grandfather, custody was removed from her and her rights to visitation were terminated. The judge said that she was causing Parental Alienation Syndrome in the child; she was too enmeshed with the child, and was falsely accusing her ex-husband.

She has not seen her son for four years. She was frozen in time and tried picketing and writing letters but largely was unable to take on the issue effectively in the context of litigation. Therefore, in her innocence she did not know that she was offending the court by writing letters, getting friends to write letters and for them to stand in front of court sadly stationed with a sign and picture of her son. Until she re-awakened the ability to reach out, she was unable to put the legal right to mother her son and protect him into workable form that would have power in the court. She now has an upcoming court date with an advocate to be by her side. She has filed proper paperwork and cited irrefutable authority that will hold up for an appeal and further action.

It will feel impossible to reframe in the midst of legal demands and trauma. However, a few moments spent on these exercises re-energize the parts of the brain that are affected by trauma will yield rich results. It is like the litigant almost in lieu of meditation or those kinds of activities that foster survival through tough times has an instant type of cure for their symptoms. Advocates will weave moments of Huffer's 8-Steps through litigation by taking short breaks or making telephone calls to the advocate when the litigants feel they cannot go on. They are then guided to specific places in this book or reminded of Reframing exercises and also that someone fully understands and validates and helps to ease their symptoms.

Litigants who've been profoundly assaulted by systems they trusted lose the conscious sense of what they want in life. If asked, they will say they just want to be left alone or never to go through such a trauma again. Those are not desires. Desires have to do with life being tasteful, satisfying, and full. Desires allude to a future with vitality. Vulnerability resulting in sweeping assumptions like "I was stupid," cripples and confuses a person's ability to desire. Pinpointed reframing statements, i.e., "I was trusting, not stupid," bring a wiser perspective. Reframed perspective allows judicious risk-taking rather than cellophane-wrapped removal from life, and opens the door to desires again.

Thus, the sufferer must begin to generate a new list of desires and dreams. It may, however, be a difficult task. Such desires and dreams were part of a past perception of life. They depended on a reality that evaporated along with friends, confidence in protective agencies, and systems that proved to be mythical. The resulting list may bring with it challenge, fear, and apprehension. Katy has now set the goal of mothering her son and getting him out of a pathological environment. Belief systems that supported past dreams have been damaged or shattered. It may feel as if there are barriers to the renewed desires. Nevertheless, this renewed list can provide the matrix and energy for the fight that must go on to give meaning to the sufferer's existence and yield the positive benefits to come by fulfilling newly reframed goals with confidence.

LWDs Reframe from Numb to Receptive to New Ideas and to Relationships

Numbness does not just dissipate. It is part of the physiological change that trauma causes. It usually eases only in micro-fragments as healing progresses. Sufferers frequently will limit discussion to one part of the trauma. They may still be in denial or unable to feel the impact of some elements of the injury. Such styles of healing from trauma are to be anticipated. The sufferer simply must start where he or she can in spite of the obstacles. This effort will begin to crowd the negative feelings out as he or she proceeds.

A significant barrier to reframing is fear of "bursting the emotional dam." Nature has generously provided our own chemical protection, numbness through natural opioids. Without opioids and desensitization, pain would render us nonfunctional. Unfortunately, the price of numbness is dullness. Victims deserve better. Thus, the advocates assist sufferers to come out of dullness and begin to interact with others and their environments, even at arms length. Katy is shedding her numb feelings and risking hope again that she can rescue her son.

Fear of the emotional dam bursting can last for years and requires patience, safety, and support. Letty was an extreme case, but it took her fourteen years to allow her emotions to be expressed and to release her trauma. A group participant, Letty, was a middle aged, single woman whose life had been consumed by her mother's domination, jealousy, and guilt manipulation. She judiciously showed up at various therapy and training groups of mine for 14 years. Letty, after all those years, began reading short, emotional poetic paragraphs to the group. The risk was eased by careful preparation of her paragraph during the week. Verbal interaction with the group followed. She began to put her feelings into poems and share them with the group.

Finally, her "emotional dam" burst. She had feared "letting go" all of her life. Her catharsis consisted of crying profusely and eating chocolate for the next two sessions while she shared a lifetime of guilt and being hooked to her mother. Letty had never been her own person. She was trained from birth to just be her mother's companion, artistic fan, and now caregiver. She had never developed her talents because her mother was talented in the arts also and she felt too guilty to compete on her mother's artistic turf.

Two years after the reframing and the dam bursting, this woman is aggressively studying art and preparing for her first art show. Fear of crying and the pain of guilt prevented her dream of a retirement career as an artist. "Emotional dams" are far more frightening in perception than reality. In twenty years, I've witnessed crying, eating, punching a wall, and pacing. All of the actions helped unlock wonderful human potential. The key to unlocking that potential is to provide an environment in which the sufferer feels secure enough to take a chance to reframe their entire self-concept.

Once the opioids decline, a short-lived identity crisis may follow (Mills, 2005). He or she is not who they were before the assaults – not the loser, liar, thief, crybaby, nor disgruntled litigant that the adversaries have characterized. But, neither is he or she the trusting, naïve person vulnerable to predatory power that they may have been before. A little defining of the new identity usually goes a long way. Time spent on this skill is always time well spent whether it is a coach, companion, supportive counselor or in formal therapy.

Author's Notes:

Techniques such as reframing are meant to promote healing of the injuries suffered prior to and during litigation. They deal with and are meant to affect the psychological health of the victim. They do not and cannot, however, address the circumstances of the court system that inflicted or exacerbated the injuries. Those situations must be addressed with legal tactics.

In essence, Reframing is one technique designed to permit the litigant to endure and to continue the fight. Participants should not make the mistake of believing that the "adversarial system" is going to change to give them an edge because of their injuries or disabilities. ADA and ADAAA have been interpreted by the Government agencies charged with their enforcement to insure "access" to everyone regardless of their disability. The current perception of these laws is that "justice" is not guaranteed just equal access toward it. Thus, the laws—if used properly and wisely—will allow disabled litigants to remain in the fight and, in some cases, protect them from some obvious abuses of the system as it operates. But, those laws and others like them do not give the disabled a pass or an advantage in their litigation. They must still know and follow the rules and understand that they are involved in what is, in fact, an adversarial system and be prepared to participate as required.

Thus, the laws passed for the disabled are no more than tickets to the stadium. Once inside, they have a right to take the field. But if they do, they must realize that the rules of the game apply equally to them, and that until the courts and the professionals who function within them come to understand what accommodations for the disabled actually mean, and how they can be effectively implemented, participants are still exposed to the potential injuries of the game itself. The laws may provide some "extra padding," but the game is still as rough and as dangerous as it ever was. Unfortunately, the only way to avoid the dangers of the game entirely is to sit in the stands as an observer or to stay out of the stadium (Goldblatt)©.

This is not to say that the laws are useless or ineffective. But, using them, as any other laws, require an understanding of both their purposes and their limits and then making them work for you as effectively as possible. But, as is the case in any other part of the judicial system, the "burden" is on the individual asserting their rights and protections. You must know what the laws say, how they are meant to work, and how the courts are required to operate within them – and be able to convince the court that your understanding and interpretation is correct.

Huffer's Log

The Triple Threat: Domestic Violence, Immigrant Status, and a Custody Battle

Tragedy is around the corner for people caught up in domestic violence. The Family Court is in crisis. It is a huge system that is putting children at risk every day.

Fortunately, after wrongly believing the defense attorney and signing herself into probation as a felon, Dagi took to Reframing as her "bread and butter" skill. She is able to use the three steps to adjust her self-concept as a matter of course. She has the process down to a brief mental exercise that she holds close while she is assaulted by false accusations, damage to her reputation in court, and rejection when she seeks employment.

Dagi's advocate had no doubt that she needed a regular regimen of reframing. She knew her client was in triple jeopardy, an immigrant, English not her first language, an ex-husband that was pathological and dangerous, and she was fighting for custody of her children.

Dagmar was raised in what she describes as a loving, extended close family in France. She immigrated to the United States after completing education in Europe. As a young adult, she traveled through Asia, the Middle East, and Europe before coming to the United States. She was educated, worldly, and felt ready for marriage. Her life had been quite ideal.

Dagmar met and married an American man who had courted her on two Continents. She had a hint of discomfort when he pursued her in Europe but agreed to marry him and move to America. He preferred to live in remote rural areas and provided a home in a beautiful part of the United States. She didn't think anything of it. Her husband was protective, charming, and strong.

But, not long after the wedding, her husband raped her. He told her it is "how Americans make love." Dagi was stunned. From then on, she was dominated by fear; afraid to leave him and afraid to stay with him. She cannot explain the hollow state she was in, but she seemed to lose her very self. Dagi did not realize she had succumbed to being a hostage progressively living in fear and resignation.

Year followed year while every day she struggled to cope with the man who by now had emerged as the ruler rather than the leader of the family. Having come from a large family she could not explain why she obeyed this ruler and gave birth to five children. She always expected to have several children but planned on more ideal circumstances. All she can relate is that when she asserted herself against him, he threatened and/or punished her. Somehow she hoped having the children would soften his demeanor.

Abuse can cause dissociation. Dagi focused on staying busy with the children, cooking, home schooling, and didn't think much about her own happiness or independence. She kept peace by acquiescing to her husband's demands. The family was the center of her life. She was surrounded by pets, children, and isolated in country life far away from her parents and roots.

Dagi has deep brown eyes that emanate pain and suffering. It seems that a reflection of pain as deep as Dagi's must have been installed in many layers over time. There came a point when she realized the sex she endured was unbearably painful. Her husband would not respond to her need for respect. Sex was punishment. One day her eyes opened seeing an unwelcome reality. Awareness of her unhappiness was like a fog slowly displacing her ability to see anything else in their home.

No one in the family was allowed to have friends, belong to social groups, attend church, or have any contact outside of the family property. She was terrorized at the realization that she and her children were more prisoners than family members. They were progressively being denied every opportunity to grow, learn, and blossom in this life or have a moment of peace. In short, no one in the family was thriving. She felt deep shame for passively allowing five children to be born into such a household. She felt guilt for her helplessness and fear. She knew that unless she treaded very carefully that even the extreme of murder/suicide was not out of the realm of her husband's reality.

At his best, her husband was coercive, invasive, intrusive, and always angry. At his worst, Dagi knew that her life was in danger. She was kept isolated and dependent as his hostage and sex slave. There were no boundaries. He allowed no locks on doors in the home so there was no privacy. He raped her at least once per month. She knew something had happened to her brain and her ability to be her own person. Her self had melted away. To outsiders the home looked healthy, rural, and her husband appeared to be devoted to his family. No one in the family could say, "no" to him. As the children got older and tried to assert their personalities, he beat them, yelled at them, forced them, and isolated them. If one of them made a move he could not control, he would appear to cooperate on the surface only to sabotage the activity in the future or brutally attack when it was not expected.

Dagi clandestinely through a friend decided to add to her education and work toward independence. She felt like a prisoner planning an escape, terrorized but energized. She had to somehow leave him and at the same time save the children. She began to study. She quietly and methodically worked her way to a certification in a health field by transferring her credits from Europe and adding to them through any means that she could manage. A plan was being put together to find work and to figure a way out of her marriage without leaving the children to be victimized by their father. She was carefully making her plans, but they were not to be carried out as she hoped. The moment came for action.

The turning point was the day her eight-year-old child was beaten and left with her face bloody; Dagi could endure it no longer. Dagi had to leave her husband immediately. She was terrified to confront him but finally worked up her courage, took a risk, and asked him for a divorce. She was surprised and cautiously relieved when he agreed to an "amicable" divorce. He left the home so she and the children could stay in it. Soon she would find out that this was his surface cooperation with scheming and sabotage to follow. She knew the pattern.

Unsophisticated in the ways of the judicial system and focusing only on protecting her children and providing for them, Dagi was blindsided by her husband. Unbeknownst to her, the children's father consulted with an attorney and formed a strategy to accuse Dagi of parental alienation. Even though their father had been coming to visit almost daily, he started to miss days of visitation and then weeks of visits, blaming a car that was not running or having to do the laundry, or some other excuse. He then executed his strategy accusing Dagi of "not letting" him visit the children for the days he had chosen to miss.

Then, the hammer dropped. Her ex-husband sued Dagi, bringing a powerful case of Parental Alienation Syndrome (PAS). The records of his missed visits perfected it. She knew nothing about the syndrome, but when he refused to visit the children and then accused her of "alienating" him, the court punished her by denying her custody. She was forced out of the home and soon the children were living with only their father. She learned from (The Leadership Council http://www.leadershipcouncil.org/) and From Madness to Mutiny (Neustein, 2005) that PAS is a trend in family court. However, it is based upon on one man's opinion not proper scientific research. With it, children are often removed from the protective parents without judges realizing that the PAS research has no scientific or factual basis that meets forensic standards.

DA
H8S

Dagi was frantic and terrified. She moved to another state and got an attorney intending to get the children removed from the abuser and protect them. She stayed with her oldest daughter who had reached adult status and was now on her own. With Dagi gone, the children could endure no more. They ran away. They showed up on Dagi's doorstep. She immediately called her attorney to intervene. Dagi went to the local district attorney's office to speak with someone at the Victims Witness program. The deputy she spoke with told her that her husband should have been put in jail many times for what he did. She spoke to the deputy for about two hours; he made a report that she counted on to rescue her children. Someone in authority had listened to her. She was greatly relieved.

To her disbelief, she opened the door one day to police who arrested both Dagi and her oldest daughter for child abduction. Her ex-husband in another state put the false accusations in motion. She spent several months in jail. She demanded the report from the District Attorney's office that caused her to be arrested. It had disappeared. Then she tracked down the assistant district attorney she had spoken with who made the report. He had left the program. Her attorney, on a pro bono arrangement, was unable to help her. She saw no public defender for four months in jail. This defied logic to Dagi who believed that laws and officials would protect her and the children. Her European background was rife with pride, responsibility, and accountability. She wondered what was wrong with law enforcement and the justice system in America. She wondered what was wrong with her.

Dagi is now an immigrant, with a felony. Her ability to practice her profession to earn a living is destroyed. No one in her family had ever been in jail. She was ashamed to talk to them but begged for their help and the help of her home country. No one helped her in a way that made a difference. She was put on probation for five years for the twisted tale told by her ex-husband. She could not have abducted her children who had run away from their abuser. She was provably in another state when they ran away. Dagi was guided to an advocate who involved her in reframing and brought her to a group of litigants who met weekly to deal with Legal Abuse Syndrome. She began reframing and although behaving normally, her sad eyes betrayed her and to this day tell the real story always lurking behind those eyes.

She presented with layers of trauma when we began her advocacy. Thankfully, she took to Reframing so a foundation was laid for her to survive the rigors of the next seven steps. We went to Empowerment after Reframing in order to assist her in obtaining resources to help her since her legal actions were immediately pending. Then we went to debriefing but limited it to the last six months in the beginning. To go much further would have bogged her legal process down. Dagi still has to grieve. That dam is left to break when she is feeling safe. Deshaming was important for her to undergo to sort out that her husband was a power-oriented person from the beginning. Blaming is broad and is still being studied because two governors are involved and two District Attorneys. A great deal of deception was used to get her to agree to the felony status.

References

American Bar Association Commission on Domestic Violence. (2009, May/June). Domestic Violence Webinar Series: *Tips and Strategies in Protecting Victim Privacy, Representing LGBT Victims and Representing Victims with Disabilities.* 07765.

Flanigan, B. (1992). *Forgiving the Unforgivable: Overcoming the bitter legacy of intimate wounds.* (pp. 187). New York: Wiley Publishing, Inc.

Hurder, A.J. (2002, September/October). ABA Urges Equal Access to Courts for Individuals with Disabilities. *Mental and Physical Disabilities Law Reporter, 26:5,* 772-3.

Mills, K.L., Tesson, M., Ross, J., Darke, S., & Shanahan. (2005). The costs and outcomes for opioid dependence associated with posttraumatic stress disorder. *Psychiatric services, 56,* 940-945.

Neustein, A. & Lesher, M. (2005). *From Madness to Mutiny: Why Mothers Are Running from the Family Courts--and What Can Be Done about It.* (pp. 26-7). Boston, MA: The Northeastern University Press.

DA
H8S

CHAPTER 9

DEBRIEFING:
HUFFER'S STEP-2 CASE MANAGEMENT TOOLS

Huffer's Step 2, Debriefing, graphs your data creating two distinctly dissimilar courses. Preparation for legal action is one path. The other combines personal coping with loss, challenge to health, and other intimate issues. If litigation is to be a successful choice, it requires this step for preparation before investing in legal fees. Organization also fosters healing and the endurance necessary to go the distance.

H8S
GRL

Problems do not just go away and time does not heal all wounds. Traumatic stress fills the soul with unrelenting pain. The problems must be worked through or else they remain, forever a barrier to the growth and development of the spirit.

M. Scott Peck

Pre-legal Preparation: Separate the Legal Positions from Emotional Interests

If litigation follows a traumatic event, debriefing must be done because it sets the parallel path for healing while simultaneously battling. After the kinds of human on human traumatic events that bring people to court, debriefing is an indispensable step in helping the person manage. They struggle with ongoing emotional reactions, material losses, demands of performance in litigation, and changes in everyday life. Debriefing also serves to lay the foundation for calculating economic loss fostering restoration. The trauma story, more importantly than in any other circumstance, needs to be conducted in a structured interview that reveals layers of facts, feelings, and losses. ADA advocates are the best resource for conducting debriefing interviews.

Advocates assist as the painful doors open and the trauma story unfolds. The first focus is initial impact of trauma, the real damages caused in the immediate day-to-day life of the victim. Ranking among the top stressors are residential and job changes or losses, expenditures of time consumed by litigation, having to assume new duties previously carried out by others, scheduling pressures, and financial restrictions. Any one of these is considered to be a major stressor in a person's life resulting in emotional fallout that is overwhelming. Processing of the feelings is laborious and threatening. In order to move from overwhelm to organized, the trauma story must be guided forth with four main questions.

1. What is happening to the litigant's life?

2. How does it make the litigant feel?

3. What losses are being sustained?

4. How are their impairments being treated?

The Debriefing process organizes the information on a graphic (Appendix A). Once the litigant sees the graphic taking shape, it helps a traumatized person to manage the overwhelming nature of feelings and experiences that create PTSD/LAS. On the one-page graphic, the traumatized person names their feelings and comes to terms with the tangible and intangible value of their losses. At this point, the debriefing story and the parallel purposes are served. Wasting a lawyer's time is wasting money. Telling the traumatic side of the story helps with healing by developing the skill of putting names to feelings and relating them to the experiences that arouse the emotions. The other is to prepare information from the story that is relevant to litigation.

Maintaining health while litigating is about identifying stressors and emotions. Why is it usually not helpful to share the story and draw from best friends and family? Even though an individual may desperately need to verbalize his or her pain and suffering, a strange thing happens when an individual begins to detail the experience. Helpers' eyes glaze over, clichés roll off the tongues of even the most sensitive, and there is that compulsion in listeners to minimize disasters with positive interpretations. Such responses only exacerbate the stress by appearing to trivialize the sufferer's feelings about what he or she has been experiencing. Those close to the litigant may volunteer help, but many times when it is requested, the friends and family withdraw.

There is controversy regarding the general value of debriefing (Kessler, 1995; North, 1999; Robinson, 1995). However, LWDs must have a detailed debriefing experience as a first step to feeling in control of their legal cases. Litigation is about redress and restoration. If there is to be any justice, the full impact of the trauma needs to be calculated in monetary terms. That is the main focus of the type of justice that a judge or jury can grant. Other than custody and visitation most adjudication is in the form of awarding "money." The injured party must come to terms with a dollars and cents "value" of his or her losses, inconveniences, and injury in sheer economic terms. In this way, "pain and suffering" comes to mean a certain dollar value, just as other aspects of "damages" inflicted by the opposing party come to have calculable dollar value.

Debriefing starts with quality listening and a safe environment provided by the advocate. Without an advocate, a feeling of safety can be the hardest for persons with PTSD to find since their stories are upsetting not only to themselves but also to the average listener (Tick, 2005). Who can be the advocate to do debriefing? Anyone that is trusted. There is no single legal or medical credentialing that qualifies a person to help another person face litigation after a traumatic event.

It is assumed that doctors and lawyers are the advocates for first line help. However, going to either before sorting out and identifying symptoms and losses can be an exercise in frustration and a waste of valuable assets. It is important that what is presented to the professional is not clouded by overwhelming stress. The litigant will not receive the best professional services under those conditions. That is why a devoted and if possible, certified, ADA advocate is usually the most helpful. They will remain the closest to the litigant in court as well as to witness their symptoms first hand. ADA advocates guide the debriefing to get the litigant ready for both legal and medical intervention using Huffer's 8-Steps outlined in this book. At all times, advocates shore up the process using the reframe exercise that underlies threatening and challenging assaults to the litigant's self esteem and psyche.

By organizing a case and setting its traumatized victim on the path to healing early on, a great deal of time and money is saved. I witness monumental waste from non-productive attorneys' fees because the litigant put forth an unclear case that the lawyer must sort out. Advocates pay for themselves many times over when cases are managed efficiently. Attorneys are not immune to legal abuses nor are they equipped to professionally deal with the symptoms of trauma. Therefore, the more the individual has clarified the sentinel issues that are appropriate for litigation, the greater are his or her chances that the case will be seen to completion with opportunity for justice.

H8S
GRL

The Debriefing Process–Getting Started

Make several copies of the Debriefing Worksheet found in Appendix A. Then, follow the instructions below.

1. The Center Circle—What Happened

Using several debriefing graphic sheets, focus first on what happened. Write it in the center circle. If debriefing is conducted in a group setting, led by an ADA advocate, each participant should have several Debriefing Worksheets. Divide the group into dyads or pairs. One member of the dyad is a listener and one shares his or her story. Then, when the first person has finished, the roles are reversed. Sometimes these dyads result in advocacy tradeoffs that assist both partners for the long haul.

Surrounding the center circle are bigger circles divided into sections. The major, initial impact experience has been written in the center circle. Then the significant resulting cumulative assaults or "ripple effects" are written in adjacent sections. All participants are listed, named, and the events are portrayed as if a picture was being painted in words. It becomes clear that the realm of the doctor or therapist is more in the feelings circle and the interest of the lawyer will be largely found in the loss circle. All facets are interrelated of course.

Debriefing is best conducted under the guidance of an advocate or one trusted person prepared to refer the litigant to a professional counselor if needed. Breakthroughs in denial are common during this experience. Either the victim or listener might break through denial at any time. They will be emotional, will usually cry and will realize unwelcome truth. It is helpful to have a supportive person or therapist aware of PTSD/LAS to turn to at those times (Herman, 61).

Consider choosing therapists who are trained in EMDR. If the person seeks or is referred for counseling, breakthroughs in denial can be an ideal time for Eye Movement Desensitization and Reprocessing to be considered as an option (www.emdr.com). Eye Movement Desensitization and Reprocessing (EMDR) is a comprehensive, integrative psychotherapy approach to manage patient treatment of Acute Stress Disorder and Post-traumatic Stress Disorder. It contains elements of various psychotherapies that have been shown to be effective in the treatment of these stress-induced disorders. A certified EMDR Therapist must do the procedure. Therefore, when selecting a therapist, try to get one that holds this certification. I have found that trauma treatment is accomplished in much less time using EMDR compared with only cognitive behavioral therapy (Shapiro, 2001).

One advantage is that EMDR can be quite non-verbal. It is an information processing therapy that uses an eight-phase approach making it very compatible with the Huffer's 8 steps in this book. EMDR allows participants to address the past experiences that are the roots of their disorder(s) that may be triggering dysfunctional emotions, beliefs and sensations. The therapy teaches participants to substitute and practice positive actions needed to enhance adaptive behaviors to restore their mental health. EMDR is a well-researched technique. My clients who participated in EMDR plus used Huffer's 8 Steps showed slightly greater improvement over those who performed the Huffer's 8-Steps only. The most beneficial skill is having the ability to reduce the symptoms of trauma and relieve pain as the debriefing and other skills proceed.

If a participant feels uncomfortable debriefing with another person or cannot be in a supportive group experience, some degree of debriefing can be done alone. Whatever the case, the litigant should take each step slowly and be prepared to respond to each of the lead-ins below. Anyone debriefing should not force him or herself to endure brutal pain without a break. He or she should be as supportive and caring with self as he or she would be with another person. If the person needs to cry, it might be good to be with someone who will hug, comfort, and care, even if the person chooses not to share specific data (Bisson, 2000).

Look again at the debriefing sheets. The initial event is now written in the center. After the initial impact data is recorded, begin the fact circle.

2. Impact of Incident or the Fact Circle

After the initial impact event has been written in the center of the debriefing sheet, the participant begins a cognitive process. Typically, he or she answers the following questions related to the fact circle:

What happened?

Who did it?

Where was each person in each event?

What was said, as close to quotes as possible?

When did each event take place?

Who were co-victims, family members, business associates, or others whose lives were dramatically affected by the assault?

Participants then mark the events that evoke the strongest emotions and/or responses with one or more symbols or keys tied to notes that can be written at the bottom of the page. If misinformation was introduced that hurt or offended the LWD, the participant underscores it. This eases anxiety regarding lies and misinformation because the litigant knows it will be revisited to be placed on a data analysis sheet for corrective action. Data analysis examples are found in the Empowerment Chapter.

H8S
GRL

3. The Feeling and Symptoms Circle

Next, the participant adds feelings and emotional experiences in the designated circle, including all physical, mental, and emotional symptoms. You are not expected to clinically diagnose PTSD or LAS. The cognitive and emotional aspects of debriefing are not designed to diagnose post trauma stress. Whether an event is merely unsettling but tolerable or rises to the other end of the continuum in terms of disruption, we will implement the healing steps as written. This leads to understanding the power of knowing what names to put to feelings versus just having a feeling. Traumatized litigants often verbalize the issues surrounding their distress in the terms listed below. If they can't verbalize their feelings, they will act out with inconsistent behaviors. Some advocates call me and ask if the litigant is bi polar because their abilities and moods change so dramatically. Usually that is not the case, they just don't have the words to describe how they feel. It is good to get the following words into the litigant's vocabulary to help them communicate their feelings with words instead of acting out:

1. Powerlessness–I'm vulnerable.

2. Isolation–I've lost control. (See the What I Can Control vs. What I Can't Control graphic Appendix A).

3. Guilt–I have frustrated feelings of responsibility.

4. Hypervigilance–How do I protect myself if the protective systems are not functioning to honestly protect me and maintain a high standard of performance?

5. Numbness–How did this happen to me?

6. Anxiety–My memories are blocked. My present life feels unbearable. I have no sense of a future that I can plan.

7. Startle responses–I jump at every little sound automatically.

8. Rage–and Beyond Rage toward respondents, bureaucracies, and courts. "I'm suffering from cumulative assaults and from those whose job it is to protect me. I remain unsafe and properly angry, but no one listens, enforces the law, or does their regulatory job for me."

9. Confusion and shame–I question my decisions and beliefs. I have lost confidence.

10. Disorientation–My life-style and belief system are in shambles. Lies are dominating the court. It is like operating in a house of mirrors.

Knowing and naming a feeling gives a litigant control over that feeling. It can be stated so others know how to help. It then supports the request for certain accommodations. Having a feeling is entirely different from knowing a feeling.

Antonio Damasio, professor of neuroscience at the University of Southern California where he heads USC's Brain and Creativity Institute and Adjunct Professor at the Salk Institute, uses an intricate neural analysis to prove that knowing and having feelings are different functions (Damasio, 335-9). Once that is realized, the litigant gains new insight that "knowing" the feeling is where power exists to control his or her environment in order to stay comfortable. "Having" feelings is automatic and can exist blindly without insight.

The traumatized have the feeling of impact/shock, recoil, and fight many times without "knowing" the feelings they are experiencing. They cannot control the feelings and are thrown into what psycho neurological researchers call "affect dysregulation." A good slang term for this state of being is "topsy-turvy." The advocate helps the litigant know and name his or her feelings relieving that instability.

Libby, a victim of intimate partner violence, has to be accommodated by allowing her to appear in court from a separate room in the courthouse. Prior to knowing and naming her feelings, she walked into the courtroom and emotionally became unhinged. She sobbed, was led into agreeing with opposing counsel's statements by shaking and nodding rather than clearly answering. Her opposing counsel began to call her incompetent and talked about getting a guardian appointed. Libby only behaved with uncontrolled emotion in court in the presence her ex and his team of lawyers. After debriefing and reframing, she realized that her feelings were helplessness, jeopardy, and fear. By geographic distance, she is able to manage those feelings now that they have a name and a place she can control. When her symptoms from having the feelings were translated into knowing the feelings, the symptoms were relieved to a great extent and communication with the court was much more constructive. It happened just in time because she was facing action to remove her freedom to manage her own affairs.

Libby exemplifies the thesis of this book, that we, as a society, compound trauma and offer little in the way of comfort or efficient response to victims of deceptive assault that exploits the functionally impaired during litigation. Another function of this book is to take the reader through steps to recovery that can be ventured alone or in a group. Whether alone or supported by others, the following lead-ins will help to develop the emotional/symptom part of the debriefing sheet, in a ritual to recovery. Gently ask the following:

"And then what...?"

"And then how were you feeling?"

"Sounds like ..."

"You felt as if ..."

"From your point of view or perception ..."

"It felt as if ..."

"It seemed as if life ..."

"You can ask yourself ..."

"At that point I just felt like ..."

"The whole world seemed ..."

"I felt like I needed ..."

"In my deepest heart I felt ..."

"My sleep became ..."

4. The Loss Circle (material and non-material)

The next step in debriefing is to identify losses in detail–material and nonmaterial– including losses to society as a whole. Victims are often very sensitive about the expansive nature of their experiences. Society's losses are sorely felt by responsible victims. Participants, therefore, record their losses in the outer loss circle.

1. First, the participant fills the circle with material losses: property, money, and treasures. They then move on to nonmaterial losses.

2. Then, the participant lists at least three (3) beliefs, and more if he or she can, that represent losses of his or her belief system. These relate to trust issues.

    "What did I believe before the event(s)?"

"What do I believe now?"

"What is happening as a result of the experience?"

"What should be happening?"

3. Next, the participant considers the philosophical and spiritual side of the losses:

"Why me?"

Who has been affected?

How do you explain the conflict or assault, if you can?

Do you relate it to past "bad" behavior?

Do I blame myself?

How deep does the damage go?

"To what am I vulnerable?"

"What can I not control?"

"What can I control?"

What feelings have changed?

What moral law was violated?

Do I feel abandoned by God or the major creative force in my life?

What losses to society as a whole exist from this experience?

What did it cost in dollars and cents?

At this point, participants may need an economist or accountant to help them ascertain the total of the various types of losses in financial terms. Without this analysis, the participant risks underestimating the value of losses needed for litigation. The goal is for the litigant to be made as whole as possible compared to the participant's pre litigation status. Therefore, these tasks are best completed before the participant sees an attorney and certainly, before he or she goes to court.

Data Derived Is Used to Perfect Legal Positions and Personal Interests

Advocates are ready for the fear factor of having to debrief prior to litigation. Fear of opening up the whole traumatic issue often prevents sufferers from being comfortable with debriefing experiences. Those around the victim become frustrated by the burden of negative information and the fact that there is often little we can do to solve the problem itself. Friends and family are fearful that they may lack the skills to deal with psychological issues, if they emerge. That is why an experienced person is the most helpful to get the information into channels and formats that serve effective litigation.

Certainly, some participants will require professional mental health services. But, instead of fearing the debriefing process, participants need to embrace it realizing that it is the key to a transition to greater mental health intended to sustain litigants through litigation. Debriefing also puts numbers, facts, and faces to losses that are needed to have an impact in court. First, however, the victim needs to be guided toward a well-defined process. The steps to recovery, as outlined in the following chapters, provide the follow-up to debriefing.

No one likes and some even fear the worms that might crawl out of the "can". We are shocked by their vileness in the can and we are nonplused as to what to do with the creatures. The eight steps prepare us to greet whatever emotions and behaviors that come forth. Instead of reacting to the symbolic worms that slither blindly to be fulfilled, litigants are gently guided toward positive actions that put the facts and feelings where they belong. Facts and feelings do not go to court equally. Advocates listening and caring throughout this journey find it a privilege, a challenge, and a pleasure. Such humanity now must be extended by demanding equal access under the ADAAA for special needs litigants in the court.

Huffer's Log

A case of crime, cover-up, intimidation, and legal abuses—LeeAnn's is a case involving depression, anxiety disorders, PTSD, and extensive and creative use of Huffer's 8-Steps. Her case runs through criminal, civil, bankruptcy, and appellate courts. She faces a large corporation protracting her litigation for years. She has had attorneys and now appears in court unrepresented. Cases like LeeAnn's have honed and tested Huffer's 8-Steps.

LeeAnn's case first revealed what I now see as "cookie-cutter" formulas that abuse the judicial system and victimize LWDs. When she first realized that law enforcement did not immediately prosecute the criminal and the insurance did not restore them for the amount contracted by the insurance, LeeAnn suffered deep depression and literally stayed in bed for six months. She found my book, *Overcoming the Devastation of Legal Abuse Syndrome* and put the protocols to work. She began to stir out of the fetal position. She reports that my book became her bible. She read it every night before bed, read it to her husband, and clung to the skills that now, after fifteen years of such testing, are called Huffer's 8-Steps.

LeeAnn contacted me during this time when her life was rather newly war torn by legal abuses. I agreed to become her advocate. As we began to establish our working relationship, what was driven home and remains a motivator for this work is the fact that, for LeeAnn and all human beings, justice is indispensable. It is a sustaining central force nudging human life toward 'better.' A public court cannot dispense justice unless the facts and the truth can be presented. Regardless of the pain caused by enduring litigation and traumatic stress, LeeAnn is compelled to react from the heart of her values.

It is 2003. I pull up to Starbucks, in Atlanta, Georgia, and see LeeAnn, who immediately knows who I am. It was one of those gossamer meetings in the beginning that steadily but ever so surely become mortar and stone. This woman had taken my book, my protocols, my advice, my insights, and integrated them from black ink on white paper, into her life. Over a decaf coffee and a little cake, looking into LeeAnn's dark and centered eyes, my work came to a new living, healing reality. It was a "solid rock" moment that inspired me to take my quest to the next level in imagining a better path to justice for people suffering various disorders.

Damn, she was smart looking, casually dressed in expensive clothes, and striking in her tall and direct attractiveness. Dark hair sleeked back into a classic bun framed her "in your face" personality emanating a confident wisdom that has proven itself over time. The legal system and its players had done her wrong and she is not going to stand for it. I agreed to come on board unaware it would take my thesis, that the legal system is injuring our most vulnerable justice-seeking public, on a rough ride through corruption, intimidation, courage, terror, and stunning official incompetence. I was thrown into a virtual house of mirrors to sort out justice in LeeAnn's case.

After authoring Overcoming the Devastation of Legal Abuse Syndrome, I have served many cases. Each, whether past or future, is and will be forever impacted by the journey that began at this first meeting at Starbucks in Atlanta, Georgia, with LeeAnn Jonas, over cake and coffee.

As she shared her story, her frustration over being inundated with the usual questions arose. Why don't you give up and get on with your life? How can you take on a legal system without an attorney? All were questions that friends and family put forth when faced with a judicial David and Goliath scenario. LeeAnn's face gets furrowed when these questions are put to her. Her forehead wrinkles up, her eyes get darker and big, her shoulders square, and her voice becomes shrill and disbelieving with a hoarse high pitch, "They will make me whole again according to the law," she declares with words underpinned by morally driven dead-on determination.

LeeAnn sees justice as a driving eternal energy source of life itself. LeeAnn cannot abandon her quest— to force the right thing to be done in her justice system. In short, it is something like…she believes God has told her to do it. I guess he told me too. Just maybe there was an ethereal presence and purpose joining us for coffee that day at Starbucks.

I have followed LeeAnns fearful road toward justice and studied how she copes with injustice using Huffer's 8 steps for healing in this book. The steps are designed to be used in any order and have been. LeeAnn's Debriefing was clear and strong as to what happened, the ripple effects to her life, and her losses. The hardest part for LeeAnn was identifying and naming her feelings. She struggles with feeling a feeling, while knowing her feelings at the same time. She chooses the safety zones of anger, being indignant, and outraged, with a powerful effort covering up the underlying emotions. I do not push her on this but gently invite her go deeper into feelings each time that we revisit Debriefing after a traumatic experience. She is unrepresented having to appear in court in the shoes of an attorney without training. Therefore, our counseling sessions are short and often triggered by crisis feelings. A great deal of time is spent on Empowerment assisting her to gear up for the next battle of the war. As her advocate, I am eternally her safe place to turn even long distance when the pressure is on or she is having a "meltdown." After Debriefing, advocates will find one or two or three skills that suit the litigant and those will be repeated. LeeAnn's first step was Debriefing, which remains the skill that she clings to even after ten years.

As LeeAnn's advocate, I have a front row seat in a battle that is relentless and desperately intense. Lawyers sometimes expect an easy win when facing off against a disabled, pro se, litigant. That is not so in LeeAnn's case. She takes the blows and does not give up. However, in 2007, LeeAnn developed PTSD as well as Depression. As her advocate, I often have to interpret LeeAnn's needs and behavior to the court and help LeeAnn to understand what has been said and done in court. She clearly demonstrates that once PTSD affects the brain, communication is severely interrupted. I then requested ADA accommodations for her while in court. Advocacy and the ADA help LeeAnn to stay in the battle by using the 8 steps and a system of data analysis to endure and stay focused or this would have been another case of attrition quite awhile back.

The Crime

After our meeting at Starbuck's, I began to learn LeeAnn's history. The story of her life fit her mannerisms precisely. It was easy to visualize her as an owner of a clothing store, displaying products with class and style, traveling as a buyer, and living the affluent life of a successful businesswoman. She married a man 23 years her senior whose family had owned clothing Stores in South Georgia for fifty-two years. They employed more than two hundred people. A business that has weathered fifty-two years of ups and downs feels as secure as any business can. Pillars supported her affluent lifestyle.

Phillip, LeeAnn's husband, is a "down-to-earth," pragmatic kind of business owner. His tastes are simple. He feels no need to boast. He is a forward thinker, very pro active in his decisions. While he trusted and had come to love his in-house accountant, Larry, he kept conservative accounting practices in place. Both LeeAnn and Phillip loved Larry so much they made him their only son's Godfather. But, even as much as Larry was trusted and almost a part of his family, Phillip's business wisdom overrode his affection. He implemented an arm's-length verification procedure of the company accounting with independent certified audits every six months. If a problem emerged, it was to be caught and dealt with early. They planned to make sure the business would survive for the next generation.

So, life was good. They lived well and had a beautiful house on a golf course. Their only child, a son, had been welcomed into arms that could provide the best for him and, of course, he would inherit his share of the clothing Stores. The auditors also liked their in-house accountant, Larry. He had been with the clothing store for years and never had the auditors turned up a problem. Then . . . it all went so wrong with one telephone call.

The store's banker called LeeAnn after hours. He informed her that a check written by the in-house accountant had not been signed. It was a large check for more than $7000. She knew that no check in such an amount should have been written on their account. The banker stayed after hours while LeeAnn raced to the bank to find that her son's Godfather had set a system in motion years before gradually robbing them *of about three million dollars. She was stunned. The independent auditors certainly should have caught this defalcation.*

Only Larry knew his ugly secret that he had embezzled $7000 per week for years. Not likely motivated by guilt but rather fear, Larry's antennae were heightened to signs of being caught. LeeAnn coordinated his arrest opportunity by agreeing to keep him at the store awaiting the police. Larry sensed that he was being exposed. He took off and was nowhere to be found. Luck and police investigation finally turned up a posh home in Atlanta purchased with stolen money and far from the address he used for work.

The police and the Jonas' rushed to the strange address and were greeted by a house full of Larry's friends celebrating Larry and his life partner's farewell as they prepared to travel to foreign destinations. The party was extravagant; the luggage was already packed and by the front door. As police surrounded the house, Larry bolted out the back door not expecting to fall into the arms of law enforcement. The thief was leaving but not to vacation out of the country. He was caught. The Jonas' felt terrible and betrayed but grateful.

After Larry's arrest, LeeAnn was confident that the law would be enforced from that day forward. Her first disappointment came when she learned that Larry had been offered a plea deal to serve only probation. I can still see her in my mind's eye with that determined and indignant look on her face and the unmistakable voice of moral clarity.

She asserted herself and appeared before the DA resisting the plea and finally Larry was tried. Her hard work and confrontation with law enforcement forced him to serve three and a half years in prison. They got back about $400,000 in liquidation of properties he had bought with their funds. However, the $3,000,000 he had stolen under the eyes of auditors put their business at risk. This was the first of many pretext- impotent official responses LeeAnn would encounter. Law enforcement looked like it was going to be effective at catching a thief bringing justice and deterring such thievery. However, their budget and internal priorities offered him a plea that would bring no satisfaction to the victims. LeeAnn fought and felt empowered by forcing the issue and getting a trial. She was now energized.

Easing their concerns was the fact that their accounting firm was insured. Phillip's proactive and conservative business style designed their protection. The Jonas' filed the necessary papers to be compensated by the insurance company. It was outrageous to the Jonas' that an ongoing embezzlement occurred in spite of the consistent oversight and certified audits that were done every six months. They paid for audits to insure that no one could embezzle as Larry had for so long. The insurer finally paid $2.4 million. To the onlooker that might seem reasonably fair. However, it was not even close to what the contract promised to the insured. When legal reality set in, the attorneys got $600,000, the court costs were $146,327 some creditors were paid and the Jonas' received less than $100,000. The insured amount was much more than $2.4, million. They were left badly damaged. Their business needed resuscitation. Their lifestyle was shattered and they were losing control of their economic lives. Insurance had not performed as contracted. It was another pretext-impotent act. The insurance was to guarantee that the failure on the part of the accountant could not put them out of business. By the insurance company paying much less than the contract, their plan was undermined. Money was made for attorneys and the court but their lives and business faced ruination.

Bankruptcy Court

They were legally advised to file for Chapter 11 Bankruptcy reorganization. Their Company of 17 retail stores was filed for reorganization with hope that they could save their business. Their assets were $8.7 million with $3.2 million of debt. This was a promising reorganization. These true believers in the American dream were certain they would recover from the crime. Faith in the justice system was bolstered. Debriefing was required again since re-traumatization and further losses were incurred. At this point the Grieving Step and Deshaming were in order to sort out the crime. A new set of requests for accommodations and court appearances were required of me as the advocate.

I didn't know on the day I committed to their cases that our therapeutic and consulting relationship would last for another six years without resolution, or that I would see this vibrant, clear headed woman hospitalized behind barbed wire for being suicidal. By now, LeeAnn had been on a 4-year rollercoaster ride largely in the dark as to how the legal system really works.

LeeAnn's case dramatizes that if the initial assault triggers a protracted legal process, the litigant stands to remain an emotional hostage for many years. Not only does the justice system move slowly but it all depends on the quality of the legal and judicial help a litigant is able to obtain. LeeAnn discovered that she had unscrupulous lawyers who deceived the court. Her trustee joined with the lawyers against LeeAnn's interests. We saw with Larry, where law enforcement creates pleas that defy truth and logic for the sake of a speedy resolution with as little effort on the prosecutor's part as possible (Napolitano, 2004). LeeAnn witnessed the destruction of the balance of her estate in bankruptcy court and had no help in forcing the insurance company to pay their contracted amount.

References

Bisson, J.I., McFarlane, A., & Rose, S. (2000). Psychological Debriefing. *Effective Treatments for PTSD.* (pp. 39-59). NY: Guilford.

Damasio, A. (1999). *The Feeling of What Happens: Body and Emotion in the Making of Consciousness.* New York: Harcourt Brace.

Herman, J. (1997). Trauma and Recovery: The aftermath of violence—from domestic abuse to political terror. (pp. 61). NY: Basic Books.

Kessler R., Sonnega, A., Bromet, E., Hughes, M., & Nelson, C. (1995). Posttraumatic stress disorder in the national co-morbidity survey. *Archives of General Psychiatry. 52,* 1048–60.

Napolitano, A.P. (2004). *Constitutional Chaos: What Happens When the Government Breaks Its Own Laws.* Nashville, TN: Thomas Nelson.

North, C., et al. (1999). Psychiatric disorders among survivors of the Oklahoma City bombing. *JAMA 282,* 755–62.

Robinson, R.C. & Mitchell, J.T. (1995). Getting some balance back into the debriefing debate. *Bulletin Australian Psychology Society. 17,* 5–10.

Shapiro, F. PhD. (2001). *Eye Movement Desensitization and Reprocessing (EMDR): Basic Principles, Protocols, and Procedures.* New York: Guilford Press. (2nd ed.).

Tick, E. Ph.D. (2005). *War and the Soul: Healing Our Nation's Veterans from Post Traumatic Stress Disorder.* (pp. 103, 120). Quest Books. Adyar: The Theosophical Publishing House.

CHAPTER 10

GRIEVING: HUFFER'S STEP-3 PRODUCTIVE, PAINFUL PROCESSING

Huffer's step 3, Grieving, is the natural reaction to loss. However, when losses are forced or caused by human on human trauma, the grief is intensified and healing takes on a new dimension. Extreme grief is a new research topic that relates closely to losses forced by unbearable court orders and denial of equal access to justice. The choices presented in this chapter reflect methods that therapeutically respond to forced grief from litigation.

"It is not suffering itself but suffering without meaning that is the real scourge of human life (1916)."

Carl Jung

H8S

Grieving during Re-traumatization

After traumatic loss, the process of grief begins. Unrelenting feelings of sadness take time to heal. Grief is part of life and there is no short cut through it. But, litigation adds a cumulative dimension to grief by its very nature. Threatened losses hang over every litigant's head. At risk are vital life's issues like losing custody of children, hard-earned assets, or privileges. The right to participate in a fair process may also hang in the balance for litigants with disabilities. As losses mount, the legal system drives grief to a more severe level. If the losses are intentionally forced by human beings, we know that trauma is intensified. There is no more important time for an advocate to be alongside the litigant with disabilities than during grieving.

Grief is a general term related to many feelings that comprise human response to loss. These feelings need to be named and attributed to a specific loss. Then the litigant's unique style of suffering through grief will be easier to process. Grieving is terribly painful, but always remember, the pain is productive. I often liken it to labor pains with clients. There are only so many, and at the end, after following the steps, there are rich rewards.

Well-processed grief awakens dimensions that stretch a person's humanity. I have clients who have turned activism into true heroism helping persons with disabilities. Litigants with disabilities need to be treated with sensitivity thereby discrimination and neglect are avoided. Our advocates know that LAS is preventable. If that disabling condition is brought to a halt by courts adopting a social model of accommodating the public, a significant stride in public health will have been achieved. This is what I believe Carl Jung meant about suffering having some meaning quoted at the beginning of this chapter.

A good first step is to believe that grief has a purpose. Next, in the context of that purpose, examine losses. It is important to figure out how and why ideals, assets, and/or relationships were lost. Get compensation for what you can. Whatever is left must be grieved. Certified advocates are trained to know that litigants in grief will tend to withdraw from life. They help litigants fight off the need to isolate. Beware that grieving in isolation fosters bitterness. Isolation also affects health. In grief the immune system has been attacked. Vitamins, exercise, eating, breathing, sometimes have to be strongly encouraged.

Anne Morrow Lindbergh (wife of Charles Lindbergh having suffered the kidnapping and murder of her child) is said to have commented on suffering, *I do not believe that sheer suffering teaches. If suffering alone taught, all the world would be wise, since everyone suffers. To suffering must be added mourning, understanding, patience, love, openness, and the willingness to remain vulnerable.*

There's the conundrum for LAS sufferers. Losses from legal malice aforethought are intentional and cruel. Legal Abuse Syndrome represents the most feared losses known to mankind. Even more feared than loss of life, are loss of trust, loss of a sense of belonging, and loss of your feeling of competence to protect yourself, your property, and your loved ones. These losses require a mourning style that calls special attention to the deceptive or bullying methods that are being used against you.

Grieving Forced Losses

An accident, an act of God, death of a loved one, or illnesses are grieved with societal support and, after a year of fairly predictable stages, shock, denial, anger, bargaining, suffering transcends to a state of acceptance of the loss. However, ADA advocates work with cases wherein the trauma is intensified because human beings intentionally cause the loss. A Diagnostic and Statistical Manual (DSM IV) study of 395 traumatized and treatment seeking participants concluded that human on human trauma was the most intense and hardest to overcome (van der Kolk, 1996).

Worse yet is when unethical lawyers behave like well-dressed thugs with all the traits of a bully, ridiculing you, scheming to weaken you, using trickery and intimidation. Mounting losses of parenting your child through custody battles or loss of your assets in court are minimized and even become a type of "gladiator team sport" by such abusive lawyers. You suffer while no ritual exists for grieving over losses forced by your legal system. In fact, you are usually advised to give it up, let it be, take your lumps, because that is "just the way it is." Loss of property is diminished as being "replaceable."

This is all wrong! The properly trained advocate sees to it that all losses are noted. Personal property symbolizes who we are. Possessions are the outward manifestations of our inner identity. We are surrounded by those items that represent an earned life style, a birthright in America, part of our pursuit of happiness, the expression of ourselves, and that which we shape to pass on to our posterity. We have a constitutional right to parent our children contributing to their futures and providing an estate to be passed on to them. Often unidentified or underestimated losses include but are not limited to:

- Friends
- Reputation
- Business
- Borrowing power
- Networking power
- Health
- Credit
- Social standing
- Pride
- Patriotism
- Faith in professionals

- Property
- Opportunity
- Relationships
- Money
- Material possessions
- Career
- Earned life style
- Trust/faith
- Law suits
- Hope
- Home/comfort/pets

H8S

Grieving Losses from Ethics Violations

I witness powerful, unethical predatory legal actions used to execute forced losses. They use the court to take property, money, assets, and children. All earned sense of security, safety, and opportunity is sacrificed. Sometimes the takings continue after the court battle is over in false claims of owed moneys, accrued interest, incompetent bookkeeping, and other means to continue to indebt. Additionally, these legal actions consume the litigant's time and energy representing a critical loss that often goes without accounting or resolution.

Litigants report that they feel like a giant legal monster lurks over them ruthlessly plucking a prized possession, a dream, an achievement, or anything of value in an insidious, ongoing, institutionalized assault. Victims state that they lose a sense of patriotism and trust in professionals when their system is used in this manner. These are takings that are illegal if done without true due process of law. The problem with special needs litigants is that that legal actions and proceedings can appear to provide due process but in fact have been no better than exploitation. With PTSD, it takes a skilled observer or advocate to know if the litigant is able to function in terms of testimony and participation during hearings and discovery.

A litigant with functional impairments and without legal representation is usually unable to defend him or herself or present their case. They are ripe for victimization through takings. Takings are methods of stealing that are concealed in procedural confusion. Powerful organizations, Governments, agencies, and/or enforcement officials can, by law, do takings. Sometimes takings are implemented by individual citizens who can pay for power and just want to take property. Having the power to take private property outright after divorce or through legal abuse or under the pretext of enforcing the law, a regulation, or somehow acting in the line of duty is not uncommon. The IRS can affect takings as can the DEA. The bankruptcy court reflects systematized takings (Stein, 1989).

Grieving Sacred Losses

The LAS walking wounded are often deprived of an easy reliance on spiritual strength because the pain has reached so deeply into the core of their existence. Some litigants feel generally betrayed by their maker. John Bradshaw throughout his work, *On the Family: A Revolutionary Way of Self Discovery*, in 1988 , refers to "soul murder," describing those whose pain and suffering prevents them from being all that they could have been in life. The pain that one must endure when trust is violated leaves the victim often unable to trust that a God exists or, at least, that a loving God exists.

Advocates sometimes find the spiritual realm awkward to approach yet important to litigants. In helping a grieving person some inquiries that help are, "I'm wondering if it feels like God has abandoned you." Or, "When the moral code is broken down to this extent, do you find it hard to figure your way in a world with no moral tenets to rely upon?" The first step is to realize that a moral compass is awry and has interrupted the litigant's belief system. A DSM IV Field Trial Study of 120 individuals found that the PTSD group was more likely to report changes in religious beliefs following the first traumatic event. (Falsetti, 2003). Organized religion sometimes has little to do with the person's ability to have a rich spiritual existence and to gain comfort from openness to a spiritual reservoir that often remains private or in question.

Whether losses come from court orders, takings, or marriage settlements, grieving litigants experience a void. How that void is filled again becomes part of a new journey. It starts with the debriefing process and acknowledgment of the intrinsic as well as dollar value of just what was lost. It is okay to grieve over personal, ridiculous appearing losses as well as the more easily accepted ones. What the loss means to the litigant is what matters and helps determine the needed value for restoration purposes. Grieving losses of pets, favorite clothes, neighborhoods and friends, a view that was enjoyed, a certain place to eat or shop are losses that might embarrass a traumatized victim. They are still important.

Certified advocates know that there is no way to qualify and no advantage to placing limits on the pain and anguish a victim feels. Losing the abusive spouse in a domestic violence relationship seems like good riddance. But, loss of the friend that the abuser was at times is still a loss. Certainly, there is no scale that can weigh or no continuum upon which one person can assess the degree of another person's pain after loss. Again, as in debriefing, it is important to accept the significance of the loss to the litigant. They need to be embraced by sensitivity regardless of the appearance of rationality or irrationality of the loss. Feelings exist without rationale. Remember Damasio, the neurologist's, findings discussed earlier in Debriefing that we feel without knowing the feeling in many cases? Grief will heal best in a milieu of respect, as part of the victim experience. Litigants need to be given a wide berth with no moral or value judgment, just supportive listening and caring. The advocate needs to keep the following words before the litigant when they are inconsolable:

Operational Principles for Acceptance of Yourself in Grief

REALIZATION–I realize that I am suffering the most profound loss known to man, loss of trust. As I predicted in 1995, our entire American culture is reeling and attempting to reassert its values as loss of trust reflects a social staple has been severely eroded throughout our major institutions.

PERMISSION TO SHED TEARS over tiers of trauma–It's okay to cry over tangible losses and history; they usually relate to significant intangible losses. Crying is a part of grieving. Victims should be encouraged to cry and feel just as sorry for themselves as they would for anyone else, no more, no less.

PREPARATION–If litigation or courts are part of my victimization, I must prepare for brutal realities of the system so I can prevent the shock stage of grief. Debrief, complete my unique application of Huffer's 8-Steps before I call an attorney and obligate myself to legal fees and costs. Planning proactively can prevent many losses.

FOCUS ON MAINTAINING YOUR HEALTH–Victims must remember to take vitamins, rest, eat (not junk food) exercise, and force it. Immune systems under recycled attack need bolstering. Litigants are preparing for a battle so they can sustain and win. Rest and focus on health are key preparation.

CONSTRICTION vs. ISOLATION–My life will be narrowed by mental censorship and avoidance of painful memories and thoughts. I won't let constriction turn to isolation. PTSD makes the past painful and blocks memory. The present is terrorizing and it is tempting to freeze and stay numb. Thus, the future is stolen costing future dreams and goals.

PATIENCE AND CONSOLATION–Silent sobbing at the helpless, endless frustration in my core is my lonely secret. No one can imagine that state of loneliness. I will be patient with my progress and pain and will console, not criticize myself. Who sits by my side, wipes my tears, listens, comforts, and doesn't run away is an eternal gift. These are spiritual connections that often come from unexpected places. After grieving, sure transcendence comes in the form of whom you now call friend. The friends and family you thought would be there often are not. New meaningful alliances form out of sharing the pain of your private grief and bubbles of joy can begin to rise even out of despair. Don't reject what fills the void, it is usually important for your future. *It suffices to say that the truth of the matter lies not in any adjective, noun, or verb but in the unrepeatable, never forgotten personal experiences that embody for their owners the annihilation of their life. Grief will always remain private and not fodder to be discussed and labeled (Wilene Gremain).*

Complicated Grief

What is it about the court of law that causes Post Traumatic Stress Disorder/Legal Abuse Syndrome? For starters, a legal case represents hope, sometimes the only hope in a life altering matter. Moreover, legal actions involve the largest investments and most important aspects of people's lives. When losses occur because of attrition or unbearable court orders following failed access to the court, the grief runs deep and lasts seemingly forever.

Advocates assess the ways and to what degree litigation affects traumatized persons with disabilities. How much of the litigant's living space is taken up by boxes, suitcases, baskets, or stacks of legal papers? Litigants all hold onto their documents because in our deepest consciousness it feels like, some day, there may be a chance at justice. Injustice plagues the human mind in many ways.

M. Katherine Shear, professor of psychiatry at Columbia University, identifies through elegant research, what she calls "a loop of suffering." She relates what she titles "complicated grief" to extreme bereavement. More than one million people per year are suffering from grief so wracking that they can barely function. She states, "It takes a person away from humanity…and has no redemptive value" (2006).

The treatment of choice, at the moment, is the same treatment as recommended for Post Traumatic Stress Disorder, i.e. exposure to the trauma in a safe environment and then encouraging the grieving person to containerize the trauma and shelve it to be processed slowly. This type of grief is new on the research horizon. I posit today that it is not only death that will precipitate complicated grief. The similarity to my clients who suffer losses from litigation is startling. For some, grief will feel unrelenting requiring long-term intervention.

The dilemma of a misbehaving court causing improper losses through intolerable court orders could not have been better stated than by Law Professor Monroe Freedman when he spoke in 1989—at a gathering of federal judges:

Frankly, I have had more than enough of judicial opinions that bear no relationship whatsoever to the cases that have been filed and argued before the judges. I am talking about judicial opinions that falsify the facts of the cases that have been argued, judicial opinions that make disingenuous use or omission of material authorities, judicial opinions that cover up these things with no-publication and no-citation rules (Freedman, 1997).

So too have my ragged clients had enough. If left without accommodations, they lose their sense of competence and trust from being immersed in disingenuous energy. Their well-prepared cases were rarely heard, lost in legal attrition. Attrition means losing by a slow perpetual erosion.

And, if their cases are heard, the merits of their cases meet strenuous obstruction. When finally put before the court, their evidence is too often hopelessly clouded in adversarial irrationality due to lies. If they finally get their cases submitted, Professor Freedman's observation is a risk. Cases are grieved throughout the litigation while the litigant is toyed with like a mouse trapped in a shoe facing a cat that is not too hungry but will eat because he can. That is where the advocate must step in and redirect the court to follow the ADAAA.

I Don't Want to Die. I Just Can't Stand to Be Here Anymore.

On a trip to Mexico in my younger days, I wanted to see a bullfight in all it's Hemmingway splendor. My mind's eye pictured bright colors, a hot summer's day, ballet, and bravery as the matador skillfully mastered the power of the bull. As expected, the day was hot. What I did not anticipate was the raw battle that ensued as the bull fought for survival, confused, being the only one who did not know the rules. The ceremony was a bloody, dusty, gradual taunting and torture of the bull. The picador cleverly lanced the bull, pricking his hide, again and again. I remember the exhausted creature with blood running over his shoulders still trying to fight. Finally, the matador put the blade through his spine at the base of his skull. It was instant death and relief. Then, to my surprise, and what I had never seen in the movies, the bull was hauled out and publicly butchered. The audience bought cuts of meat to be enjoyed with the memory of how the main course fought a war that everyone but the bull knew would end in his death. The fix was in. Even though physically dominant, the bull was not leaving the ring alive.

The use of the word, "court," in our legal system refers back to old English times and the fact that differences were settled in clashes between warriors in a "court" or arena. Unfortunately, our current system functions more like a killing sport when the law goes wrong. I flash on that bloody bull whenever a litigant is handed impossible and/or unbearable court orders. The emotional implosion or in rare cases an explosion is bound to occur. The law is too often treated as an insiders' game not a public service. Lawyers, mediators, judges, guardians have their private meetings and only the client, who has paid the bill…and pays the tax dollars to support them all, does not know the real story (Judge DeAnn Salcido ret. Abuse Freedom United Presents. http://www.blogtalkradio. com/abusefreedomlive. "The Abuse Freedom Live Show" Sunday, October 8, 2011. Whistle blower reveals the truth and is ostracized by judicial college's.) radio appearance. Clients are kept "under control," meaning compliant and in the dark. They are set up like bulls ready for the ring with its esoteric rules designed to force losses. They don't want to die. But, they won't survive, in good mental health, if they are forced into stress from unrelenting intolerable circumstances.

H8S

Where Has the Value in a Reputation Gone?

How do lawyers fit into the grief style of the invisible victim? Lawyers are the gatekeepers of the court system. As Attorney David Marston wrote in 1991 in *Malice Aforethought*, "As you already know if you have ever glanced at your bank loan agreement or apartment lease or any other legalese in your life, definitions do for lawyers what morning coffee does for everyone else; we can't get started without them." Lawyers are in every part of every business, telling people about various definitions of laws and rules. While attorneys are also guided by ethical rules, a strange evolution has taken place in the legal business. The ABA sets forth ethical guidelines but in 1988 set even higher goals held be "aspirational only" ABA Model Code of Professional Responsibility 1983. Then, by 2004 the tier of aspirational only is not apparent and the lawyers' rules of conduct are written giving great behavioral latitude to lawyers. So, if the ethical guidelines and rules of conduct are violated, there may be no place for the public to turn for proper relief ABA Model Code of Professional Conduct (2009-10).

Attorney Marston asserts that ethical rules are written to protect lawyers and it seems that lawyers function either to take advantage of this or at least to turn their heads the other way when ethical rules are violated by others. This leaves lawyers neck deep in the "taking" business and those lawyers who take no action allow the profession to deteriorate. The many lawyers and judges who are fine professionals find themselves victimized by the abusers as well. Marston's perspective focuses on those who breach their ethics, the worst of the profession. He tells us that lawyers who abuse fall into four categories:

1. Lawyers who use their legal training to break the law or commit crimes in the course of their practice.

2. Lawyers who violate any important ethical rule of the legal profession. Not surprisingly, there are big rules and little rules and lots of technicalities, so the focus here will be on significant professional misconduct, not minor infractions.

3. Lawyers who use their legal training to do things they should be ashamed to tell their mothers (including on behalf of a corporation.)

4. Lawyers who cooperate when they know there is a bad lawyer at work. Such lawyers may go through the steps but will not go up against the system on behalf of their clients. Marston calls them "Un-indicted co-conspirators."

Advocates observe their cases portraying Marston's brutal assessment of attorneys. Quite apart from the original assaults we sometimes see unethical attorneys adding outrage to existing trauma. It can be hard to identify such slick malice aforethought, but it is there, buried in legalese, and the grieving process will be profoundly compounded by it. Marston published his assertions in 1991 clearly hoping to impact the legal community (200-210).

Yet, in 2008, as Federal District Court Judge Loretta A. Preska stated, "Civil litigation is not always civil. " The high stakes and cost of much litigation today and the commercialization of the legal profession have created greater pressure on lawyers to "zealously assert the client's position under the rules of the adversary system." When that pressure leads attorneys astray, judges possess the authority to impose sanctions, under federal statutes, civil procedure rules, and courts' inherent powers. Over the past year, federal judges in high-profile litigation have invoked these powers to take action against lawyer misconduct either imposing sanctions or using their bully pulpit to put the legal profession on notice that judges will protect the public and legal consumers from abuse. (Preska, 2007).

All the while the advocate, unless a lawyer, remains solidly by the side of the LWD assuring equal access but must restrain from activist activities or crossing the line into the legal realm. The case is owned by the client and their decisions with their legal teams or without are theirs to make with supportive help from the advocate. However, listening, reflecting, guiding the client toward helpful vocabulary for their feelings and clarifying their positions can be powerful aids in their making and executing effective decisions.

Grieving Loss of Tenets: Goodwill, Good Faith, Fair Dealing

Have you ever commented that something wasn't fair and received the response, well, "Life isn't fair." Basically, "Get over it." I believe, if you are in grief over losses forced by the court system obstructing your participation, frustrating your case, promoting a war of attrition, taking your children, or property without due process of law, you are grieving loss of fairness. Fairness is an ideal. But, it is an ideal that humans must cling to and that is as significant to a healthy life as is basic trust. A rebirth validating the concept of fairness is promoted by advocacy case by case in court.

Some people who lose by takings and ugly use of their system become wiser, more compassionate. They even pity the poor lawyers who are limited to such uninspiring work as bullying and taking other people's things. On the other hand, some do not become enlightened in any way. They stay bitter, angry, jaded, withdrawn, and pessimistic. This chapter invites you to make a choice. You can face the injustice, reach for a greater sense of your authenticity and the meaning of that unique self in this puzzling and painful universe, and grieve skillfully. It is natural healing and opens new dimensions within the litigant as a survivor. Or, you could be relegated to the stress of unfinished personal growth that lends toward chronic unhappiness and resentment. I am committed to prevent that.

Today, working under the ADA, many lawyers, judges, clerks, and court personnel are responding well to my work. It has met my goal of being pertinent and useful. I am thrilled by accountability, inspired by ethics, joyful when one of my judges stretches the usual repertoire to create a fair hearing for an invisibly disabled individual. I am determined you will, with great humor and strength, make your right choice.

H8S

Huffer's Log

LeeAnn knows that insurance companies are known to try to get out of paying the amount they are contracted to pay. That is why they have spent more than a decade fighting her and wearing her down. She knows that she is not the only one impacted by this institutionalized bad faith. Therefore, her grief over financial losses has taken on an important societal purpose.

Case Example of Forced Losses

LeeAnn has had every material item taken from her and much of her health even recently being diagnosed with breast cancer. Keeping spiritual energy flowing is a daily challenge for LeeAnn. Her twilight sleep persistently replays the intentional pain engineered by the attorneys for the insurance company. They arrange the timing of subpoenas and service of documents right before holidays or when they know she is not well. The documents regularly bring bad news and catch her off guard. Backed by powerful law firms, the lawyers flaunt that they have power with the judge. When in court, they ridicule. They roll their eyes, sigh, flip their files, interrupt LeeAnn, and treat her as if she is an outcast who is fouling the formal proceedings. It is nasty artwork to observe their intimidating body language. The intent can only be to instigate and undermine her so that LeeAnn will be forced to question her very self. She asks herself, if my best does not allow me to participate, then what do I have left?

LeeAnn is sustained by a belief that she has a purpose in life. She also remembers historical figures that did not give in to corruption or wrongdoing and appreciates that we are all the beneficiaries of forefathers who paid dues facing impossible odds. Her purpose is tied to spiritual beliefs and principles. There never is a time that spiritual strength is more important than during the grieving process. Loss seems to cue us into our need for a greater perception of life. It may sound corny in today's world, but as her advocate, I am inspired by her ideals and her appreciation of forefathers with courage.

Bearing the Unbearable

LeeAnn cannot sleep. LeeAnn keeps trying to get a fair day in court. She returns to court and she pays the price. She studies and she goes to court with painful symptoms. The idea of having her rights arbitrarily denied frustrates and consumes her at night in a nebulous cloud torturing her with arrows to her heart feeling man's inhumanity to man. It is the using of her court to toy with her, to laugh at her, and use her as a dehumanized object of battle.

One night she felt so desperate, she kept taking more and more pills hoping for some rest. She had just seen the videos of the hearings in the courtroom that were not fair. The videos swirled in her brain. She took another pill. Her mediation haunts her nights. Her mediator had stood leaning over the table and foaming at the mouth yelled, "YOU WANT THESE PEOPLE (attorneys who had committed fraud on the court) PUNISHED?" Yes, she wanted those who broke the law to be properly punished. She took two more pills. She had to get some rest and relief from this. She did not put insurance companies or lawyers in a special category, not be held to their contracts and accountability. She felt outraged which awakened her more.

She took more pills. When she finally got up, she collapsed to the floor, unconscious. Her husband couldn't awaken her and called 911. She was "Baker Acted" into a mental hospital under lock and key with barbed wire surrounding the building. She woke up in a prison environment where she couldn't have any personal property, not even a toothbrush. She was monitored as a danger to herself. She admits that she can't stand the pain of life and, at times, an exit seems tempting. However, death is not her choice. We risk the loss of our lives when we are driven to the point that we can't "stand it anymore."

Author's Notes:

<u>Diagnostic and Statistical Manual of Mental Disorders</u> (DSM)-IV-TR, sponsored a study of 395 traumatized and treatment seeking participants. The conclusions aligned with the work of Bessel van der Kolk, Alexander McFarlane and Judith Herman, researchers on trauma that human on human trauma was the most intense and hardest to overcome.

References

American Bar Association Standing Committee on Ethics and Professional Responsibility. (2009-2010). *Model Rules of Professional Conduct.* Chicago: ABA Pub

Bradshaw, J. (1988). On the Family: *A Revolutionary Way of Self Discovery.* Pompano Beach, FL: Health Communications.

Falsetti, S., Resick, P., & Davis, J. (2003, August) Grieving Changes in Religious Beliefs Following Trauma. *Journal of Traumatic Stress. 16(4),* 391-398.

Freedman, M. (1997). The Threat to Judicial Independence by Criticism of Judges: A Proposed Solution to the Real Problem. *Hofstra Law Review. 25,* 729, 736.

Kensington Int'l Ltd. v. Republic of Congo, U.S. Dist. LEXIS 63115 (2007).

Marston, D. W. (1991). Malice Aforethought How Lawyers Use Our Secret Rules to Get Rich, Get Sex, Get Even...and Get Away with It. (pp. 150). New York: William Morrow & Co.

Salcido, D. JD. (2011). Blogtalk Radio. The Abuse Freedom Live Show. 9 Oct 2011. Retrieved from http://www.blogtalkradio.com/abusefreedomlive.

Shear, K., Jackson, C., Essock, S., Donahue, S., & Felton, C. (2006). Screening for complicated grief among Project Liberty service recipients after September 11th. *Psychiatric Services.* 57, 1291-7.

Stein, S. (1989). *A Feast for Lawyers.* New York: M. Evans and Co.

van der Kolk, B., et al. (1996). Dissociation, somatization, and affect dysregulation: the complexity of adaptation of trauma. *Am J Psychiatry, 153,* 83-93.

H8S

CHAPTER 11

DESHAMING: HUFFER'S STEP-4 AVOIDING AND OVERCOMING THE SHAME OF VICTIMIZATION

Huffer's Step 4, Deshaming, invites a paradigm shift in judging people. More than race, creed, social status, or sexuality, motivation toward either conscience or power divides human beings. After this chapter, the reader will look upon relationships with new, protective insight. Skills for averting and dealing with abuse of power help avoid victimization.

If one man slay another of set purpose, he himself may rightfully be slain. He who relies solely on warlike measures shall be exterminated; he who relies solely on peaceful measures shall perish.

Sunzi "The Art of War"

Sometimes the creative works of leaders loom larger than the creators could have imagined. America's forefathers did not fathom equal rights for women and it shocks some that our first president owned slaves. Yet, the documents they created opened vistas of human dignity through checks and balances that formed the basis for civil rights. The idea for this chapter was first named, "Deshaming" because shame is unfairly cast upon human beings who have been treated poorly, stripped of their dreams and dignity, and left in poverty. Need for power or desire for cooperation emanates from deep human motives; they take shape interacting throughout human lives and commerce allowing for either fairness or victimization. Motives are obscure and often hidden by pretexts and manipulative games used by people to fulfill their objective whether noble or dirty.

The terms "CC's" and "PC's" need to become everyday language after experiencing this chapter. These terms are oversimplified for the purpose of identifying those basic human motives that seed conflicts contributing most to the conditions that precipitate Legal Abuse Syndrome. PC's abuse and bully. They are the dreaded kids on a playground, the intruder on the job, unwanted online cyber attackers, and the takers of other people's things and rights. They use abusive tactics to get what they want. They do wrong and don't feel shame. Oddly, their victims somehow wind up feeling undeserved shame only because they are victimized.

PC's abuse legal processes because the legal system under certain circumstances can be converted into a tool or a weapon they can use to enhance their power. CC's make up the majority of the population. Unfortunately, PC's, who are the significant minority, grab power at every opportunity to convert systems of power for their own use. Thus, they tend to rule over the majority.

If a PC is the adversary in litigation, the CC litigants will report feeling a sick, shamed feeling. What is presented during litigation causes them to feel embarrassment/ guilt/regret/humiliation all rolled into one. Shame sneaks in through lawyer-speak including tones of voice that force feelings of disgrace and dishonor in litigants already suffering from disability and who have done nothing wrong.

Once elicited, shame hangs on the heart and in the pit of the stomach. It is there during twilight sleep. It revisits during any pause in activities throughout the day. Unprincipled lawyers know how to shame sensitive litigants, weaken a litigant with a disability, and how to demonize innocent people. After this chapter is put to work, the pain and issues of shame now and in the future will be brought to awareness notifying the litigant to shed shame releasing energy better focused on resolving litigation.

Human Motivation Simplified, Conscience Centered (CC) or Power Centered (PC)

Life's transactions are intersections of behaviors motivated by varying combinations of conscience and power. Mother Theresa is an example of a person of extreme conscience-centered (CC) motivation and Adolf Hitler exemplifies the farthest end of the power-centered (PC) scale. Most people will find their motivations clumping somewhere around the middle of the spectrum. Adolf Hitler killed to get and maintain power. Mother Theresa saved lives of homeless and helpless people that could not provide for themselves. She still has an enduring influence worldwide even though she died several years ago. Hitler, as with all power, was short lived. Both ends claim a degree of infamy; however, active power diminishes with PC's.

Conscience has nothing to do with "bleeding heart," meek or mild personalities. CC's are often aggressive, competitive, powerful individuals. However, they operate within a set of guidelines. Conscience-centered people can have power and can desire power in order to achieve their objectives. However, their goal is not to self-serve with power only to use power for a responsible purpose.

CC's differ from the power-centered whose only objective is to have power and wield it to satisfy an ego need. The traits contrasted below generally dramatize the chasm created by diametrically opposed motives. No racial, ethnic, age, sex, or other differences in humans divide us as profoundly as CC vs. PC because the true value difference is in our core motivation.

CONTINUUM of CONSCIENCE vs. POWER

Traits Reflecting Motivation of Human Behavior

CC's	PC's
CONSCIENCE CENTERED	POWER CENTERED
Feels shame	Feels Righteous
Wants peace	Needs power
Trusting	Exploits trust
Values truth	Lies=power
Respects Boundaries	Knows no boundaries
Protects children	Exploits parenthood
Follows rule of law	Abuses litigation
Seeks joy	Feels envy
Socially responsible	Serves only self
Sensitive	Cunning
Symptoms of PTSD/LAS	Smooth in court
Cares about needs of others	Compromises others
Gives	Takes
Admits wrong	Justifies wrong
Guided by conscience	Guided by superiority
Strives to be ethical/moral	Breaks all rules
Relationships from heart	Relates for advantage
Focus outward on a task	Functions to outfox
Positive sum–cooperator	Zero sum–covets
Spiritual power	Political power
Good at mediation	Coercive controller
Technologically vulnerable	Invasive/stalks/tech
Inspires to motivate	Motivates by fear

H8S

Figure 11.1 Continuum of Conscience vs. Power

Manifestation of Conscience-Centered Motives

Conscience-centered people are cooperators. Cooperation is extremely powerful when like-minded people band together cooperating with each other. The whole becomes much greater than the sum of the parts. Nothing of value can be achieved without cooperation. Without trust, true cooperation is impossible.

The cases shared in this book illustrate human beings who cooperated with their deceivers and were betrayed. Being trustworthy people, they assume they can trust others. CCs perceive the tenets of good faith to exist in other people. They enter transactions with the assumption that human beings relate or contract with others according to given guidelines. It is reasonable for people to assume that contracts, the rule of law, lawyers' advice, state and local courts act to ensure the enforcement of the law and decency.

CCs Are Good Competitors

Can a conscience-centered person be a competitor or be successful in a competitive society? Absolutely, they are our best competitors. Cooperation and competition are not opposites. In 1944, John von Neumann and Oskar Morgenstern, both mathematicians, printed their theory of games (Neumann, 1944). In 1950, Albert Tucker, mathematician, formalized the game with prison sentence payoffs and gave it the "prisoner's dilemma" name. It illustrates the difficulty of analyzing non-zero-sum games (scenarios in which one contestant's victory is not necessarily the other contestant's defeat) (Surhone, 2010). Robert Axelrod, Walgreen professor for the Study of Human Understanding at the University of Michigan, first in 1984 and revised edition in 2006, developed a computer tournament using "Prisoner's Dilemma." The game measured impulsive responses that reflected either the inclination to cooperate or defect and proved Tit for Tat to be victorious even when you are not judged on your responses (1984).

Prisoner's Dilemma: Cooperation Put to Game Theory for a Tournament

The players in *Prisoner's Dilemma* choose to cooperate or defect over no particular issue helping assess true internal motivation. Since there is no purpose or cause except to win points, the motivation that is tapped is pure. Each player looks at a card (illustrated below) and then chooses to place his finger on the box that indicates cooperation or defection in either the row or the column. The other player simultaneously chooses a column. Then each chooses a box either cooperating or defecting for points. When put together, their choices result in one of the four possible outcomes shown in the visual example below.

The Prisoner's Dilemma

Column Player

Note: The payoffs to the Row Chooser are listed first.

Row Player		Cooperate	Defect
	Cooperate	R=3, R=3 Reward for Mutual Cooperation	S=0, T=5 Sucker' Payoff and Temptation to Defect
	Defect	T=5, S=0 Temptation to Defect and Sucker's Payoff	P=1, P=1 Punishment for Mutual Defection

Figure 11.2 Prisoner's Dilemma Playing Card

If both players cooperate, both do fairly well. Both get an R, the reward for "mutual cooperation." The value is 3 points each. If one player cooperates, but the other defects, the defecting player gets the "temptation to defect" worth 5 points, while the cooperating player gets the "sucker's payoff" worth 0 points. If both defect, both get 1 point, the "punishment for mutual defection."

Neither Defection nor Cooperation Won the Tournament

The objective of the game was to gather as many points as possible as impulsively motivated as possible. Surprisingly, the winner of the tournament was neither defection nor cooperation. It was tit for tat. The winning strategy started with a cooperative mode being set down and, thereafter, the first player did whatever the opponent did. If each cooperated, a tacit rule of cooperation was established. Based upon this consistent behavior, trust eventually became a factor in the course of the game. The results suggest that the more often cooperative moves were played, the more stable was the trust. A steady building of points gained reliability for both players. Therefore, long-term interaction is assumed to be a major factor in stabilizing cooperation and building trust. On the other hand, "first blood" and "first injured" defections shattered the stability of the game. The first to deceive often found defection reciprocated. It is obvious that wars of attrition can easily destroy both players. This relates directly to the wars of attrition that are being played out in our courtrooms as "just how the game is played."

Another critical observation that relates to litigation is that defections i.e. bullying, first to lie, violation of rules and ethics altered the perceptions and behaviors of all who interacted or even observed the players. "First injured" suffered an immediate image change from player to loser in the eyes of the community. An interesting observation and a matter of concern for victims is that the "community" around the players behaved negatively toward the victim as its members witnessed the PC's defections. Further, there was contagion of punitive behaviors among community members toward the victim. The victim was now apt to receive injury from many sources. This dynamic is an example of fundamental attribution error.

This directly relates to the pattern of lawyer behavior wherein they enter the courtroom and pounce, verbally attacking the image of the opposing litigant. If a cloud of negative perception shrouds the person with a disability and/or a pro se litigant, they are more vulnerable and likely to draw sanctions and other court ordered punishments to them. This pattern and the emerging history of it may unfairly damage a case even if the motions are unfair "defections."

My interest in Axelrod's concept of cooperation came from the sad fact that our courts are a kind of game. Even though Axelrod was thinking of international peace, nuclear war, and biological evolution in the context of cooperation, his work fits litigation (2006). During litigation, the decision to serve what is good for the individual against what is good for the system and society is the dynamic that requires continual and firm checks and balances. Herein lies the need for understanding why the legal system is not working for those with special needs. They are more easily victimized triggering the community in the courtroom to subconsciously turn against them.

Just like in Prisoner's Dilemma when a player is shunned after being victimized by defection, litigants are perceived in a negative light and the community around them tends to turn on them. How have bullies come to dominate the judicial process? They create victims and then keep legal pressure on a negative, accusatory path eliciting social repercussions on the victim. LWDs often cannot sustain under the pressure. Bullying lawyers force much litigation to be nothing more than a war of attrition. Victims are driven from litigation and denied due process of law.

What can the CC do to put more clout behind being lawful and entitled to a fair day in court? Axelrod's work suggests that tit for tat may be a good way. The CC begins by cooperating and entering litigation abiding by all rules and courtesies. However, when the rules are violated and "defection" comes the CC's way, it must be judiciously addressed.

Cecilia always felt like the courtroom was dark. She could never bring herself to defame her ex-husband even though he and his attorney saw to it that court for her was nothing but her being called derogatory names and being slandered by tone of voice as well as misstatements of fact. Cecilia learned of tit for tat but knew that she had to avoid the trap of her assertions being countered by dark and nasty remarks. She could not endure that kind of behavior. Cecilia's tit for tat reached for a dimension that would illuminate in the courtroom. Her one time tit for tat statement had to shed enough light on the character, misrepresentations, and dirty motives of her ex-husband so that the courtroom could never again be quite so dark.

She planned and privately selected the one most revealing and yet embarrassing fact about him. Then she waited for her opportunity. While being cross-examined by his attorney she was able to impart that her ex-husband had represented himself as a college graduate prior to their marriage. Among other lies, she discovered after they were married, that he had not even graduated high school. She announced this exposing as much of his fraud in one tit for tat retaliatory move as she could during cross-examination and her closing statements. Except for that tit for tat response placed on the record, she returned to her usual self.

Unexpectedly, this very simple strategy did outstandingly well in Axelrod's tournament: cooperate on the first move and then copy your opponent's last move for all subsequent moves. Tit for tat (TFT) was the simple strategy and laid the groundwork for an ever-growing number of successful strategies published by Axelrod. In a similar competition with 62 contestants, TFT won again. It has three characteristics that account for its impressive performance: it is "nice" (cooperates on the first move), retaliatory (punishes defection in the prior move with defection) and forgiving (immediately returns to cooperation after one TFT response to defection of the adversary).

After seeing a pattern of tit for tat as the winning strategy for tournaments, I was curious whether it was possible to develop Axelrod's idea of "mathematical analysis" to show how cooperation based upon reciprocity can emerge in a population of egoists (PCs), like certain lawyers, with a limited number of cooperators CCs. And, what role does authority play in the dynamic of the game? (Axelrod, 1981).

"Authority" in a courtroom must technically be the Trier of Fact, the judge, to oversee that rules and laws are followed. Other authority is found in licensing bodies and professional organizations setting forth standards of practice and ethical guidelines. As I set out to design a format to study cooperation during litigation, the challenge was in narrowing the focus to accommodate research in the actual milieu of today's litigation. Three issues emerged from the Huffer/Alexander ten-year longitudinal survey that deserve further formal research.

1. In line with Axelrod's findings, we found that after misinformation attacked the character of the litigant including body language and a tone of voice that communicated disgust and distaste, a cloud of suspicion was successfully placed around the targeted litigant that changed how they were formally treated in court. Just as Axelrod found the "community" around the victim tended to reject the victim, so the judicial community can be manipulated against a targeted person in the courtroom. This dynamic is critical to wars of attrition displacing fair litigation. Authority must take a formal stand to stop PCs from using lies and insults to bully CCs in court. The effects of this technique on juries cannot be underestimated. These nebulous, but deadly tactics are commonplace in court and run rampant during litigation. Ridicule was found to be the most traumatizing type of attack that litigants sustained in court. And, lies were the number one complaint for every participant in the Huffer/Alexander Longitudinal Survey. So, ridding the courts of ridicule and slanderous lies would go a long way toward providing equal access for litigants.

H8S

2. "Defection" or betrayal stuns and distresses the target. When a litigant with special needs is discriminated against by defection, I witness embarrassment, humiliation, and responses that confuse onlookers as to whether or not they are guilty. Cooperation within a set of guidelines must be enforced with penalties for defectors in a court of law. A very experienced attorney who needed ADA accommodations for a chronic pain condition reported, "I was never so shamed in my life as having to produce medical documents to beg for my ADA accommodations." Her adversaries ridiculed her and tried to object to her accommodations, a violation of ADAAA and all decency according to this seasoned lawyer. It is tantamount to objecting to a paraplegic using a wheelchair to challenge accommodations needed by those with invisible disabilities. This attorney risks her client's wellbeing when she is maltreated because her reactions as counsel could send the wrong signals to the judge or jury.

3. There needs to be a study measuring the difference when two issues are addressed: First issue is the awareness of the effects of feeling shame put to Huffer's 8-Steps to avoid devastation from Legal Abuse Syndrome. Second issue is the difference when clients approach the court with pride and confidence. Advocates recommend that clients dress like a lawyer, walk into court like a lawyer, have papers organized, and do not allow shame to overtake their emotional state or appearance.

The Impact of Zero Sum Behavior

Power-centered people will cheat in order to win and then bask in the glow of victory. They will use "whatever it takes" to win, thus destroying the spirit of the endeavor. That is why power-centered people are considered "zero-sum." Zero sum means, if I have something or I win, the power-centered person feels a loss. The PC has conceptualized others' gains as direct defeats for him. Envy is the emotion that causes the PC to assume that, if the other is succeeding, they must be losing. This distortion vindicates, in their minds, acts of deception and other sleazy moves. Obviously, the result is an unjust loss or for those who play fairly. Vehemently, however, these liars and cheaters share, with those they betray, the desire not to be deceived (Bancroft, 2002).

The work of neuroscientists is enlightening as to the very inner workings of the human brain as it responds to power plays by deception, noted in LWD cases. My oversimplified concept of those motivated by sheer power, PCs, and those who are conscience-motivated, CCs, is an effort to help the litigant with disabilities envision, in a tangible way, how human traits cause victims and victimizers. The deceiver as well as the deceived are interesting to study.

Deception appears to be a hardwired human tendency. Giorgio Ganis and Julian Paul Keenan quote William Hazlitt (1778-1830), a British writer who wrote, "life is the art of being deceived." Ganis and Keenan published in *Social Neuroscience* that deception is a core feature of human nature (2009). Therefore, from the beginning of recorded history and reported from a vast array of societies throughout all facets of human interaction, deception is a factor to be considered. No one wants to be deceived, but to deceive is human.

The power-centered strive for a feeling of significance in relationships but are thwarted by their power moves that bring them ego status but little in the way of satisfying relationships. The farther toward the power end of the continuum their motivation lies, the more the PC will lack ability to cooperate, an essential trait for maintaining good relationships.

When PCs encounter a problem that demands cooperation with others, it throws them into tension. Since they can't be trusted, they feel incapable of trusting others. Risking trust is another major component of healthy relationships. Therefore, two critical elements of healthy relationships are missing with PCs. They can't cooperate and they can't trust. Once you realize you are relating with a PC in business or personally, it is usually wise to run not walk away from the PC if possible. If you are entrenched in a relationship with a PC, then protecting yourself becomes paramount. A PC parent might be generous and fun, but ultimately the narcissistic side of their efforts will be exposed. They groom their target people to comply with their demands. PCs interpret compliance as affection. When their children simply want to make independent decisions or their partner expresses an opinion, the PC will feel rejected and often behaves punitively toward the child or partner. They feel insulted by noncompliance. PCs do not feel like they abuse their relationships. They feel completely justified in punishing the noncompliant person who rejects their coercion. Being blind to cooperation and compromise, they righteously swear that they are not abusive. Awareness of this distortion is critical if you are facing litigation, mediation, or arbitration. The PC will often convince others to back their position because they sincerely believe they are right plus they emanate power. Prior to any hearings or meetings this dynamic must be exposed. The expert used by the advocate or attorney can say, "PC has a different language of love or business management than the LWD." "He/She interprets compliance as affection." "He/She feels rejected and unloved or not respected when those he oppresses don't comply." "Then, he/she uses punitive means to force compliance." "This is an unhealthy dynamic that must not affect the outcome of the proceedings."

At the beginning of a relationship, PCs give all appearances of being a perfect mate or business partner. But, over time, it is apparent that they do not listen to another's ideas, cannot cooperate, and they do not care about the other person's needs, feelings, or opinions. PCs are incompetent relating with others emotionally and culturally.

PCs who perversely pursue power do so from a posture of imagined superiority. They spend their energies outwitting others and the law. Power seekers envision themselves to be more cunning than they are. The ability to deprive others of their property, to have command of life and death, to prove one's own importance at the expense of others, and to deceive others creates and endorses their superiority (Tucker, 1985).

Responses to the Zero Sum

It is critical to know the initial strategy, strengths, and weaknesses of the other player in a contest or the other person in a relationship. You need to know if you are facing a PC or a CC. If you are in litigation, remember litigation is a contest. If the opponent steps in with deception on the first move, the cooperator can lose everything. You can begin to predict whether or not your opponent is likely to violate the rules and defect once you sense what motivates the person. Advocates need to summarize with the litigant, coaching them as to CC and PC behaviors by asking the litigant the following questions. Remind the litigant of the dynamics indicating basic motives:

1. Carefully observe the opponent. Are they too good to be true in the beginning? PCs first know how to disarm the opponent by charm, dazzle, intelligence, or whatever works. They groom the target. Once groomed, PCs know how to deliver a few major blows that stun and neutralize their prey. "Lame duck" status is awarded to all who appear to falter. It becomes an open door to exponential attacks and spurning (Axelrod, 2006). PC deceivers zero in on the CC person's sensitivity, vulnerability, and desire for cooperation. As PCs move in for the "kill," instinctively they seem to know that their vicious assaults are sure to damage their target's image.

2. Does it first seem like progress is made to benefit all and then hidden agendas emerge benefiting only or mainly the suspected PC?

3. Does the opponent seem to use reckless strategies that betray the rules and the common good for self-interest?

4. It seems an agreement is being negotiated and then they pull out the stops in an ambush. You find that they are engaging in any number of deceptions, i.e. in rumors, slander, libel, accusations, stealing of assets, forcing bankruptcy, filing harassing motions, lawsuits, or false charges. They damage the opponent's credit, make threats, interfere with business relationships, and harass on the job.

5. Does the opponent violate boundaries i.e., spy, terrorize, and blackmail, to name a few? This kind of tactical subterfuge is ruinous, and yet remains largely un-actionable in terms of the victim's ability to effectively assuage a damaged reputation or find relief through litigation once it is in full force.

6. Every person needs to be cognizant of CC/PC dynamics and keep them in mind when they meet others. Advocates can assist with observations noticing telltale traits displayed by the adversary and counsel during litigation.

7. A few simple side questions about family, jobs, or the current state of the economy can open doors to begin to sense if the opposition is PC or CC driven depending how they respond.

Power orientation leans toward extremes in self-serving actions and crime. Since power strivers are bold, visible, and influential, they will often be politicians, presidents, dictators, and famous leaders in their fields. Many times they are the abusers or cheaters in domestic violence relationships. This brings into focus myths to be dispelled.

MYTH 1: Criminals are often geniuses. Intelligence does not seem to be a factor in crime or immorality. It can appear as intelligence because criminals get away with considerable crime before they're caught. Their daring can cause them to look heroic or they momentarily win favors through intimidation or reckless success at their craft. Time and energy accomplishes. Equal time and energy on a legal endeavor would produce accomplishment as well.

MYTH 2: All public servants who are elected or hired to serve the public do so. The list of cheaters who enjoyed undeserved public trust and faith is too long to list in this work. However, they are corporate executives (even toy makers), financial "wizards," presidential candidates, sports champions, religious leaders, politicians, medical innovators, celebrities, leaving few identifiable positive role models for our posterity. No cloak assures honesty and authenticity. We must know how to look beneath and beyond the trappings.

Do not vote for PCs. CCs are too often kept out of public service and/or limited as to their terms by PAC's (Political Action Committees) viciousness of campaigning, and the resistance to positive change by those in power. Those with integrity withdraw from public service in droves every year. They point to chicanery, pressure from lobbyists, or their supervisors to violate their values causing difficulty in dealing with their promises to constituents as reasons for withdrawing from public service. PCs in CC clothing are naturals to sit in family portraits in front of a flag, chameleon-like charming their way to power. However, once in place, they do not serve the best interest of the public, only themselves.

Richard Nixon is a good example of a PC in high office. On June 23, 2009, the Nixon Library released 5,000 pages of previously held documents. The PC side of Nixon is apparent in the comments and attitudes portrayed in these documents. After elected President, he broke the rules to assure his next win, determined to hold onto the power of the presidency. He did this in the face of an almost sure re-election that was predicted (Volkan, 1997).

The criminal scandal of Watergate was set into motion and finally cost him the presidency by resignation. The Watergate "break in" initiated by Nixon was to learn the Democrat's election strategy. It was unwarranted and showed very poor judgment not only because it was illegal, but Nixon was the favored to win. In the *Frost/Nixon Interview*, he actually stated that, "When a president does it, it is not against the law." When he resigned the presidency, he blamed the media. He attempted to interfere with the Washington Post's communications licensing since they broke the Watergate story that brought him to his presidential demise. His is a rise and fall that truly dramatizes the PC and the consequences of the public not identifying these traits but blindly voting for a party or being fooled by an appearance.

MYTH 3: PC Abusers need psychotherapy to deal with early bad experiences, low self-esteem, or emotional problems. Once these painful experiences are relieved, their behaviors will change. That is not born out by research. PC's customarily are stuck with feelings of superiority, choices that serve self, and an unwillingness to undergo the rigors of counseling. These types of PC's often make comments that reveal that they perceive the population as "stupid" while they manipulate behavior,

H8S

finances, polls, images, and votes.

In fact, the population of trustworthy CCs is slow to fathom the wiles of PCs that can look and sound sincere. Therefore, PCs are often elected and once in office use myriad tactics to stay in positions of power.

Working with Systems of Power

Who makes things happen the way they do? Who has the power to design the behavioral setting and to maintain its operation in whatever way it is manifested? Dr. Phil Zimbardo, Professor Emeritus, Stanford University in Psychology asks: "Who is responsible for the consequences and outcomes?" "Who gets the credit for successes or pays the dues for failures?" "System Power" is what he calls the force that emerges punishing and controlling people as power is amassed (Zimbardo, 2007).

If the systems espouse ideology that is in tune with the people, they may be easily accepted as the "authority." Thus, the justice system is our authority.

Zimbardo, has spent years examining dynamics of persons placed in positions of power. His work consistently demonstrates that humans must have oversight and checks and balances on power. The judicial system is relied upon to oversee the courts. Within this powerful arm of Government rests deep-seated motives of human beings who, if they wear a black robe, can take your house, your money, your life, your child, and your freedom and leave the litigant in shame and pain. If questioned, judges can often claim absolute immunity. Unchecked power is a sobering concept for a human being to prudently manage. We expect super human prudence from judges in today's environment of ethical relativism. See examples at www.zimbardo.com.

Therefore, people must monitor their interactions with others for self-protection. At all times, in all endeavors, litigants must examine the motives of those they encounter as to conscience versus power. The Power Centered (PCs 10-15%) are the smallest part of the population, but they are compelled to grab for power. The majority of people are Conscience Centered (CCs 80-85%). They wind up too often in forced compliance through employment or under other power of PCs where they are squeezed between their values and what they must do to stay safe or employed.

In this high tech age, PCs ability to use coercion through stalking and intrusion are reaching unimagined dimensions. Their ability to manipulate the media is unprecedented. Therefore, as litigants become enmeshed in legal battles, a new sophistication for litigants with disabilities must be born along with it. Certified advocates can bring to impaired litigants a new mentality, innovative and broadened vocabulary, and force a paradigm shift to all involved as part of the enrichment they bring to litigation. It is critical to upgrade ways to protect and rescue those taken hostage by the disparate motives of the Power- Centered who defy science fiction in their abilities to commandeer new intrusive technology. This is discussed in detail in the Empowerment section.

Senator Pell, author and supporter of Pell Grants that have helped many people go to school, said, *"I have always felt that we needed more psychiatrists in government."* He foresees a role for psychiatrists in understanding the motivations and behaviors of world leaders. He hoped that such influence would help them to free themselves from acting upon unconscious conflicts in their power roles.

Having a power-centered president, boss, judge, spouse or banker poses an immediate threat of victimization. The classic worst-case scenario for litigation is having a power centered offender aided and abetted by a power-centered judge. The analysis in this book is meant to help the litigant and client understand and avoid such predicaments and deshame early on so as not to encourage the "community" to mistakenly go against the victim. It is a perception issue that can cause the wrong party to be punished so very unfairly.

Appropriate Selfishness

Litigation is a forum entertaining a collision of self-interests. It is appropriate selfishness to protect oneself from abuse. Ending a relationship with a PC who has violated the CC through deceptions, invasions of boundaries, use of force can be filled with more confusing twists and turns than a Grisham novel. The PC will call the CC selfish for wanting anything for themselves and their children. The CC will feel selfish and wonder in self-doubt because of the history of influence of the convincing PC. They once trusted the PC. If deception is to work, there have to be those who trust first and are prone to self-doubt. Trusting comes naturally to the CC. So they become vulnerable (Ringer,1977).

Convergence of power-centered and conscience-centered people, in their purest forms, will inevitably result in the conscience-centered person being victimized. It is a marriage of deathly complementary value systems upon which the power-centered thrive. They literally tend a garden of trusting relationships while perpetrating hidden agendas. Such marriages fail and wind up in court for years on end with the court unable to sort out the issues. Mediation fails. The PC always accuses the CC of the PC's wrongdoings. It is the worst of he said/she said. The court grows weary and impatient leaving the CC unprotected, even punished. The courts attempt to be therapeutic by ordering litigants for evaluation and counseling but the entire premise of the therapeutic environment, trust, choice, reduced stress, cannot flourish when court-ordered. Threat overhangs and necessary trust cannot build.

A frightening thing often happens as CCs try to end litigation. The CC offers to give up every asset in trade for custody, peace, and safety. This is a huge mistake if custody of children is involved. Because once the PC and CC have made their asset settlement, it seems to be etched in stone. The CC walks away from all assets in exchange for full custody bargaining to be left alone in safety and peace. What would the natural instinct of the PC be? The custody is never etched in stone. So, with the CC's assets used against them, the PC now goes after custody. The CC is deceived and victimized once again and is left with no assets to support the litigation. CCs must accept enough selfishness to assure they have equal assets from the marriage to protect them. CCs must be appropriately selfish, self-protective, and savvy. That is just good management.

Methods for CC Protection

Advocates must help the litigant develop sight, insight, and foresight. "I just didn't see it coming," litigants tell advocates. "How could I have been so blind?" they ask. Three tasks combine to develop sight, insight, and foresight, the first protective goal.

Task 1–See the game. See both players, in your mind's eye, on the continuum. Don't be blinded by dreams, hopes, or wants, but be aware of what you want, specifically. Don't buy verbal promises and don't act too fast. Take time for history to develop through a few moves. Do not be motivated by fear or intimidation.

Task 2–Gain insight into the motives of the other player. Even if the first few moves are cooperative, caution is in order. When you know what you want and what motivates you, then ask yourself, "What motivates the other player?"

Task 3–Verify every statement and document. Trust if you wish, but verify nevertheless. Visualizing human beings in transactions on the continuum helps discern just where on the scale the other player falls in terms of his motivation.

Don't Envy or Emulate PC Behavior

Caution: a PC will use defection in a symmetrically accelerating negative manner. It looks easy, just pick defect every time and get 5 points. The first and second time works, but then the other player catches on and begins defecting also in tit for tat fashion. In litigation, this defection translates to an action that cancels or slows the momentum towards a resolution to the litigation, e.g. filing a false accusation that must be responded to before we can continue forward. These tit for tat cycles are crudely called "pissing contests" by lawyers and can become the dreaded "he said/she said" droning on in likewise defections (Ringer, 2009).

Stick with Your Conscience

Very important harbingers for society are found in that, in using tit for tat, never did one player have to do better than the other in order to do well for himself. The overriding lesson is that doing well for oneself is a most successful goal in and of itself not contrasted with the other player's performance.

Bill Clinton's campaign staffer, Lee Atwater, used defection when he published terrible lies about people and hurt many irreparably. While dying, he called and apologized to some victims of his politically motivated defamations (Atwater, 1991). The staff kept a 24-hour rapid response team on alert to immediately and publicly counter negative attacks. Tit for tat was applied. However, it was abused by Atwater to powerfully crush opponents surpassing their first defection. Human systems of care are not to be used to destroy human beings or the delicate moral foundations that must exist for humans to share the planet. Lee Atwater, on his deathbed, brings perspective to destructive behaviors of those who will abuse the courts of law, their professions, elections, and the rule of law. In a February 1991 article for *Life* magazine, Atwater wrote:

> *My illness helped me to see that what was missing in society is what was missing in me: a little heart, a lot of brotherhood. The '80s were about acquiring— acquiring wealth, power, prestige. I know. I acquired more wealth, power, and prestige than most. But, you can acquire all you want and still feel empty. What power wouldn't I trade for a little more time with my family? What price wouldn't I pay for an evening with friends? It took a deadly illness to put me eye to eye with that truth, but it is a truth that the country, caught up in its ruthless ambitions and moral decay, can learn on my dime. I don't know who will lead us through the '90s, but they must be made to speak to this spiritual vacuum at the heart of American society, this tumor of the soul.*

I don't believe it will be elected officials or officers of the court that will lead us correctly into the mid 2000's. It must be the disenfranchised, the disabled, those who see beyond ego, power, and acquisition. Those who already possess the wisdom that Atwater so painfully and tardily attained. It will also be their advocates who know that wisdom needs to come from looking back and looking forward and then designing the present with balance and fairness as CCs and PCs must intersect.

Huffer's Log

Case of Deshaming-Tit for Tat Applied

Opposing counsel in Libby's case would walk into the courtroom loudly announcing to all who were present that she was "unstable, unpredictable, dangerous to her children, and refused to obey court orders." By the time court opened its session, the perception of Libby, held by all court personnel and onlookers, was damaged. Such slander is powerful, shaming, and nearly impossible to cure once it is put into the mind of the court. The "community" was turned against Libby before she entered the courtroom.

Libby must be cognizant that her image has to be repaired as a matter of presenting her case. She has believed that she should rise above such slander by not responding. In fact, she has refused to attend court on many occasions due to the degrading attack on her and the pain that it arouses. Unfortunately, while she is on what she perceives as a higher road, she is being held in contempt, sanctioned, and has bench warrants issued for her arrest. All of these punitive actions reflect only defamation and not the true person who is a kind cooperator simply unable to play the game of legal attrition. Yet, she is now in the position of being punished severely by the court simply because she cannot tolerate the war of attrition any longer.

Author's Notes:

Several citations in this book are aged more then ten years. When they are included in this work, the purpose is to show the conditions that originally contributed to Legal Abuse Syndrome as contrasted with how litigants find the courts today. For example, Robert Axelrod has had an international impact on research pertaining to the value of cooperation from 1984 to the present. Many attitudes have strengthened or been altered in the past decades.

European Journal of Work and Organizational Psychology (EJWOP), 1996, whole issue devoted to bullying and its effects, including PTSD. Published by Psychology Press, 27 Church Road, Hove, East Sussex BN3 2FA, UK.

Leymann, Heinz was one of the first people to identify the symptoms of injury to health caused by bullying as PTSD.

Stein, Sol. (1992). Feast for Lawyers. New York: M. Evans and Company, Inc. Owner of Stein and Day lost his publishing company in an abusive Chapter 11 bankruptcy that he works to expose by telling his story.

Andersen, Donna. (2010). Love Fraud: How Marriage to a Sociopath Fulfilled My Spiritual Plan. New Jersey: Anderly Publishing is mentioned prior to publishing.

Donna Anderson takes her reader on a very personal journey through an intimate relationship with a sociopath. The book spans more than 600 pages of her story and other selected stories of what she has termed, "Love Fraud." This is not a book to be read for research or pleasure. It is a critical book to be experienced in the manner of having a close friend stop by for tea that knows the shocking and isolating pain of trusting a person without a conscience. When you need to explore the experience, your friend is there with empathy, guidance, and finally a spiritual awakening that spiritually enriches the awful memories of life. Donna Anderson opens her heart and soul as a friend does over time and over tea. The reader comes away wiser and comforted knowing that there is a bigger purpose to this life. And, alert to the subtle traps that await any of us from the charm, wit, and magnetism of the sociopaths among us.

(http://nixon.archives.gov/virtuallibrary/documents/jun09.php

Torts – Abuse of process, intentional infliction of emotional distress (If all abuses were to become torts it would bankrupt each state and the nation.)

1. The courts need to take strong action to stop being used as weapons, tools of intimidation by PC's. A Canada case provides a good example. Court refuses to be pawn in divorce case: Ontario judges reject appeal of man they say used legal system to punish former spouse

By Cristin Schmitz , The Ottawa Citizen January 23, 2010

Ontario's top court has warned high-conflict spouses it won't be used as a weapon of marital destruction.

Recently, Ontario Court of Appeal unanimously quashed the appeal of Darko Danicic from a groundbreaking decision last year that ordered the Toronto photographer to pay nearly a quarter of a million dollars in damages and court costs to Traci McLean for threatening and harassing her in a failed bid to get her to drop her property and spousal support claims. A panel of three judges said Danicic was dragging his heels in an effort to thwart his ex-common-law spouse's efforts to end the litigation and collect her judgment. They dismissed the case on Jan. 15, 2010 "The appeal appears to be vexatious and a continuation of a previous pattern—as a result, we are of the opinion that the appeal is an abuse of process."

"The court has a right to control its own process." McLean's lawyer, Georgina Carson, said "the case has exposed a small but real and very dangerous element of quasi-criminal behavior in family law. Hopefully, the case will have a long-term chilling effect on others seeking to threaten a more vulnerable spouse into relinquishing their valid claims."

The trial decision broke new ground in Canada last year because it was the first to order one spouse to pay damages to the other for the intentional infliction of mental and emotional suffering in a case that was not accompanied by a physical assault.

According to the trial judge, Danicic's "outrageously unreasonable conduct" included writing McLean crudely abusive letter, denying their romantic involvement, unsuccessfully trying to get her lawyer disbarred, and threatening to send to her grandmother private, intimate photographs he took when they were a couple.

"He has made no effort to bring the appeal forward and seeks to obstruct and increase the costs to (McLean)," they said in a decision to be reported in The Lawyers Weekly. Danicic was ordered in June to pay McLean $15,000 for intentionally causing her mental distress, plus $228,500 for the legal costs he forced her to incur.

Since then, McLean's lawyer says she has heard from dozens of people in high-conflict separations who complain they are being harassed by their ex-partners. "It seems to have touched a chord," Carson said. "Although we like to believe we live in a society where justice will prevail, the fact is, in family law, spouses frequently give up their rightful claims in the face of seemingly overwhelming emotional, physical or financial pressures from a spouse. In this case, I am proud to say that the victim was protected by the system and the bully punished."

H8S

The trial judgment says Danicic's psychologically abusive conduct toward McLean ranged from his "extremely hurtful" claim that they were only ever landlord and tenant, to him sending her "hostile" and "frightening" letters, one of which spoke of putting a bullet in her head.

McLean wound up under a doctor's care and taking anti-anxiety medication.

Danicic faces trial on related criminal charges of threatening and extortion.

References

Atwater, L. (1991, January 28). Apologies for Campaign Tactics. U.S. News and World Report. 110(16).

Axelrod, R. (1984). *The Evolution of Cooperation*. New York: Basic Books.

Axelrod, R. & Hamilton, W. (1981). The evolution of cooperation. *Science, 211(4489)*, 1390-6.

Bancroft, L. (2002). *Inside the Minds of Controlling Men: Why Does He Do That?* New York: Berkley Publishing Group.

Ganis, G., & Keenan, J. P. (Eds.). (2009). The cognitive neuroscience of deception. *Social Neuroscience, 4 (6)*, 465-472.

Ringer, R.J. (2009). *The Search for Truth*. Retrieved from www.robertringer.com.

Ringer, R.J. (1977). *Looking Out for Number 1*. Beverly Hills: Los Angeles Book Corp.

Surhone, L., Timpledon, M., & Marseken, S. F., (Eds.). (2010, June). *Prisoner's Dilemma: Game theory, Merrill M. Flood, Melvin Dresher, Albert W. Tucker, Framing Device, Experimental Economics*. Germany: Betascript Publishing.

Tucker, W. (1985). *Vigilante: The Backlash Against Crime in America*. New York: Stein and Day Pub.

Volkan, V. D., Itzkowitz, N., & Dod, A.W. (1997). *Nixon: A Psychobiography*. New York: Columbia University Press.

von Neumann, J. & Morgenstern, O. (1944). *Theory of Games and Economic Behavior*. Princeton: Princeton University Press.

Zimbardo, P. (2007). *The Lucifer Effect: Understanding How Good People Turn Evil*. (pp. 9-10). New York: Random House Trade.

CHAPTER 12

OBSESSIVE-COMPULSIVE HYPER-VIGILANCE (OCH): HUFFER'S STEP-5 REGAINING CREATIVE CONTROL

Obsessive-Compulsive Hyper-vigilance (OCH), Huffer's Step-5, is a condition that drives lawyers to distraction. Do not discredit a person because of irritating suspicion, anxiety, fear, and caution. Look to when the behavior happens and why they need the behavior. The skills for OCH bring rationale to quirky behavior that helps to alleviate the symptoms. Then onlooker, look in the mirror.

A man is but the product of his thoughts. What he thinks, he becomes.

Mahatma Gandhi

Obsessive-Compulsive Hyper-Vigilance or OCH feels like anxiety and paranoia, but it is not a mental illness. It is part of the PTSD/LAS experience. The sufferer knows where it came from and what will relieve it. A person afflicted with a mental illness does not know how it happened or what will cure it. ADA advocates are trained to refer litigants to a medical or mental health professional when needed. But, in most cases, advocates provide a satisfactory level of supportive counseling while working through the protocols (Huffer's 8-Steps). That usually suffices. Litigants who sustain a psychic injury are substantially improved when they regain control over their lives. That is what identifying OCH and its manifestations help to attain.

In the meantime, the advocate knows that the richness of the litigant's ability to experience the "now" is being compulsively diverted to ritualized behaviors due to OCH. Rituals are essential for maintaining balance in an imbalanced environment. So, when the sufferer feels crazy, unbalanced, or persecuted, he or she may develop a defensive obsession as a normal post trauma reflex action. This is not uncommon while the litigant works to help regain control of his or her environment. I have

H8S

named it OCH because it really is hyper-vigilance in response to trauma, not customary obsessive-compulsive disorder.

In such a circumstance, OCH must be identified, treated, and managed. And, in court, the advocate acts as a rudder to keep the litigant redirected to the present moment. This can result in a huge tug of war between the natural responses of a traumatized person with their emotions feeling tied to survival versus the tactics of adversarial litigation. There is no substitute for preparation for this moment in court.

In the throes of litigation, natural survival instincts take over at a primitive level that will supersede cognitive judgment in the moment. That is why advocates must be able to speak for the litigant from their prepared statements. This does not put the advocate on par with an attorney; no legal advice is imparted or legal procedure improperly entered. It is the voice of the litigant interpreted when they are unable to communicate fully provided for under the ADAAA.

Courtroom Centralizes Traumatic Exposure Precipitating OCH

After or during trauma, while the litigant's internal protective physiology forces him or her to be normally obsessed, the sufferer's mind must figure out what happened or is happening. They are driven to form a basis for feeling safe again. Survival preoccupies the individual's life.

Cues signaling danger may be picked up only by the LWD. Being in the courtroom with the abusive spouse and/or the team of attorneys representing the abuser emits many subtle warning signals of danger. The aroma of the abuser, certain looks, gestures, tones of voice trigger the limbic system in the brain. The hippocampus, important in decision-making, has been shown to actually shrink in size with prolonged trauma (Hunter,2009; Nadel, 1996).

Right when the judge makes a pronouncement or the litigant is called upon to speak the sufferer's brain may be symptomatic reflected by reactions of recoil, fight/flight or freeze. What defines a critical symptomatic moment is the flashback, the degree of helplessness experienced while simultaneously feeling jeopardized. Every LAS survivor at some point feels that he or she has been in significant jeopardy and has been absolutely unable to do anything about the perceived threats or hostile actions. That stress, coupled with his or her feelings of impotence, precipitates fear-motivated OCH (O'Brien , 1997).

Herein lies the crisis presented by family court for domestic violence victims. The aggressor usually has commandeered the finances and tirelessly lobbied the court and community toward their power interests. Having taken control of the moneys the controller can afford lawyers that go up against an abused, broke, and fearful victim. The very architecture of the court is all wrong when this happens. Family courts function with an insider system of mental health professionals being appointed by judges. Such evaluators, guardians, investigators appointed by judges can represent an unintentional ganging up against the litigant with a disability. The appearance of a conflict of interest cannot be avoided. It is a set-up for disaster before the litigation begins. Then, lies are introduced;

intimidation is put into full force; and soon, the litigant with special needs is symptomatic and unable to function. Simple changes in those patterns and practices would go a long way to offering a good social model for litigants with disabilities in family court.

Meanwhile, ADA advocates assure that litigants do not overlook their strengths: 1) a powerful law in the ADAAA, 2) each other as supporter/advocates, 3) treatment, starting with Reframing and continuing through Empowerment found in Huffer's 8-Steps, and 4) an advocacy system set up to positively affirm and accommodate the litigant in the court. Focus remains on functionality of the litigant.

The following case shows how developing OCH escalates into an emotional hyperbole that erodes the functionality of the LAS victim. The demands of daily living become exhausting. LAS litigants will usually have a window of energy early in the day and then find themselves completely exhausted by evening (Pert, 1999). They may need to go to sleep early but are troubled especially during twilight sleep at dusk and dawn. They become exhausted and ask, "What's wrong with me?" and many times reply, "I've gone completely nuts." No, it is OCH. You are just feeling like you are nuts.

Hyper-vigilance As an Obsession—Is Not Paranoia

Thriving in this culture as a human being depends on enjoying a sense of belonging, being able to trust, and being confident in self worth. For many LWDs to stop litigation would mean succumbing to the devastation of feeling they:

- belong nowhere;

- trust nothing;

- are annihilated as a person.

Hanging on to litigation gives the sufferer some sense of meaning and purpose. It represents one tiny shred of hope. Sometimes it is the simple hope that the litigant's humanity can be restored. This unrelenting force for survival, Obsessive-compulsive Hyper-vigilance, often plagues the courts and distorts the purpose and meaning of litigation. It opens the door for legal abuse on one side and a human being's need for survival on the other.

H8S

Family courts typically struggle to deal with these compelling, nebulous self-survival forces that materialize in Obsessive Compulsive Hyper-vigilance. One person can be viciously abused, attacked, and out powered by a cruel and coercively controlling person and the court may mischaracterize it as a "high conflict" case. There is no conflict. It is predator and its prey struggling to survive. Family Court makes these mistakes because virtually no court is equipped to deal with the emotional dynamics that underpin the causes of hyper-vigilance in litigation. Until there is a method for acknowledging deep human dynamics in litigation and improve the treatment of justice seekers, family courts will be a wasteland that satisfies no one and that fails in their social mission. Bullying is the force that most often creates OCH. Whether on the street, on the job, in the boardroom, or in a court of law, PTSD is accurately deemed a psychiatric injury, not a mental illness and therefore must be curtailed as a health threat. Litigation seems to pose a threat to health in the bullying category that would fit Center for Disease Control requirement to post a warning label, LITIGATION MAY BE HAZARDOUS TO YOUR HEALTH. However, to avoid the risk, it is not as simple as advising a litigant to stay away from litigation. Seeking justice is engrained and entrenched in litigants and their cases. LWDs often give the impression of being mad hoarders with their stacks of boxes filled with files and papers. Litigants customarily cling to the voluminous legal papers as a symptom of OCH because they represent a lifeline to hope that someday they will attain justice. They hold onto the every shred of the case for years unable to part with one page or trust legal documents completely to scanners. It is important to respect that LWDs have a right to their health and justice they should not have to choose one or the other (Daniel, 2006).

Certain components comprise Obsessive-Compulsive Hyper-vigilance:

1. The sufferer manifests a dogged determination not to lose – never will give up. The court system has cases that are decades old and need to be resolved. Yet, the fragility of litigant rights combined with the profitability of litigation that has turned into commercialized business perpetuates OCH in cases that are deadlocked for decades on end.

2. The sufferer fights for justice every day and can think of little else. The cause often becomes larger than self. Personal, moral, and professional values are viewed in ethical and moral terms. The gap widens between (a) the reality of compromised ethical and moral expectations of attorneys and court personnel and (b) those ideals that the litigant holds. Intrinsically, the litigant is right, but "right," then conflicts with "reality."

3. The sufferer feels vulnerable and fearful once he or she discovers that knowing the law and the rules does not make a litigant a successful litigator. The litigant feels unfairly incompetent because the harder they try, they do not get a clear win. There is a set of rules that litigants do not know. It is obvious that some insider force is in play. They still believe it is important to put forth the values of fair dealing, rules, laws and they expect reasonable ethical behavior. To let go of those values is unacceptable and feels irresponsible to them.

4. Symptoms of mental illness are situational and reactive, not organic. Yet, the adversary will many times try to use symptoms of psychic injury or mental illness if it exists, to discriminate against the sufferer. Such litigation trauma further triggers the sufferer's symptoms. Even though the HIPAA and ADAAA laws protect the litigant against violations of their medical confidentiality, many judges do not know these laws or follow them. They will flagrantly violate confidentiality and provide the adversary with a great weapon to use against the special needs litigant.

5. The sufferer obsesses on litigation and preoccupies themselves with the behavior of the adversary or opposing counsel as the cause of their injury. Fixing the bad behavior is

perceived as potentially curative. Unethical, fraudulent, and discriminatory behavior by the adversary or opposing counsel is immoral and unethical defying professional standards according to the litigant. But, reporting may fall on deaf ears. Therefore, The data analysis process is designed for the purpose of guiding the litigant as to how to speak to the court so misinformation is illuminated improving their chances of correcting the record.

6. The sufferer is articulate, but trauma physiologically prevents him or her from speaking for him- or herself when under stress. If the court prevents others from speaking for the sufferer, he or she is left without an influential voice. The advocate must speak for the litigant when they are unable to speak for themselves. This act of interpretation is clearly intended by the ADAAA.

7. The sufferer, against all odds, holds out hope that their legal system and the adversary will recognize the errors of their ways and correct wrongdoing. Sufferers cannot fathom the intentional infliction of pain and suffering he or she is experiencing.

8. The sufferer feels undeserved personal worthlessness. Rejection and incompetence in court add to feelings of worthlessness and helplessness. These feelings create ongoing symptoms manifesting Complex Post Traumatic Stress Disorder emanating from cumulative trauma as delineated from Post Traumatic Stress Disorder from one traumatic event.

9. When Prescription drugs are offered and may even help the symptoms of PTSD/ LAS, they are often resisted because the sufferer feels an obsessive need to cure the societal problem as part of healing. They do not want to be medicated allowing the pattern of wrongdoing to go uncorrected while they dull a critical reality. Here is where the law protects under what is called the "eggshell skull theory," that whatever predisposing factors s exist for the trauma the negligent or intentional offender must accept responsibility for the injury as it occurs including all damages. When violation of principles is at the base of the suffering, litigants do not want to take a pill and let it go. They feel that to do so is to sacrifice important values of society. Those values are what create satisfaction in their lives and bring happiness to human beings. In their opinion, they will not support a commercialized endeavor that has ripped the fairness and justice from their legal system.

10. Symptoms improve when the sufferer is away from litigation or his or her adversary. Abandoning litigation is a very personal decision that depends upon the degree of OCH and how deeply personal survival is tied to the issues being litigated. The intricacies of those deep-seated emotions tied to survival must be explored to realistically evaluate when to quit or how to continue to pursue protracted litigation. Whenever the court orders and litigation are unbearable, OCH is likely to result.

A New Age Invokes OCH: Stalking and High Tech Intrusion

People who are bullied, stalked (even online), threatened, and who have no safe haven are more likely to develop symptoms of Obsessive Compulsive Hyper-vigilance. In fact, the severity of a person's obsessive symptoms is connected to the number of traumatic events he or she has experienced in his or her lifetime. Therefore, since even one single traumatic event can cause PTSD, multiple events from protracted adversarial litigation is a predictable explanation of PTSD/LAS manifesting full-blown symptoms of OCH.

Not all symptoms will rise to the level of OCH. But, the more a litigant is forced to bear unbearable court orders or is stalked and intruded upon by "legal" discovery abuses, (i.e. snooping under the pretext of being proper surveillance and discovery), traumatic stress reactions are certainly more likely. There is little or nothing that can be done about these kinds of intrusions. Police do not have the manpower or tools to handle stalking and intrusive terror of individuals as it is and are hands off when it comes to legalized intrusions.

I worked on a case that involved tens of millions of dollars as part of an inheritance. Denise, one of the heirs, would get out of her car, lock it and go into a store. When she came out, documents and other items would be rearranged and her car locked as she left it. When she arrived home, her apartment had been invaded and things moved, yet no evidence existed, except in her mind and memory. Nothing was stolen. Her OCH revolved around stark terror. Her inheritance being more than $100,000,000 could buy her death through "accident." The first task was to assure Denise that she had support and a witness. Denise never got to court. All preparation that was done helped her to personally plan how she could realistically live well and protect her life. Once debriefing was done and the pre-legal/medical path designed, Denise decided to take a much lesser amount. She was in a battle for such a large inheritance that business funds were available to the other heirs. They used the business of which she was part owner to hire professionals to invade her email, compromise the locks on her apartment and automobile, and terrorize her by letting her know they had access to every part of her life. She was kept isolated, unprotected, exposed, and had to remain in a vigilant state. Police could not tell if she was just paranoid or telling the truth. They admitted they could do nothing to help her except tell her to leave the area.

I was the only one who believed her according to Denise. She would call me from supermarkets and public places and then we had to talk in a code. The code was never preplanned, it grew out of what we understood as we talked and twisted words. We planted tape recorders in her apartment to catch the intruder's noises. The noises were there. But, it would have taken an FBI crime lab to unravel it all. She was offered twenty per cent of her inheritance by the heirs in control. It was substantial so she took it. She is still gripped by trauma and injustice that her father's wishes as stated in his will were ignored by the court. But, her safety was a major issue and she was being sent threatening "messages" reminding her that she had no protection. Her symptoms subsided once she settled her part of the estate. She will always feel cheated and sad about her father.

Litigants feel terrorized and are sometimes the only ones who know they are being stalked. Opportunities for violating privacy are wide open today. High tech stalkers have an expanded arsenal of weapons to further abuse their opponents by using the legal system as just one. "The information revolution has vastly increased the scope of technologies of intrusion." Feeling you are being abused by technical stalking, may, in fact, be correct in an era of easily available high technology spy gear and "Trojan Horse" software tools (Spitzberg & Hoobler, 2002). Advocates know that if the litigant sounds paranoid and terrorized by intrusion and stalking, they are usually accurate. Advocates listen when no one else will.

More than one billion people now use the internet (techcrunch.com, 2009). It is nearly impossible to determine the level of internet, e-mail, cell phone, or other technical stalking that is occurring in one's life. But, when data appears in legal documents that were never printed only transmitted by e-mail to two or three people, it can produce a chilling moment of terror to an OCH sufferer. Delineating the dispensable obsession from true fear for safety has become more and more difficult. Lora routinely found that in court her private email and telephone conversations were being revealed. Her attorney husband had many private investigators at his disposal. Privacy was not protected in any form for Lora. Worse, "evidence" was "planted" that she planned to kill her husband. She was jailed and her life virtually put at risk because the jail did not attend to her daily medication needed to sustain her life. The accusation was a last straw destroying her dignity adding the humiliation of jail to her downfall as her husband threw her away.

Advocates know that these dirty legal games deprive a litigant of sanctuary and needed rest to recuperate from the battlefront conditions. Accommodations in such instances must include rest. Therefore, it is urgent that harassment through technology, intrusion, be taken very seriously. In assisting PTSD/LAS sufferers–particularly those experiencing OCH–it is our mission to always respect the sufferer's fierce need to maintain control and safety over their lives. The advocate communicates to the court that OCH symptoms reflect normal automatic internal reactions to threatening circumstances. Accommodations are designed to reveal and quell unnecessary threatening acts or at least the impact of those acts. Denise was grateful that someone, I, believed her. It helped her to think things through rationally and finally make her decision.

H8S

Litigants will look normal even while their impairment is compromising their ability to function in the courtroom. Author, E. Hatfield, in his book *Emotional Contagion* illuminates the vulnerability of the PTSD litigant by showing how human beings are susceptible to a tendency to emulate behaviors of others especially if facing power through authority, position, or protocol. Hatfield's work claims that the synchronization of behaviors happens within 50 milliseconds (Hatfield,1994). In fact, almost all individuals respond to their environment in very measurable ways—often cited as changes in heart rate, blood pressure, skin conductance, muscle activity, motor behavior, and autonomic system activity that is shaped according to emotion (Bloom, 1998). Appearance is not reliable as an indicator of functionality during litigation. Coercive controllers work to damage the court's perception of their opponent and work to enhance their image falsely. LWDs usually have a habit of struggling to appear capable but may be grossly disadvantaged during litigation.

An individual does not choose their initial reaction to a traumatic assault. Their responses will typically be "knee-jerk" reactions that reflect their assessment of their level of safety. In court, litigants will appear to behave in concert with those around them while suffering profoundly damaging trauma. Their blood pressure may reach stroke levels damaging their kidneys. Their digestive systems shut down. LWDs look fine while their hearts pound, but they feel broken. They are robbed of sleep, yet they are instructed to shut up and stay stoic in the court. And, they often do, at a great price to their health.

Characterization of OCH

LWDs, whether represented or not, carefully prepare evidence for court and spend a large portion of their legal budget on discovery. Then they find that a disproportionate percentage of time in and around litigation is spent obstructing the evidence rather than getting it on the record. Motions that limit information allowed into the court record, objections take up time and energy that the litigant needed to address what appears to be substantial evidence at hand. Litigants with disabilities report they are frustrated being prevented from talking in court.

Litigant　　　　　　**Court**

Figure 10.1 Surviving Litigation

These activities can turn into a type of consumption trick. It is used by some lawyers who take up the court's time telling the court all the rotten things they can contrive about the litigant leaving little time for an unrepresented litigant with a disability to present their case. As if that was not frustrating enough for a person trying to solve a problem, there is the recycle trick. Old decisions/orders are misinterpreted and brought forward to crowd out newer orders or authority pretending that an old order more favorable to their side had never been replaced. Years of legally layered confusion keep cases active, wasting our nation's most precious resource, human capital (Berardinelli, 2008).

Over the years, authors like Beverly Flanigan, in *Forgiving the Unforgivable,* and I, in *Legal Abuse Syndrome,* have attempted to characterize styles of obsession. There are common characterizations of obsessive styles that will uniquely combine into OCH affectations. It can help the litigant to visualize and communicate about the effects of their obsessive styles. Advocates ask the litigant to look them over to see if some combination of them hits home. Once a litigant identifies with one or more of these characterizations, it is a first step in managing those feelings and the rituals that are motivated by the feelings.

1. "Pilot–in–command"–This person is the master of his habitat. His control relies on the assumption that others will be somewhat predictable in their reactions to him or her. When that trust is violated, he must quickly try to restructure his belief system. Obsession revolves around the question, "How can I bring things back into control?" The question is urgent to the pilot in command because he has never faced his vulnerability. This type of controller can be brought to his knees by one event. They have functioned as the pilot of enterprises fostering predictable behaviors from family, employees, and the business community. Suddenly, the "pilot is grounded" due to no fault of his own.

2. "Dependent"–The dependent type of orientation causes one to feel that others are in control. This type of person needs protection. Every relationship is set up for the purpose of satisfying dependency needs. There is a strong assumption that the system functions to help in time of need. Deceptive crimes followed by betrayal by the system cause a critical loss of faith in life itself.

3. "Mathematician"–Recovery for this type of person is the toughest. His obsession forms around the question, "What are the rules?" Rules guide everything. He listens for formulas. Examples are "God protects us if we are good," and "If something bad happens to me, I must be getting paid back for something I did in the past." The therapist or helper must force clear identification of rules that have failed the victim. Otherwise, this type of individual will obsess around forming a new set of commandments (Flanigan).

4. Fierce, Natural Protector–The head of household who fears the family is threatened or a mother's entire hormonal and intuitive system being in force to protect her young against danger.

5. Activist–The person commits to solve the problem for society. Many valuable non-profit organizations have been born, motivated by obsession after a traumatic event.

6. Anti-dependent–This individual goes far beyond independence, to "I don't need anyone for anything," and "To Hell with the whole world." These statements characterize the anti-dependent person in times of stress. The danger in being anti-dependent emerges when the victim needs advice or help and he or she has shut out the world. Imminent consequences do not motivate this type of person to accept help from others. Whatever the price of anti-

dependence, it does not seem as menacing to the victim as mingling with the world.

7. Indecisive–This type of obsession leaves the person unable to feel comfortable with decisions – even to the point of driving between locations unable to decide which place to go, if anyplace. They will go shopping and come home with nothing.

8. Figuring it out–The person spends most waking moments and many asleep trying to figure out why the deception happened or trying to make it fit some logical schema. It feels like finding a reason for the occurrence might make it all right.

9. Inventorying–The victim perceives that everything is disposable. There is an overwhelming sensation that, at any time, anything might randomly disappear.

10. Control of the uncontrollable–They rigidly try to control the uncontrollable. These people expend extraordinary amounts of energy in an attempt to control regular eventualities.

11. Security Guard–The security guard is never going to be "duped" again. He spends his life suspecting everyone, with squinted eyes he hopes to see through deception. He keeps checking and rechecking windows, doors, locks, receipts, or the locations of valuables and often carries mace and other weapons.

Fig. 12.2 Hoarding as a symptom of OCH

12. Hoarding–The hoarder stores things, worries about scarcity, hides a stash of money, paperwork, food, alcohol or anything he values. This is related to but reflects the habit of saving legal documents.

13. Night terror–Nightly rituals characterize the night terror types. Daunted by nighttime, they struggle to cope. All-out efforts are mobilized to contend with fear of going to sleep or not going to sleep. They're rapt with meanings of nightmares and impending dreams or sleepless nights.

14. Lifeguard–An overwhelming sense of foreshortened life rules this type. Health is the obsession for the lifeguard. Status checks on family members, trips to the doctor, and taking pets to the veterinarian are common. A sense of well-being is never felt.

15. Revenge–Immersion in recompense drowns this type. He feels life can't go on until he gets even. It is important to help this person realize that revenge is strictly for fantasy. It

backfires on decent people when carried out in reality.

16. "World Sucks"–The awful preoccupies the mind. If there is negativity, "World Sucks" will find it. If there isn't, he'll perceive it. It's hard to have a good time with "World Sucks" types. It's hard to be around or to be motivated to help them.

17. Mt. Everest climber–Exhaustion greets every task. If there is a chore, Mt. Everest must be climbed before the chore is efficiently completed. These are truly the sick and tired, the walking wounded.

18. Perfect Sufferer—From an idealistic stance, this individual can submit, in detail, that he was right at all times. Being right, doing the right thing, and all it should have bought the victim has been violated. He is consumed by the fact that "wrong" won. This person suffers a great deal of anxiety as his obsession spirals. The victim is indignant due to the inversion of his belief system about justice and fairness as the reward of the righteous. This type will be defensive and able to list every wrong the other side committed. Every motion to the court will have too much extraneous wrongdoing packed into it unless the advocate is in the picture.

A Voice for OCH

During litigation, language is the tool of competence. The dichotomy of needing to fight and having all survival mechanisms in your brain telling you to avoid the intimidating legal environment immobilizes PTSD sufferers. There is simultaneously both a survival force and a counterforce intruding in the brain, interfering with language, preventing the court user from being an effective litigator (Flanigan,1992)..

What to Do about OCH

- Name it
- Face it
- Own it
- Accept it
- Manage it
- Communicate it

1. Name It (or Them) - Any combination of the styles described might make up the sufferer's obsessive style. It is also possible that other, unnamed, styles may emerge from a sufferer. Once the obsessive style can be identified and categorized, the sufferer has chosen one route to mastery.

2. Face It - A sense of humor is often a principle asset when dealing with obsession. The ability

to laugh at oneself and with others relieves anxiety and lends to self-acceptance. Almost all victims have unexpected and/or unorthodox reactions after being assaulted. Individuals suffering loss of their children through court battles, facing possible incarceration or other insults added to losses cannot predict their reactions. Dissociation and denial are often common symptoms. But, once the sufferer sees his or her OCH in his or her mind's eye, the negative effects often begin to diminish.

3. Own It - The sufferer's combination of obsessive behaviors is often unique. Rarely do obsessions manifest themselves exactly alike among different victims in spite of the common characteristics. However, sufferers can readily take ownership of their obsessions after they face them. But, until the sufferer grabs the obsession and owns it, it will grab and own them.

4. Accept It - The sufferer should accept obsession as a natural part of the response process. Fighting obsession or feeling guilty about it is not productive in dealing with it. Resisting or succumbing in secret to the obsessions often intensifies them. Obsessions manifest themselves as healthy and natural reactions to devastating circumstances. They offer a gentle way out of the psychological dilemma the sufferer faces.

5. Manage It - By analyzing "what I can control" from the Debriefing list, generated by the sufferer, the advocate helps the individual create new goals designed to empower some positive actions. Compartmentalization of time is the main component of management of OCH. Setting a time period with a beginning and an end is the first task. This scheduling acts as a promise to self that certain hours of the week will be spent on empowerment in the areas where control has been lost. In other words, the sufferer schedules his or her way out of obsession. Compartmentalization helps in the following ways:

    A. It validates the victim's need to own and deal with the issues that cause fear and loss of control.

    B. Well-planned activities are more productive than non-directed, obsessive, and intrusive thoughts.

    C. Completion of empowering activities relieves the intensity of the obsessive feelings.

    D. It substitutes for revenge and bitterness and prevents an obsessive spiral producing sardonic, disillusioned reactions.

6. Communicate it - The litigant must take responsibility for communicating feelings, rituals, and manifestations of their OCH - always, with a tone of dignity intended to garner respect from those who may attempt to use the OCH symptoms in a disparaging way. When symptoms emerge it is without an LWD's permission. Symptoms are frightening. The ADA advocate helps the LWD to verbalize relieving the pain of the symptoms so they begin to feel more in command not allowing the adversary to exploit a disability.

When the energy consumed by symptoms is defined, communicated, and directed, it then appropriately can be shifted to more efficient use by addressing pertinent litigation.

Obsessively fighting on provides hope in what feels like a hopeless situation. Some cases are driven by obsessions that truly do not stand to arrive at a good outcome in court. OCH challenges the court system and desperately needs to be identified, clearly defined, and put into terms that reveal underlying dynamics leading to better management of cases involving those with special needs. Forcing settlement conferences and mediation prior to trials are attempts at relieving the court of the deep emotions and conflicts that causes litigation to be hopelessly stuck. Unfortunately, they too often fail. The legal professionals involved do not fathom the underlying forces that drive the OCH sufferer to insist on continuing to a disastrous end rather than working toward a reasonable settlement. Or, the perpetrator knows that by forcing protracted litigation, the OCH sufferer stands to be destroyed.

Use of the court as a weapon needs to be curtailed. Legal professionals often describe a "successful settlement" as one in which neither party is happy with the result. But, the OCH sufferer is probably incapable of understanding and accepting that concept and the perpetrator refuses to be even a little unhappy since abuse through the court can be serving a perverted need. The most vulnerable, LWDs unrepresented, are at risk of being injured by the very legal process that is instituted to provide a right and reasonable solution to a conflict. Esoteric and adversarial language of litigation places an insurmountable barrier for many who cannot speak for themselves and cannot afford legal counsel.

It is unacceptable that a public service creates psychic injuries such as OCH that mocks paranoia. Medical research has reached a point of proving by scans and brain chemistry the changes in the brain from stressful events. Behavioral researchers are rapidly producing elegant research that documents how institutional actions, such as those in our judicial systems, impact life, health, and even death of some who come in contact with them. Systems interactions with the human beings that need services remains a critical matter for future study and improvement.

Huffer's Log

1. Cases of OCH

Lora was married to a successful big city lawyer, a marriage that made her parents much happier than Lora. She lived in a prestigious house and attended lawyers' wives luncheons. She was able to give her children more than they needed. But, regardless of her comfortable, luxurious lifestyle, she suffered a lingering feeling that emptiness was crowding out all other aspects of her life. She believed that she wasn't "exactly abused." She just "felt bad" every time she had an encounter with her husband. Lora finally realized that she was oppressed, interrogated, commanded, criticized, embarrassed, and made to feel stupid by the very tone of voice her husband used. It was emotional abuse and hard to define and communicate. Still she endured and made the best of what was good about her life.

Then, one day her husband literally pounced on her with divorce papers. She discovered he had a relationship with another woman and intended to replace her. She was to move out so the new woman could move into her house. The children were to stay. The high stakes legal game was on. She was forced through hearing after hearing and motion after motion, often losing before she got to the courthouse or opened her mouth. Her husband knew every legal move ahead of time and was clearly monitoring her telephone and emails. No attorney wanted to do battle with her powerful husband and his firm and usually only stayed on her case briefly before finding a "conflict" after the retainer had been quickly consumed. She was systematically stripped of her assets while the kids were charmed with toys, trips, and special diversions by their father. She was belittled and demeaned in court and called crazy. Her parents added a crushing blow. Right when she felt ugly, hurt, and undesirable and cast aside, her parents repeatedly asked her what she had done wrong and what she could do to fix it.

As the pressure increased relentlessly, her OCH took firmer and firmer hold on her psyche. Lora had a chronic illness and now suffered traumatic stress. She asked for the ADA office at the court and none could be found. She was denied the very act of applying for accommodations.

Once the OCH manifested, she could not let go of ritualistic letters to the judge, the mayor, the attorney general, the governor, all regulatory bodies. She was in a cycle of ineffective behavior but could not stop: it would be unbearable. What became clear to her while immersed in litigation is that the abuse she endured from her husband was very similar to the abuse she was subjected to in court. His adversarial team used sarcasm, trickery, intimidation, and humiliation and, in her guts, she felt the same sickening feeling of verbal abuse she had come to know well from her ex-husband's prior behavior.

Lora's advocate helped her to implement protections and to identify the coercion and mischaracterizations that defines her domestic violence. Then, her disabilities were accommodated and equal access became the focus. It took several bouts of reframing to heal the damage done to her self-esteem for many years. Debriefing helped her to focus and quit shot-gunning letters that just aggravated her angst. She had to accept the political power she faced while learning the Empowerment skills. She improved her legal writing and adjusted her work to better impact the local power structure by educating about the ADA through her documents. She quit writing letters realizing that telling her story was not making a difference. Her ADAAA rights were so blatantly violated that she found a civil rights activist lawyer who is helping her file a federal lawsuit for relief.

Lora hadn't clearly seen or defined the spousal abuse in time to address it. Now, it was complicated by economic exploitation. And, during litigation, the horrible verbal gang rape she sustained was endorsed by her court of law. She pitifully filed with the court year after year and appeared in court by herself. She always wore his favorite color, red, to court. Why? She did not know.

2. Case of OCH

Observing LeeAnn's house for a day can give the observer a quick understanding of OCH. The garage walls are hidden behind stacks of boxes full of legal files. The dining room is stacked with more such boxes. A savored formal holiday dinner is tainted by being surrounded by the symbols of more than ten years of *devastation and dashed hope represented in carefully labeled bankers' boxes surrounding the dining room table. The family room and kitchen are the "office." Virtually every life activity serves, "the case." The only thing that stands between them and getting their normal lives back, they believe, is the moral turpitude by the insurance company and lawyers willing to cooperate with it. LeeAnn's OCH reached a peak upon receiving new evidence of fraud on the court in her case.*

Not long ago, a document that LeeAnn suspected was forged, altered, and fraudulently submitted to the court was put before a nationally known document expert at LeeAnn's expense. That expert confirmed that the document had been altered with no other possible scenario than that the attorneys and trustee of the bankruptcy court had committed fraud on the court. The evidence is clear. LeeAnn reports that the insurance company is obligated to pay the Jonas' in the vicinity of $60,000,000 according to their contract. The attorneys and trustee who committed the alleged wrongdoing could lose their licenses and be imprisoned. Therefore, it appears that in order to avoid the obligations of their contract and the responsibility of their personal wrongdoing, more wrongdoing is required. The stakes are now huge, the family members' lives have been destroyed and progressively re-damaged during sixteen years of litigation in which various professionals have to all appearances conspired to use the justice system to obstruct justice.

When LeeAnn presented the evidence to the court, LeeAnn's Judge denied every motion. She denied an evidentiary hearing. The judge refused to hear the facts of the case. She would not look at the report of fraud.

Like the child considered a slow learner in the schools of yesterday, LeeAnn faces opposing counsel's ridicule and ongoing theatrical demonstrations of impatience at her ignorance continuing to relegate her to "dunce" status of not knowing "how the system really works." Simultaneously, LeeAnn watches the judge bury the facts using artful, verbal bullying from the bench and legalized confusion. LeeAnn faithfully and competently appears in court submitting the facts, rules, and laws guaranteeing she will prove fraud if allowed to put her evidence before the court. She waits.

Author's Notes:

ADA Advocates

Differences between mental illness and psychiatric injury and the intensity of symptoms help to determine when the client needs professional counseling help. The length of time symptoms persist after Huffer's 8-Steps are employed is a sign as well. At first symptoms will be intense but should lessen in both intensity and length of time symptoms persist as the 8-steps are put into place.

David Kinchin, 2001, UK expert on the effects of bullying has illustrated clearly how a psychiatric injury is different from mental illness. Kinchin's work was done in the context of employment bullying but if considered in the light of complex PTSD and the official bullying that exists in Legal Abuse Syndrome, it is similar helping to clarify for the litigant and the court the differences. The first graphic shows the difference between paranoia and hypervigilance and the second graphic illustrates psychiatric injury versus mental illness.

Paranoia	Hypervigilance
• paranoia is a form of mental *illness*; the cause is thought to be internal, e.g. a minor variation in the balance of brain chemistry	• is a response to an external event (violence, accident, disaster, violation, intrusion, bullying, etc) and therefore an *injury*
• paranoia tends to endure and to not get better of its own accord	• wears off (gets better), albeit slowly, when the person is out of and away from the situation which was the cause
• the paranoiac will not admit to feeling paranoid, as they cannot see their paranoia	• the hypervigilant person is acutely aware of their hypervigilance, and will easily articulate their fear, albeit using the incorrect but popularized word "paranoia"
• sometimes responds to drug treatment	• drugs are not viewed favorably by hypervigilant people, except in extreme circumstances, and then only briefly; often drugs have no effect, or can make things worse, sometimes interfering with the body's own healing process
• the paranoiac often has delusions of grandeur; the delusional aspects of paranoia feature in other forms of mental illness, such as schizophrenia	• the hypervigilant person often has a diminished sense of self-worth, sometimes dramatically so
• the paranoiac is convinced of their self-importance	• the hypervigilant person is often convinced of their worthlessness and will often deny their value to others
• paranoia is often seen in conjunction with other symptoms of mental illness, but *not* in conjunction with symptoms of PTSD	• hypervigilance is seen in conjunction with other symptoms of PTSD, but *not* in conjunction with symptoms of mental illness
• the paranoiac is convinced of their plausibility	• the hypervigilant person is aware of how implausible their experience sounds and often doesn't want to believe it themselves (disbelief and denial)
• the paranoiac feels persecuted by a person or persons unknown (e.g. "*they're* out to get me")	• the hypervigilant person is hypersensitized but is often aware of the inappropriateness of their heightened sensitivity, and can identify the person responsible for their psychiatric injury
• sense of persecution	• heightened sense of vulnerability to victimization
• the sense of persecution felt by the paranoiac is a delusion, for usually no-one is out to get them	• the hypervigilant person's sense of threat is well-founded, for the serial bully *is* out to get rid of them and has often coerced others into assisting, e.g. through mobbing; the hypervigilant person often cannot (and refuses to) see that the serial bully is doing everything possible to get rid of them
• the paranoiac is on constant alert because they *know* someone is out to get them	• the hypervigilant person is on alert *in case* there is danger

• the paranoiac is certain of their belief and their behavior and expects others to share that certainty	• the hypervigilant person cannot bring themselves to believe that the bully cannot and will not see the effect their behavior is having; they cling naively to the mistaken belief that the bully will recognize their wrongdoing and apologize

Other differences between mental illness and psychiatric injury include:

Mental illness	Psychiatric injury
• the cause often cannot be identified	• the cause is easily identifiable and verifiable, but denied by those who are accountable
• the person may be incoherent or what they say doesn't make sense	• the person is often articulate but prevented from articulation by being traumatized
• the person may appear to be obsessed	• the person is obsessive, especially in relation to identifying the cause of their injury
• the person is oblivious to their behavior and the effect it has on others	• the person is in a state of acute self-awareness and aware of their state, but often unable to explain it
• the depression is a clinical or endogenous depression	• the depression is reactive; the chemistry is different to endogenous depression
• there may be a history of depression in the family	• there is very often *no* history of depression in the individual or their family
• the person has usually exhibited mental health problems before	• often there is *no* history of mental health problems
• may respond inappropriately to the needs and concerns of others	• responds empathically to the needs and concerns of others, *despite* their own injury
• displays a certitude about themselves, their circumstances and their actions	• is often highly skeptical about their condition and circumstances and is in a state of disbelief and bewilderment which they will easily and often articulate (*"I can't believe this is happening to me"* and *"Why me?")*
• may suffer a persecution complex	• may experience an unusually heightened sense of vulnerability to possible victimization (i.e. hypervigilance)
• suicidal thoughts are the result of despair, dejection and hopelessness	• suicidal thoughts are often a logical and carefully thought-out solution or conclusion
• exhibits despair	• is driven by the anger of injustice
• often doesn't look forward to each new day	• looks forward to each new day as an opportunity to fight for justice
• is often ready to give in or admit defeat	• refuses to be beaten, refuses to give up

Figure 12.3 Kinchin Tables

References

Berardinelli, L., JD. (2008). From Good Hands to Boxing Gloves: The Dark Side of Insurance. (pp. 139). Oregon: Trial Guides LLC.

Bloom, S. & Reichert, M. (1998). *Bearing Witness: Violence and Collective Responsibility.* (pp. 17). Binghamton, NY: Haworth Press.

Daniel, T.A. (2006, August). Bullies in the Workplace: A Focus on the "Abusive Disrespect" of Employees. Society for Human Resource Management.

Flanigan, B. (1992). *Forgiving the Unforgivable: Overcoming the bitter legacy of intimate wounds.* New York: Wiley Publishing, Inc.

Hatfield, E., Cacioppo, J.T., & Rapson, R. (1994). *Emotional Contagion: Studies in Emotion & Social Interaction.* New York: Cambridge University Press.

Hunter, R.G., McCarthy, K., Milne, T., Pfaff, D., & McEwen, B. (2009, November 23). *Regulation of hippocampus H3 histone methylation by acute and chronic stress. Proceedings of National Academy of Sciences.* Online Rockefeller University.

Kinchin, D. (2005). *Post Traumatic Stress Disorder: the invisible injury.* United Kingdom: Success Unlimited.

Nadel, L. & Jacobs, W.J. (1996). *The Role of the Hippocampus in PTSD, Panic, and Phobia.* In Kyoto, Japan, Nobumasa Kato, ed. *Hippocampus: Functions and Clinical Relevance.* Amsterdam: Elsevier: Science & Health News.

O'Brien, J. T. (1997). The 'glucocorticoid cascade' hypothesis in man. Prolonged stress may cause permanent brain damage. *British Journal of Psychiatry, 170,* 199-201.

Pert, C., Phd. (2002). *The Molecules of Emotion.* New York: Scribner Books.

Spitzberg, B. & Hoobler, G. (2002). Cyberstalking and the technologies of interpersonal terrorism. *New Media &Society, 4(1),* 71-92.

Resource

European Journal of Work and Organizational Psychology (EJWOP), 1996, 5(2), (whole issue devoted to bullying and its effects, including PTSD.) Published by Psychology Press, 27 Church Road, Hove, East Sussex BN3 2FA, UK.

CHAPTER 13

BLAMING: HUFFER'S STEP-6 ACCOUNTABILITY AND ATTRIBUTION

Blaming is inevitable and necessary. It acknowledges that human beings must attribute wrongdoing somewhere. Unresolved personal interests that have not found a legal path for resolution are ripe for creative blame. A Blaming action is chosen for its potential for fostering accountability and bringing justice to the injured in ways that courts are often unable to do. Selecting the best target(s) and method(s) for a blaming action requires analysis. A successful blaming action uses imagination and brings a sense of affordable justice.

Do What You Can, With What You Have, Where You Are.

Theodore Roosevelt

Blame the Bastards…but How in a No Fault Society?

Blaming actually centers on our sentinel and eternal need to continually move toward a better life for ourselves and our progeny. However, a fresh approach to resolving conflicts is needed. I see a great opportunity to end a certain amount of psychic injury for LWDs by widening the avenues of choice for attaining justice beyond the judicial system.

The more human-to-human solutions we can find, the more rewarding it is for all concerned. After an assault, a crime, abuse, fraud, or a conflict, most litigants find that lawsuits, law enforcement, and regulators cannot jump in and fight for them vigorously, affordably, and fairly. As a result, they are left with the huge responsibility of protecting themselves, then attributing the violation, and finally correcting it.

Most people cannot let go and just accept a profound injustice, so-called "turning the other

H8S

cheek." If they try to just turn the other cheek, they wind up with two sore cheeks and a gnawing sense of unfinished business that eventually turns to bitterness. Moreover, social failures are left unaddressed and imbalanced. And, that is not the way civilization naturally is intended to evolve. Human history is filled with people who have creatively sought attribution for wrongdoing by swinging a pendulum that blamed and then naturally came to rest at a fair and a balanced center. Such has been the history of the disabilities movement in America.

Today, our culture resists assuming blame, accountability, and responsibility. Ever since lawsuits arose as the populist way to solve problems, we have become as "no fault" as possible (Olson, 1991). The no fault pendulum has swung too far. The destructive force of denying responsibility is too great to allow. Compromised food quality, safety in construction, and falsification of legal and medical records, and institutional predatory behavior results when accountability and responsibility are not aggressively enforced and culturally valued. Blaming and responsible whistle blowing are naturally intended to head off human tragedy.

However, blaming as a cultural function has been supplanted by the lawsuit. It seems like talking out a problem or working to be fair has been replaced by posturing against a feared lawsuit. Business and social intercourse communicate in defensive, destructive "gotcha" games instead of working toward a sensible and fair solution to conflicts. Doctors and hospitals have adopted policies of refusing to disclose mistakes costing the needed education and wisdom that mistakes teach. *Sorry Works!*, a 2008 book by Doug Wojcieszak, is timely and addresses these problems through the Sorry Works! Coalition. They teach methods of disclosure to head off the current trend toward patients losing trust in our medical systems.

Through the Sorry Works! Coalition, hospitals and doctors are finding that honest disclosure and assuming blame/responsibility is becoming economically wiser than refusing to disclose out of fear of being held liable. Turning to the legal system did not work nearly as well as face-to-face meetings with the offended parties with skilled disclosure and working out the best solution under the circumstances. It is the simple act of human caring that seems to turn the matter around.

Productive blaming needs to replace the defensive, fearful stance that threat of lawsuits has perpetrated. When wrong is done, i.e., a spouse hurts a mate, a boss unfairly fires or abuses a worker, a parent abuses a child, or a lawyer sets out to take from instead of serve the client, blaming is in order. However, it feels like the proverbial "hot potato" to manage in the beginning and then, like the Sorry Works! Coalition is reporting, human-to-human blaming and resolution works more satisfactorily than lawsuits if the players will cooperate(48-66).

Who to Blame

Exactly who to blame is the first critical task. In a court of law, a great deal of pretext, misinformation, and obstruction can be used to keep the accountability stuck to the victim in order to protect the wrongdoer. If the blame is not properly targeted, a typical outcome is that the most vulnerable party will be blamed. That is usually the innocent victim, protective parent, special needs person, mate who trusted the wrong spouse, boss, court system, or lawyer. Accountability is deflected while the perpetrators avoid accepting responsibility.

Look in All Directions and All Places

Who is the bad guy? Is there more than one? Are some guiltier than others? Who and where is the target for resolution? Is it possible to just let it go and do nothing?

ADA advocates are called upon to firmly guide the blaming process. Typically, litigants get expansive. They shotgun their blaming reporting to agencies, law enforcement, filing complaints, picketing, and come away with little but frustration. The toughest task is to containerize the impulse to file too much and focus on the most important issues at hand. What holds the wrongdoer accountable and brings relief to the victim? Refer back to the Debriefing Graphics.

1. Initial Incident—Think who or what force is still victimizing you now.

2. Reaction to Initial Incident—Move inward to the reactive forces that sap the litigant's resources. Litigants suffer from how one human being can hurt another and how systems of care do not seem to care.

3. Intentionality of Wrongdoer—Determine if pain is purposefully inflicted. If humans intentionally hurt the litigant, it makes the hurt worse. When the perpetrator knows the buttons to push to cause harm and pain and then exploits the vulnerability by persisting, it is the worst of human on human trauma.

4. Inappropriate Guilt—Discover that floating, unconscious shame that perverts blame. Guilt is the undetected monster that forces the litigant to accept undeserved blame. Litigants usually won't report the feelings as guilt, just a nasty feeling of punishment, in fact, "cruel and unusual punishment." The advocate needs to point out the distortion of guilt solely caused by feeling helpless. If not corrected, undeserved guilt actually serves the adversary. Oddly, guilt is a usual reaction to being victimized. It is an embittering force.

5. Ten behaviors that signal guilt are:

    1. Distrust

    2. Shame

    3. Rage

    4. Terror

    5. Suicide ideation

    6. Homicide ideation

    7. Hatred

H8S

8. Withdrawal

9. Grief

10. Defensiveness

If suicide tempts the litigant, it often relates to guilt. To properly blame, help the litigant realize that feelings listed above are undeserved. Guilt, rage, and anger need to be directed where they belong, at the offender(s).

6. Establish New Boundaries—It is painful to plunge through denial only to be struck by horrific emotional pain. What does denial look like? How does it feel? The litigant often cries and utters words like "upset" or "angry" as the protective layers of denial are lifted. However, it is clear that vocabulary fails to express the intensity of their feelings. Advocates can respond with, "I know how deep down your feelings go and that there don't seem to be words." "Upset" and "angry" are secondary feelings that cover up more intimate feelings. It is more productive to identify the underlying feelings.

Blaming Styles

As is true of OCH and grieving responses to victimization, the litigant's style of blaming is not completely a conscious choice. It tends to be a spontaneous and a dynamic process.

1. Self–Blame

"I Did It–Somehow, someway, it is ultimately my fault." A prevailing myth provides that the victim somehow causes their assault. Self-blame is convenient and will be quickly affirmed by onlookers and an adversary. It gets everyone off the hook. If victims are responsible for their plight, then the bad guy goes free, onlookers feel safe again, and responsibility is not assigned. Deep down litigants almost hope they are to blame. It is a trick of the mind that if you are to blame, then you can fix the problem. There is a false sense of relief with the concept. Unfortunately, it is usually not healthy to take that route for long. Self-blame is wrong in most cases. At most, litigants with disabilities are only partially to blame, not totally. When dealing with forgiveness issues in therapeutic settings, encouraging the release of anger at self may be one way of reducing self-blame (Barber, 2005).

A. Self–Blame Checklist:

Check the statements that describe how you feel about your victimization.

1. _____ I feel responsible.

2. _____ I took a chance and shouldn't have.

3. _____ It happened because I've done wrong in the past.

4. _____ I should have seen it coming.

5. _____ I was stupid.

6. _____ If I just hadn't.....

7. _____ It was an expensive education.

8. _____ How can I be so gullible?

9. _____ I got what I deserved.

10. _____ I knew better.

11. _____ I've hurt so many people.

12. _____ I wish I had it to do over again.

B. Self–Blame Complications:

Those people who are Conscience-Centered (CC's) are especially prone to self-blame. Here is where codependent overlays complicate the recovery process. The codependent person accepts responsibility too quickly for the wrongdoing of others. The codependent spends energy searching to understand the crime from the criminal's point of view by saying, "Maybe he came from poverty," "Maybe he was a victim of society," or "Maybe he needed whatever he stole to feed a starving family or a wounded ego." It may sound compassionate, but it is abuse of self.

Self-blame is dangerous. If you take it too far then you, not the offender, will look guilty. When a person exudes guilt, he or she will act in ways that draw suspicion. It is important to shape the experience so you don't take on another's guilt (Bard, 1986).

1. Self-blame can be turned on litigants in court by clever attorneys tricking them into admitting some unconscious complicity or they create a guilty image through pointing out flushing in the LWD's face or a moment's hesitation in answering a question.

2. Police officers or prosecutors who sense this self-blame might view the victim with suspicion. An entire crime can be misperceived as a result of a guilty appearance of the innocent.

3. Self-blame can cause those around the victim to hold back supportive behavior and even to make remarks that demean the victim or otherwise mirror the self-blame.

4. Self-blame removes a victim from being entitled to restitution, community resources, and comfort.

5. Self-blame lets the offender get away with wrongdoing. It perpetuates and reinforces the violating behavior.

H8S

2. They Blame

Another mode of blame comes in a road form called "they" blame. "They Blame" blames nebulous forces. They blame feels safe. It is popular because accountability is never placed.

A. They Blame Checklist:

If Not for "Them/It," It Would Not Have Happened! Examples of "they":

- Divorce rate

- Failures of churches and schools

- State of modern medicine

- Corrupt politicians

- Permissiveness

- Offender protected society

- Broken judicial system

- Corrupt lawyers

- Permissive parents

- No truthful media

B. They Blame Complications

1. "They" blame allows the victim full entitlement to feel righteously angry without learning from the experience.

2. Sense of hopelessness increases because the target is so large that there is little the victim can do to affect it. Yet, they may put out energy that doesn't bear fruit.

3. The victim may become generally accusatory with law enforcement officers or court personnel or others and alienate those from whom he needs help.

4. The victim's support system, family and friends, can be put on the defensive by other blaming remarks and, therefore, not be there to help the victim.

5. "They" blaming can cause further personal resentment if, for example, there is blame of a spouse's employment, political affiliation, partnership that ripples into the social and business relationships taking attention from the personal choices and responsibility.

3. Revenge-Blame

A compelling need to get even dictates the third blaming style. Acts of revenge bring momentary pleasure and are useful in imagination but not in reality (Barber, 2005). Revenge is punishment and acts as a cognitive equalizer. Drawbacks to revenge are found in the fact that:

1. Immediate, impulsive counterattack may attack the wrong person or entity on insufficient evidence.

2. Well-planned and successfully executed revenge takes tremendous amounts of time and energy. When compared with spending that same time and energy on alternative appropriate blaming actions, the risk often outweighs the rewards and revenge does not prove to be efficient.

3. Revenge, in the end, may violate the values of the victim. Eventually, it stands to bring more shame and guilt. "How can I have been so mean?" clients will ask, shocked at their ability to avenge.

4. Revenge, taken too far, destroys the conscience-centered person's self-esteem. They fear that they are becoming corrupt. They've violated their own standards.

5. It magnifies flaws contradicting Huffer's 8 steps to improve self-image.

6. If revenge moves accelerate on both sides, they will tend to be accelerated symmetrically (Flanigan, 1992). It may be a war wherein retaliation becomes the only focus.

However, revenge is great in fantasy and a little fun to explore. Revengeful thoughts are not to be worried about as long as they are fleeting contemplations. Further, they have proven to actually torment the person further unless done in a safe environment and dismissed (Herman, 1997). Momentarily, they help in provoking creative thinking that sometimes assists in finding the most appropriate blaming processes.

Qualifying Who Deserves the Blame

Who violated the moral contract? Could the violator have foreseen the pain he was causing whether the violator was a precursor causing litigation or some member of the legal process abusing during litigation? Did the violator know in advance that the victim would be injured as a result of his actions?

1. Justifiability–Was the violator coerced in any way that might justify the assault?

2. Intentionality–Was it intended? Were the results known and the decision to hurt the other planned? This evil intent weighs the scale dramatically toward blame.

3. Foresee ability–Could the violator have foreseen the pain that would follow their actions?

4. Cause–Did it happen to me as a coincidence or was I the target?

5. Association–Was a relationship of trust violated by this action?

6. When the violator was informed that you were suffering an impairment, did actions continue or get worse?

7. Do the violator's actions risk damage to an entire regulatory or justice system setting off exponential destruction? (Flanigan,1992)

For example, the following chart demonstrates how to qualify blame by degree using the above criteria.

Categories for Assessing Degrees of Blame

Violation

1st Degree Blame

- Trust is violated, professional or personal—violation was done under the pretext of doing a service with an underlying hidden agenda, i.e. racketeering/money laundering, violations of honest services by trusted, or insider favors compromising regulatory or legal services.

- The intent is to cause suffering.

- The injury to the victim is foreseeable.

- The perpetrator initiates an assault.

- The perpetrator uses the protective systems to continue to offend.

2nd Degree Blame

- The legal system joins the violator inadvertently through abuse of process.

- Part of a group violates.

- Actions are destructive to societal good.

- "Hired guns," expert witnesses who lie is used.

3rd Degree Blame

- The person is forced to violate.

- Non-intentional violating, one is misled into violating.

- One quits when aware of violation.

- Part of job or contract–eviction by manager.

After the degree of blame is assigned to the various violators, a blaming action can be instituted. The degree refers to the amount of personal investment in blaming that is appropriately assumed by the victim. If the violator intended to hurt the victim personally and could have foreseen the pain his actions would cause, it is a personal blaming issue for the victim. If a corporation rip-off occurred, the violator is harder to personally identify and blame. More impersonal blaming actions are chosen in those cases.

Challenges to Allocating Blame in Court

Debriefing, step two, provides the information to be legally postured for the court. Once the litigation process begins, the opposition seeks ways to divert or invalidate blame emanating from the legal position. All the while, there are personal interests that do not meet forensic standards and cannot be litigated. An example is found in Minnesota law that does not legally recognize emotional damage from domestic violence. Therefore, unless the violence is provably physical, there is no way to position emotional pain for litigation. In states like Minnesota, it is good that litigation is but one method of blaming.

Once the litigant looks deep within their own values, the salient questions emerge. What do I really want to happen as a result of blaming? Are you satisfied if the violator is prevented from assaulting or hurting another person again? Do you want restitution? Very often, confronting the blamed is the first step toward rebuilding trust. We have ascertained that loss of trust is the greatest loss known to man. Deception and willful destruction of trust is a transgression recognized by every victim. Since society cannot sustain itself without trust, this too is added to your responsibility as a citizen. How does basic trust rebuild?

The "filtering process" activates when one establishes who is to be blamed for what and then what is to be done with the offender (Shaver, 1985). Normally, there are many offenders of varying dimensions mixed into the assaults of the LAS victim. Degrees of blame need to be assessed accordingly. Then, a blaming action is selected.

Blaming actions will either be personal or impersonal. Personal actions require the offended to take personal responsibility for initiating a blaming action. Some of the best personal blaming actions are achieved when the victim is allowed to have an eyeball-to-eyeball, heart-to-heart encounter with the offender to inform the offender of the violation of the moral code. Profoundly effective are personal confrontations resulting in sincere apologies, changes in behaviors, and restitution for the victims. Much success in blaming rests on satisfaction that the moral code has been recognized and preserved.

If the blaming action is effective in causing the offender to genuinely realize the moral law that was broken and to apologize, make restitution, and actively do what is agreed upon as the right thing to do, recovery may occur after the blaming stage. Indeed, if the blaming action causes justice to occur, such as the court process working as it was intended, recovery is imminent.

MADD (Mothers Against Drunk Drivers) http://www.madd.org/ instituted victim impact panels. The survivors and victims of drunk drivers confront the offenders in exactly the manner prescribed above. It has been effective in promoting victims' and survivors' recoveries. Change in behavior and attitude of the drunk driver is a major factor in the victim sensing that justice has been accomplished. How many times do we hear victims of horrific assaults say that they have gone public simply to try to prevent the victimization of any more people? Societal correction is at the heart of a real victim's need to blame.

You Must See It to Correct It: Analyzing, Correcting Misinformation, and Managing Self-perception in Court

Carl Sagan, in his series *Cosmos*, in 2009, used an astronomer's term, "good seeing," conditions needed for ideal viewing or "seeing." It is when looking through the gigantic telescope out to the undiscovered expanse of unknown galaxies, debris is minimal, interference is reduced, allowing the astronomer to look toward the undiscovered truly seeing and learning the reality of what is there. You need "good seeing" when it comes to blaming.

You can be in situations where the debris of protocol, the traditions are well entrenched, and relationships and power that affect them are so potent that the LWD doesn't have "good seeing." You can also be in a position where the intent of those in power over a case is at cross-purposes with the LWD. In order to attribute responsibility for what is wrong, the task is to reduce the matter to the simplest terms and see the underlying truth.

Caution: The courts can be conned by PC's. The Power motivated, those who put self interest first, are often most charismatic spending their time politicking for their cause. The CC parent, who is doing the job involving all of the rigors of attention to homework, brushed teeth, and chauffeuring children, cannot lobby for their cause and are often misunderstood and outshined by a vulnerable court.

Studying and Designing Blaming Actions

Blaming must encompass the culture as well as the violator. Dormant in the consequences for wrongdoing are practical actions and vocabulary that foster the moral code. Words like pride, reputation, morale, character, courage, responsibility, professionalism, good/ faith, and fair dealing have been sacrificed in their purest forms. They once tied people to behavioral expectations that foster trust. Further, shunning and shaming punishments are rarely used even though we know that shunning and shaming are extremely powerful consequences for immoral and illegal behaviors. A judge in Texas forced a sex offender to put a sign on his lawn stating "I am a sex offender" after a violation of his parole.

The following are further examples of both personal and impersonal blaming actions:

A.   A woman was denied her ADA rights in a doctor's office. She has traumatic brain injury and an arterial degenerative disease. The sound of the promotional television set in the waiting room was torturous for her auditory processing problem. She asked the office manager to turn off the TV or to turn down the volume. The office manager refused, was rude, and invited a power struggle, all of which was very stressful, putting this patient at risk. The patient found a mail order device called "TV-B-Gone." It was thirty dollars. She carries it with her and turns off such television sets.

B. A patient found that her doctor revealed her medical records to her adversary on a subpoena that should not have been honored. She filed a complaint with his medical licensing board. But, more than just mentioning the ethical violations, she cited the laws that were broken. Reported legal violations strengthen a complaint to a licensing board. Make the complaint short without too much history and emphasize if there has been a pattern and practice of the behavior.

C. A company placed a negative on a lawyer's credit report and would not remove it when properly challenged with evidence. The consumer filed a lawsuit against the erring creditor for libel. It was successful. Now, the lawyer does it for her clients.

D. Remember Bernie Madoff, the Ponzi scheme crook that left many investors and organizations broke? For Ponzi schemes to work, some investors must make money. According to the Idaho Supreme Court in Christian v. Mason, those who lost money have a right to collect money from those who made money. As the trend of predator and prey expands in this culture, the same logic could apply in all schemes that pay a small group at the top knowing the entire multi-level concept is a house of cards that can easily collapse on lower level investors.

E. An example of a blaming action was one case that had been stalled in court for several years that jarred loose when the litigant discovered from new transcripts that the adversary had lied to his mortgage company understating his assets when his home was foreclosed upon. The mortgage company welcomed information that the adversary had a substantial jury award that he had been concealing. Now, the litigant waits for poetic justice. Justice can come in many forms even through third parties.

Active Blaming

We hear that you can't change the system. I disagree. Litigants must change the system as hard as it may seem. Changing the system might involve refusing to use it. Boycott is a successful tool for reform. The opposite is true as well. Aggressively pursuing your case with resolve can force the system to work as intended in certain instances. There is a way to affect change in your own style. Phil Zimbardo, 2008 preface p.x, in *The Lucifer Effect*, writes about changing or preventing undesirable behavior of individuals or groups:

> ....*That means adopting a public health approach in place of the standard medical model approach to curing individual ills and wrongs. However, unless we become sensitive to the real power of the System, which is invariably hidden behind a veil of secrecy and fully understand its own set of rules and regulations, behavioral change will be transient and situational change illusory.*

Litigants and advocates are the voice of moral and ethical codes in our culture. It may or may not be a topic in vogue, but betrayal, deceit, and theft (takings) are unacceptable violations of humans seeking justice. First and foremost, the moral code and foundation of our system addresses abuse of power. Regardless of the adversarial system, from the beginning of time a moral code has existed among human beings that generally follows these tenets: (1) I may not violate your right to live and enjoy what you have earned, (2) We all must strive to live in a climate of freedom, to think and function as we wish within a set of rules equally enforced and (3) Your actions will not violate my right to live and enjoy what is mine and to think and function according to my conscience. If a violation occurs, then I have the right to confront you and inform you that you have violated the moral contract. All justice systems are designed and obligated to stand for and enforce that code. Or, they are useless to civilization.

Huffer's Log

Case of Blaming

There may be one or more perpetrators. Each violator may qualify for a different degree of blame. *Darlene's husband beat her mercilessly and clearly is the first-degree perpetrator that caused Post Traumatic Stress Disorder. However, he has been able to involve the court and influence a host of others to perpetuate the abuse for more than four years, many of which were hired in official capacities privately as well as appointed by the court.*

The court appointees are doing their jobs putting them at a third degree blame level. However, if less than professional and honest services are rendered, it moves the blame upward on the rating scale. These appointees work together creating a team around the judge. If one of the appointees is influenced, there is a pattern of the others going along and reinforcing one another's opinions. Certainly, the opinions are accepted in the inner circle without rigorous scrutiny.

At my first meeting with Darlene, I opened the door to see a beautifully chiseled face framed by reddish/brown hair. This slender, clear-eyed woman sat down in my office. Unlike many who show up at my door with laundry baskets or suitcases full of wrinkled and stained papers, Darlene was organized. She led me through her papers and like a tapestry unweaving as a thread is pulled and pulled, she related the unraveling of her life in family court.

Unfortunately, I knew the theme of her story well. It has become sadly typical. Girl meets boy; they get married; and, they have children. Boy is an abuser-controller, a PC, and must oppress. Boy beats girl in front of the children. That is the final straw. Girl fears for her life and well-being and does not want children to witness abuse. Girl gets a lawyer and, upon advice, reports the abuse to the authorities and files charges against boy. He admits the abuse but minimizes the charges. One would think the story is predictable from here... wrong.

Girl leaves relationship, files for divorce and custody, and becomes a protective parent following the law, as she knows it. Darlene was a successful computer programmer and had been in the same industry for more than 10 years. Her husband lost his job, began to drink heavily, and was abusive when he drank. He told her if she left him, he would ruin her and she would never see the children. She did not believe him. She had never done anything wrong and was stable.

Darlene entered the court confidently. A custody evaluator and minor's counsel were appointed. Before it was all over, the children were appointed a psychologist, a custody evaluator, a lawyer, a supervisor for visitation, and judge, but no one could have foreseen that soon they would have no mother. This team would prove to formulate a twisted formula for destruction of a mother's bond with her children and financially destroy a successful businesswoman.

The Custody Evaluator knew that Darlene suffered from PTSD and yet, behind closed doors, with no hearing, recklessly engineered a change of custody to award the children to the admitted abuser ex parte. Darlene was thunderstruck by the news. She had no advance warning and no access to any hearing or proceedings. It was not only shocking, it was against the law. It is unlawful for children to be put in the sole care of a domestic abuser in violation of state law, according to Darlene's careful research. Secondly, the law provides for the children to be held away from a party that has committed domestic violence within the past five years. In defiance of the law, the children were picked up from school and did not see their mother for one year while she fought to get visitation and custody.

Picturing the children being taken by strangers kicking and screaming is an unbearable vision. Darlene's inexperience with legal matters left her naive as to the power structures that surround the world of family law, the courts, and the generalized fear of litigation that is felt in society. It is shocking to Darlene, but well exposed as a destructive pattern in family court, that the children's team of experts now advocate for the abusive father.

Hearing by hearing through misinformation Darlene is stripped of any power against the coercive behavior of her husband. Darlene has not found protection from any official resource. Her ex-husband comes from a family with wealth. Darlene continues her efforts to expose the manipulation of the legal and public systems that are serving her husband's unhealthy need to exert destructive power on her. Through excessive demands, threats, charm, lobbying, legal fees, and 'the family resources to control the justice system and all of the services that support it,' he remains the final arbiter.

Darlene's state of mind was no less than controlled terror and grief during our next few meetings. I wondered what species could stand by seeing their offspring placed in harm's way and not violently attack the abductor. It seems only humans are expected to relinquish their children without a fight. I heard all about the deconstruction of Darlene's motherhood, career, estate, and life over the past three years and heard again that familiar and penetrating sound when the human voice expresses Legal Abuse Syndrome.

In Darlene's case, without notice, without a hearing, without a reason, and before the Child Protective Service investigation was completed, Darlene's children were handed over to the admitted abuser giving him full custody. The mother/children bonds were annihilated and ignored; the children were in a forced abandonment by their mother. Their mother lives in perpetuated grief and desperation. It has been nearly five years as of this day.

Darlene's PTSD is now complicated by her husband simply moving the abusive and controlling *behaviors to the legal machinery. His team feeds misinformation and blocks the Court from receiving the factual data that would benefit Darlene. It is important to note that Darlene suffers from a psychiatric injury, not a mental illness. Her condition is a normal reaction to an abnormal circumstance. If Darlene did not have PTSD, she would not be normal considering her state of affairs.*

Darlene immediately filed for ADA accommodations. The Minor's Counsel interfered with the accommodations at every turn. This is absolutely prohibited by the ADA laws. However, every effort Darlene made to get her lawyers, five in all by the end, to take action against this behavior was ignored by the lawyer. They promised to do so going in but neutralized her position once the legal action was in play.

Darlene's first-degree offender is her ex-husband. Then, the Court appointed the mental health professionals and evaluator who have 'rubber stamped" one another taking the position that this mother, who suffers from PTSD, is a danger to her children. This could be a consideration except none of them have met with the mother or are able to produce any research to back their positions. Darlene has undergone four psychological evaluations, all of which found her a fit mother and turned up nothing remarkable. Yet, the minor's counsel is leading the pack against her with the story that she is mentally ill and refuses treatment.

Darlene's blaming began by hiring attorneys who were badly treated by the court appointees and, after five, she tried one more who compromised her case and did not protect her ADA rights. The expenditure was more than $200,000 to pay lawyers to oversee the destruction of her estate. She wound up in bankruptcy and on Social Security Disability because the volume of hearings, motions, and paperwork that assaulted her overwhelmed her ability to cope. She cannot work to this day although it is her dream to return to work. After the succession of attorneys and the disastrous results, Darlene will not give up. She keeps fighting and was finally placed on supervised visitation although there were no indicators from her history that she is any danger to her children. She was told in court that the domestic violence did not matter and she was not to bring it up. Yet, it is the central point in her case. So, if she is to see her children, she must do so supervised to ensure she does not mention abuse.

In cases like Darlene's, one of the most important functions is the supportive counseling and assistance to stay the course. As Minor's Counsel threw one obstacle after another between Darlene and her children, she stayed in the battle taking the blows. Without the advocate to call when she was at her wits end and someone to organize and listen while she strategized, she may have succumbed to the pain.

Darlene took on a blaming action that has been making progress in her state. She began to join activist efforts to reform the family court system. Her group was successful in causing an audit of the family courts in one county in their state. She has met with the media with no positive results for her individual case, but her involvement helped with the group's efforts.

Darlene knew that her email and phone were being monitored. One day she decided on a personal blaming action that, to her, met the criteria of stopping short of real revenge. She visited the spy shop to learn about protecting herself. While there, she learned about "fart spray." Knowing that her ex-husband is vain and always boosted his ego by his dress and grooming, she purchased an aerosol can. In a few well-chosen private moments, around the courthouse she was able to spray some in his car, on his briefcase and once, well placed, on him unbeknownst to anyone. He just finally smelled as he behaved.

Darlene, with the support of her advocate, has gone forward without an attorney. It certainly wasn't her first choice but became a necessity. She is under ADA accommodations that have helped her to gain continuances and to sustain in court. As an expert witness, I testified in court that she is no threat to her children and urged the court to return custody of the children to Darlene. The court has demanded repeated mediations and psychological examinations of Darlene and none from her ex-husband. Minor's Counsel continues to repeat the same misinformation to the court and prolongs the case keeping Darlene on supervised visitation. The visitation costs $800 per month.

I addressed that minor's counsel was falsely reporting on the record that Darlene had depression and refused to take prescribed medication. I further pointed out that Darlene's risk of suffering such symptoms were actually less than that for lawyers as a profession (Sweeney, 2010).

Darlene continues to support the activist group that pickets the judge's house and publishes his decisions that harm children. They have achieved legislative hearings where Darlene testified. Darlene's Minor's Counsel has crossed many ethical lines. Yet, when Darlene looks to file complaints, she finds that there is no regulation on Minor's Counsels in her state. She filed a Bar complaint, but the bar reported they do not supervise such a role. Every formal avenue has been disappointing regarding the ethical obligations of her attorneys and Minor's Counsel, but the activists and creative activities have helped the cause. Her ADA advocate stays in touch and acts as a liaison with the court when needed.

Darlene finally filed a writ of prohibition to the appellate court exposing the violations in the lower court. The writ was immediately denied. BUT, the next day when she went to court, she was taken off supervised visitation and her case appeared to have been positively affected by simply filing the facts.

As advocates, we will never know what goes on behind the scenes. However, it appears that hanging in there and not allowing wrongdoers to bluff the client out of their rights, eventually does affect the situation.

Additional Web Site Reading

http://www.protectiveparents.com/.
http://corp.sorryworks.net/.
http://www.isc.idaho.gov/opinions/Christian%20opinion.pdf.

References

Barber, L., Maltby, J., & Macaskill, A. (2005). Angry memories and thoughts of revenge: the relationship between forgiveness and anger rumination. Personality and Individual. *Differences, 39*, 253-262.

Bard, M. & Sangrey, D. (1986). *The Crime Victim's Book.* New York: Brunner/Mazel, Inc.

Flanigan, B. (1992). *Forgiving the Unforgivable: Overcoming the Bitter Legacy of Intimate Wounds.* New York: Wiley Publishing, Inc.

Herman, J. L. (1997). *Trauma and Recovery.* (pp. 189). New York: Basic Books.

Olson, W. K. (1991). *The Litigation Explosion: What Happened When America Unleashed the Lawsuit.* (pp. 19). New York: E.P. Dutton/Truman Talley Books.

Shaver, K. G. (1985). *Introduction to Attribution Process and The Attribution of Blame, Causality, Responsibility and Blameworthiness.* New York: Springer-Verlag.

Sweeney, M. J. (2010). *The Devastation of Depression: Lawyers are at greater risk—It's an impairment to take seriously.* Retrieved from http://www.abanet.org/barserv/barleader/22-6dev.htm.

Wojcieszak, D., Saxton, J. W., & Finkelstein, M. (2008). *Sorry Works!* (pp 48-66). Bloomington, Ind.:Authorhouse.

Zimbardo, P. (2007). *The Lucifer Effect: Understanding How Good People Turn Evil.* New York: Random House Trade Paperbacks.

CHAPTER 14

EMPOWERMENT: HUFFER'S STEP-7 FEARLESSLY SELF-PROTECT, RESEARCH, AND CONFRONT ETHICAL CHALLENGES

Huffer's Step 7, Empowerment, imparts a range of skills that empower the individual litigant regardless of disabilities. Litigants with disabilities must master self-protection and a sense of safety in the expanding dimensions of a high tech age. They need crackerjack ability to observe the background dynamics and activities in the courtroom, and to implement positive forward thinking challenging outdated and destructive patterns of bias. Using accommodations, and affirming their cases through effective communication strengthens the litigant with or without legal representation.

Today I will do what others won't, so tomorrow I can accomplish what others can't.

Jerry Rice

CADAAs Facilitate LWD's Self-reliance

People get swept into court. Then, they can easily lose control to protocols, traditions, intimidation, their lawyer's, and their opposition's legal games. Many emerge from litigation feeling as though their case was never effectively heard. Litigants look back with regret on their few precious moments in court wondering what they could and should have done differently. Bringing together the preparation from Huffer's six steps of the eight accomplished thus far, in the context of the brutal realities of the case at hand, lends to the skill and wisdom needed to now boost the litigant's personal resources for greater self advocacy. Advocates will notice that clients need less from them as they progress through the steps. LWDs may need to be encouraged to progressively take more responsibility for their cases. Most decrease their dependency over time.

EC
GRL
H8S

Empowerment Section 1: Insight into the Dynamics of the Court

Electric words that project a charge outward from the integrity of the litigant can be deliciously powerful but so hard to plan and execute in a court of law. Rarely do litigants with disabilities get to speak, uninterrupted, to a receptive court. They report that they are mostly told to be quiet.

The advocate's role is inextricably tied to helping the litigant effectively communicate in court, both listening and speaking. Advocates, through the debriefing process, first help the litigant uncover the significant issues that lend to selection of the right words that will affect the court whether spoken or written. Once the litigant has selected key legal issues, then the litigant's words must be choreographed to fit the odd dance of litigation. The advocate is usually the only player in this legal game that protects the special needs litigant during a legal process that is wreaking havoc with their emotions while simultaneously forbidding expression of that emotion. A whole underlying communication dance is played out in courtrooms, many times unbeknownst to the public.

While advocates function under the ADAAA of 2008 promoting the original intent of the ADA, the details of constructing meaningful accommodations are left to wide interpretation. Advocates are invaluable in pinning down the details needed to design and deliver powerful accommodations. Do not depend on the ADA Access Coordinator to be able to design accommodations for a disabled litigant. The litigant or ADA advocate must do it and see that it is done timely. Having the accommodations clearly in place is critical before litigation begins. It is advisable to file for accommodations before or at the same time as filing the legal action if possible. However, some jurisdictions will insist upon the legal action being filed and scheduled first. In that case, the disadvantage to the litigant with disabilities lies in no time to grieve or appeal if needed accommodations are denied. Therefore, unless a formal rule of procedure prohibits early filing it is time to use tools of persuasion with the ADA Administrative Office.

Persuasion does not stop with the ADA coordinator and court administration. The value of looking at the court through the eyes of a judge can be helpful in polishing off the LWD's preparation for court. In a book written for lawyers, Supreme Court Justice Antonin Scalia discusses the art of persuading judges. At first blush, it is a shocking book in that the judge's power seeps through the pages of this book in a manner that smacks of catering to an emperor whose very whim might strike you down. Yet, once the reality of that perspective sinks in, the book has advice that can assist both represented and unrepresented litigants. The most important for LWDs are:

1. Be sure you are in the right court that has jurisdiction.

2. Lead with your strongest arguments affirming yourself, not being defensive.

3. Assume a posture of intellectual equality with the bench.

4. Arrive in court early well prepared.

5. Have your opener down pat.

Unrepresented LWDs often feel they lack the ability to write a motion or a brief that will be accepted by the court. Scalia's advice is welcome for the non legal public. Judges value clarity over pomp. Simply state the facts and the relief desired in the most straightforward manner possible. There is much more in this book, but these five simple items are powerful and go a long way towards efficiency of the pro se LWD (Scalia, 2008).

Uses and Abuses of Obstruction of Information and Lying in Court

One of the worst culprits that steal justice in the courtroom has to do with the disproportionate amount of litigation time consumed limiting or obstructing information. According to our observations up to 80% of speaking time in court is often spent in efforts to obstruct the salient points rather than putting facts and evidence on the record. These are subtle forces that interfere with fair access to the court by wearing litigants down. A major challenge for every litigant lies in preserving the valuable time of the court for weighing of the admissible evidence, the laws, and facts. Many who suffer disabilities cannot sustain years of obstructive legal game playing. The advocate is key to keeping litigants focused on main points once they are clarified. Then by using Huffer's 8 steps they extend the litigant's endurance while preventing exploitation of the impairment inadvertently by habit and routine of the court.

Lying and Trickery as Litigation Tactics

Human beings are stung after being tricked. The consequences loom greater than mere resentment at being deceived. When a major institution like the legal system deceives, public health is endangered. Psychologists and sociologists tell us that if social ecology traumatizes its members through prolonged interpersonal trauma, such as the legal system does, the population becomes a subordinate group embedded in abuse and exploitation (Courtois, 2009). This refers to the population at large. Some lawyers especially those representing corporations routinely trick citizens who are asserting their legal rights. Much of this is done through sophisticated deceit using pretext of lawful actions to cover wrongdoing committed by unethical attorneys (Berardinelli, 2008). Each litigant suffering from impairment is already relegated to being part of a subordinate group from the outset. They must be skillfully buoyed to face the legal system.

For litigants suffering from Post Traumatic Stress Disorder (PTSD), Traumatic Brain Injury (TBI), Attention Deficit Hyperactive Disorder (ADHD), Autism Spectrum Disorders (ASDs), and other invisible disabilities, tricks and lies take on a more severe dimension. Protecting vulnerable litigants from deceit is a critical part of the accommodation picture. Just as if a toxic chemical was used in the courtroom that affects the functionality of a person with disabilities, lies are toxic to those with invisible disabilities. Lies disorient them to the point that they often become symptomatic and cannot function during stressful litigation. Therefore, a system of data analysis has been developed to correct the misinformation threatening to wipe out their equal participation in court.

EC
GRL
H8S

A typical scenario occurs when opposing counsel or the opposition lies damaging the litigant's case on the record. The target litigant will become symptomatic and sometimes cannot restrain themselves from speaking out directly to the opposition denying the lies or doing a "He said, She said" interchange that does not belong in litigation. Or, the attacked litigant cries, wrings hands, gets ill, or displays other manifestations of their symptoms. At that point, they are functionally impaired and unable to perform; they are damaged by the behavior of their opposition. Then by symptomatic reactions they further damage their own case by lending to a negative perception.

Due to fundamental attribution error/correspondence bias, data analysis is a critical accommodation for LWDs with invisible disabilities such as traumatic stress or brain injuries. There are times that opposing counsel or the adversary will use misinformation, gratuitous statements, scurrilous remarks, ridicule, and bullying for the sole purpose of eliciting symptoms in the LWD diminishing or preventing them from defending themselves or presenting their case. If there is no proper and sustained objection, the inaccurate material placed on the record can prevent the trier of fact from adjudicating fairly according to facts in evidence.

The accommodation of data analysis prevents this exploitation of the LWD, preserves the court's obligations under ADAAA and HIPAA and the economy of the court. It is a simple process whereby misinformation is recorded by the LWD on a sheet patterned to list misinformation in one column during testimony rather than speaking out. The other column lists evidence refuting the misinformation. Then the exploitative misinformation along with the forensically acceptable evidence is provided to the trier of fact for correction of the record. This eases the symptoms of the LWD during the attack and stands to assist all involved to stay with the facts that serve the case in chief. If done well, this is a service to the court as it alerts the opposition that they must not discriminate or exploit a disability, and serves the cause of expedience and justice well. The ADAAA is clear that no person is to be discriminated against due to a disability. Inciting symptoms with intent to disarm is such discrimination. Data analysis puts the LWD in a position of power to respond and not be victimized.

Some attorneys file a motion for a hearing including the data analysis if the material stands to strongly influence the case. The accommodation is put in place providing for those moments when lies are being told that stab the litigant's heart and twist their image. In addition to proper legal objections, the litigant has an opportunity to list the misinformation calmly averting symptoms.

Trickery under the pretext of law truly is abuse but is so common that it rarely is identified and corrected. Abuse is defined as the harmful use of insults, offensive language, and/or maltreatment. Through data analysis of use of misdirection, confusion, and exploitation of those with invisible disabilities is caught in the act. For litigants with autism, tricks kill their chances for a fair hearing. They are not able to distinguish tricks from truth. Autism and other disabilities render the person especially vulnerable to being deceived. Thus, exploitation is certain without clear accommodations and preparation ahead of time to manage the toxic disorientation.

The Pervasiveness of Lying

Lies are interesting because some lying is expected in court. Other lying in our culture is accepted as acts of kindness as humans relate with one another. Lies warrant a quick look back into history to gain perspective as to the lies that must be eradicated because they deny access to persons with certain invisible disabilities versus those lies that are part of human interaction.

Lies must not, on their own, determine a crime has been committed or be the determiner in establishing a life altering judicial decision. Therefore, judicial notice is in order.

6. Some lies are crimes in and of themselves i.e. fraud, making false statements to the court or investigators, or committing perjury. Yet, those crimes are rarely punished.

7. However, investigators often assume that lying proves the person knows he or she is guilty. This assumption may be valid for the general population but cannot be relied upon in cases of autism, schizophrenia, traumatic brain injury and other invisible disabilities. Persons with these disabilities will confess under pressure, say what they are told, or impulsively speak out unrelated to the topic at hand. Moreover, many times the person will not realize that what comes out of their mouths can criminally jeopardize them.

In fact, in many cases, under the pretext of "zealous representation," and with full cooperation of the court lawyers have taken unfair advantage of any weakness in the litigant. The ADA advocate defines "weakness" in terms of disability to be offset by accommodations. This is done with the intent and spirit of ADA protection and preserving human dignity. In the face of the ADAAA, certain lawyers will still challenge the veracity of invisible disability. When the ADA advocate approaches the court for accommodations for a litigant, the functional impairments have been well determined. And, interestingly, usually the least medically qualified person to opine on medical conditions is opposing counsel. Under the new ADAAA the litigant is protected from having to prove the disability under such conditions.

Contrary to most litigants' original beliefs about getting a lawyer and going to court, litigation does not present a forum where conflicts are freely worked out. In a court of law, careful parsing of data excludes human emotion and shapes it into a legal format. It is an artificial process and tough to manage for even the strongest of human beings when struggling with conflict. Litigants with special needs usually do not easily blend into such a litigation process. The ugly unqualified suspicions and accusations that the disability does not exist or is being exaggerated need to be aggressively curtailed as discrimination, strictly prohibited by law.

EC
GRL
H8S

Respondents reported in the longitudinal survey (Huffer/Alexander, 2007) that lying in the courtroom is the biggest problem they faced during litigation. Lying puts the true purpose of going to court in a chokehold. Lies assault the special needs litigant's brain cumulatively fulminating traumatic stress. Lies work like parasitic worms permeating every legal action, halting progress, and eating away at due process rights. Lies obstruct justice. Sunlight on the "can of worms" sends them scurrying. I recommend starting this process in two ways: 1) telegraph the adversary's game to the court, and 2) data analysis to correct misinformation submitted to the court that could skew a judicial decision unfairly against the litigant with disabilities. These techniques help to provide irrefutable evidence needed for the trier of fact to adjudicate without misperceiving the litigant or the case.

Fundamental Attribution Error and Data Analysis

Fundamental attribution error/Correspondence Bias abounds with litigants crying fraud. Then they carefully expose the fraud before the court under Federal Rules of Civil Procedure requiring another tier of litigation. Fraud reported to the court rarely brings satisfaction to the litigant with disabilities or correction and punishment of the fraud.

The reopening of a case due to new or corrected information presents an opportunity to deal with fraud but simultaneously adds another burdensome remedy if misinformation or blocking of information has brought a bad result. A litigant, already struggling with disabilities, may not be able to deal with furthering legal battles. Each procedure requires monumental planning for accommodations and strain on an impaired individual.

Therefore, data analysis, a system that identifies attribution error and solves it while in progress is more conducive to serving litigants with disabilities and preserves the economy of the court. Data analysis identifies the misinformation on the spot heading off the need for additional legal actions. It is a simple process that attends to personal interests and helps to keep them out of the legal arena as well as protecting the positive perception of the client with functional impairments.

This method is put forth to ensure that the public's most vulnerable to fundamental attribution error has confidence in the judicial system. The courts are filled with attorneys attempting to confuse the truth and submit proof that does not reflect quality evidence. Many of these discriminatory behaviors slip by a judge if not parsed out and exposed through an accommodation such as data analysis.

Data analysis is a tool intended to organize, itemize, define, and clarify the misinformation that has impeded fair accesses to court under the Americans with Disabilities Act and/ or HIPAA. As a document of record, it alerts the court of the violation and places it for Judicial Notice or other action. This form speaks to violations of the ADAAA, HIPAA, and abuse of process for litigants with disabilities. The following are basic elements to be included in the data analysis. Every case weighs data differently, so customize your own report form as best simplifies and puts forth the misinformation that represents violations of your client's right to dignity, due process rights, ADAAA accommodations, and medical rights to privacy.

Sample Form for Data Analysis Prior to ADAAA:

DATA ANALYSIS SAMPLE CUSTOMIZED STATEMENT

Name: _____ Docket/Case No._____

Directions:

Attach all completed copies of this form to the information given on first page. Make copies of your work.

Use the terminology given below to clarify the data you are disputing.

Be specific as to the violation you are citing under the ADAAA Title II & III or HIPAA.

When writing your detailed explanation, include names, dates, actions, labels, form numbers, etc.

If you spoke with or are relying on an outside authority to substantiate your dispute, include all contact information, documents, citations, conversations, etc. of importance.

Clearly explain attachments, other than additional exhibits, and their significance.

If you require additional exhibits or more room, retype following the sequence.

Be concise. Edit. Verify. Copy. Data analysis can be performed as needed.

Include Signature.

The case submitted below is an actual case that demonstrates severe bungling of the accommodations needed by a person with Depression and PTSD. This case is followed due to the longevity, severity of legal abuses, and challenges it presented to the advocate.

Attachments to Case Example of data analysis for LEANN JONAS

CASE NO. 99-21062 CA 15

Submitted by: Dr. Karin Huffer, ADA advocate

Case of: LeeAnn M. Jonas, Georgia resident, 16-year long litigation

ADA Violations with Nine exhibits (description of exhibits only due to volume):

1. Violation of due process of law for denying equal access for person with disabilities

2. Violation or threatened violation of ADAAA confidentiality/HIPAA protection

3. Violation of approved ADA Accommodations

EC
GRL
H8S

Exhibit 1-Violation 3- Date: June 24, 2008 - Letter to Honorable Trier of Fact, from Dr. Karin Huffer. The Judge had demonstrated concern that Litigant may be "holding the court hostage." (1) Letter informs the Judge that the ADA request for accommodations had been filed with the clerk of the court. (2) The letter affirmed the accommodations and asked for an additional accommodation to be added to those approved on July 16, 2008 to wit Litigant Jonas be included on the service list as is a usual protocol of court. And, (3) The Judge was assured that our organization, LVAA, monitors our clients ruling out malingering or any ill intent and affirms that the basic rules, courtesies, and protocols are adhered to since they are the foundation on which ADA accommodations rest and succeed.

Exhibit 2-Violation 3—July 11, 2008 – Letter to Mr. Wodatch, Department of Justice, from Dr.Karin Huffer. Letter requests guidance due to denial of basic procedures required for ADA accommodations to be effective. NO RESPONSE RECEIVED.

Exhibit 3-Violations 1 and 3—July 11, 2008 –Copy of letter to Civil Rights Division from Dr. Karin Huffer. Letter requests guidance for unprecedented denial of basic rules and courtesies for ADA Accommodated Litigant. NO RESPONSE RECEIVED.

Exhibit 4-Violation 1—July 16, 2008-Transcript. Litigant attended hearing with ADA advocate Dr. Karin Huffer, clothing store's owner, Jonas, and their Attorney, Ms. Levin, and John Swenson, former attorney for LeeAnn Jonas as a witness. Also present were Opposing Counsel, and Judge. (1) ADA Accommodations were personally approved by Judge, page 4 (lines 21-25), page 5 (lines 1-25), page 6 (lines 1-25), page 7 (lines 1-25), page 8 (lines 1-25), page 9 (lines 20-25), page 10 (lines 1-6), page 22 (lines 24-25), page 26 (lines 14–20), pages 29 (lines 21-24), page 37 (lines 7-25), page 37 (1-25), page 39 (lines 1-25), page 45 (lines 17–21), and page 45 (lines 1-21); (2) Transcript contains discussion of specific need for misinformation to be corrected and procedure followed due to litigant having been denied service of documents and having the judge adjudicate on a matter that was not read according to three witnesses, pages 13-14; (3) Court: "I will make every accommodation in your request," page 47 (lines 1-5 and lines 19-21), and page 51 (lines 7–20); (4) Generally agreed litigant would have an avenue for correcting misinformation, page 78 (lines 1-25); and, (5) Agreed on same rules for all. Examples include all evidence to be clearly heard with rules equally applied laying the foundation for access through accommodations and for adjudication to be determined on evidence alone. Intimidating and exploitative body language from opposing counsel is to be curtailed, pages 80-81. All accommodations are approved at this point.

Exhibit 5-Violation 3—December 10, 2008 - Transcript, page 3 (lines 3-21) Litigant experiences Administrative Failure of ADA Accommodations. (1) Judge claims that the ADA Administration knew nothing of the litigant's request or history of approvals even from Judge. (2) Judge informs special needs litigant that no accommodations are in place (See Exhibit 9 #2). (3) Based on Exhibit 1 and Exhibit 4 #1-5, Litigant has undergone nearly six months of litigation with Judge Crawford. (4) Litigant was led to believe that proper administrative procedures were followed by Judge who held a hearing on the matter. Litigant had filed for accommodations timely. Litigant cannot be held responsible for the Judge violating proper administrative procedures pursuant to enforcement of ADA accommodations.

THE COURT six months after July 16 hearing approving accommodations stated: The first thing that I'm going to require is this: I've spoken to my ADA Accommodation people. I should have done this a long time ago... think that it is necessary in order that we are not requesting things that are not viable or appropriate requests pursuant to the ADA. All right. Here is our ADA form. All of the information on here is laid out. Mrs. Jonas is going to have to fill this form out, go to the ADA office, and try to get an accommodation. If they deny it or any part of it, she will have an administrative remedy, she can appeal it through the administrative process. All right. We have a whole ADA office set up. We are equipped at ways to do this, how to do it, whether to do it, when to do it, why to do it, and if she is not happy with it, then she can appeal it through the ADA process. Here is your form.

THE COURT: I just wanted to know what my timeframe was. I just want it to say that she was suffering. The other thing is, I don't know why she has never filed for ADA accommodations.

MS. LEVIN, Attorney for Clothing Store: I believe she was in contact. I can't

THE COURT: No. My ADA office says they have no record of her.

MS. LEVIN: I believe she did.

THE COURT: They said she hasn't. She may have done it in the federal court or the bankruptcy court, but she never did it here. So, anyway, let's do this my way, please, and go ahead and talk to me about Mr. Jonas's individual claims.

Exhibit 6-Violation 1&3—December 3, 2008 - Letter to Judge from Dr. Karin Huffer (1) Letter addresses Litigant accusations of malingering by Judge and other concerns. (2) The letter clarified that Litigant needed her accommodations and in no way was manipulating the court according to our assessments. (3) Litigant's condition was deteriorating as a result of the stressors created by the Judge not following the plan set in place in July 2008 at the hearing allowing all evidence to be heard, rules to be equitable, and for accommodations agreed upon in the hearing of July 16, 2008. The Court has made many rulings without Litigant having fair access and due process due to confusion over ADA accommodations. That is no fault of Litigant.

Exhibit 7-Violation 3—December 10, 2008 - Transcript page 1, page 14, page 32 (lines12 -25) and page 33 (lines 1-9) (1) Responses show Failure of Court to Protect Administrative Confidentiality. (2) Quotes demonstrate confidential information unprotected violating HIPAA and ADA Title II, as ADA Accommodations are confidential, ministerial, administrative not adversarial.

Exhibit 8-Violation 1,2, &3—March 3, 2009 – Letter to Heidi Johnson-Wright Director, Office of ADA Coordination from Dr. Karin Huffer (1) Letter informs of severe problems for Litigant in this court. (2) Request made for change of venue under an additional accommodation. And, (3) Notifies that Litigant's health is dramatically deteriorating under present circumstances.

Exhibit 9-Violation 1,2,&3—March 12, 2009 – Letter to Access Coordinator for Court, from Dr. Karin Huffer with the report and proof of filing attached, . (1) Letter requests explanation of Judge comment that administratively, the ADA Access Coordinator had no knowledge of Litigant.

(2) Proves ADA Access Coordinator failed to process this request. (3) Letter explains how the effort to gain fair access and fair accommodations has precipitated and exacerbated symptoms in a most insidious manner. (4) The letter described Litigant's demise with examples of denigrating statements from the Court that are discriminatory of Litigant's symptoms and condition (See Transcript 12-10-08, page 75 lines # 1-25). The resulting deterioration of Litigant's condition required emergency hospitalization. (5) ADA Coordinator affirmed Ms. Jonas's accommodations and qualifications for same. (6) Now, after six months of damages inflicted on a defenseless litigant without consistent accommodations and being accused of malingering, Judge disassociates herself from the American with Disabilities Act. And, (7) Judge, at this juncture, in a coup de grâce of irrationality, hands the disabled litigant an ADA form to fill out, submit, and start all over asking for ADA Accommodations. It is nothing less than a public health crisis when a citizen seeks justice through the civilized court of law and through incompetence or corruption is left predictably worsened from being denied basic civil rights.

Common Problems Requiring Data Analysis Improved Since ADAAA

Completing a data analysis usually requires an advocate to assist. There is no substitute for detailed quotes and pertinent exhibits. For those with PTSD, reintroduction of the trauma can cause the LWD to become symptomatic. The advocate also needs to watch for common problems that discriminate against persons with disabilities:

1. Functional impairment being ignored

2. Functional impairment worsened with no intervention allowed by the court.

3. Legal capacity inhibited by no funds for or access to counsel leaves them vulnerable for exploitation as a pro se litigant.

4. Procedural harassment- wasteful, abusive paper demands, court dates with no substantive accomplishment, attempts to impede process and obstruct justice for the sole purpose of diminishing the LWD's functionality.

5. Basic rules of court and courtesies are denied the special needs litigant who is also pro se but were disproportionately afforded the adversary.

6. The special needs litigant is denied equal access to transcripts or a record of hearing.

7. LWD is not put on the service list.

8. LWD is denied discovery.

9. LWD cannot access documents with same courtesies and ease as attorneys even though a pro se is their own attorney i.e. electronic systems.

10. The court's websites or e-delivery and filing of documents are user unfriendly or denied to disabled litigants.

11. Court's rulings conflict with formal rules and laws provided to special needs litigant ignoring accommodations.

12. Procedure is unclear or there are no published instructions for receiving ADA accommodations.

13. The court forces excessive assistance beyond needs of ADA Advocates, for example, involuntary contracts with court appointed counselors, guardians, masters that are prohibitive in cost. The court ignores the litigant's concern that many court appointed guardians have little regulation, cannot be terminated even when bias is apparent, and they are abiding by no formal enforced description of professional duties.

14. The court allocates assets unfairly.

15. Long court days, pressure from deadlines, difficulties with legal research, expenses, and battle take the litigant beyond their tolerance.

Once these factors have worn the litigant down there is diminished capacity to function. Progressively their impairments worsen, their finances are depleted, and a war of attrition causes them to give up.

Blocks to Communication:
Anger and Defensiveness Damage Perception of LWD

Advocates need to analyze these emotions in order to manage the litigant's ability to perform. From the outset, two major blocks to effective communication are anger and defensiveness. Debriefing offers the first clues that the litigant may get stuck on these secondary emotions. It is critical to work with litigants to name the feelings that precede anger and defensiveness. There are always underlying emotions such as fear, sense of rejection, humiliation, and helplessness when anger or defensiveness surfaces. They need immediate intervention using the following tools so as not be exploited by the adversary.

Use Deflectors to Maintain Focus when Verbally Attacked

Much of empowerment is being skilled at selecting from a plethora of deflecting skills. If you are in an adversarial communication, learn to toggle. First act as the authority presenting your material. Keep all parties on focus by shifting gears between asserting authority and hearing opposing responses. After listening reflecting your understanding, and acknowledging the other's position, reassert your demand and authority.

EC
GRL
H8S

If your opposition calls you a "filthy, flea ridden, fungal, pervert" the answer is: "Regardless of my adversary's false assertions, we will focus on the pertinent issues in this case." Then move on with the points you need to make. When the focus begins to be diverted from your goal, use deflective responses:

Adversary says, "He is a 'lying, cheating, rat'."

Answer, "Nevertheless." Then go on with case presentation.

Lead in with deflectors like:

"Regardless"

"Nonetheless"

"Notwithstanding"

"It doesn't matter"

Now, bring the presentation back to your point. After the negative diversionary statement is made, use the following in order to begin restating the other's position:

"I hear you"

"I understand"

"It sounds like"

"Yes"

"From your point of view"

Take their words and deflate them. Example: *I know you disagree that our son needs medical treatment, I hear you, NEVERTHELESS, the medical professionals overwhelmingly support our son being treated.* Then, by turning the conversation back with the deflective lead-ins above restate your authority, and your demand continuing to force the focus back to your point.

When you use your words defining and exposing the other's attacks on you, it takes the power out of them. Mothers and fathers are easy prey to statements about the children loving or not loving them or wanting to be with them. Attorneys often state, "Her or his children don't want to see her or him." This is a classic attack to disarm and emotionally stab the heart of the opponent parent. The response needs to be, "From your point of view, a lawyer representing a person who wants to win this case, you hope I will collapse in emotional pain from that statement. Unfortunately for you, I know that statement to be untrue." Then the capper is to endorse both sides by a statement such as, "Our children love both parents." No court can fault that statement.

The adversary's goal is to ambush, shock, or frustrate the litigant from effective action. Eventually, the surprise attacks divert attention and waste the court's time. Time represents the litigant's money, which runs out before fair adjudication when a litigant with disabilities is so lost in lies and the resulting false paper trail that they can't endure more and give up. Advocates help you force the focus to present your case by taking breaks, using cue cards, reminding you of your words and to re-energize like reframing, allowing the litigant to argue accomplishing the intended objectives without defensiveness (Bodenhamer, 1992).

Mental Toughness:
A Little Known or Used Technique to Keep Focus during Litigation

Focus is the final key to effective communication. Do not go down paths set by your adversary. Use mental toughness. Mental toughness is a term used in sports and business. Toughness of the mind relates to the ability to concentrate and execute a planned performance under difficult conditions. The ability to envision yourself and your desired result is fundamental to staying on focus regardless of your emotions (Sheard, 2010).

Court is not unlike a competitive sport; unfortunately, the issues of court are deadly serious and it would be better if they were not cast as a win/lose game. Yet, some attorneys and judges approach litigation with a game mentality. This perverted court/sport is of Olympic importance and challenge. No one jumps into the Olympics without training, coaching, and focus. Litigation deserves nearly equal preparation.

I work with litigants and advocates to develop mental toughness, coaching them to rehearse and picture themselves presenting their cases in court or sitting for depositions. They practice non-response to lies, deflectors, telegraphing, and continue to use analysis of behavior, needs, and demand accuracy of data on the record. They redirect emotional reaction when they begin to get upset. Advocates help litigants improve their visualization skills by using three fundamental principles. They repeat:

1. Stay in the moment. Affirm, "I visualize only myself at this moment and the performance that I can control." Refuse to succumb to emotions from the past and fear of the future.

2. Act, do not react. "I will not engage when the adversary is trying to make me angry or lose control. I will deal with their lies through data analysis correction." "I will use deflectors, silence, telegraphing, and reframe."

3. Advocates help to research and keep the rules clearly before the litigant. Know the rules and become skilled. "I will be prepared knowing the rules and laws remaining confident that I belong here and I will perform without losing focus on my goal blocking everything else, all deceptive legal games and bait from my mind."

If the adversary succeeds in forcing the litigant to become angry or defensive, they have taken a giant step toward winning unfairly. Once those emotions are felt and reacted to, they block the litigant's ability to read the adversary's background emotions. Feeling defensive is also a critical barrier to the sufferer's reception of information. That is why the adversary is eager to elicit these communication blockers.

EC
GRL
H8S

Litigants must not display anger and/or defensiveness. When they arise a cue needs to be worked out between the advocate and litigant. The advocate helps the litigant to be wise to multiple tactics simply used to provoke symptoms. If the litigant gives away to anger or defensiveness, even for a moment, it is a huge payoff for the adversary. Litigants need to be coached again and again to stay calm and alert practicing effective responses to every possible, painful verbal attack that could come their way in court. Georgia was easy to set off. She has Tourettes Syndrome and impulse control problems. Now she is without medication. Even the strongest of litigants will have "buttons" that when pushed are triggers to the two responses that must be avoided at all cost in the courtroom, anger and defensiveness. The advocate and Georgia have worked out a cue squeezing the hand or arm of the other when needing to deal with anger and its partner, defensiveness.

Example of LWD Using Mental Toughness by Telegraphing

Paula is a very intelligent adult who suffers from autism. It is a developmental condition, not a mental illness. She manages it well and has been in the military, effectively adopted and raised a daughter to early teens, and is working on an advanced degree. When conflicts arose with her life's partner and "other mother" of the child, Paula found herself overcome by litigation and trickery. Before the proceedings could start, opposing counsel would say, "Before we begin, your honor, I just need to say…." Then a rash of attacks would devastate Paula disarming her for her hearing. Knowing that Paula is autistic, the attacks were designed to trigger her symptoms that included talking very fast, rocking in her seat, showing stress in her face, and all of that combined with her a typical autistic symptom of rolling her head as she thinks. Sometimes she does this on the witness stand. Without ADA interpretation to the court she can look out of control.

The opposing counsel moves in for the kill misrepresenting the behaviors to the court at every turn. Her opposition fabricated a scenario as to how the child is being harmed by this "mad woman" demanding a psychological evaluation and asserting that she must be on supervised visitation. Paula had never had a complaint from a school, any complaint filed with a child protective agency, and mostly, the child was happy well adjusted and loves her mother, Paula. This child was accustomed to her mother's autistic traits and had begun to perform poorly in school because she missed Paula. The adversary claimed that Paula schemed to cause the child to do poorly in school and behave badly in order to make the "other mother" look badly in the eyes of the court. The ignorance of this adversary was demonstrated by the fact that autistic people customarily do not scheme and deceive. Further, they cannot be evaluated in the usual manner ordered by the courts without being severely discriminated against.

Studies on autism clearly demonstrate that a trait of an autistic adult is their purity and naiveté as to manipulative behaviors by others. They are bound to the truth almost innocently and can become agitated but are not expected to be dangerous. Frustration is more internalized than externalized. Autism is not a mental illness it is a pervasive developmental disorder.

After protracted litigation took its toll, Paula also showed symptoms of PTSD. She filed for ADA Accommodations for the PTSD, but none was needed for the autism. She retained an advocate. The advocate immediately could see the game that was played while Paula was denied her due process rights. Paula prepared for the next hearing.

When the adversary jumped up to speak first and take control, Paula was ready to telegraph. She got up and said, "Your Honor, I need to speak first with a brief statement to the Court." *Ms. "Opposing Counsel" is going to tell you, before proceedings even start, that: 1) I am an unfit mother. 2) The child does not want to see me. 3) I am "crazy" because I have an injury for which I am receiving accommodations in this court. And, 4) they will repeat earlier assertions that I am the party that stalls the momentum of the court and first filed an action against them. These are serious misstatements to the court. I am the defendant your honor. Regardless of these and other false assertion made at the beginning of each hearing, I have the evidence to challenge each one. I request that we begin proceedings without allowing Ms. Opposing Counsel to misinform the Court for the purpose of exploiting my disability and preventing me from exercising my due process rights.*

Now, if Ms. Opposing Counsel gets up and says what Paula has telegraphed, the effect has been lost. It virtually takes the wind out of their sails. It is a neutralization technique. The litigant or their attorney has to be ready to jump up and take the floor before the other side deprives them of opening remarks when the rules dictate that they are entitled to opening statements. Opposing counsel has grabbed the stage using the technique for the past several appearances. With no cross-examination, no notice to the other side of what will be spoken so Paula can be prepared they get away with casting the negative image. It is an ambush and exploitation. Telegraphing is a "tit for tat" move that if done well (Chapter 11, Deshaming), once, can deny the opposition their opening salvo. If not, that salvo damages the perception of the litigant being attacked creating a fundamental attribution error or correspondence bias in the court.

Empowerment Section 2: Overcoming Invasive and Faulty Psychological Evaluations through Accurate ADA Accommodations Reports

Abusers first call LWDs crazy and then set out to prove the perception. Legally abusive tactics, unfortunately, will often include attacking a litigant's sanity by creative attempts to violate privacy rights under HIPAA and ADAAA. Advocates and LWDs need to weigh all options and proceed with great caution if they allow anyone to evaluate their psyche. They need to know the law, privacy rights, and stand firm.

An unethical invasive trend has developed, especially in family court, rising from the common claims that the "other" litigant in the conflict is "crazy." Psychological evaluations should be a responsible, objective measure provided to the court. However, they have too often become a fishing expedition into the litigant's mind by court appointed personnel that seriously suggests bias. If the judge orders and appoints a particular mental health professional, how often do they disagree with results provided by their appointees? How many of those evaluations are performed properly and ethically in view of the invisible disability? Unfortunately, I have witnessed flawed and biased evaluations left unchallenged by judges in cases that have hurt the very children the law intended to protect.

EC
GRL
H8S

Psychiatrists and psychologists must not be seen in a mystical light with litigants believing mental health professionals can analyze a litigant's mind. No one person can analyze the mind of another. Mental health professionals must rely on what is presented to them by the litigant and certain standardized tests. Such professionals have no magical key into a litigant's brain. It is important to approach psychological evaluations as you would any important negotiation. You need to know the qualifications of the evaluator, who the evaluator reports to, and the relationship between the mental health professional and the court. It is not impolite to challenge an appearance of a conflict of interest or insufficient qualifications (Courtois, 2006).

Many litigants quickly agree to psychological evaluations because they want to look cooperative, confident, and show the court that they have nothing to hide. Many of those same litigants later regret having been too willing to agree to psychological testing and find that the style of revelation of the results was secretive, damaging, and unfair. When the PC states that the litigant is crazy, it is not a qualified medical opinion nor are the lawyers and judges qualified to render a medical opinion. However, once the litigant has succumbed to examination by a mental health professional, it will be that forensically qualified person who will provide information to the court. In the event of a misdiagnosis, or damaging results due to using a wrong battery of tests for an LWD it will be expensive and difficult to challenge wrong opinions or inaccurate results.

There are many reasons for a person with PTSD to score with inaccurate results on psychological testing. One is the numbing caused by opioids released into the system blocking the litigant from responding with predicted emotion. Opioids produce a sense of numbness when the pain of trauma is overwhelming. This can elicit certain answers to questions that will seem emotionally blunted (Goleman, 1990). These hormonally driven answers risk being misinterpreted as indications of "personality disorder." The evaluator naively notes that the litigant doesn't "feel" normally in response to certain stimuli in the test. A personality disorder is the diagnostic area that suggests criminal behavior, borderline personality disorder, or disorders that cause one to have little conscience. It is a dangerous misdiagnosis.

Specialized Testing Required for Some Invisible Disabilities

I have patients who are being forced to repeat psychological testing more so in family court than other venues. Persons with disabilities many times cannot take standardized tests or the results are biased against them. For example, autistic litigants cannot be assessed by usual psychological evaluation. Forcing a disabled person through improper testing is highly discriminatory and denies access completely. No person can "prove" sanity. No testing is without severe limits and flaws. Much more valuable to the court is a behavioral analysis and a disability report as to the litigant's awareness and management of the disability. Further, behavioral analysis overcomes ethnic barriers in cases of language and cultural differences considering the immigration salad bowl that represents our current society. The behaviors of the litigant are more pertinent than intangible educated guesses that come from standardized psychological testing. It is assumed that custody evaluation accomplishes this. However, most custody evaluators are not trained behavior analysts and are vulnerable to hearsay, lobbying, and fundamental attribution error.

The more testing is repeated, the less accurate it will be. Keeping an unrelenting demand of psychological intrusion is a tactic used in court wars of attrition that prevent fair litigation. Before any assessment is agreed to in an adversarial environment the patient must feel free to insist upon the following:

A. Question issues of confidentiality. Reports submitted under the ADAAA are kept confidentially with the ADA Administration Office. Results of psychological testing are not to be made public and used as ammunition in an adversarial system. Unless you sign a release of information form, confidentiality is to be respected. Further, rapport with the psychiatrist or psychologist is critical to a thorough and valid report being compiled. There must be trust in the professional to abide by ethical and legal requirements and not be biased. If there is no atmosphere of trust, the results of the battery of tests will be skewed. The report should contain:

   1. the purpose of the examination including documentation of the patient's understanding of the purpose of the examination and appropriateness for the litigant's impairments,

   2. consent in writing by the patient to being examined,

   3. time and place of the examination and who pays for the evaluation,

   4. conclusions, reports, and all test results are to be given to the patient including raw data from testing,

   5. personal history will be and should be taken,

   6. psychiatric history should be taken,

   7. surrounding circumstances or the patient's involvement with the legal issues or situation without subjective judgment from examiner,

   8. results of mental status examination and psychological testing given to the patient in raw form, and the appropriateness of the battery of tests and

   9. diagnosis and impressions complete with prognosis and recommendations.

   10. the client may need accommodations for the testing process.

B. The ADA advocate must be allowed to be present sitting quietly out of the sight of the patient. Another health professional can substitute for the advocate as an observer if that is preferred. Again, the observer stays out of the patient's line of sight during the evaluation. I have observed many evaluations sitting well behind the client. Ethical professionals have never resisted my presence.

C. The report should be extremely accurate and objective regarding pertinent data in the form of a summary. Psychiatric symptoms, problems, and impairments are to be discussed without going into detailed discussion of psychodynamic factors.

D. Ensure that ADA and ADAAA reports are considered either in lieu of or at least alongside of the psychological evaluation. When a good ADA Report and Request is considered, we are finding that the ADA report has many times replaced the need for the court ordered psychological evaluation invasively demanded by an adversary. Since psychology is an inexact science, more weight needs to be put on the fact that no scientific research has ever proven that mental illness or injury alone interferes with parenting, employment, or independent living. Therefore, the path through psychological testing can easily become an egregious waste of resources with no sound basis for being ordered.

A Case Example of Using an ADA Assessment in Lieu of a Psychological Evaluation

Libby was in the throes of her adversary getting a court order forcing her to be evaluated by a specific evaluator. She refused to be tested by that evaluator and instead completed her evaluations for ADA Accommodations. Once her ADA Accommodations were approved and her confidential information was provided to the judge, he accepted that she had responsibly met the terms of the court order for psychological evaluation. The Judge wisely took into account that the litigant with a disability took responsibility for it and could articulate not only the disability but also what accommodations were needed for her effectiveness. What more would responsible psychological evaluations impart? The adversary's motion for contempt for not completing their biased psychological testing was denied.

The disabilities outlined in this book, related to stress, are usually situational. In other words, under some circumstances the litigant can function effectively even quite normally and is not symptomatic. Conversely, in stressful, threatening situations, the litigant becomes symptomatic. The demands of normal living are often met by the litigant remaining symptom free. Litigants with disabilities will need accommodations to allay symptoms during litigation due to the additional stress. Accommodations must be included during the surrounding depositions and accompanying meetings, mediations, and other legal activities as well. Most legal activities fall under ADA Title II, but some legal events will fall under the ADA Title III that covers private organizations serving the public.

Empowerment Section 3: Developing Legal Positions from Emotional Dynamics

Our society must continue to develop alternatives to litigation. Legal reform will not come fast enough to meet the needs of many who are being devastated in wars of attrition in our courts. Too much emotional need is left unfinished with our current family court model. The adversarial model routinely fails to serve the best interests of litigants with disabilities and devastates children and families. It clearly is more harmful than helpful in the win/lose power game when the adversarial system is used as a weapon. People in crisis do not need to enter additional conflict, expense, and adversity more than they already experience. Further, the stickler in the traumatized brain immersed in litigation is found in the physiology, a virtual internalized volcanic disruption can be caused by the methods of adversarial litigation.

The first problem is trying to fit the many dimensions involved in family dynamics and/or the challenges of special needs into a legal framework. The emotional, social, psychological, and cultural traditions of family life or dealing with a disability in our culture cannot be legalized. Yet, there are legal components to every divorce. After the court has determined whatever legal issue is appropriate, there are still underlying residual emotional dynamics that may be worsened.

Too often, these unresolved deeply personal dynamics play out tragically. Parents wind up in court for years on end motivated by what the court cannot and is not qualified to address. They struggle to fit personal interests into legal positions. The family assets are depleted, parental abductions take place, sometimes murder/suicides result from unbearable circumstances, depression is rampant, PTSD/LAS is added to the existing pain that brought the family to court in the first place, and crushing of ambition and careers comprise the fallout from forcing the court to do what it simply can't. Children's trust accounts are invaded for legal fees and costs and aged parents are mortgaging paid-for homes to help their children. The law is not the appropriate forum for assisting dysfunctional families to function better (Olson, 2009).

The courts guarantee each litigant the "right to zealous representation." However, that right often collides head on with ADAAA protection against discrimination and exploitation and the best interests of all litigants, especially the children. Confidential and sensitive information needed to bring cooperation, functionality, and health to a critical human conflict is sometimes twisted under the pretext of zealous representation. Lawyers are trained to attack the vulnerable person, which is tantamount to ripping the wheelchair out from under a paraplegic and then forcing them into a litigation foot race. The spoils of these ill-gotten gains represent loss of equal access to litigation and worsening of the disability by adding psychiatric injury only furthering the functional impairment of the litigant with a disability. Thus, through attrition, the grievances, appeals, and avenues for righting the wrong may be pushed out of the emotional reach of those with disabilities.

Children and those with disabilities need to be able to prepare for any stressful event. They must predict how they will respond in given situations. Proactive foresight is critical to providing for their needs to ensure that they do not become symptomatic destroying their effective participation. An extra burden exists for litigants and advocates in identifying what triggers symptoms and untoward behaviors and then arranging the experience to avoid those triggers. The court, as it stands, deals largely with history. LWDs need it to carefully deal with their present and future needs during litigation.

EC
GRL
H8S

Unfortunately, history is only one facet in dealing with the needs of human beings. For example, a family is an ever evolving, dynamic system of personalities and relationships interacting with a community and society as a whole. Parenting styles and methods change after a divorce and continue to adjust as children grow. A snippet of parenting evaluations and plans at the time of divorce is extremely inadequate to determine the futures of children. The traditional legal approach in family court requires a judgment of the family dynamic based on layers of data collection from persons with questionable qualifications, and little regulation of court appointees and decision makers, resulting in snapshot decisions that do not serve the best interest of the child or the accommodations for litigants with special needs.

Personal interests must not be ignored as part of legal disengagement. However, the pain of abandonment, rejection, feeling unloved, being insulted, downright devastated will not respond to a protective order or a judge's admonishment. Families are created to function in a milieu of privilege, sensitivity, and shared wellbeing. The morphing of a family into a win/lose business model alone is a stimulus for profound destruction. There must be a therapeutic facet, trusted by all members of the family apart from litigation.

Advocates assist in helping the litigants find this type of mitigating activity that helps to divide loss from abuse-born, forced insulting loss that breeds bitterness and revengeful feelings. Each advocate plays a critical role bringing the element of listening to the feelings of the players and then demanding dignity and safety for the litigants as well as opening doors to therapeutic interventions.

Different Perceptions–Where is the Error?

Families in conflict perceive the same situation very differently. In a significant twenty-five year longitudinal study of children of divorce, sixty California families of divorce were selected for study. Consistently, it was shown that the spouse who initiated the divorce perceived the children as adjusting well to the separation. The parent who disapproved of the divorce saw the children in crisis suffering from the separation. Rarely was divorce a mutual decision. This is the dynamic that most contributes to litigation strife (Wallerstein, 1996). Usually, neither parent is accurate. Mediation routinely fails to get to the underlying dynamics that feed protracted litigation through emotionally based perceptions. The courts, whether it is litigation or court ordered mediation, are not designed to sort out such problems.

The court needs to move in the direction of using research and evidence based science and not be vulnerable to junk science and unreliable evaluations and traditions. Awareness of Fundamental Attribution Error and efforts at quality correction of the record through data analysis can assist the trier of fact to adjudicate more fairly. Additionally, instead of favored court appointees, any state licensed professional of the litigant's choosing needs to be allowed to do analysis for the court. Court appointees present as biased and therefore do not enjoy the respect of the public.

Empowerment Section 4: Safety and Self-protection

The eventual goal is that the litigant with a disability is self sufficient and able to face their cases self-advocating. Litigants with disabilities are too often easy prey lacking sophistication in elements of basic self-protection. Thus extra steps need to be taken to assist LWDs to feel safe during litigation or the entire issue of justice is sacrificed. I am struck by the number of litigants who live in terror because of intimidation, intrusive behaviors, and the many ways an adversary can use the courts as tools of bullying and torment.

Additionally, lawyers use pretexts and their positions to invade and intimidate even the opponent's counsel. If the client does not feel safe, it has to be determined if the LWD is in physical danger v emotional danger. If there is physical risk inform the court, ask for protective orders and alert the police department. In the end, safety depends on the client taking every measure to protect self. Tell your clients:

1. Trust your instincts—If you suspect the adversary knows too much or has accessed information not made public, it is cause for alarm. Stalkers of all types can act in incredibly persistent and creative ways to maintain power and control through technological means. High tech is a stalker's dream play toy. Court is his theater.

2. Avoid the predictable—vary your actions, schedule, and habits.

3. Do not give your social security number out anywhere—ask why the entity needs it and arrange an alternative method of identification. Form an organization with a tax id number and use it.

4. Under a different identity—and address give to charities and do volunteer work Political parties and charities will publish information on the internet.

5. Plan for safety—Navigating violence, abuse, and stalking is very difficult and dangerous. Advocates at the National Domestic Violence Hotline encourage you to consult with them if you believe you are being stalked. Some litigants have even brought the matter to Homeland Security if their adversary is highly technologically savvy.

6. Avoid social networking sites and blogs—Stalkers mine search engines, blogs, social networks, organization web sites and public records, i.e. birth, marriage, death, legal, property ownership, vehicle licensing, drivers licenses, professional licenses, employment records, media announcements, directories for social, educational or any résumé's submitted online, leases for residency, credit and debit card or ATM data, utility bills, subscriptions, catalogs, store discount cards, product registrations, warranties, and contest entries.

7. Stalkers get information—Be aware of information brokers who mine and sell information or gain information under a pretext. Examples, Intelius, Acxiom, PeopleData, Veromi, and Docusearch. Answer no surveys or questions over the phone.

EC
GRL
H8S

8. Opt Out—The following link is a comprehensive list of organizations where you can opt out. This also helps to protect your HIPAA rights. http://www.privacyrights.org/ar/infobrokers-optout.htm

9. Lie on databases—Infuse inaccurate information into databases any time you can without compromising legal requirements or pertinent health information.

10. Use a safe computer—Change to a computer the abuser has no access to or has not used. You may wish to use a public computer at a library, community center, or internet café, or a friend or acquaintance's computer.

11. Create new email accounts on a regular basis—Use an anonymous name and account. Do not give accurate information about yourself when you set up accounts.

12. Check your cell phone settings—Keep your cell phone off when not in use. Do not use a phone provided by the abuser or adversary. Lock the keys on the cell phone so it does not automatically answer.

13. Change passwords and pin numbers often—Change passwords & pin numbers everywhere using nothing that is familiar with you.

14. Do not use cordless phones or any device that broadcasts widely, like a baby monitor—Use donated cell phones if discussing sensitive information preventing a phone log to be connected with you. Contact your local hotline program to learn about donation programs that provide new cell phones and/or prepaid phone cards to victims of abuse and stalking.

15. Check your records often—Many court systems and Government agencies are publishing records to the Internet and have records on you open to the public.

16. Ask every organization and agency how they protect or publish your records—Request that your court, Government, post office records and other public agencies seal or restrict access to your files to protect your safety.

17. Use a private mailbox and don't give out your real address—When asked by businesses, doctors, and others for your address, have a private mailbox address or a safer address to give them. Try to keep your true residential address out of national databases. Have someone do a Google search for your name in the internet at least twice per week.

18. Check phone directory—Remove your name and any printed information (sometimes even unlisted names will show up on phone directories.)

19. Computer monitoring software—Check for computer monitoring software on any computer used or "SpyWare" as it is sometimes called. VERY IMPORTANT THIS TYPE OF SOFTWARE CAN BE INSTALLED REMOTELY. THE ABUSER DOES NOT HAVE TO HAVE PHYSCIAL ACCESS TO YOUR COMPUTER. There are no reliable programs that remove this type of monitoring software. Do not trust them and do not put private information out over your computer.

20. Keystroke logging hardware—It can be inserted between the keyboard cable and the back of the computer. They are really small hard drives that record every key typed, including all passwords, personal identification numbers (PIN), websites, and email. Installation of this device does require physical access to the computer.

21. Email & instant messages—Every type of identity theft and pretext is used through email and IM. You can be threatened, you can be impersonated, and your private information is mined. Don't believe that deleting an item leaves it untraceable. Email is vulnerable with no protection we can find.

22. Don't be Bluffed into signing anything—Attorneys will bluff you that you have to be deposed or to give privileged information. They will use intimidating tactics. Don't fall for it and take the bait. Stand firm that your privacy is to be protected. Don't believe attorneys when they say a law forces you to put your privacy or safety at risk. For HIPAA Privacy information go to www.HHS.Gov.

23. Don't be Bluffed out of your accommodations. The court will say, "You don't need an accommodation for breaks, video or audio recording, telephone appearances or whatever you have requested." The court allows them without ADA accommodations. However, if you are not approved through the ADA Administration, the opposition can object and have a say. Then you risk being slowly stripped of your needed accommodations as the trial proceeds. You have a right to ADA; so, do not compromise.

24. Caller ID—Cancel caller identification that provides the name and number of the caller. Some even provide the address of the caller. If your adversary gets a hold of your telephone, your social history is available.

25. Fax Machines—Do not put a header or the correct date on your fax machine. Abusers and stalkers use the fax header on faxed documents to locate their victims.

26. TTY/TTD Teletypewriters (TTY) and Telecommunications Devices for the Deaf (TTD) are text based telephones—People who are deaf or hard of hearing use to communicate that can record and save the history of conversations.

27. Never assume you are not being recorded. Video key chains, buttons, pens, and a host of spy equipment can be purchased online and must be assumed to be everywhere. (ABA/DOJ webinar, 2009)

EC
GRL
H8S

List any of the above you have been subjected to and the inconvenience of protecting yourself. Put a price on it. These are part of the litigant's damages.

Empowerment Section 5: Making the Decision to Quit Litigation

Each day has a value, lessons to be learned, principles to be reinforced, joy to be sought, meaning to be realized, and health to be maintained and protected. Whenever you decide to quit litigation, I respect your decision. However, it is best if the cessation of litigation is a decision and not a reaction. Many cases die of attrition. So, you are not alone when you can't fight any more or the means to fight are exhausted.

Before quitting, it is crucial to return to the protocols. Review reframing and debriefing all the while identifying where resilience has weakened. Usually, repeating exercises from Huffer's 8-Steps resuscitates the dignity, determination, and desire to continue. There is a time to quit but it must be a wise decision made timely to enhance the person's situation. Clients must never be forced out of their courts because emotionally, financially, or physically, they are denied equal access to their public services.

The worst cases are those wherein one party desperately wants to end the litigation; however, their adversary is a controller of the PC type who is determined to ruin them financially and emotionally. They keep the litigation pressure on regardless of the disabled litigant's efforts to stop it. Unfortunately, the aged, those with disabilities, and the poor are the most vulnerable to these kinds of motives.

PC corporations will persevere with litigation to ensure that the litigant is wiped out to the point that they are no longer a threat. A great deal of spying and intrusion is done by ethically challenged law firms and private investigators they hire. They cross boundaries denying their target sanctuary and equal access to the court further traumatizing the victim. They dive into privileged relationships and confidential data demanding access to protected information. All belief that your doctor/patient relationship and lawyer/client relationship is sacred is dashed further crippling the litigant's ability to function effectively when violations of privacy succeed.

These events provide opportunity for the advocate to listen while revisiting the debriefing skill. ADA advocates can focus on the following two points: 1) If the quality of life is improved by quitting, then it might be time. 2) However, if quitting causes the client to writhe in bitterness and anger feeling an awful sense of unfinished business, then it is probably time to change strategy or the method of the fight but not time to quit.

Some People Are Incompatible with the Judicial System

Could you perform your work in the middle of a surgical suite with blood and innards surrounding you while you tried to concentrate? Most judges, lawyers, and court personnel stop and think when I ask this question. Yet, the courtroom is as repelling and viscerally intolerable to some individuals as an active surgical suite is to others. Adversarial litigation is incompatible with CC's who like to discuss matters fairly and cooperate in a milieu of respect, dignity, and trust. Therefore, before any disability is considered, some people need help to block out certain stimuli from the surroundings before they can function. Accommodations allow that such LWDs are afforded distance appearance, by telephone, Skype, or to be in the courthouse in a separate room videoed into the courtroom.

What make the litigant "tick?" What can be adjusted environmentally that will improve their chances of a fair hearing? Advocates and litigants must identify their incompatibilities. If litigants do not move beyond their feelings of helplessness and court devastation, there is immediate risk that the litigant's normal support system will become frustrated and leave the litigant isolated. Internalization of ever-increasing trauma to basically gentle souls is common and very dangerous. Gentle people have a hard time doing the aggressive actions that hurt the adversary even when the adversary desperately deserves it. CC litigants would never, in their own belief system, engage in the types of behaviors that they are now forced to contend with in a win/lose adversarial environment.

It is vital to justice to be aware that these gentle souls have suffered a psychic injury that is a normal result of abnormal circumstances not to be mischaracterized as a personality disorder or a mental illness. An example of the mischaracterization of an abuse victim would be in a setting whereby a gang rape of a teenager occurred; certainly, the adolescent would show extreme symptoms as a result of the trauma. This in no way indicates the rape victim to be mentally ill, simply traumatized. To add yet another layer of dysfunction to the suffering already incurred is, in every sense, to re-victimize the sufferer for being human and showing human trauma reaction.

Trust needs to be learned again. Litigants with LAS must start as an infant does in learning to trust the environment, checking each relationship for integrity, and non-gratuitous behavior. Once you have identified your relationships that are filled with integrity and true concern for your wellbeing, you take a huge risk and trust again. It won't be a blind trust. You will check and verify, but in your life are those who truly love you and have earned a position of trust.

Empowerment Section 6: Ethics Leading the Way—Making a Difference

In 1982, The Supreme Court identified an ethical challenge. In Griggs v. Duke Power Company (Appendix B) The Supreme Court described "built-in systemic headwinds", obstacles used in employment discrimination preventing a target group of individuals from equal oportunity for advancement. Persons with disablilities are often greeted by built-in system headwinds as they seek accommodations.

The following objectives align with the standard of care for LWDs under ADAAA overcoming obstacles in the system (Appendix B):

1. Identify and effectively treat stressors caused by litigation, intimidation, and adversarial experiences or bullying.

2. Manage internal symptoms of traumatic stress helping LWDs cope with injustice.

3. Respond skillfully to unfounded accusations, ethical violations, manipulation, and lawsuits.

4. Give advice regarding the Americans with Disabilities Act within professional ethical boundaries (ABA, 2010).

5. Mitigate disputes using Huffer's 8-step process plus therapeutic mitigation (Chapter 17).

EC
GRL
H8S

6. Manage filings with court administrations assisting all personnel to never be induced or misled into violations of HIPAA Laws, ADAAA or privacy protections during legal processes.

7. Skillfully manage confidential information and protect self during sworn testimony, in powers of attorney, affidavits, and advance directives.

8. Create safeguards for informed consent, confidentiality, and subpoenas.

9. Know limits and range of expert witness testimony (Weinstein, 1999).

10. Provide greater patient/client accessibility to services utilizing the Americans with Disabilities Act.

11. Recognize the role that power differential plays in ethical violations.

12. Be a leader serving on committees, boards, and forums that create and enforce ethics.

Questions for Refreshing an Ethical Stance

1. How do you recognize an ethical issue? It is an ethical issue if there is a choice that could result in a potential wrong, a conflict, or situation that could damage people or the community. Ethics are about human beings improving the quality of their interactions. Ethics also loom larger than the law or an institution. It profoundly affects people's dignity, rights, hopes, inspiration, and ability to improve an empathic life with one another.

2. How do you define and create your ethical stance? Study the relevant facts, the history, and the potential risks to the quality of human life. Consider the influences on each side of the issue. What groups are affected and what do they have at stake? What individuals are affected? What do they need? Finally, reach the quiet meditative place inside you and listen to your pre-reflective intuitions. Instantaneous moral intuitions or pre-reflective intuitions are unexamined conscience-based responses to behavioral choices. Unlike the law, ethical codes of professional behavior draw directly from our moral intuitions. A legitimate way to test ethical principles is to connect your deep internal reaction to the ethical issue at hand. Then consider the end goal or outcome while balancing your personal principles of fairness and honesty. Hadfield's work claims that the synchronization of behaviors happens within 50 milliseconds (1994). In fact, almost all individuals respond to their environment in very measurable ways—often cited as changes in heart rate, blood pressure, skin conductance, muscle activity, motor behavior, and autonomic system activity that is shaped according to emotion (Bloom, 1998). These are pre-reflective intuitions, "gut" feelings. Ethics tap intuition, professional judgment, courage, character, and a commitment to place the client's or patient's well being above or at least equal to self-interest. Humaneness, the subjective moral side of values, has waned over the past decades. However, personal investment in deeply caring about their careers and contributions is not dispensable for most professionals;

yet, it is being in some instances disregarded as an important facet of professional practice. Objectifying the consumers in systems of care is usually done reluctantly and defensively by the professional out of fear of liability, being professionally intimidated, or attempts to control the paperwork history that affects appeals, accreditations or evaluations.

3. How do you decide which actions to recommend or follow?After acknowledging "gut" intuition, evaluate alternative actions reflecting various moral and ethical perspectives (reflective sense) and answer which option will produce the most good and do the least harm. Be aware of cognitive dissonance from demands that conflict with the LWD's ethical stance or the advocate's. A major challenge lies in how to communicate disagreement when confronted by power differential (employers, media, hidden agenda that goes against your "gut." The temptation is to bend your ethics–called the agentic shift, when ethics are progressively related. "If the organization bends rules, so can I."

4. As an ethics leader how do you evaluate the process that determines the content of a professional ethical code?Give the matter time and observe. Ask yourself if the process is empathic, pure and fair? The process is the key and must be preserved with integrity. Are the rights and dignity of each individual respected? And, does the process encourage the participants to involve themselves more in the future without fear or dread?

5. Can you be ethical without being taught an ethical code?An established ethical code helps to promote consistency in the behaviors of the group but is less important than doing the right thing. In fact, many ethical people in this world do the right thing without ever having studied ethics or working under a formal ethical code.

6. How does a professional adhere to limitations posed by ADAAA and HIPAA yet offer ADA accommodations for LWDs? A lawyer, other professional or advocate cannot properly ask if the person has a disability. Therefore, a professional is better off preparing a document as part of an engagement handout or agreement inviting a person with disabilities to confidentially consider disclosing limited medical information if they need ADA Accommodations.

7. What is ethical relativism? It is a decline in ethical standards due to non enforcement that slowly lowers expectations until the behaviors formerly prohibited are more and more accepted among the members of a group. Examples are: When changes occur rapidly as is the case in the modern world of technology, it is found that professions avoid identifying a standard of care largely due to the climate surrounding legal liability. Examples are 1) the current CPR "guidelines" that move away from the term "standards" by the American Heart Association due to fear of creating a legal vulnerability conveying a legal obligation; 2) the ADAAA took effect in 2009 and has no established standard of care and the weakened enforcement of ethics suggested by the American Bar Association by stating that many of

EC
GRL
H8S

the standards are "aspirational only" (Black's, 1991).

8. If it is legal, it is ethical. Laws do not supersede ethics. California courts established that involvement in nonviolent civil disobedience acts does not exclude a person from a professional license and "would ultimately deny the community of many highly qualified persons of high moral courage" (California State Bar, 1966). Many acts of civil disobedience are tied to values, morals, and ethics.

Ethical Relativism, a Scary Trend

In order for professional ethics to thrive, a cultural covenant of good faith and fair dealing has to be protected. Phil Zimbardo, Professor Emeritus at Stanford University, states that a cucumber cannot stay sweet in a barrel of vinegar. However, if you are the cucumber, you know if you are slowly being pickled.

What if the community agenda is tainted or corrupted? Listen to the news, read the paper. Chicanery, fraud for profit is becoming tolerated as expected corporate and professional behavior. The Judicial System does not ensure a civilized path to justice or endorsement of right over wrong. Every day litigants are disoriented in legal proceedings by having their "apples" not only called but also adjudicated to be "oranges" with grave consequences.

Ethical relativism refers to an act being considered right or wrong whenever the majority in any given society accepts it as "the way it is." If the majority accepts it (or endures it or perceives that it is endured), it becomes informally approved. If a certain distasteful behavior is forced upon a population for a lengthy period of time, the population adapts to the cruelty or abuse. Today's media promotes illusion portraying public perception of popular approval even if the majority does not agree. Ethical relativism exists in the form of consumer rights violations becoming commonplace; however, ethical relativism, as understood here, is not a valid ethical principle and is not to be promoted as such.

Creating an Ethical Stance

In a predatory business environment, fear of lawsuits motivates many decisions as to the policies that dictate professional behavior. Health and legal professionals are pulled two ways at the same time determining self-protective policies while maintaining the highest level of care for their clients and patients. The following are challenges that professionals face as they attempt to provide a crisp statement of mission and ethical policies while attending to that deep moral fiber that resonates beneath all ethical decisions.

Ethics are created either by considering the result or by giving weight to the means to an end. Regardless of intellectual or philosophical view, public trust is the central issue when considering an ethical code. Safeguards, (ethical codes) of public trust recommend, but do not guarantee an individual's behavior.

1. Ethical violations can be extremely intimate and subtle. Intimate unethical behavior will be felt as a betrayal, an assault in that secret chamber in the heart and gut that wounds your very soul.

2. Ethical violations can be blatant having broad societal impact. Larger impact usually stems from greed-driven unethical behavior. Such unethical behavior may ride in on a credit card contract alteration in light and fine print written in tiny letters, buried in gray language. Or, it can be fraud, misinformation about you used in a court of law or another forum to tarnish your character.

3. Ethics can be violated in a moment of carelessness or poor judgment. We live in a time of rampant violations by professionals, government officials, clergy, institutions and shockingly by those who are trusted as professionals, conscience-oriented people with clean motives. Abiding by "political correctness" and following our leaders' examples can be dangerous. Adhering to the concept of political correctness can even lead to cover ups. Some unethical behavior emanates from carelessness, ignorance of professional obligations, or simple mistakes with no evil intent. Nevertheless, the recipient of the unethical behavior will feel profoundly betrayed and will suffer damages.

4. Ethics can be violated, strategically planned, and carefully executed over time.

5. Ethics violations cannot be predicted. The Stanford Prison Experiment- Professor Zimbardo's Prison Experiment shocked the consciences of behavioral scientists the world over. He could not have predicted the transformations in character that took place during the experiment he created many years ago that randomly assigned healthy, normal intelligent college students to play the roles of prisoners or guards in a projected 2 week-long study. He was forced to terminate the study after only 6 days because it went out of control. Pacifists were becoming sadistic guards, and normal kids were breaking down emotionally. The best and brightest of our young people succumbed to egregious behaviors causing harm simply by being placed in an experimental "vat of vinegar" of a prison environment.

Trust Is a Motivating Factor Encouraging Ethical Behavior in Professions and Institutions

Professionals are trusted to facilitate positive change within their expertise. When one group of humans dictates or endeavors to change another's behavior, it is of ethical and moral concern and great responsibility exists.

EC
GRL
H8S

Trust is a social staple. Processes set up to enforce ethical behaviors cannot be underestimated. Enforcement processes that are fair and that effectively maintain ethical, responsible, and lawful behaviors must protect the most vulnerable in society.

It is thought that the threat of a lawsuit strikes fear in the heart regardless of the circumstances. However, it is the irrationality of the current justice system, in an atmosphere of huge financial burden that terrorizes the population. The Judicial System in the United States is extremely fragile. It can be corrupted; it can be misused as a weapon to destroy a professional person simply by a complainant filing a false action against him or an LWD suffering from an impairment.

An ethical violation cannot occur in a vacuum. Ethics refers to how human beings treat one another within systems of accountability. However, if the system for accountability becomes compromised in any way, the process fails leaving the ethical codes to have no meaning and offering no substantive guide or protection for ethical professionals. Power motivated organizations lobby the regulatory boards, agencies, legislatures, and try to pro-actively influence decisions that impact their profits and growth. In such cases, ethical and legal codes are violated and the good of the public is compromised. A part of every ethics training needs to address this dilemma.

The leader in ethics design and enforcement must consider the impact of ethical violations on every level of social intercourse.

Huffer's Log

Case Example of the Power of Background Emotions

Georgia's story, told below, illustrates invisible forces that dominate much of what occurs in courtrooms today. The advocate is sometimes the only observer truly privy to the effects of what Damasio calls "Background Emotions" (52). Without a word being spoken, when a hearing begins, it is actually possible to detect a state of being of the litigants, the attorneys, and even the judge. Each will emit some aura, some sense of being stressed, tense, relaxed, confident, edgy, unsure, worried, exhibited by subtle details. If one reads the litigant's body posture, hand movements, eye focus and movement, facial movements, and breathing, the general essence of those facing off in court can be perceived. Those emotions often dictate the outcome of the proceedings more than the words that are written and spoken. The ADA advocate is trained to perceive background emotions, especially in the client. The less stress the litigant succumbs to in the courtroom the more they can accurately perceive the influence of background emotions around them.

Georgia suffers from bi polar disorder, ADHD, and Tourette's Syndrome. Before having an advocate, she began her part of the court proceedings by blurting out in the direction of her ex-husband and his attorney, "Screw You Hamburger Face!" The court did not know she had a disorder and punished her severely ordering terminating sanctions (her case was virtually wiped out) and even removed her children from her custody. She was "punished" by the court for her symptoms. Everything she valued in her life went down like dominoes from that day forward. She lost her home. She has been unable to work. She lost her doctors and now cannot afford medication so her symptoms are worsened.

Once Georgia found an Advocate, her disability was properly defined to the ADA Administrative office of the Court. The accommodations were approved and the court was apprised of her medical conditions. The advocate designed accommodations to assist Georgia. Georgia was able to sustain her court dates without losing control by exiting at times to either take a break or allow the advocate to fill in for her momentarily. It became easy to read opposing counsel's behavior using the concept of background emotions. He would become agitated in his seat forewarning that he was about to jump up to ask to make a comment designed to elicit an impulsive response from Georgia.

The advocate would alert Georgia and then interrupt opposing counsel's momentum. At that point, the Judge worked very well with the advocate. The advocate would signal the Judge that Georgia needed a break and sometimes as issues were winding up and her stress level was high, Georgia would exit to the hallway and her advocate would communicate Georgia's words for her. However, a great deal of damage had already been done to Georgia and her case that put her at a disadvantage. So, the first items at hand were undoing the terrible wrongs that had been done.

It helps that Georgia is very bright and, although she cannot afford an attorney, she intellectually understands legal procedure. She researches and is able to substantially contribute to her case. But, when a court date begins and she has to face her ex-husband and his attorney, she cannot control her emotions or words without serious accommodations. Her ex-husband and his legal counsel are continually and impatiently scrutinizing Georgia when she sets foot in the courtroom. The lawyer chooses the most prickly, sensitive topics and sends them like verbal arrows to pierce Georgia's heart, her brain, and to challenge her conditions. He gores her, baiting her so she will spout off again. When this process begins, the advocate must be on alert to insist upon respect and dignity for the client and identify the best moment that a break from the proceedings is needed for review of the skills. A moment in the hallway might be taken to do quick reframing. The advocate checks to see if the litigant is staying with the plan for the day. Also, discrimination and exploitation need to be revealed to the judge through data analysis and correction of misinformation. Otherwise, the litigant is subject to a flawed judgment through fundamental attribution error/Correspondence Bias.

Case Example of a Deadly Result of Uncorrected Misinformation in the Court

Molly shot and killed her ex-husband. He had stalked, abused, terrorized, and threatened her for nearly two years. She caught him masturbating in front of their 18-month-old daughter. She tried to get away from him and protect the child, but he was allowed to have the child for unsupervised visitation. Molly finally met with her now ex-husband and they worked out that he would terminate his parenthood if he did not have to pay child support.

He was facing jail time for domestic violence and for some hearings he could not even show up to court because of warrants out for his arrest. Finally, she felt that she and their daughter could be safe. She came to court with the agreement to be approved and watched a visiting judge who had no understanding of the terror she and the child lived under slowly undo the agreement. When court was over, the father told Molly that he had hired someone to kill her.

Molly bought a gun, one box of bullets, and learned to shoot. She did not know who would be coming out of the shadows to kill her also endangering her mother who helped care for their daughter and child. One day when transitioning the child to her ex-husband, he said. "Wait just a minute. I am going to put a bullet in your head." She knew he carried a gun in his vehicle. He turned toward his truck and she reports only having a loud noise in her ears. She shot him with one bullet out of the one box she had bought. Then, she went to the police and reported that she had hurt him. They found him dead.

Three separate mental health professionals determined that this was self-defense. She had no intent to ever kill anyone. When trial came it was miserably handled and she was sent to prison for murder. The child was given to the father's family. The court did not call one of her mental health witnesses. No one testified as to her traumatized mental state. The jury did not know of the undoing of the agreement by a visiting judge that had no knowledge of the history of the case. The judge inadvertently protected the father's rights to stalk, abuse, visibly sexually abuse by masturbating in front of the child, threaten Molly's life, and break into her home taking what he wanted whenever he had the urge.

She did not want her ex-husband to die, just be held accountable for his behavior. Molly needed to mother her child in reasonable safety. The judge needed to do his homework. In cases where behaviors are questionable and litigants have worked out agreements, more information is needed for the court that cannot be perceptually perverted by judicial personnel. Unarguable facts are the answer.

Behavior analysis is a system for observing and reporting behaviors objectively. This method offers an avenue for more clear information to be garnered and put before the court. Laying this information out graphically eliminates or at least minimizes some of the negative legal games that are inherent in forcing the round pegs of human behavioral/medical issues and complex family systems into the square hole of the legal system. A Behavioral Analyst graphs actual behaviors in various targeted environments. The analyst is able to report irrefutable behaviors along with insights and recommendations to the court as expert recommendations.

Case Examples of a Contrived Legal Position Creating Fundamental Attribution Error

Case example 1, Carol came to a Behavioral Analyst broken and beaten by the legal system protracted litigation over ten years. She was forced to sell her home to pay the attorneys. She had been insulted and left terrified when she needed critical information from the schools regarding her son. He suffers from multiple disabilities needing a host of special services. She was shocked when the faculty treated her as if she had no right to her son's information. Unbeknownst to her, her ex-husband, who had severely abused her, flooded the schools and community with the slanderous story that she had abandoned her son and was disreputable. Every time she petitioned the court for help, she was considered "hysterical" by the court after the recycled degrading misinformation was put onto the court record causing her to break down with her symptoms of PTSD. Worry about her son forced her into a terrified state as the court forced her to turn her child over to the abuser.

She had to relocate out of state with her parents to regain some footing and control over her life. Her ex-husband would not help her financially and so severely damaged her reputation in the community that she could not get work. She fled the area hoping to set up a peaceful and therapeutic environment for herself and her son. Her ex-husband got temporary residential control of the child even though Carol maintained custody during her move. That was her big mistake. She pled her case to the court for five years to move the child to be with her in another state, each time being denied.

After ten years, Carol has a good job as a medical professional. She is well established in her new community and decided to change her strategy. She did not rely on the attorneys to tell the truth in court. Carol realized that she suffered from PTSD as a result of the domestic violence. She knew she would need ADA accommodations. Carol hired expert witnesses in the mental health field to present to the court the actual hard facts about her son's needs and the advantages to him moving to live with her.

The Behavioral Analyst conducted a comprehensive behavioral study of the child, the parents, and the environments. This assessment explored all aspects of the environments of this child. The school environment, each parent's home, and how the child reacted in community settings with each parent were personally observed. Teachers and parents were observed and asked to document the child's behaviors in graphic form.

This analyst compiled a comprehensive report for the court detailing the behaviors of the child in the abuser's environment and the behaviors of the child in the mother's environment. The analyst testified as to the exact methods the abuser used to reinforce the inappropriate and acting out behaviors of the child in his environment. Due to his disability, this information is critical to him being socialized and able to function socially. The analyst provided evidence from school records demonstrating that this father did not effectively intervene when the child endangered himself or others. On the other hand, behavior analysis distinguished for the court that this mother extinguished the child's negative behaviors, which had decreased in the mother's environment. This testimony could not be argued. It was based on actual proof (behavior reports from school) and not on hearsay evidence, psychological theory, or a visiting judge's inaccurate impression.

Additionally, the behaviors can and will continue to be documented in both environments by a trained behavior analyst. This information clearly must be in place if there is further litigation. Behavioral Analysis takes the matter completely out of the "he said/she said" realm that wearies the courts. High conflict individuals use children as pawns in the court system. They may claim that the other (victimized) parent is causing the child to act out inappropriately. This was the accusation that Carol's ex-husband claimed when he repeatedly reported, "The child has begun to be physically and verbally aggressive at school because the mother keeps dragging me back into court." Meanwhile the behavior analyst was able to document how permissive and passive dad was regarding inappropriate behavior, which reinforced the child's acting out behavior. In this case, the child called other kids in his class, "dummies." Dad laughed with the child, instead of quelling the mean behavior. The Behavioral Analyst waited to hear from the dad, "Do not call your classmates this name again." No correction was forthcoming. This is the pertinent information that cannot be manipulated and is needed by the Trier of Fact.

Consequently, the analyst recommended that the child be allowed to relocate with the mother. Additionally, the analyst recommended that the child have a trained behavior analyst work at the father's home and continue to document behaviors, to help train the father ensuring that the father will reduce his reinforcement of the child's acting out behaviors. This analyst was able to diminish lies and speculation from the court hearing. The court heard the evidence and the facts, not the father's accusations, or the attorney's accusations.

Behavior analysis is a researched profession. These professionals demonstrate to companies, parents, and institutions how wanted or unwanted behaviors are being reinforced, thereby increasing the probability that the behavior will be repeated. The evidence is clear, when a behavior is rewarded, the probability is that behavior will increase.

Case Example of a Contrived Legal Position to Serve Personal Interest

Many cases that come to court are based upon emotion and issues that are not legal in nature. The pretext of some legality may be merely contrived. Sam was a successful businessman. His former wife petitioned the court several times for an increase in alimony. Sam hired accountants and attorneys who took his money and were not able to help show the court reasons to deny an increase in alimony. Each time the court awarded an increase in alimony it directly diminished the quality of Sam's life to the point that today he lives in a state of depression. Sam is being held hostage by the court and his former wife.

Sam needs to hire a behavior analyst. This analyst would be able to present to the court the motivation behind the court petitions. Were her trips to Paris necessary? Were the spa weekends necessary? The analyst could also show the court, the pattern that has emerged demonstrating that each time they award this type of domestic piracy, they are increasing the probability of the former wife asking for modification based upon want rather than need. The court appears to award her a treat each time she petitions. All the while, Sam is punished by being robbed of his creativity, his incentive to grow financially, and to be all he can be in his life.

Case Example of Being Bluffed by Defense Counsel

Dagmar Reframes and then participates in activities through the City Parks and Recreation that are free allowing her to expose her skills. She led some sessions for no pay in a healing Legal Abuse Syndrome group. Dagi persevered in the court, used the ADA for accommodations along with all of her wit and skills, and she was finally awarded custody of her children. At this point, the entire criminal matter should have been reversed because the new judge obviously did not take the original charge of child abduction (as her ex-husband accused after the children ran away) seriously or he would not have granted her custody. Further, all the papers that support her arrest have been "lost" by the DA so there is no legal documentation as to why

Dagi was arrested in the first place. She is finding that no matter what evidence surfaces after a plea, that it is nearly impossible to get the plea reversed.

Dagmar's strength remains in her ability to reframe, socialize, and reach out. She takes each negative and is able to reframe so her basic self stays intact. She is empowering herself through networking. However, those dark, sad eyes still reveal that she has emotionally been forced into places that no human being should experience.

Dagi has learned that once a person admits to a crime whether guilty or not, it is extremely hard to undo. She continues to file papers trying to extricate herself from the false posture as a felon where she is stuck. The prosecuting attorney threatened Dagi with 7 years of prison if she did not sign a plea bargain. She counted on a trial to show her innocence and the absurdity of the situation. Dagi did not intend to admit to something she did not do. The public defender replied that none of her witnesses would be allowed to testify. Their testimonies were considered "irrelevant". Domestic violence and child abuse issues were "irrelevant" and not to be brought up during the trial. He told her she would not be allowed to present her case.

If she signed a "West Plea", her public defender explained, it was a plea that meant she had not admitting to committing the crime. Never thinking that he was deceiving her, she signed the West Plea. When she "woke up" to reality, she realized that she was now an admitted felon. The public defender had manipulated and conned her. She was placed on probation for 5 years for a crime she had never committed. In desperation, she sought to appeal the West Plea but found out that by signing she had given up all rights to appeal. That false felony destroyed her career as a Ph.D. in Natural Health.

References

American Bar Association Commission on Domestic Violence, in collaboration with the United States Department of Justice, Office on Violence Against Women (OVW). (n.d.). *Tips and Strategies in Protecting Victim Privacy, Representing LGBT Victims and Representing Victims With Disabilities/Cyber-Abuse and Civil Protection Orders* [Webinar #07782]. Retrieved April 29, 2009, from http://www.abanet.org/domviol.

American Bar Association Standing Committee on Ethics and Professional Responsibility. (2009-2010). *Model Rules of Professional Conduct*. Chicago: ABA Pub.

Americans with Disabilities Act Amendments Act of 2008, 42 U.S.C. §§ 12101 *et seq.*

CELDF: Community Environmental Legal Defense Fund. (2002). *PA Township Bans Corporate Involvement in Governing*. Retrieved from http://www.ReclaimDemocracy.org.

Bazelon, D. JD. David L. Bazelon Center for Mental Health Law: Retrieved from http://www.bazelon.org.

Berardinelli, D., JD. (2008). *From Good Hands to Boxing Gloves: The Dark Side of Insurance.* (pp. 15). Portland, OR: Trial Guides LLC.

Bernstein, B. E., & Hartwell, T. Jr. JD. (2000). *The Portable Ethicist for Mental Health Professionals: An A-Z Guide to Responsible Practice*. New York: John Wiley & Sons.

Black's Law Dictionary. (1991). (6th ed.). St Paul, MN: West Publishing Co.

Bloom, S., & Reichert, M. (1998). *Bearing Witness: Violence and Collective Responsibility.* (pp. 17). NY: The Haworth Maltreatment and Trauma Press.

EC
GRL
H8S

Bodenhamer, G. (1992). *Back In Control.* (pp. 47-50). New York: Simon & Schuster.

Citizens United v. Federal Election Commission, 558 U.S. 08-205 (2010).

Courtois, C., & Ford, J. (eds.). (2009). *Treating Complex Traumatic Stress Disorders: An Evidence-Based Guide.* (pp. 16, 90). New York: Guilford Press.

Damasio, A. (1999). The Feeling of What Happens: Body and Emotion in the Making of Consciousness. (pp. 35-37, 52). New York: Harcourt Brace.

Daniels, N. (1997). *Justice and justification: Reflective equilibrium in theory and practice.* Cambridge: Cambridge University Press.

Goleman, D. (1990, June). Key to Post Traumatic Stress Lies in Brain Chemistry, Scientist Find. New York Times. Retrieved from http://www.nytimes.com/1990/06/12/science/a-key-to-post-traumatic-stress-lies-in-brain-chemistry-scientists-find.html?scp=1&sq=Key%20to%20Post%20Traumatic%20Stress%20Lies%20in%20Brain%20Chemistry,%20Scientist%20Find&st=cse.

Hadfield, G. K. (2010). Higher Demand, Lower Supply? A Comparative Assessment of the Legal Landscape for Ordinary Americans. *Fordham Urban Law Journal*, 129.

Health Insurance Portability and Accountability Act of 1996 (HIPAA), 42 U.S.C. § 300gg *et seq.*

Huffer, K., & Alexander, J. (2007). Huffer/Alexander Longitudinal Survey. Appendix.

Olson, K. B. (2009). Family Group Conferencing and Child Protection Mediation: Essential Tools for Prioritizing Family Engagement in Child Welfare Cases. Family Court Review: Association of Family and Conciliation Courts. *47 Fam. Ct. Rev. 53*, 203-215.

Sandberg, J., & Juth, N. (2010. June 11). Ethics and Intuitions: A Reply to Singer. *Journal of Ethics*.

Scalia, A., & Garner, B. (2008). Making your Case: The Art of Persuading Judges. (pp. 1-5). New York: Thomson West.

Sheard, M. (2010). Mental Toughness: The mindset behind sporting achievement. (pp. 197-204). New York: Psychology Press.

Studdert, D. M., et al. (2005, June 1). Defensive Medicine Among High-Risk Specialist Physicians in a Volatile Malpractice Environment, *Journal of the American Medical Association, 293(21)*.

Tersman, F. (2008). The reliability of moral intuitions: A challenge from neuroscience. Australasian. *Journal of Philosophy 86(3)*, 389–405.

Wallerstein, J., & Kelly, J. B. (1996). *Surviving the Breakup: How Children and Parents Cope with Divorce.* (pp. 235-9). New York: Basic Books.

Weinstein, J. B. (1999). Expert witness testimony: a trial judge's perspective. *Neurology Clin, 17*, 355-362.

Zimbardo, P. (2007). The Lucifer Effect: Understanding How Good People Turn Evil. (pp. 320-1). New York: Random House Trade Paperbacks.

CHAPTER 15

RECOVERY: HUFFER'S STEP-8 TRAUMA OVERRIDDEN

Huffer's Step-8, Recovery, orchestrates the healing protocols into a rhythm of self-assertion and skilled management of trauma in the face of abuse, injustice, anywhere at any time. This last step in the 8-step therapeutic set of protocols soothes and redirects the brain while undergoing re-traumatization. Each protocol helps to retrain the brain to override the limbic system bringing the LWD to Recovery, that path where brain function is guided toward normalization. It is achieved by the LWD being empowered, treated with kindness, supported, and coached through the toughest of human circumstances. All protocols are potentiated by the CADAAs forcing fair legal processes under the ADAAA law. Recovery reflects a skilled way of living that allows the LWD to release internal negative forces that disrupt affect and cause physical symptoms. That release, while different from forgiveness, does not preclude it. As the fabric of recovery and healing are woven, henceforth and broadened into society, one major ideal of a civilized society looms large on the horizon. Humans treating each other as they would wish to be treated winds up being the targeted ideal as the judicial system moves toward the "Court of the Future."

We promise justice, but we deny access. We promise equality, but we deny access. We promise fairness, but we deny access. We don't seek your sympathy. We don't want your pity. Just remove the barriers, and let all have access.

Chief Justice Lewis, Florida Supreme Court

The Recovery Path

Recovery does not mean the end of a journey. It means controlling what we can and feeling competent facing the myriad challenges that come with life. At any time, in the middle of litigation, prior to being in court, after litigation, re-traumatization may occur. The 8 steps hit home for LWDs by replacing fear and an awful sense of helplessness with skill. The brain is trained, through 8-steps,

DA
H8S

to override symptoms of trauma. Recovery means being ready and armed, calling upon the normal brain functions that come quite easily once trauma is processed.

First comes the LWD's vision of being effective. They picture themselves capable of enduring insults, bias, assaults on their character and humiliation. They relegate these negative assaults to an envisioned container—called containerizing. Containerizing adds to their shield of support and protection. Adversaries' attempts at using legal abuses to crush LWD's spirits while prolonging trauma are met with clear-headed responses that adhere to legal requirements. Threat has no meaning. Power plays are rebuffed and deflected. Like a weak muscle feels energized and excited when strengthened allowing the person new range of motion, the brain is a miracle of pliability and resilience. When retrained, power surges over the old trauma; all the dynamics that created the hostage, the victims, are changed. With ADAAA accommodations, the LWD has a fair chance in court and that is all we can expect.

Recovery is rooted in a sense of safety. However, for LWD's safety is nearly impossible to feel in usual ways. In the worst cases, LWDs have lost their homes and, due to the intrusive nature of litigation, they have lost any sense of a physical safe place. Process servers have brutally served threatening documents where they live, at odd hours of the day, on their jobs, and embarrassed them in social situations or at work. Courts have ordered unreasonable mediation, forced them to turn over private and treasured property and information, and invaded their brains through psychological tests that fished for evidence to use against them. The definition of safety is forever altered. Many have their children excised from their lives and placed under the authority of sociopaths, abusers, and coercive controllers.

Confidence in the 8-step skill-set for living becomes the only real sanctuary for LWDs. Researcher, Bessel van der Kolk cites Bowlby's work demonstrating the crucial role that an "early secure base experience" for children plays in achieving maturity (1996). For LWDs and the children who suffer from Legal Abuse Syndrome, a safe place environmentally may have been stolen from them long ago. Therefore, a new safe base is not a physical place but a "state" of recovery-being armed with confidence, validation of the self, having internalized coping strategies and achieving a trust with a CADAA followed by self-advocacy that endures.

How Recovery Works and Looks:

1. Reframe—*Linda was served a document that threatened her parenthood. Without her having been psychologically evaluated, a mental health professional claimed she had a personality disorder.* This diagnosis is very serious because it suggests lack of conscience and possible criminal tendencies. *As a result, she was formally charged with child neglect.* Typically, when such painful and fearful legal documents rained on her, she would panic, become defensive, begin to criticize those who perpetrated the scheme, and she was left teeming with self-doubts.

    Linda did not fall into her usual reactive pattern of focusing on her self-doubt now that she understands the power of the recovery path. She can't prevent them from filing inaccurate information, but through data analysis, she can bring judicial notice to it. She can alter how she feels about herself in the circumstance. She also can strengthen her self-image thereby affirming herself to the court denying her adversary the opportunity to create a false persona before the judge. In completing the three steps of reframing (self appraisal, facts in perspective, what is the wisdom gained? Huffer's Step-1), Linda realizes it is a serious situation wherein she is facing misinformation being filed into the court to remove her parenthood. She affirmed herself as a parent and a person capable of sorting the matter out and legally responding to create a record. As she identifies herself to the court, she creates, at that moment, her own image and exposes the opposition's strategies to mischaracterize her. "Your honor, I'm conscientious and a good mother contrary to what this court has been told. "Given an opportunity, I will demonstrate that today." Wisdom gained from her reframing gives her validating information about her and her parenthood to communicate to the court. She realized that all the time she criticized those who attacked her; no one was filing positives about her into the record. The affirmations served her well personally and legally.

2. Debrief—Chris suffered from TBI, traumatic brain injury, and PTSD. In court or even in preparation for court, words to him moved in a fog with questionable meaning. Debriefing took him through the trauma of coming home from deployment only to be asked for a divorce and loss of custody of his children. He was in a safe place while the debriefing graphic took shape allowing him to see what happened, learn to name his resulting feelings, and begin to override the trauma. His losses were unclear to him leaving him in no position to self-protect. He identified his losses and began to recognize areas of destabilization. He isolated what he can control and what he cannot control. Graphing his experience helped him to connect with the words that were spoken. He learned that his brain was preventing expressive speech and his ability to grasp and remember the words spoken in court. His CADAA rehearsed with him prior to court. His accommodations helped him to slow speech down in court and take breaks to review his audiotape to ensure he has enough language proficiency to participate. Debriefing served many functions for Chris. It processed trauma in a safe place, outlined the case plan dividing legal and personal issues, and clarified losses for restoration.

3. Grieving—Linda struggles with her opposition's continual efforts to prejudice the record against her by slipping in misinformation. The children were abruptly removed from her custody based upon misinformation. The children call her crying and complaining, but if she attempts to assist them, she is accused of interfering with her ex-husband's time with the children and finds herself being defensive. Defensiveness is a weak posture for court. Linda loves her children and has always conscientiously parented them. She is virtually in a

DA
H8S

lose-lose posture where her children are concerned. If she helps them, she faces contempt. If she doesn't, it breaks her heart and they feel abandoned. She must grieve shamelessly. Crying is what we do when there seems to be nothing we can do at the moment while the loss or threat is of extreme importance.

4. Blame—Chris knew he had assistance coming from veterans' services, but he was confused as to accountability. He knew he had been faithful to his wife and now found that she had not been equally faithful. His children inspired him to serve his country and then get home. He dreams of raising his children, educating them, playing with them, and making up for lost time. He can't bear the thought of not living with them. Who does he blame for his predicament? Who is accountable?Chris had a rolling anger/resentment, that kept him in a state of foggy symptoms that mostly manifested in depression from anger turned inward. Once he finished analyzing degrees of blame, he realized that his wife qualified for first-degree blame. She deceived, schemed, and exploited his disability in the court– accompanied by her attorney. The wife's attorney deserved third degree blame.

5. Deshame—Linda feels guilty about her children being unhappy and abused by her ex-husband. She feels incompetent, coerced, and enmeshed in destructive behaviors. How does she go forward? How did she get involved with a PC like her ex-husband? Linda welcomed the definition of PC traits and how CC's deal with them and preferably avoid them if possible. She appreciated herself as a CC more after this step. Her values were reaffirmed. She felt stronger and without shame once she saw the true dynamics that had dictated their relationship.

6. Obsessive Compulsive Hypervigilance—Chris trusted no one. He could not complete paperwork needed for his case. He would work on it but could not get it as perfect as he wanted, so he would avoid it. The work he completed was excellent but he did not believe it. He became a slave to his files organizing and reorganizing waiting for the moment when he plowed through and finish the job. He worried over the files and documents that were becoming so voluminous that he needed five-inch binders to hold them. He and his advocate decided to make a time each week to address the files and the rest of the time he had to turn away from them. They limited the scope of the work to be done in the compartmentalized time so he would not have one issue lead him endlessly to the next. Chris got a scanner and reduced the files to his computer. He names his feelings referring back to the debriefing graphics to identify his emotional reactions to litigation. As he worked through the steps for dealing with OCH, his anxiety lessened allowing him to make decisions about his paperwork rather than being driven.

7. Empowerment—Linda embraced communication skills, deflectors, and mental toughness. She also caught her ex-husband intruding into her email through high tech spy ware. The more she refused to be defensive and manipulated by his usual tactics, the better she felt.

She is nearing the point that she believes she can go into the court unrepresented. She has paid hundreds of thousands of dollars to lawyers and now is without the ability to hire another.

The above is what recovery looks like. When needed the 8-steps are used in any order that works. It is like wearing an emotional tool belt.

Recovery has a rhythm. It takes great concentration to switch gears from trauma controlling the brain to the brain overriding trauma. At first there is panic as risks are taken, fear, suspicion, and stress triggered by the trauma brain's automatic responders to perceived danger. However, with kindness and encouragement of a CADAA, new coping skills awaken the plasticity of the brain, awareness develops, and after processing feelings of simultaneous helplessness and jeopardy, a new habit is established. Normal brain function is natural; so, once practiced, it falls into place allowing a rhythmic momentum to override the symptoms of trauma. Recovery occurs like a rhythmic dance. With the 8-steps integrating as second nature to the LWD, it flows to the beat of breathing, in and out, changing the pattern of adversarial litigation.

Weaving Justice into Our Immediate Surroundings

Healing is not contingent on the PC finally doing the right thing. The truly power centered person has a pathological personality that leaves emotional scar tissue over the wounds they inflict that may still ache when it rains memories of the trauma. Most PC's will never apologize, never feel truly sorry, or have empathy. Waiting for them to acknowledge the reality of what they have done that bullies, torments, hurts others or for them to learn from their mistakes is likely to fail. They will not bleed for forgiveness. In fact after many years, the PC type may still be arrogant and righteous, even though they are dead wrong. If sociopathic wrongdoers could ever truly look the offended in the eye and from their heart reveal deep contrition, litigants with disabilities probably could bypass the 8 steps and be fine. Since that is a rarity, the 8-steps offer the best relief.

An unexpected and true gift for LWDs is found in the people they meet on the way to seeking justice. They are the other victims of legal abuses who share your values and know your pain. They are the majority of the population motivated by their consciences, CCs, who both know and care. Most care about the greater picture as well as themselves. You join those who are sculpting a better future.

Forgiveness

Forgiveness has numerous definitions and perspectives. Enright states, *"People, upon rationally determining that they have been unfairly treated, forgive when they willfully abandon resentment and related responses (to which they have a right), and endeavor to respond to the wrongdoer based on the moral principle of beneficence, which may include compassion, unconditional worth, generosity, and moral love (to which the wrongdoer, by nature of the hurtful act of acts, has no right"* (Enright, 2000).

After or during litigation, forgiveness is a personal issue to be determined by the offended.

Forgiveness is not a prerequisite for an LWD to be considered a healthy balanced person. LWDs must never be pressured nor made to feel obligated to forgive or to let go; a person chooses to forgive when it is real and when it's time, if at all. But, when the LWD is no longer a victim, a hostage, or feels at the losing end of the game, forgiveness is often a natural event. Rarely, there will be the type of rich and rugged encounter of offended and offender shouldering the courageous task of standing for the virtue and honor required for basic trust to rebuild. Forgiveness is more a second stage of letting go after releasing negative emotions.

One does not forgive from a hostage stance. Forgiving while being punished is a faux forgiveness that is really abuse accommodation syndrome or a type of Stockholm syndrome. Holding on to an angry memory is an important part of not being able to forgive oneself (Barber, 2005). Lingering winner/loser stances prevent the desired human yearning to overcome conflict and cold separation as illustrated in the play, "Playland." Fugard touches on the intimate type of forgivness human beings need.

This South African playwright, Athol Fugard, dramatizes in *Playland* forgiveness in a socially profound discovery of "each other" set against the severe injustices of African apartheid, through two characters, a Blackman and a Whiteman. It is eyeball-to-eyeball and face-to-face. It is a multi-layered conflict between two individuals who wrestle with social histories of collisions and atrocities. These two sinewy figures portray rugged forgiveness in a one-on-one encounter involving deep emotion and, finally, forgiveness as a heart wrenching choice transcending pain, habit, history, hate, and power differential. Authentic forgiveness is achieved when humans feel equal and sorry for moral violations in a type of rebirth of virtue.

LWDs will not forgive as was done in *Playland*; but rather, it will be a letting go. They now re-enter the game of life. They will win again, lose again; risk is bearable because they will use their 8-step coping skills ready to effectively greet the next assault. They also construct life with proactive measures for self and asset protection. They cautiously trust again with a lot of verification and sense of risk.

Restoration

The justice system is all about restoration—it's why you went to court. Court is not about personal issues. The court does not take on your healing, your recovery, and your forgiveness. Society cannot forgive for an individual. Restoration is separate albeit related; it is the legal position. Restoration means getting back what was wrongfully taken or its equivalent, your house, your business, your parenthood, your job or money to compensate. Any organization aimed at justice for victims or any legal system or governmental agency responsible for serving the populace usually has as an ideal some sort of material restoration of what was wrongly taken.

During litigation, LWDs need to press for restoration within their realm of power. CADAAs help them organize any potency they possess toward being restored. Within every victim's realm of power is the ability to advocate for expanded restorative services. LAS victims deserve disaster loans, restitution, and material relief. For those who want to address reform and social change, it is necessary to toggle between the LWDs case and a broadened societal stance. Litigants often become activists, take a stand, assert rights under law, and reset the moral and ethical compass. It is critically important that these efforts take into consideration the human traits that have brought the system to fail justice-seeking citizens to the extent that we witness. LWD's represent a giant step toward enriching the nation with wisdom that was not available to the founding fathers. What an exciting thought it is that America could grow up truly providing justice for all. And, it appears that it will be the afflicted, the impaired, those with disabilities who will lead.

Moral neutrality is not an option for me. Whatever the price of facing the reforms necessary for those with disabilities and the citizens who get injured by their justice system, it must be paid. Do not be fearful that this work will go away and some unsavory perpetrators will win another immoral victory. I assure you this effort to preserve due process will not run scared. Most courts appreciate our work, with the thread of support for LWDs going all the way to the top. The President signed the UN Treaty for the Disabled in 2009. Congress, the Bar Association, and the Department of Justice have clearly spoken through the ADAAA of 2008 that reinforced the structure and intent of the ADA. These acts intend to protect disabled litigants and advocates from harassment and intimidation while their right to a fair court is assured by law. To borrow the words of Harvard Professor Judith Herman, M.D., "I will inevitably have to face the perpetrator's unmasked fury. And, for me and many of us there can be no greater honor."

Huffer's Log

Case of Linda's Recovery

The first sense Linda felt after engaging her CADAA was having a bubble of protection around her. After feeling confused, hopeless, and fearful, her days were no longer spent in frozen apprehension. Waiting for the other shoe to drop had eaten up her energy for years. Her brain felt like a tormenting tyrant forcing flashbacks, memory loss, fear, often leaving her dumbstruck. She experienced the plasticity of her brain and with training Linda began to experience control of her life again. It was a rigorous path. Linda gained insight into the defensive stance she took to every comment, behavior, and wrongdoing of her ex-husband. His assaults were artfully put forth, utterances in court, nasty, combined with false accusations from his attorney setting forth rumors that would come to her from hearsay in the community and the children, letters, and messages on her voice mail. All had overwhelmed her senses taking her focus off of her case.

Linda didn't realize that when she was accused she gave the false allegations power by aggressively defending herself against each accusation by denying them verbally. This allowed her ex-husband to control their time in court. The court never heard how good she was. It was all focused on her ex

DA
H8S

husband's negative issues about her. Therefore, in court she usually lost because her side was never heard. She didn't know how to deal with the humiliation. Fear for her children's wellbeing was growing and becoming overwhelming. Yet, she was stuck in a trauma cycle.

The CADAA surrounded Linda with a sense of safety and hope. This bubble of protection provided the matrix for the rigors of Huffer's 8 protocols. As each step was addressed, Linda's countenance relaxed. Her forehead released furrows and it was visible that her energies were no longer being sucked down wasteful drains of defensiveness and terror. She achieved a release of negative emotion from her innards improving her health.

Linda's effectiveness in court improved after she forgave herself for being helpless when gripped by trauma and for succumbing to manipulation by her adversaries. Once clarity began to replace terror, Linda was no longer blind to the fact that much of her opposition's behavior was intentional baiting. He planted outrageous statements and toyed with her by dropping verbal threats and bending court orders. He knew he could send her down the path of reacting to him instead of proactively protecting her legal position. She was regularly spending huge sums of money fighting some fabricated charge by her ex-husband.

Linda is now her own best advocate claiming her rights and managing what she can control in her case. Through debriefing she isolated and then separated the legal and personal tasks. She reframes as needed leaning on the wisdom and balance that reframe fosters. The court record has been corrected through data analysis.

Linda is shocked at how different the courtroom environment feels to her now. She is empowered and finally able to speak using exercises that override Broca's area that had allowed trauma to halt expressive speech in her brain. Her toolbox is quite full of skills and strategies. She worries less about court corruption because, now that her hearings are fair, she is winning her share of motions. Linda is still on edge and will be hyper-vigilant and compulsive until her children are safe and thriving. However, the obsession is serving her work now instead of preoccupying her.

Linda grieves with her advocate by her side. She is comforted albeit still facing losses. Blaming sorts out for Linda the dynamics that are working against her. Her adversarial actions are now well placed and effective. Linda actually got a judge disqualified for bias.

She has let go of the bitter, internal pain of being hurt to her core and forgiven herself for being victimized. Linda once again sees a future for her and her children. She wants to one day help others to overcome trauma as a defeating and impoverishing factor in life. She feels hopeful every time she experiences her brain literally reshaping to normal responses instead of leaving her hostage to the pain and terror that trauma wrought on her prior to having a caring CADAA and experiencing 8 simple but challenging steps.

References

Barber, L., Maltby, J., & Macaskill, A. (2005). Angry memories and thoughts of revenge: the relationship between forgiveness and anger rumination. *Personality and Individual Differences, 39*, 253-262.

Bowlby J. (1995). *A Secure Base: Clinical Applications of Attachment Theory*. Hove: Routledge.

Enright, R., & Fitzgibbons, R. (2000). *Helping Clients Forgive: An Empirical Guide for Resolving Anger and Restoring Hope*. Washington, DC: American Psychological Association.

Herman, J.L. (1997). *Trauma and Recovery*. New York: Basic Books.

van der Kolk, B., et al. (1996). Dissociation, somatization, and affect dysregulation: the complexity of adaptation of trauma. *American Journal of Psychiatry, 153*, 83-93.

DA
H8S

ACTIVELY IMPROVING THE JUDICIAL SYSTEM: COURT CAN BECOME RATIONAL, EMOTIONALLY SAFE, AND USER FRIENDLY FOR LWDs

This chapter emphasizes experts' recommendations for improvements to the justice system that save money and better serve the whole of the population.

1. Recognize and accommodate Limited Language Proficiency (LLP).

2. Relax laws on unlicensed practice of law.

3. Create a centralized intake center for access to court.

4. Multidisciplinary medical/legal approach to management of ADA accommodations.

5. Modernize and economize through technology to accommodate special needs.

6. Trust in institutions and professionals needs to be restored as a social staple.

7. Minimize re-traumatization and recognize need for ADA advocacy.

When Spiders Unite, They Can Tie Up A Lion.

Ethiopian Proverb

Experts' Recommendations for Improvement

Bond's finding puts a group, as few as three, in a social situation where acceptance is at stake; "Social identity theory (Tajfel, 1981, 1982) and self-categorization theory (Onorato, 2004) emphasize that the implications of agreement or disagreement with others will depend on whether they are perceived as in-group or out-group members." This explains how judges, lawyers, evaluators, guardians, and court appointees inadvertently and quite naturally become court insiders. They are the constant. Litigants then perceive themselves as outsiders whether an individual or as part of a

GRL
DA
ADA

group, the public, who come and go, comprising the absentee owners of the justice system. This helps explain why unrepresented litigants feel shunned even though they stand in the shoes of an attorney.

Pro se or unrepresented litigants with disabilities are burdened by having to challenge the social morays that currently exist. The litigant with disabilities and advocates armed with ADA accommodations have an opportunity to confront and force those with power to have the courage to refuse to conform to stigmatizing behaviors that were accepted, even commonplace before passage of the ADAAA. Many LWDs cannot withstand the rigors of court and are denied their fair day. Some disabilities are misunderstood such as ADHD and autism incarcerating innocent people who cannot communicate effectively and are pushed into plea deals, not by guilt or innocence, but for expedience.

Relax the Laws on Unlicensed Practice of Law

Gillian Hadfield, professor of law and economics at the University of Southern California in Los Angeles suggests that relaxing the laws on unlicensed practice of law would go a long way in expanding access to the justice system. In these economic tough times, we must look to nontraditional methods of delivering service to justice seekers. Hadfield cites operations such as LegalZoom, an online service that allows individuals and businesses to create their own legal documents, although it does not offer legal advice on specific matters. Similarly, JustAnswer makes lawyers available to answer questions submitted online, but it side steps UPL rules by answering only general questions (Podgers, 2011). Herman cites that some survivor's missions become pursuit of justice. She tells of Sarah Buel, once a battered woman who became a district attorney now working to help others who are abused to have hope through her understanding (Herman, 1997).

Figures from ABA Task Force, May 29, 2011 show that eighty-four per cent of family court litigants, twenty seven per cent of civil cases, and ninety per cent of housing cases are unrepresented. Therefore the courts must provide specific assistance for these taxpayers. Hadfield who has done international comparative research on justice systems reports that significantly more people in the U.S. "lump it" are able to do nothing to resolve their legal matters than residents of other countries.

Create a Centralized Intake Center

Rebecca L. Sandefur, a senior research social scientist at the American Bar Foundation, the ABA's Chicago-based research affiliate, discusses an idea that would substantially assist LWDs. A centralized intake center would receive all cases for the purpose of matching them up with a customized plan streamlining their contacts to only those pertinent to their cases. Instead of bouncing litigants around the court searching for the resources, paralegals and ADA advocates could man such an intake services and save the court countless dollars by assisting the public to focus on only the meaningful legal actions needed. This type of service could also direct the public to non legal options. All matters that come before the court are not best solved in the court.

Sandefur refers to "referral fatigue" wherein litigants are exhausted by inefficient referrals and give up on pursuing their cases. LWDs are particularly vulnerable to this due to having to apply for accommodations and wait for approval. If approval is denied, they must exhaustively grieve the decision, but must continue their attempt to gain some type of help if they are to compete at their best (Podgers, 2011).

Modernize and Economize through Technology

The most current discussion among judicial experts occurred at an American Bar Association Task force meet on May 26, 2011. Improvements were explored to address the budgetary crisis in the courts. Various states were analyzed as to measures that successfully addressed the problems faced by the various judicial systems. Technology emerged as the greatest hope for improving access for the public and saving money for the courts. LWDs benefit greatly by:

- telephonic appearances;

- electronic filing requiring fewer trips to the courthouse;

- use of a technological business model for managing the courts reducing the paperwork and duplication of efforts to bring cases to court; and,

- true and accurate records of hearings need to be technologically and inexpensively provided to litigants. LWDs suffer from serious amnesic moments under stress. When they are denied their transcripts, they virtually are denied access to due process.

Multidisciplinary Medical/Legal Approach to Management of ADA Accommodations

Once we know that human suffering can be alleviated, it is incumbent upon responsible people to make necessary changes. From the "man on the street" opinion to the ABA's 1999 study on Public Perception of the Judicial System, to current research on traumatic stress and neuroimaging, it is clear that involvement with the judicial system has evolved into a public health risk. Scientific evidence cannot be ignored. Patterns of neurology that affect LWDs during their litigation directly influence the outcome of their cases.

A simple neurological pattern guides human behavior (Damasio, 334-335). The central nervous system predicts what is ahead and then mobilizes appropriate action. A sensorimotor image based upon the senses, i.e. hearing, touch, sight, smell, contextualizes and synchronizes the external world with internal awareness. Combinations of sensations, physical actions, and emotions are then put to work guided by rationality (Damasio, 334-335). Rationality is not disrupted for the judicial insiders who are wise to the use of lies. However, for the LWD who is shocked and ambushed by lies in court, 'due process of law' is often lost owing to internal factors beyond their control.

The anatomy and physiology of a person confronted by a lie often wields the death knell in legal cases and precipitates a decline in mental and physical health. The actual effect of lying on LWDs

GRL
DA
ADA

and judicial personnel is rarely explored in the context of a court of law. The lie has evolved as a key tool during litigation because it carries such nebulous and far-reaching power. Therefore, a method for offsetting the destructive effect of a lie on the litigant, i.e. using the data analysis process or some other method for reducing the irrationality caused by misinformation needs to be faced head on by medical and legal personnel in addressing equal access to the legal process.

Neuroimaging studies of PTSD demonstrate that when exposed to traumatic reminders, participants have cerebral blood flow increases in the right medial orbitofrontal cortex, an encompassing part of the brain that mediates decision-making via a process that also involves emotion and cognition (Cavada, 2000). Traumatic memories always forced during trials also affect blood flow to the insular cortex (often called insula, insulary cortex, or insular lobe) the part that helps humans understand what it feels like to be human. It has been called the wellspring of social emotions eliciting feelings like lust and disgust, pride and humiliation, guilt and atonement. It stimulates moral intuition, empathy and the capacity to respond emotionally to music. Also deprived is the Amygdala - this almond shaped structure is thought to be critical in regulating emotion and in guiding emotion-related behaviors. It is related to fear and anxiety with circuitry connecting the frontal cortical regions of the brain that may be critical in a relative deactivation in left anterior prefrontal cortex specifically Broca's area the expressive speech center in the brain.

Sissela Bok, in her work on lying, claims that once a lie enters the forum, the forum itself becomes irrational (1978). In the Preamble and Scope of The American Bar Association Model Rules of Profession Conduct, it is made clear that the Model Rules are rules of reason. Since irrationality and reason are polar opposite states of functionality, lies and model rules of professional conduct cannot coexist without rendering the forum dysfunctional. Therefore, unless lying in the courtroom is stringently curtailed, litigation is held in an irrational environment compromising the rules of reason (ABA, 2009-10). Philip Zimbardo, professor emeritus of psychology at Stanford University, asks in *The Lucifer Effect*, "Can you be judged sane in an insane place?" A committee of medical/legal community members to oversee LWD's needs under ADAAA could help to reverse the sense of insanity that LWDs experience when they enter the esoteric legal world.

The Need to Minimize Re-traumatization and Recognize Need for ADA Advocacy

The judicial system traditionally has treated neurology as a factor only in determining competence to stand trial. The convenience of having an attorney equalizes access in the eyes of the court even if the client has invisible functional impairments. The attorney is a legal advocate but without specialized training, legal counsel is not a qualified ADA Advocate.

The new demands of ADAAA, HIPAA, and the burgeoning unrepresented population appearing in court, require specialized advocacy to offset certain impairments.

The Need to Recognize and Provide
for Situational Limited Language Proficiency

Damasio, van der Kolk, McFarlane, Foa, and Herman, to name a few, have concluded that when people are reminded of a personal trauma they activate brain regions that support intense emotions, while decreasing activity of brain structures involved in the inhibition of emotions and the translation of experience into communicable language. These and other findings related to neuronal activation in response to traumatic reminders serve as the foundation for Huffer's 8-steps. They provide the reliving of the trauma in a safe environment relieving the need to stay on guard.

By acknowledging invisible disabilities and the effects of re-traumatization, articulation of a new language of accommodating LWDs is put forth. That new language must include a category for "Limited Language Proficiency (LLP)." LLPs may suffer language deficits that may have known or unknown origin, but fall under similar protection as those who have a first language other than English and limited English proficiency (LEP) or who suffer sensory impairment. It defies logic that a court will provide a foreign language interpreter but not an interpreter for an autistic person or for those suffering from TBI and PTSD knowing that Broca's Area is immediately diminishing their abilities to manage expressive speech.

The U.S. Department of Justice Civil Rights Division made it clear in a letter of April 16, 2010 regarding LEPs (limited English proficiency):

> *Dispensing justice fairly, efficiently, and accurately is a cornerstone of the judiciary. Policies and practices that deny LEP persons meaningful access to the courts undermine that cornerstone. They may also place state courts in violation of long-standing civil rights requirements. Title VI of the Civil Rights Act of 1964, as amended, 42 U.S.c. § 2000d et seq. (Title VI), and the Omnibus Crime Control and Safe Streets Act of 1968, as amended, 42 U.S.c. § 3 789d(c) (Safe Streets Act), both prohibit national origin discrimination by recipients of federal financial assistance. Title VI and Safe Streets Act regulations further prohibit recipients from administering programs in a manner that has the effect of subjecting individuals to discrimination based on their national origin. See 28 C.F.R. §§ 42.1 04(b) (2), 42.203(e).*

Returning soldiers need their families to understand that they will likely not be able to effectively use expressive speech for some time. As they process the trauma in treatment, expressive speech becomes unblocked allowing them to override the trauma. Until that happens, damaged communication risks marital problems and family conflicts. If those veterans wind up in court they may find they are unable to use expressive speech that must be offset by advocacy. If not, veterans feel that all they fought for is not his or hers when they arrive home. Their service and all that was sacrificed, represented by the disability, can feel like they fought for and were involved in, "a terrible lie" (Werner, 1989).

GRL
DA
ADA

Recognize the Impact of the Social Context of the Courtroom on LWDs

Zimbardo uses a term called "essentializing" referring to roles people are assigned for a given situation that directly applies to the cruel and unusual punishment that parents torn from their children and grieving heirs who are barred from carrying out the wishes of the deceased and others report as they sustain losses from litigation (320-1.) The question as to what extent humans are willing to hurt one another and under what circumstances was the subject of an ambitious study. Basically, Phillip Zimbardo studies a research question, "What variables and principles are involved when ordinary people engage in torture?" He cites Susan Fiske's research from Princeton University encompassing a compilation of 100 years of research and 25,000 studies representing 8 million people. More than 300 meta-analyses were involved and then reanalyzed narrowing the focus to specific influences people have on one another. Social psychological evidence points to the power of social context. It seems that the interpersonal environment profoundly influences behavior in the directions of both good and evil (323).

I often sit in court when the process is abused, and wonder who opposing counsel really was before being a lawyer in this courtroom. When the "spin" that is intended to damage my client rolls out of his or her mouth like the stench of halitosis permeating the courtroom, I am struck by what insanity emanates from the bench, the bar, and posture of the Bar Association. I watch it manifest in a courtroom turning some attorneys into ugly and cold facilitators of pain for profit. They become embedded in the judicial system that transforms them into people capable of hurting children for profit, destroying careers, taking people's property, taking unbalanced fees, and defaming with impunity because their positions as Bar members in a courtroom allows it. Humans hurting humans always comes with a huge personal and social price.

It is time for a gold standard to be applied to legal and medical ethics coming together to prevent torturous and dangerous litigation. Public health must come first and all other motives of the judicial system must bow to it.

Recognize and Elevate Coercive Control from a Second Class Misdemeanor to a Human Rights Violation

Evan Stark, Ph.D., award winning researcher, forensic expert, and advocate wrote how systems fail to protect women against domestic violence due to an obscure but devastating style of abuse. He finds that in millions of abusive relationships, men use a pattern of abuse that expands to legal abuse as well, called "coercive control." Stark's revelation is based upon thirty years of experience and sound documentation. Likewise, I see coercive control in a smaller percentage showing up against men as well. Coercive control is legal abuse, usually making false accusations and setting protective systems unfairly in motion to block/gain control of the proceedings. It is an extension of dominance using taxpayer systems as tools of abuse. (Stark, 2007)

Most abused women who seek help do so because their rights and liberties have been jeopardized not because they have been injured. The coercive control model Stark develops resolves three of the most perplexing challenges posed by abuse: why these relationships endure, why abused women develop a profile of problems seen among no other group of assault victims, and why the legal system has failed to win them justice. It is important to recognize and elevate coercive control from a second-class misdemeanor to a human rights violation, Stark explains why law, policy, and advocacy must shift their focus to emphasize how coercive control jeopardizes women's freedom in everyday life.

Therefore, it is reasonable to posit that the social context in the courtroom profoundly influences both good and bad behaviors. Safeguards of high standards built into and stringently enforced are necessary or public trust is lost. Litigants, especially with disabilities, are the consumers who are in the best position to take this need to the next step when safeguards fail. Advocates are the keys. LWDs learn from their effective behavior. They model effective behavior, raise awareness, and support litigants with afflictions. They confront appropriately in the courtrooms, when access is threatened or denied through deception. LWDs progressively pick up these skills and once on the recovery path are able to call on what they have learned.

Trust in Institutions and Professionals Must Be Restored as a Social Staple

The research of Rod Bond (Tajfel, 1981), concludes that those cultures with more collectivist values are more likely to be concerned with maintaining harmony through caring for people with disabilities. Since America is known for emphasis on individuality, it appears that rugged individualism is being challenged by corporate power demanding corporation-mindedness of its employees putting the collective good of the company ahead of original thinking, imagination, and creativity.

Using an Asch paradigm on conformity described below, Asch speculates that essential trust is lost as the number of people we depend upon to adhere to our nation's values and the ideals of the justice system disappoints us. An example of this is the realization that there can be court insiders who are court appointed and who rubber stamp each other destroying the individual's opportunity to make independent choices. In these cases, the family court feels like the wagons are circled and the court is a closed system. This whole dynamic is interesting to me since I see many LWDs feeling defeated as court outsiders who ask if there is a second set of rules they know nothing about.

Asch asserted, "That we have found the tendency to conformity in our society so strong that reasonably intelligent and well-meaning young people are willing to call white, black is a matter of concern." He urged that we look at our methods of education, values promoted by our behavior in society, and our conduct (34). He points out that there is a danger of polluting our culture through conformity if we subscribe to a subset of behaviors as those that I have observed evolving in the adversarial system. For example, litigants struggling with side effects from medications for schizophrenia, fibromyalgia, or ADHD were cruelly taunted by opposing counsel. If the disability can be dragged into the argument, it is used to discredit the afflicted stripping them of parenthood, pride, and independence without merit. It is perverted bias drawing on outdated stigma (1996).

Compassion is then wrung out of litigation. Opposing counsel's retort to my demands for compassion are often accusations of the LWD malingering. Asch encouraged the fostering of what Zimbardo now calls the search for situational determinants of behavior. He asks, "What factors are present when conformity compromises the basic conscience that guides a human being's sense of right versus wrong?" This goes to the heart of the power versus conscience as basic human motivators. Where does inner strength and will power to resist all temptations and situational inducements come from? Can individuals truly rise above their surroundings in the face of criticism, rejection, economic threat, and political pressure?

Zimbardo points to his 30 years of research when he argues that, "The influence of the social situations, the Situationist approach, exerts much greater power over human actions than has been generally acknowledged by most psychologists or recognized by the general public." It appears from my observations that the CC, the conscience-centered individual, is more likely to stand firm for the right thing in the face of social pressure. Those who pursue power for its own sake tend to bend their behaviors to serve their need for power only in the present moment.

This division, between the drive of the individual and the force exuded by the social situation, gives the public a kernel to chew on as they wonder how lawyers can behave in ways that damage and destroy instead of resolving conflict. Some disparity or faulty conformity allows lawyers to claim zealous representation as they contort simple fact to exhaustive litigation and defend it as serving the public. Considering Zimbardo's alternative orientation, rectification comes not from changing the individual but by altering what is considered appropriate behavior in the social setting of a system that allows denial of empowerment of the disabled as socially acceptable. Historically, conforming to "group think" results in isolation and maltreatment of those with disabilities. The ADAAA is an opportunity to assert choice over conformity and to restore a sense of basic trust needed for a culture to survive. All it takes is a commitment by all to equal access for every person.

LWDs Case Law Resonates into the Future

The judiciary is an especially critical system of care because whatever it does sets precedent. That precedent then launches a trajectory wherein predators can defy ethics spreading contagion of contempt for citizens, laws, rules, and codes. Arbitrary rulings become commonplace. Judge Napolitano ended his book, *Constitutional Chaos*, with the words, "…government lying to its citizens, stealing their property, tricking them into criminal acts, bribing its witnesses against them, making a mockery of legal reasoning, and breaking the laws in order to enforce them…is not your friend" nor is it a system of care. Our institutions must be confronted and forced to provide honest services or we have nothing but chaos (2004).

A nation can only grow for a finite period in a culture of predatory takings. Capitalistic societies have historically failed because hoarding, greed, and unwillingness to share during tough times have fatally undermined the capitalistic cultures. When a population is reduced to prey, energy is sucked into defensiveness, self-protection, shock, and reaction to trauma. Communities die if there is no recourse through a strong and fair justice system.

Sometimes litigants get caught in battles that blind both the warriors and the victims. They get so enmeshed in reacting emotionally and legally to one assault after another that they lose a vision of their future or doing better. Advocates help litigants to realistically decide what they want to come away with in a context that balances pragmatism with matters of "principle." Some issues just cannot be resolved in a court of law, i.e. living with the injustice of a destructive court order. Examples are found in being ordered to pay a thief money who won in court unfairly and pay his or her lawyers fees and costs or being forced to turn an abused child over to the abuser who won by lying to the court.

In each case, I work to find the chink in the armor where the response can be on the spectrum of kindness and not adversity. Somewhere in any organization there are individuals with values, who appreciate kindness and, unlike PC's, don't take it for weakness to be exploited. In your court, your bank, your lawyer's office, someone knows. Keep your antennae out for those people and create a network of contacts that respond to and build upon kindness. Someone "on the inside" that connects through kindness can indirectly be very powerful. They can clue you in with a look when someone is steering you wrong. They can hold documents, save documents, find documents that make all the difference. These are beacons of help in the midst of what can be institutionalized chaos or wrongdoing. Listen to them. Be kind and friendly to them. Establish rapport.

Fear feeds adversity that invites abuse to abound. Therefore, when viewing the conflict, look for where fear is breeding. Target the areas of fear and alleviate them. Calmly, confidently, refuse to engage in ugliness. A choice, from the range of kind responses, disarms the legal warrior and sometimes turns the matter around. I often ask each party what they are afraid of happening if they cooperate with the other. Every time there is a chance, try the kindness response. Abusive lawyers are too often feeding the adversity and quelling the clients' desire to stop the litigation. Advocates in these cases alert the litigants to the option of Therapeutic Mitigation. Litigation can be put aside and through a skilled liaison and new level of communication is established. Therapeutic Mitigation described in the next chapter is an experimental program designed to assist certain cases for which neither mediation or litigation is working.

Author's Notes:

Larry Berardinelli, attorney and insurance specialist, investigated and exposed McKinsey & Company documents, which promote highly lucrative and unethical practices, *From Good Hands To Boxing Gloves*, in 2009, (129, 1337-1338).

Asch's work was largely done in the 1950's. It is seminal work in conformity and deserves to be

GRL
DA
ADA

considered even with a decades old citation.

When ADAAA rights have been violated, litigants ask about void judgments. There are people living under judgments, suffering while not knowing that they judgment is void. Some recovery occurs when bad judicial decisions become void judgments. The following are some of the laws that dictate void judgments.

Void judgments:

1. Judgment is a void judgment if court that rendered judgment lacked jurisdiction of the subject matter, or of the parties, or acted in a manner inconsistent with due process, Fed Rules Civ. Proc., Rule 60(b)(4), 28 U.S.C.A.; U.S.C.A. Const Amend. 5. Klugh v. U.S., 620 F.Supp. 892 (D.S.C. 1985).

2. Elliot v. Piersol, 1 Pet. 328, 340, 26 U.S. 328, 340 (1828): Under federal law, which is applicable to all states, the U.S. Supreme Court stated that if a court is "without authority, its judgments and orders are regarded as nullities. They are not voidable, but simply void; and form no bar to a recovery sought, even prior to a reversal in opposition to them. They constitute no justification; and all persons concerned in executing such judgments or sentences, are considered, in law, as trespassers." [Elliot v. Piersol, 1 Pet. 328, 340, 26 U.S. 328, 340 (1828)]

3. World-Wide Volkwagen Corp. v. Woodson, 444 U.S. 286 (1980) "A judgment rendered in violation of due process is void in the rendering State and is not entitled to full faith and credit elsewhere. Pennoyer v. Neff, 95 U.S. 714, 732-733 (1878)." [World-Wide Volkwagen Corp. v. Woodson, 444 U.S. 286 (1980)]

4. Void judgments are those rendered by a court, which lacked jurisdiction, either of the subject matter or the parties. See: Wahl v. Round Valley Bank, 38 Ariz. 411, 300 P.955 (1931), Tube City Mining & Milling Co. v. Otterson, 16 Ariz. 305, 146 P. 203 (1914) Milliken v. Meyer, 311 U.S. 457, 61 S.Ct. 339, 85 L.Ed. 2d 278 (1940)

5. A judgment obtained against a party, which lacked either subject matter or personal jurisdiction is void as a matter of law, Balding v. Fleisher, 279 So. 2d, 883 (Fla. 3rd DCA, 1973) Nigerian Airforce v., Van Hise, 443 So. 2d, 273 (Fla. 3rd DCA, 1983). Black's Law Dictionary, Sixth Edition, p. 1574: Void judgment. One which has no legal force or effect, invalidity of which may be asserted by any person whose rights are affected at any time and at any place directly or collaterally. Reynolds v. Volunteer State Life Ins. Co., Tex.Civ. App., 80 S.W.2d 1087, 1092. One which from its inception is and forever continues to be absolutely null, without legal efficacy, ineffectual to bind parties or support a right, of no legal force and effect whatever, and incapable of confirmation, ratification, or enforcement in any manner or to any degree. Judgment is a "void judgment" if court that rendered judgment lacked jurisdiction of the subject matter, or of the parties, or acted in a manner inconsistent with due process. Klugh v. U.S., D.C.S.C., 610 F.Supp. 892, 901.

References

American Bar Association Standing Committee on Ethics and Professional Responsibility. (2009-2010). *Model Rules of Professional Conduct*. Chicago: ABA Pub.

Asch's Studies of independence and conformity... meta-analysis of studies using Asch's (1952b, 1956) line judgment task line judgment task. Psychological Bulletin, 119, 111-137. Post Traumatic Stress Disorder in Trauma Exposed Adults. *Journal of Consulting and Clinical Psychology, 68,* 748-766.

Bok, S. (1978). *Lying Moral Choice in Public and Private Life*. New York: Pantheon Books.

Bond, R. & Smith, P.B. (1996). Culture and Conformity: A Meta-Analysis of Studies Using Asch's (1952b, 1956) Line Judgment Task. *Psychological Bulletin. American Psychological Association, Inc., 119(1),* 111.

Cavada, C. & Schultz, W. (2000). Special Issue: The Mysterious Orbitofrontal Cortex. Cerebral Cortex. *Oxford University Press, 10(3),* 205.

Damasio, A. (1999). *The Feeling of What Happens: Body and Emotion in the Making of Consciousness.* (pp. 35-37, 334-5). New York: Harcourt Brace.

Herman, J.L. (1997). *Trauma and Recovery.* (pp. 209). New York: Basic Books.

Napolitano, A.P. (2004). *Constitutional Chaos: What Happens When the Government Breaks Its Own Laws.* (pp. 190). Nashville: Thomas Nelson.

Onorato, R. S., & Turner, J. C. (2004). Fluidity in the self-concept: the shift from personal to social identity. *European Journal of Social Psychology, 34(3),* 257-278.

Podgers, J. (2011). Sustaining Justice: 10 Experts Tell How Courts Can Do More with Less. ABA *Journal in Law News Now Section.*

Stark, E. (2007). *Coercive Control: How Men Entrap Women in Personal Life*. NY: Oxford University Press.

Tajfel, H. (1981). *Human Groups and Social Categories: studies in social psychology*. Cambridge, UK: Cambridge University Press.

Werner, E. E. (1989). High Risk Children in Young Adulthood: A Longitudinal Study from Birth to 32 Years. *American Journal of Orthopsychiatry, 59,* 73-81.

Zimbardo, P. (2007). *The Lucifer Effect: Understanding How Good People Turn Evil.* (pp. 320-3). New York: Random House Trade Paperbacks.

GRL
DA
ADA

CHAPTER 17

THERAPEUTIC MITIGATION (TM): COOPERATIVE CONSTRUCTIVE COMMUNICATION

TM's goal is effective communication. Therapists have used proxy voice interventions for years in therapy. The therapist will paraphrase or say what one person really is saying or means as a sort of role-play. This skill and Huffer's 8 supportive counseling steps are put to the symmetrically accelerating conflicts commonly found in family court. TM streamlines simple communication issues. It is proving to save money, time, and relieve the families and the court of much cost, strife and stress. For LWDs struggling with expressive speech, proxy voice works like interpretation. Greater public satisfaction is expected when win/lose is averted.

This is a court of law young man, not a court of justice.

Oliver Wendell Holmes

Meeting Disengagement Needs beyond the Parameters of Court

Therapeutic Mitigation offers more than mediation and is complementary to litigation. TM offers an innovative service with therapeutic features underpinning a new mitigation method. When necessary, TM reaches the underlying emotions that create traps keeping a case stuck in a "high conflict" category. Further, TM meets the needs of being affordable, stays with a case as long as needed, and is more attentive to true human interests than either litigation or mediation. Litigation is necessary for legal disengagements. However, once litigation begins, adversarial positions are formed and a type of battle ensues. Usually prior to litigation, mediation is recommended or required by the court. Mediation can be successful but has limitations due to working from the legal positions formed for the adversarial arena. As defined by Mnookin, who delineates between positions and interests, neither litigation nor mediation addresses the interests and needs of the litigants from a human standpoint (2010). A void is created that puts the outcome of litigation at risk of being influenced by emotional pain and resentment instead of sound objective decision-making.

Courts look at behaviors and listen to demonizing statements rarely considering the influence of the context of the court setting on the issues at hand. Social psychologists call this the "fundamental attribution error." Therefore, when negotiation presents as an option, many litigants refuse, caught in negative traps emanating from the court context rather than the pure issues. I find that litigants fear one another and grab onto the lesson in the Faustian parable quoted by Mnookin that reflects LWD's apprehension especially if their adversary is a PC:...*you must never negotiate with the Devil. He's clever and unscrupulous. He will tempt you by promising something that you desperately want. But, no matter how seductive the possible benefits, negotiating with evil is simply wrong: it would violate your integrity and pollute your soul* (Mnookin, 2010). Therapeutic Mitigation relieves those deep-seated intractable fears and lingering emotions that negatively affect the wellbeing of children and adults long after disengagement. Sometimes we have to "negotiate with the devil" and TM offers a way.

On the other hand are the leftovers of love that intertwine with the fear of the opposition. Antonio Damasio, Neurologist and Researcher, writes of the "autobiographical self." So many court cases involve family matters that are layered in conscious and unconscious "selves" emanating from the similar family experiences and drenched in the same genetic pool. Litigation exerts a pull on the "memories, desires wishes, goals, and obligations," of the selves (1999). Therapeutic Mitigation gives an opportunity to hear, respect, resolve conflict, and avoid the tragedy of ended or ongoing conflicted relationships.

Unless you have a talented, professionally responsible, and caring attorney, they will work from a "position"–what is wanted and demanded–rather than your personal "interests"–your fundamental needs and concerns within the reality of your whole self. You can spend your entire legal budget on arguing "positions" year after year without getting to your interests. There is a difference. Frustrated love, mistrust, feelings of betrayal and your basic goals and needs, short term and long term, are tied to your interests. This is a differentiation that is served by TM referring back to Debriefing, Step 2.

Legal positions in friction with deep personal interests create potential for cognitive dissonance, an unrelenting, unsettled self-contradictory psychological state. The self-contradictions are rooted in the person's beliefs, attitudes, and actions. Dissonance results when an individual faces a contradiction between behavior and attitude. For example, when under a court order, behavior is forced (loss of visitation rights) that can brutally collide with the litigant's attitudes reflecting strongly held personal interests (the mother's instinct to protect and nurture the child) (Festinger, 1957).

Tavris and Aronson, in their book, *Mistakes Were Made, but not by Me*, assert that dissonance is hardwired in the human being but how we think about mistakes does not have to be. They describe the brain as being designed with blind spots that psychologically trick us into covering up our mistakes by justifying them, diminishing them, or isolating them as one event that did no harm. Unfortunately, the person who is rigidly justifying wrong behaviors is usually unaware or unconcerned about the feelings of those he has hurt. This is seen when prosecutors will refuse to recognize new evidence after they have perfected a conviction in their minds, or a mate cannot admit wrongdoing regarding behavior that has caused a marriage to break up. Instead of admitting error, they justify by calling the mate "crazy." In the extreme, dissonance drives ridicule, reckless accusations, and in some cases unethical and illegal behaviors (Tavris, 2007.)

The greater the investment, the more dissonance will be felt if the significant investment is not paying off. You have hired an attorney at great cost, however the attorney is unable to bring about any favorable decisions. Dissonance exists between your belief that you have paid for the service of the attorney but you are frustrated by your attorney's lack of/slow progress in your case increasing the cost. Dissonance could be eliminated by deciding that it's okay since any voice in court is better than abandoning the litigation and you couldn't do it on your own (reducing the importance of the belief) or focusing on the attorney's strengths such as reputation, standing in the eyes of the court, knowledge of law (thereby adding more consonant beliefs). The dissonance could be eliminated by getting rid of the attorney and starting over with new representation or going pro se, but this behavior is more difficult than changing your opinion.

A better understanding of cognitive dissonance is needed in protracted litigation. Elliot Aronson hypothesizes on the Principle of Effort–the more effort invested in a behavior the more dissonance is experienced. Litigation requires an adversarial effort that compounds with the nature of protracted battle. Three factors are believed to intensify dissonance, 1) the importance of the decision (i.e. I must fight; my children's welfare is at stake); 2) the difficulty of the decision (i.e. Do I confront my abuser or walk away?); and 3) the irreversibility of the decision (Either way, the court's decision will stand). Additionally, the enormous cost causes the litigation to feel irreversible.

What TM Looks Like–Proxy Voice Intervention

TM starts by choosing or being ordered to try a less expensive communication model from litigation (Seedall, 2006). The following are suggested readings prior to choosing Therapeutic Mitigation:

- *Bargaining with the Devil: When to Negotiate, When to Fight* (2010) by Mnookin

- *Most Difficult Conversations: How to Discuss What Matters Most* (1999) by Douglas Stone, Bruce Patton, Sheila Heen.

- *Dividing the Child: Social and Legal Dilemmas of Custody* (1998) by Maccoby, Eleanor and Robert Mnookin.

- http://www.gordontraining.com/parentingclass.html—*Parent Effectiveness Training* by Thomas Gordon – "Method III Conflict Resolution."

After reading or perusing the above, consider the following usual reasons why litigating adversaries choose TM. Check the reasons that would support therapeutic mitigation:

1. _____Power and control to parent your children is being removed from parents and placed in the hands of the court/ court-appointed personnel. This resigns the children to being

raised "in and by the legal system."

2. _____The wellbeing of the children is consistently negatively affected by litigation. Grades go down; they act depressed at school; they lose respect for adults; and, they are torn between parents. Children complain that they are not heard.

3. _____The economics of the case force extreme stress draining the family's assets to the detriment of the children and litigants. Retirement and education funds are being converted to legal fees; children's enrichment activities are restricted; and, the family's financial plan and portfolio are compromised to perpetuating the "case". Litigation has long passed being a reasonable business decision. The parties involved agree that the moneys could be better spent elsewhere.

4. _____There is no closure in sight for litigation to end bringing responsible resolution to the original positions of conflict. Litigation has become a consumptive war.

5. _____Litigation stress is causing or exacerbating health problems. The doctor has advised that to continue litigation risks the health of any or all of the family members.

6. _____You are ready to surrender on certain points of conflict and explore therapeutic alternatives to adversarial techniques for the sake of ending litigation. TM offers an opportunity to overcomes obstinacy, abuse, vindictiveness, and often relieves much of the pain that persists after marriage fails.

7. _____You need an ongoing service that treats the conflict through many ups and downs not limited to a one-time negotiation.

8. _____You are fed up with the legal system enough to test another method of resolving differences, such as collaborative divorce.

9. _____The legal system is fed up with your case or cannot assign blame and orders you to try a better method of communicating eradicating "He Said–She Said" from the legal process.

Once the decision to try TM is made by one, both, or all parties, the following steps are usually taken:

Step 1—The parties agree to dispense with active legal action for a period to be agreed upon. Then, an evaluation of the mitigation program is scheduled in nine months or a year at which time the litigants can always resume litigation if desired.

Step 2—Both parties commit that the wellbeing of the children is the major focus subordinating all matters to that end. If there are no children to be considered, then the health and wellbeing of the litigants are the main focuses.

Step 3—Communication is mainly done through the advocate where it is filtered to reflect the interests of each party transmitted with the greatest degree of respect preserving the dignity of all parties. Words are edited to carry the intended message, but no inflammatory words or phrases are transmitted. All words pertaining to legal contracts and legalese are omitted and substituted with informal language. Most cases deal with transitioning with visitation.

Step 4—Advocates are uniquely trained to identify the roadblocks to communication and the emotional bases upon which they persist in litigants. They function under the direction and supervision of qualified mental health professionals and legal experts.

Step 5—Anger, resentment, and intransigence are often rooted in a strongly held principle being violated. A major trap lies in the unforgivable nature of these offenses that cause relationships to disengage. Pain from unforgivable offenses that resides in the hearts of litigants is not relieved by divorce decree. There is no appropriate expression or treatment for that type of pain in court. Further, if one party is unaware of abusive behaviors such as coercive controllers or PCS display, they will spend years in court attempting to justify their behaviors. Yet, it is a circuitous ball of energy perpetuates litigation without much merit. Moreover, court personnel are not qualified to therapeutically respond to such pain. Therefore, without an intervention that addresses these underlying factors, the abuse will continue long past the divorce.

It frustrates the litigant when the most crucial issues underpinning the disengagement are being shunned and ignored by the court. ADA advocates keep the blaming process close at hand when TM begins. It helps to process the pain from unforgivable injuries so that frustration does not intensify. Litigants are wary that the behaviors that hurt them will be officially condoned. That anxiety is relieved after they complete the Blaming process.

Step 6—The parties agree to generate a volume of possible solutions to a problem before critiquing them.

Step 7—Parties agree that the goal is not for a "win" but a communication process that is productive. The advocate/mitigator may not be neutral. They care and will often commit strongly to the best interests of the children. The advocate does not assume a position of power. Advocates are merely skilled liaisons. One advocate reports that she is both a "referee" and a "coach" as well

Step 8—Mitigation is not usually done in person but through writing, telephone, fax, email, text, Skype, or whatever works. The key is that the communication is filtered through the advocate using plain and human language taking all threat out of the encounter.

Step 9—When or if an impasse occurs, then a qualified therapist personally approaches the matter with therapeutic skills or referrals if needed to overcome the emotional hurdles. Toxic communication patterns are identified and addressed.

Step 10—The arrangements are not binding except as the court may order or the participants may want to contract with one another. Who is legally responsible? The TM is not held responsible or liable for outcomes and is protected against retaliation. TM is a good faith, informal service designed to assist in communications. There will always be a margin of error in proxy voice communications. It is the participant's responsibility to correct errors prior to transmission. Are records of conversations available for review by court? They are only if court ordered or agreed upon by participants. All matters are kept confidentially by the CADAA as much as possible.

Eleanor Maccoby, in her book written with Mnookin, *Dividing the Child*, studied 1100 divorcing families. She makes the point that families don't break up at one point in time, but the disengagement takes years and is a dynamic process (1998). If the adversary is a PC type, then it is more difficult to use Therapeutic Mitigation but not impossible. A PC will do what serves their self-interested needs best. I have worked on cases where parents have been willing to terminate parenthood in exchange for no financial obligations and sometimes other surprising tradeoffs.

Communication Standard of Care

Communication must meet three criteria:

1. Issue must be clearly identified.

2. Dignity and self esteem must be in tact after communication.

3. Parties comfortably return to the process.

TM mitigators have a front row seat to the communication patterns of participants. Similar to mood is a force called dispositional affect. Simply meaning, does the person communicate from a positive or a negative stance? Research shows a correlation between dispositional affect and decision-making, negotiation, psychological resilience, and ability to cope with stressful life events. It is shown that positive affectivity lends toward more efficient, flexible and creative negotiations. Agreements are more readily sought using compromise and cooperation. Those with negative affectivity used more competitive strategies missing opportunities for agreements due to zero sum type thinking. It is not unusual to have TM dealing with one party having positive affectivity and the other negative. Once this is identified, it is good to point out to the person with negative affectivity along with the communication styled to compensate (Festinger, 1957). The first task is to remove negative slurs and pessimistic statements replacing them with a communication style of basic facts set in respectful words that convey the distinct, meaningful message. All underlying insults and personal attacks are removed.

Many PC's need and want to stay involved with their children even though their language of love is unhealthy. And, sometimes their motive is to ruin their opposition by continuing litigation. In these cases, TM has the potential of shedding light on unhealthy behaviors and untoward motives. However, logic and reason may be of little use. The liaison deals in the PC's reality as a point of departure to mitigate. While improved communication has an ameliorative effect, the goal of TM is to clearly and effectively communicate the specific issue at hand. The CADAA purifies the messages clearing them of manipulative language, legalese, offensive comments, and with no eye contact, facial expressions, gestures removed, it becomes efficient correspondence. Once power plays don't work, the dynamics of the relationship have to change.

If TM is court ordered, the court may insist upon a status report from time to time. This also motivates a PC to cooperate with the communication program. In time, without inflammatory or legal language, some cases relax into a style of cooperation. It is impressive how powerful language and attitude can foster either cooling off or accelerating of conflict.

On the other hand, there are attitudes that can cause a person to be unable to constructively assert themselves in the negotiations necessary to carry out disengagement and custody arrangements. Many people cannot tolerate facing the traits of the opposing party. One characteristic of war that is found in litigation is the dehumanization of the other causing a defensive reaction. Or, each side may feel morally superior perceiving evil in the other and become trapped in that stance (Mnookin, 2010). Each attitude or trap is described as having a cluster of reinforcing prisms that distort judgment.

One objective of Therapeutic Mitigation is to gradually reveal the traps giving litigants an opportunity to release themselves from them. Once this is accomplished, a list is created of what is most important to each party. Sometimes an agreement hinges simply on framing and reframing the statements. Mnookin gives an example of presenting an offer without much legalese or detailed terms. "Let's agree to a parenting plan that uses no label at all…and agree that the children will spend a certain amount of time with each parent, but let's not call it shared physical custody." Therapeutic Mitigation gives the advocate/communication liaison a chance to frame the deal in flexible terms that do not arouse the fear of legal terminology that can cause the litigants to feel "pinned down" and as though they are losing choices (2010).

One of the saddest outcomes of probate is what Mnookin calls "sibling warfare (2010)." Therapeutic Mitigation needs to replace a great deal of probate litigation. Litigation comes at an emotionally high impact time. Good lawyers help to mitigate differences, but many unfortunately drag the probate out and feed conflict among the heirs. Estates and the intentions of many deceased are lost to poor communication during emotional times.

Requirements for Successful TM with PCs

Lundy Bancroft, author, workshop leader and activist on trauma, abuse, and healing, in his book, *Why Does He Do That?*, offers services in the area of domestic violence. He confronts PC behaviors outright and outlines the components that stand to make a difference in changing PC behavior in the context of domestic violence. Scientifically, there are few encouraging results for change since the PC's stance is one of self-assurance, high self-esteem, and being self-serving and relationally incompetent (2002). Nevertheless, a constructive communication pattern can sustain for years even without the human efforts listed below. If any of the following traits are observed, the chances for success of therapeutic mitigation improve dramatically. Bancroft asserts that the abuser can change only if willing to do the following:

- must be willing to admit fully to their abusive history,

- must admit it was wrong without question,

- must take responsibility for making a choice to be abusive,

- must recognize the effects their abusive behavior had on the family (and community regarding PC's),

- must admit compulsion to control is out of step with cooperation and good relationships,

- must reevaluate their perception of those that were abused showing some empathy,

- must make amends for the damage that was done,

- must accept the consequences for the abusive actions, and

- must commit to not repeating the abusive behaviors; be willing to give up the privileges that the PC's gain from their behavior; own that the changes are a lifelong process not a quick fix (6000-6006).

Since the only way that PC's have been willing to change is if it is self-serving, when the PC is caught, inconvenienced, or loses something every time he or she defects, then they change out of self-interest. They take on the appearance of cooperation but in pretext only. Cooperation of any kind is preferable to no cooperation at all. However, when the cost of litigation is destroying both health and wealth, it is self-serving to face the realities of the conflict and try alternatives.

The question remains, should one negotiate with the devil? In my experience, yes, most of the time it is worth a try. Moral principles, revenge feelings, and extreme narcissism of the P.C. have parameters that, while the experience may not be inspiring, can be productive. The final consideration may rest in the intuitive hearts and guts of the litigants. These parents once loved one another. Once these family members shared people they loved and business partners respected one another. They may have hurt each other and even hate each other today. But, many times the legal team's ability to destroy the life of the opposition exceeds the true motive and comfort level of these parents to hurt one another. They also intrinsically know that to hurt a parent or remove a parent from the child hurts the child irreparably.

Because of the extreme behaviors triggered by divorce cases, it is rare for two parents to finally agree to quit litigation at the same time. However, once they try Therapeutic Mitigation, they usually stay with it and believe they did the right thing.

Huffer's Log

Case Example of Therapeutic Mitigation

I noticed that Georgia's husband did not look happy in court. He had all the money; his attorney had destroyed Georgia in court; and, if victory was to be savored, he hadn't realized it or surely didn't reflect it. He always left court quietly shaking his head, physically removed from his lawyer and with a slump in his shoulders. His sandy colored hair blended with a grey pallor that made his face appear nondescript.

Intuitively, it felt like he still loved this woman but couldn't deal with her. Whatever she had rent in his heart and soul was a deep wound that he struggled to overcome. Sometimes after annihilating her in court, he would give her some money or do her a favor on the side. The kids were with him and resented being taken from their mother. They weren't kind to him and were old enough and smart enough to challenge his authority.

He and Georgia decided to try Therapeutic Mitigation. This ex-husband felt like the profound and conflicting feelings represented by this family were funneled through the keyhole of litigation and, even though he legally won, something very ugly came out the other end. Georgia and her ex-husband decided to apply the money that was being consumed in the legal battle to buy houses not much more than a block from each other. This eliminated the children traveling to visit one or the other and eased the burden of custody on the children. The children had more say as to which parent they needed and budgeted their time accordingly. The Judge had punished Georgia by taking all custody from her, but her ex-husband knew that the children were suffering and that the pain for this mother and the children outweighed the value of the power it bought him in the war.

Over the next nine months while the parents communicated through the ADA advocate, we were able to define to each person some of the basic emotional dynamics that were in play as destructive forces. It was almost as if an oppositional part of their personalities had been thrown up as protective capsules and now those capsules were dissolving. The lawyer's animus toward Georgia in court exceeded the anger that her ex-husband felt. Once the threat was removed of adversarial action or attempts for one to hurt the other, the protective capsule could be completely absolved. The children are doing much better, the finances begin to improve, and, while their marital relationship will not resume and the love has been forever quelled as a bond between them, they are being truly responsible parents. It is less than perfect but is working better than litigation was for this family.

References

Bancroft, L. (2002). *Inside the Minds of Controlling Men: Why Does He Do That?* New York: Berkley Publishing Group.

Baruch Bush, R. A., & Folger, J. P. (2011). *The Promise of mediation: The Transformative Approach to Conflict.* San Francisco: Jossey-Bass.

Damasio, A. (1999). *The Feeling of What Happens: Body and Emotion in the Making of Consciousness.* (pp. 35-7, 225). New York: Harcourt Brace.

Festinger, L. (1957). *A Theory of Cognitive Dissonance.* Stanford, CA: Stanford University Press.

Maccoby, E., & Mnookin, R. (1998). *Dividing the Child: Social and Legal Dilemmas.* Cambridge, Mass: Harvard University Press.

Mnookin, R. (2010). Bargaining with the Devil: When to negotiate, when to fight. (pp. 124-32, 359, 399, 448-455). New York: Simon & Schuster.

Seedall, R. B., & Butler, M. H. (2006, October). The Effect of Proxy Voice Intervention on Couple Softening in the Context of Enactments. *Journal of Marital and Family Therapy, 32(4),* 421-437.

DA

GRL

Stone, D., Patton, B., & Heen, S. (1999). *Most Difficult Conversations: How to Discuss What Matters Most*. New York: Viking Penguin.

Tavris, C., & Aronson, E. (2007). *Mistakes Were Made (but not by me), Why We Justify Foolish Beliefs, and Bad Decisions, and Hurtful Acts*. Orlando, Florida: Hardcort, Inc.

Websites

www.transformativemediation.org

Mediation Training Institute International: www.mediationworks.com

Acknowledgments

Barton, T. D. (1999, December). Therapeutic Jurisprudence, preventive law, and creative problem solving: An essay on harnessing emotion and human connection. *Psychology Public Policy and Law, 5(4)*, 921-943.

Daicoff, S. (1999, December). Making Law Therapeutic for Lawyers: Therapeutic Jurisprudence, preventive law, and the psychology of lawyers. *Psychology, Public Policy and Law, 5(4)*, 811-848.

Wexler, D.B. (2000). Therapeutic Jurisprudence: An Overview. *Thomas M. Cooley L. Rev*, 125.

UNTIL IT HAPPENS TO YOU

WARNING: LITIGATION-INDUCED STRESS MAY BE HAZARDOUS TO YOUR HEALTH

In a nanosecond, any life can be dramatically altered leaving a person disabled and in a legal limbo for years–or, even decades. Through no fault of the person injured, one odd turn on the road, a failed marriage, custody challenges, a false accusation, or regrettable business decision can injure you and/or land you in court. Sometimes you get sued. Sometimes you choose to file suit. Either way, once you are embroiled in litigation, it is expensive and complicated. If you have or develop a disability, it further complicates stressful litigation. Pursuing a fair hearing that includes equal physical access, participatory access, and testimonial access becomes more and more like treading on loose stones between the law and the disability. An established standard of care implemented through ADA advocacy using Huffer's 8-Steps, stabilizes the loose stones reversing the current trend that inadvertently denies approximately 60 million persons with disabilities to be denied equal access to their public and private services.

Litigants enter court with a simple expectation. "Justice will prevail." When it doesn't, litigants find themselves driven to the ends of their ropes, often developing a form of Post Traumatic Stress Disorder (PTSD), a psychic injury. Such PTSD is sometimes caused by litigation and is now referred to as Legal Abuse Syndrome (PTSD/LAS). In other words, the stress of protracted litigation in and of itself can exacerbate or induce a psychological injury.

In view of the fact that stress unarguably negatively affects health along with the Huffer/Alexander Study that concluded that litigation was a major factor in somatic symptoms resulting from litigation stress, a standard of care for LWDs must demand adoption of the social model for determining ADA Accommodations. After many years of submitting hundreds of cases requesting accommodations, a common thread emphasizes that most accommodation needed by persons with disabilities reflected no addition economic burden for the court simply a shift toward kindness and consideration toward special needs. Compared to the medical model currently used, the social model will save money, improve service and align with Department of Justice and American Bar Association recommendations.

People with disabilities are not a disparate group. Potentially, they are any of us. Disability is but a bad experience away from virtually any person. When the first Americans with Disabilities Act was passed by the United States Congress, there were approximately 43 million disabled Americans. Psychological conditions were a fraction of that number. Today, according to the National Institute of Mental Health (NIMH), one in four American adults "suffers from a diagnosable mental disorder in a given year." Exceeding the 1990 figure for all disabilities, mental disorders alone now claim 57.7 million people and yet are rarely recognized as needing special accommodations during litigation. Mental disorders represent the "leading cause of disability in the U.S. and Canada for individuals 15-44." The World Health Organization (WHO) cites depression alone as affecting 121 million people worldwide. In 2008, the American Journal of Psychiatry estimated that in the U.S. major mental disorders cost $193 billion annually in lost earnings. The cases you read about in this book demonstrate that "toxic litigation" is costing our nation billions of dollars—not to mention the waste of contributions that these people could be making if they were free to function at their best. Yet this single, preventable, major public health "issue of the century" is largely kept locked in the shadows–until now.

When litigation goes wrong for a person with disabilities and they feel at the end of their ropes, litigants are often forced to go on Social Security Disability—Supplemental Security Income (or SSI)—income at taxpayers' expense. Many of these people could work if they were not entrapped in their protracted litigation and exhausted by their legal system.

Differentiating which mental disorders are preventable injuries, such as PTSD/LAS as outlined in this book, will profoundly relieve the burdened economy. Relieving taxpayers of supporting PWDs (persons with disabilities) who desperately want to be creative contributors will boost the economy. All they need is simple accommodation to assure a level playing field. Instead of litigation creating low income PWDs due to excessive costs of litigation and crushing pride and hope, justice will be not only unlocked but stabilized. My therapeutic program asserts that if the psychic injuries caused by toxic human systems are delineated and properly addressed, statistics regarding psychic injuries are largely reversible. It is within our power to eliminate significant human suffering under my innovative advocacy program.

Appendix A

Recommended Readings

Foa, E. B., Choate-Summers, M. L., Garcia, A. M., & Moore, P. S. (2008). *Effective treatments for ptsd: practice guidelines from the international society for traumatic stress studies.* (2nd ed.). New York, NY: The Guilford Press.

Foa, E. B., Coles, M., Huppert, J. D., Pasupulet, R. V., & Franklin, M. E. (2009). Development and validation of a child version of the obsessive compulsive inventory. In *Behavior Research and Therapy* (OCI-CV ed.).

Freeman, J. F. et al. (2008). Increased error-related brain activity in pediatric obsessive-compulsive disorder before and after treatment. *American Journal of Psychiatry, 165(1),* 116-123.

Hadfield, G. K. (2010). Higher demand, lower supply? A comparative assessment of the legal landscape for ordinary Americans. *Fordham Urban Law Journal,* 129.

Herman, J. M. D. (1997). *Trauma and recovery: The aftermath of violence—from domestic abuse to political terror trauma and recovery.* New York, NY: Basic Books.

Hopper , J., Frewen, P. A., van der Kolk, B. A., & Lanius, R. A. (2007). Neural correlates of re-experiencing, avoidance, and dissociation in ptsd: Symptom dimensions and emotion dysregulation in responses to script-driven trauma imagery. *Journal of Traumatic Stress, 20(5),* 713–725.

Khanna, M. S., March, J. S., Foa, E. B., & Franklin, M. E. (2009). The pediatric obsessive-compulsive disorder treatment study ii: rationale, design and methods. *Child and Adolescent Psychiatry and Mental Health, 3(4),* 1-15.

Schmidt, A. B. et al. (2008). A randomized, controlled trial of cognitive-behavioral therapy for augmenting pharmacotherapy in obsessive-compulsive disorder. *American Journal of Psychiatry, 165(5),* 621-630.

Simon, N. M. et al. (2008). Paroxetine CR augmentation for posttraumatic stress disorder refractory to prolonged exposure therapy. *Journal of Clinical Psychiatry, 69(3),* 400-405.

Simpson, H. B., Zuckoff, A., Page, J. R., Fanklin, M. E., & Foa, E. B. (2008). Adding motivational interviewing to exposure and ritual prevention for obsessive-compulsive disorder: an open pilot trial. In *Cognitive Behavior Therapy, 37(1)* ed., 38-49.

Simpson, H. B., Maher, M., Page, J. R., Fanklin, M. E., & Foa, E. B. (2010). "development of a patient adherence scale for exposure and response prevention therapy. In *Behavior Therapy, 41(1)* ed., 30-7.

Simpson, H. B., Cheng, P. E., Huppert, J., Foa, J., & Liebowitz MR, E. (2008). Statistical choices can affect inferences about treatment efficacy: a case study from obsessive-compulsive disorder research. *Journal of Psychiatric Research 42(8),* 208-18.

Ulrich, O., Cahill, S. P., Foa, E. B., & Maercker, A. (2008). Anger and posttraumatic stress disorder symptoms in crime victims: A longitudinal analysis. Journal of Consulting and Clinical Psychology, 76(2), 208-18.

Related Recommended Reading

http://www.ncbi.nlm.nih.gov/pubmed/19488073

Chrousos, G. (2009, July). Stress and disorders of the stress system. *Nat. Rev. Endocrinol, 5(7),* 374-81.

Charmandari, E., Tsigos, C., & Chrousos, G. (2005). Endocrinology of the stress response. *Annu. Rev. Physiol, 67,* 259-84.

Johnson, E. O., Kamilaris, T. C., Chrousos, G. P., & Gold, P. W. (1992, Summer). Mechanisms of stress: a dynamic overview of hormonal and behavioral homeostasis. *Neurosci Biobehav Rev., 16(2),* 115-30.

Chrousos, G. P., & Gold, P. W. (1992, March 4). The concepts of stress and stress system disorders.

Overview of physical and behavioral homeostasis. *JAMA, 267(9)*, 1244-52.

Chrousos, G.P. (2000, June 24). The role of stress and the hypothalamic-pituitary-adrenal axis in the pathogenesis of the metabolic syndrome: neuro-endocrine and target tissue-related causes. *Int. J. Obes. Relat. Metab. Disord. Suppl., 2*, S50-5.

Imparato, Andrew J. (2005, May/June). Addressing Mental Illness in the Legal Workplace, *Diversity & the Bar*, 60-63.

Data Analysis Form- Part A

GENERAL GUIDE TO INVESTIGATE, DECIDE, AND RESOLVE VIOLATION DISPUTES UNDER TITLE II AND III OF THE ADAAA and HIPAA

In accordance with the American Bar Association/ Department of Justice, Webinar Series 2009, Americans with Disabilities Act Titles II and III, and Prevention of Exploitation of Cognitive Impairment of Traumatic Stress Suffered by Litigants, this Data Analysis is provided for correction of record.

__[Attorney name]____[Address]____[Phone]__Attorney for __[e.g., Plaintiff]__, _[name]__ _ _ _ _ _ Court, County of _ _ _ _ _ _[_ _ _ _ _ District]__ __ _ _ _ _ _) No. _ _ _ _ _ _ Plaintiff(s)) vs.) REQUEST THAT COURT TAKE) JUDICIAL NOTICE OF _ _ _ _ _ _ _ _ _ _ _) __[SPECIFY NATURE OF MATTER Defendant(s)) TO BE NOTICED] _____) Hearing: __[date; time]__ Department: _ _ _ _ _ __[Estimated length:_ _]__ __[Discovery cutoff: _ _ _]__ __[Law and motion cutoff: _ _ _]__ Trial Date: __ [if set]____[E.g., Plaintiff]__, __[name]__, in support of __[his/her/its]__ motion for __[specify nature of order sought]__, asks the Court to take judicial notice of the following: 1. Under California Evidence Code section __[451/452]__, __[specify records, facts, and other matters to be noticed and reasons the court should take judicial notice of each in numbered paragraphs]__.Date: _ _ _ _ _ _ [Signature] __[Typed name]__ Attorney for _ _ _____ _

Data analysis is a tool intended to organize, itemize, define, and clarify the misinformation that has impeded fair accesses to court under the Americans with Disabilities Act and/ or HIPAA. As a document of record, it alerts the court of violations. This form speaks only to violations of the ADAAA, HIPAA, or similar protective laws.

DATA ANALYSIS FORM -Part B

Name: _____ Docket/Case No._____

Directions:

1. Attach all completed copies of this form to the information given on first page. Make copies of your work.

2. Use the terminology given below to clarify the data you are disputing. Add exhibits if needed.

3. Be specific as to the violation you are citing under the ADAAA Title II & III or HIPAA.

4. When writing your detailed explanation, include names, dates, actions, labels, form numbers, etc.

5. If you spoke with or are relying on an outside authority to substantiate your dispute, include all contact information, documents, citations, conversations, etc. of importance.

6. Clearly explain attachments, other than additional exhibits, and their significance.

7. If you require additional exhibits or more room, retype following the sequence.

8. Be concise. Edit. Verify. Copy. Data Analysis can be performed as needed.

Date: _____

Data Analyzed: 1._____ 2._____

                    3._____ 4._____

ADA/ Violation(s): 1._____ 2._____

HIPAA   3._____ 4._____

Exhibit 1- Date:

Statement of your concern:

Detailed explanation of document, conversation, etc.:

Outcome/ Response:

Therapeutic Mitigation Intake Form
Legal Victims Assistance Advocate

Agreement:

Step 1—The parties agree to dispense with active legal action for a period to be agreed upon.

Step 2—Both parties commit that the wellbeing of the children is the major focus subordinating all matters to that end. If there are no children to be considered, then the health and wellbeing of the litigants is the main focus.

Step 3—Anger, resentment, intransigence often rooted in a principle being violated are invited to be expressed.

Step 4--ADA advocates keep the blaming process close at hand when TM begins. It helps to process the pain from unforgivable injuries so that frustration does not intensify. Litigants are wary that the behaviors that hurt them will be officially condoned. That anxiety is relieved after they complete the Blaming process.

Step 5—Parties agree that the goal is not for a "win" but a communication process that is productive. The advocate does not assume a position of power.

General information:

1. Your responses to the questionnaire provide the boundaries of your communication and will reveal common concerns between parties for the advocate.

2. Dialogue between you and the advocate will separate litigation topics from topics of personal interest which are the main concerns when participating in TM.

3. Both parties will be requested to generate numerous possible solutions to obstacles. All will then be proposed for consideration.

4. Determining goals, lofty or small, is a group effort.

5. Unlike litigation, agreements reached in TM are achieved through honest speech and not in legalese.

6. Either party may decide to return to litigation ending TM.

7. Your comments and responses will be edited for inflammatory speech and devoid of emotion when delivered. The other party will hear only concerns/issues/responses/ or opinions.

8. Communication with advocate to parties and parties with each other will be through email, phone, etc.   One-on-one communication will happened only if agreed to.

9. The advocate is trained. And, behind the advocate is a mental health professional and legal expert.

Directions: *Please respond to the following as indicated. If your desired response or concern is not listed, write it in.*

Check *the issues that apply to your case.*

1.____*Power and control to parent your children is being removed from the parents and placed in the hands of the court and court-appointed personnel. This resigns the children to being raised "in and by the legal system."*

2. ____*The wellbeing of the children is consistently negatively affected by litigation. Grades go down; they act depressed at school; they lose respect for adults; and, they are torn between parents. Children complain that they are not heard.*

3.____*The economics of the case force extreme stress draining the family's assets to the detriment of the children and litigants. Retirement and education funds are being converted to legal fees; children's enrichment activities are restricted; and, the family's financial plan and portfolio are compromised to legal costs and fees. Litigation has long passed being a reasonable business decision. The parties involved agree that the moneys could be better spent elsewhere.*

4.____*There is no closure in sight for litigation to end bringing responsible resolution to the original positions of conflict. Litigation has become a consumptive war.*

5.____*Litigation stress is causing or exacerbating health problems. The doctor has advised that to continue litigation risks the health of any or all of the family members.*

6.____*You are ready to surrender on certain points of conflict and explore therapeutic alternatives to adversarial techniques for the sake of ending litigation. TM overcomes obstinacy, abuse, vindictiveness, and relieves much of the pain that persists after marriage fails.*

7.____*You need an ongoing service that treats the conflict through many ups and downs not limited to a one-time negotiation.*

8. ____*You are FED UP with the legal system enough to test another method of resolving differences.*

9. *List what is most important to you. Often legalese confuses a need to agree on a simple visiting arrangement, "Let's agree to a parenting plan that uses no label at all...and agree that the children will spend a certain amount of time with each parent, but let's not call it shared physical custody."* _____

_____
_____
_____
_____
_____

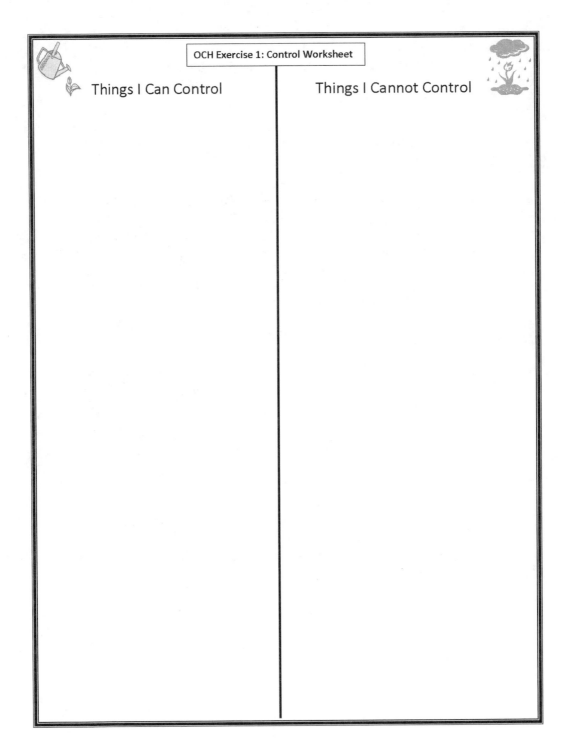

Things I Can Control	Things I Cannot Control

Debriefing Graph

The Debriefing wheel is your tool to prepare to see an attorney or to direct your case. The following functions to separate legal issues and perpetrators from your emotional losses. Do not introduce emotional issues as they waste your court time and cloud your case. Number the loss. Follow up on next page.

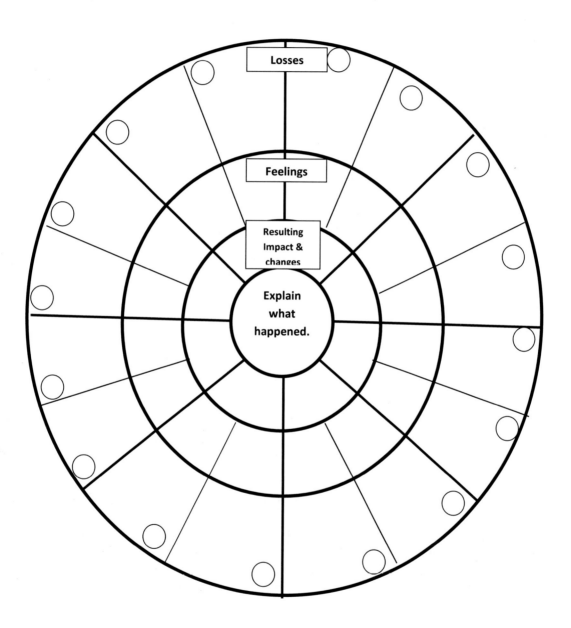

Appendix B

In appreciation to:

C. Ann Huffer, Editor

Don Alan "Mo" Frederick, Esq., Assistance with Citations

Gary Zerman, Esq., Research

Mary Alice Gwynn Esq., Research

Kenn Goldblatt, Research history of maltreatment of persons with disabilities

The following guide to legal authority supporting use of the ADAAA is offered with basic explanation as to application of the law.

General Legal Information Every Advocate Should Know:

The ADA/ADAAA can be found at: 42 USC § 12101 *et seq*

Title IEmployment

Title IIPublic Services (The Courts, Public Assistance, transportation, etc…)

Title IIIPrivate Serving the Public (Lawyers, Restaurants, etc…)

Title IVTelecommunications

Title VTechnical Provisions

The implementing regulations for the Americans with Disabilities Act are in the Federal Code of Regulation:

29 CFR Parts 1630, 1602 (Title I, EEOC)

28 CFR Part 35 (Title II, Department of Justice)

49 CFR Parts 27, 37, 38 (Title II, III, Department of Transportation)

28 CFR Part 36 (Title III, Department of Justice)

47 CFR §§ 64.601 *et seq*. (Title IV, FCC)

A disability is a condition that "substantially limits" the ability of an individual to perform a major life activity as compared to most people in the general population. The term "major life activity" includes, but is not limitedto, caring for oneself, performing manual tasks, seeing, hearing, eating, sleeping, walking, standing, sitting, reaching, lifting, speaking, breathing, learning, reading, concentrating, thinking, communicating, and working. Many impairments, such as deafness, blindness, epilepsy, diabetes, cancer, autism and bipolar disorder, will practically always beconsidered covered disabilities.

CADAA Protection

The regulation that protects advocates is in (42 USC § 12203), 28 CFR 36.206. Retaliation or coercion:

A. No private or public entity shall discriminate against any individual because that individual has opposed any act or practice made unlawful by this part, or because that individual made a charge, testified, assisted, or participated in any manner in an investigation, proceeding, or hearing under the Act or this part.

B. No private or public entity shall coerce, intimidate, threaten, or interfere with any individual in the exercise or enjoyment of, or on account of his or her having exercised or enjoyed, or on account of his or her having aided or encouraged any other individual in the exercise or enjoyment of, any right granted or protected by the Act or this part.

C. Illustrations of conduct prohibited by this section include, but are not limited to:

    1. Coercing an individual to deny or limit the benefits, services, or advantages to which he or she is entitled under the Act or this part;

    2. Threatening, intimidating, or interfering with an individual with a disability who is seeking to obtain or use the goods, services, facilities, privileges, advantages, or accommodations of a public accommodation;

    3. Intimidating or threatening any person because that person is assisting or encouraging an individual or group entitled to claim the rights granted or protected by the Act or this part to exercise those rights; or

    4. Retaliating against any person because that person has participated in any investigation or action to enforce the Act or this part.

Responsibilities of the ADA Access Coordinator:

A Coordinator is obligated "to give primary consideration to the accommodation requested" by the individual with a disability. Cf. 28 C.F.R. § 35.160(b)(2) (2009) (under the ADAAA, "[i]n determining what type of auxiliary aid and service is necessary, a public entity shall give primary consideration to the requests of the individual with disabilities")

Section 504 of the Rehabilitation Act (29 U.S.C. § 794) and Title II of the ADAAA; both acts explain that anyone:

"[w]ho, with or without reasonable modifications to rules, policies, or practices, the removal of architectural, communication, or transportation barriers, or the provision of auxiliary aids and services, meets the essential eligibility requirements for the receipt of services or the participation in programs or activities provided by a public entity"

The Equal Protection Clause of the Fourteenth Amendment to the United States Constitution provides that, "no state shall … deny to any person within its jurisdiction the equal protection of the laws." U.S. Const. amend. XIV, § 1. See also Due Process Clause

Grievances, Appeals, Redress for Violations of the ADA:

1st Amendment right to redress the government for grievances

Title II governs all the operations of a State, which plainly encompasses state conduct subject to a number of other constitutional limitations embodied in the First, Fourth, Fifth, and Eighth Amendments and incorporated and applied to the States through the Fourteenth Amendment.

Violence Against Women Act

Department of Justice Reauthorization Act of 2005

42 U.S.C. 1983

Civil Rights Act of 1964

Developmental Disabilities Act of 1984

From ADA to Empowerment 18 (1990) (Task Force Report)

See, e.g., Rule 1.100 of the California Rules of Court ("Requests for accommodations by persons with disabilities"); Colorado Judicial Department, Access to the Courts: A Resource Guide to Providing Reasonable Accommodations for People with Disabilities for Judicial Officers, Probation and Court Staff; Georgia Commission on Access and Fairness in the Courts, A Meaningful Opportunity to Participate: A Handbook for Georgia Court Officials on Courtroom Accessibility for Individuals with Disabilities (2004); State Court Administrative Office of Michigan, Model Policy: Requests for Accommodations by Persons with Disabilities (1998)

Cases:

The ADAAA rejected (4) Supreme Court Cases:

The ADAAA overturns the ruling in *Sutton v. United Airlines* (1999) and its two 1999 "companion" rulings (*Murphy v. UPS* and *Albertsons v. Kirkingburg*) on "whether an impairment substantially limits a major life activity is to be determined with reference to the ameliorative effects of mitigating measures"

The ADAAAA overturns the ruling in *Toyota v. Williams* (2002), which "narrowed the scope" of being "substantially limited" with respect to "manual tasks"

The ADAAA overturns EEOC's definition of the term "substantially limits," which required individuals to be "significantly restricted" with respect to a major life activity

The ADAAA overturns the ruling in *Sutton* as it relates to the "third prong of the definition of disability" (being regarded as being disabled) and reinstates "the reasoning of the *Supreme Court in School Board of Nassau County v. Arline*, 480 U.S. 273 (1987), which set forth a broad view of the third prong of the definition of handicap under the Rehabilitation Act of 1973."

These are critical changes that will enable ADA plaintiffs to more easily overcome the hurdle of proving they are *disabled* within the meaning of the ADA.

The ADAAA explicitly rejected the Supreme Court's definition of "substantially limits," in *Toyota Motor Manufacturing, Kentucky, Inc. v. Williams*, 534 U.S. 184 (2002), 224 F.3d 840, and clarified its intention that the primary object of attention in ADA cases is whether the entity has complied with its obligations and "the question of whether an individual's impairment is a disability under the ADA should not demand extensive analysis."

Cases That Turned the Tide for Persons with Disabilities:

In the landmark case *Tennessee v. Lane et al.*, 541 U.S. 509 (2004), it was established that States are ~~not~~ protected from suit in federal Court under the Eleventh Amendment's Sovereign Immunity Doctrine. ~~The ADAAA overturned this protection~~. Further the Lane court found that, "[w]hile Congress may not have had enough evidence of disability discrimination to waive sovereign immunity for equal protection claims, it did have enough evidence of due process violations (such as non-handicap-accessible courthouses) to waive the sovereign immunity doctrine for due process claims." It is additionally important to remark that *Tennessee v. Lane et al.*, noted the expansive reach of 28 C. F. R. 35.150(a)(1): "Public entities need only ensure that each service, program or activity, . . . when viewed in its entirety, is readily accessible to and usable by individuals with disabilities." 28 C. F. R. 35.150(a).

Anderson v. Gus Mayer Boston Store, 924 F. Supp. 763, 771 (E.D. Tex. 1996), "Unlike other legislation designed to settle narrow issues of law, the ADA has a comprehensive reach and should be interpreted with this goal in mind."

Once thought to mandate only equal physical access to courthouses, disabilities rights law also obligates all public entities, including court systems, to facilitate equal *participatory* and *testimonial* access. In re: *Ruby McDonough*, 457 Mass. 512. 2010.

Olmstead v. L.C., 527 U.S. 581, 606 n.16 (1999). Title II may be enforced through private suits against public entities. 42 U.S.C. § 12133. Congress expressly abrogated the States' Eleventh Amendment immunity to private suits in federal court. 42 U.S.C. § 12202.

The Supreme Court in *University of Alabama v. Garrett*, 531 U.S. 356 (2001), reaffirmed that Congress had the power to abrogate States' Eleventh Amendment immunity to private damage actions under Section 5 of the Fourteenth Amendment, which authorizes Congress to enact "appropriate legislation" to "enforce" the rights protected by Section 1 of the Fourteenth Amendment.

The Supreme Court specifically reserved the question that the district court addressed, whether Title II's abrogation can be upheld as valid Section 5 legislation. The Supreme Court noted that Title II "has somewhat different remedial provisions from Title I," *id.* at 360 n.1, and that the legislative record for those activities governed by Title II was more extensive, see *id.* at 372 n.7. Less than a week after deciding *Garrett*, the Supreme Court denied a petition for certiorari filed by California and let stand the Ninth Circuit's holding that Title II's abrogation was valid Section 5 legislation.

See Dare v. California, 191 F.3d 1167 (1999), cert. denied, 121 S. Ct. 1187 (2001).

To the extent that Title II enforces the Fourteenth Amendment by remedying and preventing government conduct that burdens these constitutional provisions and discriminates against persons with disabilities in their exercise of these rights, Congress did not need to identify irrational government action in order to identify and address unconstitutional government action. *See Popovich v. Cuyahoga County Court of Common Pleas*, 276 F.3d 808, 813-814 (6th Cir. 2002) (en banc); id. at 820 (Moore, J., concurring) ("The fact that Title II implicates constitutional violations in areas ranging from education to voting also suggests that heightened judicial scrutiny under both the Due Process and Equal Protection Clauses is appropriate.")

Historic Discrimination: The "propriety of any § 5 legislation 'must be judged with reference to the historical experience . . . it reflects.'" *Florida Prepaid Postsec. Educ. Expense Bd. v. College Sav. Bank,* 527 U.S. 627, 640 (1999). Congress and the Supreme Court have long acknowledged the Nation's "history of unfair and often grotesque mistreatment" of persons with disabilities. *City of Cleburne v. Cleburne Living Ctr.*, 473 U.S. 432, 454 (1985) (Stevens, J., concurring); see *id.* at 461 (Marshall, J., concurring in the judgment in part); *see also Olmstead v. L.C.*, 527 U.S. 581, 608 (Kennedy, J., concurring) ("[O]f course, persons with mental disabilities have been subject to historic mistreatment, indifference, and hostility."); *Alexander v. Choate*, 469 U.S. 287, 295 n.12 (1985) ("well-cataloged instances of invidious discrimination against the handicapped do exist")

In L.C. v. Olmstead, 138 F.3d 1485 (11th Cir. 1998), the Supreme Court held, "[T]he states' need to maintain a range of facilities for the care and treatment of individuals with diverse mental disabilities must be recognized. In determining whether a state can successfully assert a "fundamental alteration" defense (i.e., claim that providing community-based services to an individual would fundamentally alter the state's service-delivery system), courts must consider not only the cost of providing community-based care to the litigants, but also the state's obligation to mete out services to others with mental disabilities in an equitable manner."

The *Olmstead* decision should encourage states to begin planning implementation strategies to comply with the ADAAA's integration mandate, spelled out in regulations requiring that services be provided "in the most integrated setting appropriate to the needs" of people with mental or physical disabilities.

"Prejudice, once let loose, is not easily cabined." *Cleburne*, 473 U.S. at 464 (Marshall, J.). "[o]utdated statutes are still on the books, and irrational fears or ignorance, traceable to the prolonged social and cultural isolation" of those with disabilities "continue to stymie recognition of the[ir] dignity and individuality." Id. at 467

In re Marriage of James, 158 Cal.App.4th, 1261 (Three reasons to deny ADA requests). a trial court may deny an ADA accommodation request when the court determines:

- "[t]he applicant has failed to satisfy the requirements of this rule. (CA Rules of Court, rule 1.100)"

- "[t]he requested accommodation would create an undue financial or administrative burden on the court."

- "[t]he requested accommodation would fundamentally alter the nature of the service, program, or activity."

Boston Hous. Auth. v. Bridgewaters, 452 Mass. 833, 845-848, 898 N.E.2d 848 (2009) (housing authority had notice of tenant's disability despite lack of express notice from tenant, and although tenant did not request accommodation expressly, tenant's acts and assertions "amounted to a request for an accommodation"; "[t]o make a reasonable accommodation request, no 'magic' words are required")

Robertson v. Las Animas County Sheriff's Dep't, 500 F.3d 1185, 1197 (10th Cir.2007), and cases cited (when need of individual with disability for accommodation is "obvious," individual's "failure to expressly 'request'" accommodation is "not fatal" to ADA claim).

Badillo-Santiago, 70 F. Supp. 2d at 89: If a Judge makes a ruling regarding a litigants ADA accommodations they do such as an administrator and not a judge. Thereby an administrative function does not give judicial immunity under the 11th Amendment.

Lanman v. Johnson County, 393 F.3d 1151, 1155-56 (10th Cir. 2004) (ADA harassment prohibited)

In *Horgan v. Simmons*, (No. 09 C 6796, ND IL, 2010), the court held that an HIV-positive man who was terminated after disclosing his medical condition to his supervisor could pursue an employment discrimination claim under the ADA.

Judge Frank Montalvo of the United States District Court for the Western District of Texas issued an opinion denying the defendant's motion for summary judgment in *Molina v. DSI Renal, Inc.*, --- F.Supp.2d ----, 2011 WL 6076178 (W.D.Tex., Dec. 5, 2011). The case is a standard-issue back pain/lifting restriction case, but it nicely shows the impact of the ADA Amendments Act. (The case was brought under the Texas Commission on Human Rights Act, which the Texas legislature amended in 2009 to conform to the ADAAA, so the court relied on its interpretation of the ADAAA.) In denying that plaintiff Molina's back injury was a disability, the defendant employer made a number of arguments that would likely have been successful under pre-ADAAA law, but which the court rejected based on the new statute.

In *Gibbs v. ADS Alliance Data Sys.*, No. 10- 2421, 2011 U.S. Dist. LEXIS 82540 (D. Kan. July 28, 2011), the court denied defendant's motion for summary judgment and held that carpal tunnel syndrome that is debilitating in one hand may constitute a disability under the ADAAA. The court stated that under the new law, "Congress intended to convey that the question of whether an individual's impairment is a disability under the ADA should not demand extensive analysis and that the primary object of attention in cases brought under the ADA should be whether entities covered under the ADA have complied with their obligations."

In *Kinney v. Century Services Corporation*, No. 10-787, 2011 U.S. Dist. LEXIS 87996 (S.D. Ind. Aug. 9, 2011), plaintiff had isolated bouts of depression, which was debilitating when active, but did not impact her work performance when it was inactive. The district court denied defendant's motion for summary judgment and held that although intermittent depressive episodes was clearly not a disability prior to the ADAAA's enactment, plaintiff's depression raised a genuine issue of fact as to whether she is a qualified individual under the Amendments Act.

In *Feldman v. Law Enforcement Assoc.*, 10 CV 08, 2011 U.S. Dist. LEXIS 24994 (E.D.N.C. Mar. 10, 2011), one plaintiff had episodic multiple sclerosis and the other plaintiff had TIA, or "mini-stroke." The court found that the multiple sclerosis was clearly a disability under the ADAAA, as the statute specifically states that "an impairment that is episodic or in remission is a disability if it would substantially limit a major life activity when active." In addition, the recent EEOC regulations for the Amendments Act specifically list MS as a disability. As to the plaintiff suffering from TIA, the court held that "while the duration of [plaintiff's] impairment may have been relatively short, the effects of the impairment were significant", and therefore, he also alleged sufficient facts at the initial stage of the case.

In *Chamberlain v. Valley Health Sys.*, 10 CV 28, 2011 U.S. Dist. LEXIS 12296 (W.D. Va. Feb. 8, 2011), plaintiff adequately alleged that she was "regarded as" disabled as a result of her visual field defect which made fine visual tasks more difficult. The court denied summary judgment and held that the issue of whether the employer believed that plaintiff's impairment "was both transitory and minor must be decided by a jury" given that plaintiff submitted an affidavit stating that one of her supervisors insisted that plaintiff was completely unable to work as a result of her vision problem.

In *Cohen v. CHLN, Inc.*, 10 CV 514, 2011 U.S. Dist. LEXIS 75404 (E.D. Pa. July 13, 2011), plaintiff alleged that he suffered from debilitating back and leg pain for nearly four months before his termination. The court denied summary judgment and held that under the less restrictive standards of the ADAAA, plaintiff has offered sufficient evidence to raise an issue of fact as to whether he was disabled at the time of his termination. While defendant claimed that his condition was of too short a duration, the court disagreed and found that the ADAAA mandates no strict durational requirements for plaintiffs alleging an actual disability.

In *Norton v. Assisted Living Concepts, Inc.*, 10 CV 91, 2011 U.S. Dist. LEXIS 51510 (E.D. Tex. May 13, 2011), the court denied summary judgment and held that renal cancer qualified as a disability under the ADAAA. The fact that plaintiff's cancer was in remission when he returned to work is of no consequence since there is no dispute that renal cancer, "when active", constitutes a physical impairment under the statute. Moreover, cancer, when active, substantially limits the major life activity of normal cell growth, as defined by the statute and the EEOC regulations regarding the Amendments Act. See also *Meinelt v. P.F. Chang's China Bistro, Inc.*, 10-H-311, 2011 U.S. Dist. LEXIS 57303 (S.D. Tex. May 27, 2011) (denying summary judgment where plaintiff had an operable brain tumor).

In *Lowe v. American Eurocopter, LLC*, No. 10 CV 24, 2010 U.S. Dist. LEXIS 133343 (N.D. Miss. Dec. 16, 2010), a court held that obesity may qualify as a disability under the ADAAA. Plaintiff alleged that she was disabled as a result of her weight and that her disability made her "unable to park and walk from the regular parking lot." The court found that because "walking" is specifically listed as a major life activity in the Amendments Act, plaintiff had adequately stated a claim for purposes of Rule 12(b)(6) by asserting that her obesity affected her major life activity of walking.

Propria Persona or Pro Se Cases:

As a litigant appearing In *Propria Persona*, pleadings are to be considered without regard to technicalities. *Propria*, pleadings are not to be held to the same high standards of perfection as practicing lawyers. *See Haines v. Kerner*, 92 Sct 594; also *See Power*, 914 F2d 1459 (11th Cir1990); also *See Hulsey v. Ownes*, 63 F3d 354 (5th Cir 1995). Finally *See In Re: Hall v. Bellmon*, 935 F.2d 1106 (10th Cir. 1991).

In *Puckett v. Cox*, it was held that a pro-se pleading requires less stringent reading than one drafted by a lawyer (456 F2d 233 (1972 Sixth Circuit USCA). Justice Black in *Conley v. Gibson*, 355 U.S. 41 at 48 (1957) "The Federal Rules rejects the approach that pleading is a game of skill in which one misstep by counsel may be decisive to the outcome and accept the principle that the purpose of pleading is to facilitate a proper decision on the merits. According to Rule 8(f) FRCP and the State Court rule which holds that all pleadings shall be construed to do substantial justice."

There is legal sufficiency to show Plaintiff is entitled to relief under her Complaint. A Complaint should not be dismissed for failure to state a claim unless it appears beyond a doubt that the Petitioner can prove no set of facts in support of his claim, which would entitle him to relief. *See Conley v. Gibson*, 355 U.S. 41, 45-46 (1957) also *Neitzke v. Williams*, 109 S. Ct. 1827, 1832 (1989). Rule 12(b)(6) does not countenance dismissals based on a judge's disbelief of a complaint's factual allegations. In applying the Conley standard, the Court will "accept the truth of the well-pleaded factual allegations of the Complaint."

If Going to Federal Court be Aware of:

Ashcroft v. Iqbal, 129 S. Ct. 1937, 1949 (2009) ("To survive a motion to dismiss, a complaint must contain sufficient factual matter, accepted as true, to 'state a claim to relief that is plausible on its face.'") quoting *Bell Atl. Corp. v. Twombly*, 550 U.S. 544, 570)

Younger v. Harris, 401 U.S. 37 (1971), was a case in which the United States Supreme Court held that United States federal courts were required to abstain from hearing any civil rights tort claims brought by a person who is currently being prosecuted for a matter arising from that claim.

The Rooker-Feldman doctrine is a rule of civil procedure enunciated by the United States Supreme Court in two cases, *Rooker v. Fidelity Trust Co.*, 263 U.S. 413 (1923) and *District of Columbia Court of Appeals v. Feldman,* 460 U.S. 462 (1983). The doctrine holds that lower United States federal courts other than the Supreme Court should not sit in direct review of state court decisions unless Congress has specifically authorized such relief. In short, a federal court must not become a court of appeals for a state court decision, the litigant must exhaust all state remedies.

Examples of Historic Maltreatment of Persons with Disabilities:

Congress found that its hearings, investigations, and other sources revealed severe prejudice and discrimination towards disabled persons persisted in this country. Persons with disabilities, especially those with severe, noticeable disabilities, were told outright that they had been excluded because others would feel uncomfortable around them. *See, e.g., S. Rep. No. 116, 101st Cong., 1st Sess. 7 (1989), and H.R. Rep. No. 485, 101st Cong., 2d Sess., pt. 2, at 30 (1990)* (a New Jersey zoo keeper refused to admit children with Downs syndrome because he feared they would upset the chimpanzees; and, from remarks of Rep. Vanik, citing as an example of discrimination on the basis of disability from *Alexander v. Choate*, 469 U.S. 287, 307, 83 L. Ed. 2d 661, 105 S. Ct. 712 n.29 (1985), a child with cerebral palsy was excluded from public school, although he was academically competitive and his condition was not actually physically disruptive, because his teacher claimed his physical appearance "produced a nauseating effect" on his classmates); 135 *Cong. Rec. S10720* (daily ed. Sept. 7, 1989) (statement of Sen. Durenberger) (applicant with cerebral palsy described being told she was not qualified for job in metropolitan hospital because fellow employees would not be comfortable working with her); *Senate Comm. on Labor and Human Resources, Rep. on the Americans with Disabilities Act, S. Rep. No. 116, 101st Cong., 1st Sess. 7 (1989)* (applicant "crippled by arthritis" denied employment in higher education because "college trustees" [thought] "normal students shouldn't see her"); *House Comm. on Education and Labor, Rep. on the Americans with Disabilities Act, H.R. Rep. No. 485, 101st Cong., 2d Sess., at 42, reprinted in 1990 U.S. Code Cong. & Admin. News 303,324 (1990)* (testimony of Virginia Domini) ("The general public doesn't want to see you doing your laundry, being a case worker, a shopper, or a Mom. It is difficult to see yourself as a valuable member of society, and sometimes it is hard to see yourself as a person worthy of so much more respect than you get from the general public.

Guidelines for Assessment of and Intervention with Persons with Disabilities:

These guidelines were developed by the APA Task Force on Guidelines for Assessment and Treatment of Persons with Disabilities. The task force members included Kurt F. Geisinger, PhD (University of Nebraska, Lincoln, Nebraska); Kay Kriegsman, PhD (independent practice, Bethesda, Maryland); Irene W. Leigh, PhD (Gallaudet University, Washington DC); Elina Manghi, PsyD (Adler School of Professional Psychology, University of Illinois at Chicago, Chicago, Illinois); Izabela Z. Schultz, PhD (University of British Columbia, Canada); Tom Seekins, PhD (University of Montana, Missoula, Montana); and Greg Taliaferro, PhD (Cincinnati Psychoanalytic Institute). Drs. Schultz and Taliaferro were the Task Force co-chairs.

The task force wishes to acknowledge Izabela Schultz, PhD for her foresight regarding the need for guidelines and for initiating their careful development. In addition, the task force is grateful to Rosemarie Alvaro, PhD, Thomas Bartlett, PsyD, Jim Butcher, PhD, Susan Drumheller, PhD, Michael Dunn, PhD, Stephen Flamer, PhD, Alan Goldberg, Psy.D, ABPP, JD, Virginia Gutman, PhD, Dara Hamilton, PhD, Roger Heller, PhD, Tamar Heller, PhD, Rosemary Hughes, PhD, William Kachman, PhD, Monica Kurylo, PhD, Kurt Metz, PhD, Sharon Nathan, PhD, Rhoda Olkin, PhD, Sara Palmer, PhD, Diana Pullin, JD, PhD, Jeff Rosen, PhD, Cheryl Shigaki, PhD, David Smith, PhD, Martha Thurlow, PhD, Michael Wehmeyer, PhD, Julie Williams, PsyD, and Gerry Young, PhD for their assistance in providing important feedback on several earlier drafts of the guidelines; to Diana Spas (University of Montana, Missoula, Montana) for her thorough and thoughtful review and editorial suggestions; to APA's governance groups who reviewed this document and provided valuable feedback and suggestions; and to the myriad other individuals for their careful review and comments. The task force also wishes to thank Anju Khubchandani, Director of APA's Office on Disability Issues, who assisted and provided counsel to the Task Force throughout this project, and to her administrative coordinators, Sara Laney and Mara Lunaria. Dr. Taliaferro wishes to thank the Research Fund of the Cincinnati Psychoanalytic Institute for its support.

The late Greg Taliaferro, PhD served as a member and co-chair of this task force. Greg made an indelible impression with not only his professionalism and determination, but his grace, his courage, and his puckish sense of humor. The Task Force dedicates this report to his memory. At its February 2006 meeting, the APA's Council of Representatives approved the Task Force and allocated $18,500 from 2006 discretionary funds. In 2007, the Council of Representatives allocated $13,500 from its 2007 discretionary funds to support two additional Task Force meetings. No other group or individual contributed financial support, and no Task Force members or their sponsoring organizations will derive financial benefit from approval or implementation of these guidelines.

This document will expire as APA Policy by February 2021. After this date, users should contact the APA Practice Directorate to determine whether this document remains in effect.

Guideline 1: Psychologists strive to learn about various disability paradigms and models and their implications for service provision

Guideline 2: Psychologists strive to examine their beliefs and emotional reactions toward various disabilities and determine how these might influence their work

Guideline 3: Psychologists strive to increase their knowledge and skills about working with individuals with disabilities through training, supervision, education, and expert consultation

Guideline 4: Psychologists strive to learn about federal and state laws that support and protect people with disabilities

Guideline 5: Psychologists strive to provide a barrier-free physical and communication environment in which clients with disabilities may access psychological services

Guideline 6: Psychologists strive to use appropriate language and respectful behavior toward individuals with disabilities

Guideline 7: Psychologist strive to understand both the common experiences shared by persons with disabilities, and the factors that influence an individual's personal disability experience

Guideline 8: Psychologists strive to recognize social and cultural diversity in the lives of persons with disabilities

Guideline 9: Psychologists strive to learn how attitudes and misconceptions, the social environment, and the nature of a person's disability influence development across the lifespan

Guideline 10: Psychologists strive to recognize that families of individuals with disabilities have strengths and challenges

Guideline 11: Psychologists strive to recognize that people with disabilities are at increased risk for abuse and address abuse-related situations appropriately

Guideline 12: Psychologists strive to learn about the opportunities and challenges presented by assistive technology

Testing and Assessment

Guideline 13: In assessing persons with disabilities, psychologists strive to consider disability as a dimension of diversity together with other individual and contextual dimensions

Guideline 14: Depending on the context and goals of assessment and testing, psychologists strive to apply the assessment approach that is most psychometrically sound, fair, comprehensive, and appropriate for clients with disabilities

Guideline 15: Psychologists strive to determine whether accommodations are appropriate for clients to yield a valid test score

Guideline 16: Consistent with the goals of the assessment and disability-related barriers to assessment, psychologists in clinical settings strive to appropriately balance quantitative, qualitative, and ecological perspectives, and articulate both the strengths and limitations of assessment

Guideline 17: Psychologists in clinical settings strive to maximize fairness and relevance in interpreting assessment of data of clients who have disabilities by applying approaches which reduce potential bias and balance and integrate data from multiple sources

Interventions

Guideline 18: Psychologists strive to recognize that there is a wide range of individual response to disability, and collaborate with their clients who have disabilities, and when appropriate, with their clients' families to plan, develop, and implement psychological interventions

Guideline 19: Psychologists strive to be aware of the therapeutic structure and environment's impact on their work with clients with disabilities

Guideline 20: Psychologists strive to recognize that interventions with persons with disabilities may focus on enhancing strengths well being as well as reducing stress and ameliorating skill deficits

Guideline 21: When working with systems that support, treat, or educate people with disabilities, psychologists strive to keep clients' perspectives paramount and advocate for client self-determination, integration, choice, and least restrictive alternatives

Guideline 22: Psychologists strive to recognize and address health promotion issues for individuals with disabilities

Communication Access in Federal Courts:

When you expect to be in a federal court for any reason, you or your lawyer must contact the court in advance to request the accommodations that are necessary for you to understand the court proceedings. The Americans with Disabilities Act (ADA) does not apply to the federal courts. However, the Judicial Conference of the Administrative Office of the United States Courts has adopted a policy that all federal courts will "provide reasonable accommodations to persons with communications disabilities." Policy requires sign language interpreters or other appropriate auxiliary aids and services, at no charge to deaf or hard of hearing court participants. Federal court policy allows federal courts to decide whether to provide accommodations for court spectators who are deaf or hard of hearing. These guidelines are published in Vol. I, *Administrative Manual, Chapter III, General Management and Administration, Guide to Judiciary Policies and Procedures.* These guidelines are reprinted below. You may also print this page to inform your lawyer or a federal court about your rights.

The NAD advocates for federal courts to provide accommodations for deaf and hard of hearing people in federal court, for any reason.

Guidelines for Providing Services to the Hearing-Impaired and Other Persons with Communications Disabilities

1. General Policy.

As adopted in September 1995, it is the policy of the Judicial Conference that all federal courts provide reasonable accommodations to persons with communications disabilities.

2. Sign Language Interpreters and Other Auxiliary Aids and Services.

Each federal court is required to provide, at judiciary expense, sign language interpreters or other appropriate auxiliary aids or services to participants in federal court proceedings who are deaf, hearing-impaired, or have other communications disabilities. The court shall give primary consideration to a participant's choice of auxiliary aid or service.

"Auxiliary aids and services" include qualified interpreters, assistive listening devices or systems, or other effective methods of making aurally delivered materials available to individuals with hearing impairments. "Participants" in court proceedings include parties, attorneys, and witnesses. The services called for under these guidelines are not required to be provided to spectators, although courts may elect to do so in situations where they determine such to be appropriate, for example, providing an interpreter to the deaf spouse of a criminal defendant so that the spouse may follow the course of the trial. "Court Proceedings" include trials, hearings, ceremonies and other public programs or activities conducted by a court. "Primary consideration" means that the court is to honor a participant's choice of auxiliary aid or service, unless it can show that another equally effective means of communication is available, or that the use of the means chosen would result in a fundamental alteration in the nature of the court proceeding or in undue financial or administrative burden.

3. Jurors.

The determination of whether a prospective juror with a communications disability is legally qualified to serve as a juror is one for the judgment of the trial court under the Jury Selection and Service Act, and that determination is not governed or effected by these guidelines. However, where an individual with a communications disability is found so qualified, a sign language interpreter or other appropriate auxiliary aid or service should be provided under these guidelines.

4. Procedures.

Each court is required to identify a specific office or individual(s) to serve as access coordinator from whom participants in court proceedings may request auxiliary aids or services. The access coordinator must be familiar with the judiciary's policy of providing reasonable accommodations to persons with communications disabilities, to ensure that the policy is properly implemented. The access coordinator must have a ready working knowledge of the types of auxiliary aids and services available to serve the needs of disabled persons and of the local sources from which auxiliary aids and services may be procured. Personnel in each court are to be instructed as to the judiciary's policy and the identity and location of the access coordinators in their particular court. Each court shall appropriately publicize the identity and location of its access coordinator through courthouse signs, bulletin board announcements, pamphlets, announcements in the local press, etc.

Courts may, but are not required to, establish specific procedures through which requests for auxiliary aids and services are to be submitted, such as requiring that they be submitted to the access coordinator in writing or that they be submitted in advance of the court proceeding involved. Courts may also establish procedures through which persons dissatisfied with the court's proposed provision of auxiliary aids and services may seek review or reconsideration. Any such procedures must be appropriately publicized. These guidelines are not intended to, nor should they be construed to extend or modify existing law.

5. Reporting.

In all situations in which services are provided under these guidelines, regardless of whether any direct new costs are incurred, courts are to file reports with the Administrative Office on forms provided for this purpose.

6. Effective date.

These guidelines are now in effect.

Where a court determines such to be appropriate, computer-assisted real-time [also called CART] reporting is one of the services that may be provided under these guidelines, but solely in furtherance of the limited purposes for which the guidelines have been adopted. Thus, real-time reporting should be provided for only as long as and for the specific purposes required by a participant: for example, only for the duration of the deaf witness's testimony. Real-time reporting is to be used solely to assist in communication and is not to be used in lieu of conventional means of producing the official record. Real-time service provided under these guidelines shall be limited to a video display of spoken words, and shall not include enhancements such as key word searching or the provision of unedited daily transcripts. Courts may not use this policy as an authorization to purchase and install real-time court reporting equipment in the courtroom. Such purchase is controlled by Judicial Conference policy relating to the methods of court reporting.

Office of Federal Contract Compliance Programs (OFCCP):

Section 503 of the Rehabilitation Act of 1973
The Americans with Disabilities Act and EEOC and Affirmative Action Guidelines for Federal Contractors Regarding Individuals with Disabilities

The mission of the U.S. Department of Labor's Office of Federal Contract Compliance Programs (OFCCP) is to ensure that companies doing business with the federal government comply with their contractual obligations to provide equal employment opportunity and to develop positive programs to recruit, hire, and promote workers who traditionally have been discriminated against in the job market — minorities, women, persons with disabilities, and Vietnam era and special disabled veterans.

Basic Provisions

For the past two decades, OFCCP has enforced Section 503 of the Rehabilitation Act of 1973, as amended, (Section 503), which requires federal contractors and subcontractors with Government contracts in excess of $10,000, to take affirmative action to employ and advance in employment qualified individuals with disabilities.

Additionally, since 1992, OFCCP has had coordinating authority under Title I of the Americans with Disabilities Act of 1990 (ADA), which prohibits job discrimination by employers, with 15 or more employees, against qualified individuals with disabilities. The Equal Employment Opportunity

Commission (EEOC) has primary authority for enforcing the ADA. Most Government contractors are covered by both Section 503 and the ADA.

Persons Protected

Section 503 and the ADA cover persons with a wide range of mental and physical impairments that substantially limit or restrict a major life activity such as hearing, seeing, speaking, walking, breathing, performing manual tasks, caring for oneself, learning or working.

Section 503 and the ADA also protect qualified individuals with records of substantial mental or physical disabilities. Individuals who have recovered from their disabilities may face job discrimination because of their past medical records. Finally, individuals who are perceived as having disabilities, when in fact, they do not, are protected by Section 503 and the ADA as well.

Only **qualified** individuals with disabilities are protected by Section 503 and the ADA. The person must have the necessary education, skills or other job-related requirements. The person also must be able to perform the essential functions of the job — the fundamental job duties of the position he or she holds or desires — with or without reasonable accommodation.

Reasonable Accommodation involves making adjustments or modifications in the work, job application process, work environment, job structure, equipment, employment practices or the way that job duties are performed so that an individual can perform the essential functions of the job.

Medical Examinations and Pre-employment Inquiries

It is generally unlawful for the contractor to require medical examinations or to make inquiries as to whether an applicant or employee is an individual with a disability or as to the nature or severity of such disability. The contractor, however, may make pre-employment inquiries into the ability of an applicant to perform job-related functions, and/or may ask an applicant to describe or to demonstrate how, with or without reasonable accommodation, the applicant will be able to perform the duties of the job.

The contractor may also require a medical examination or make an inquiry after making an offer of employment but before the applicant begins his duties, and may condition the employment offer on the results of such examination, if all entering employees into the same job category are subjected to such examination or inquiry. In addition, the contractor may require a medical examination or make an inquiry of an employee if it is job-related and consistent with business necessity.

Enforcement & Compliance Complaint Investigations

Individuals who believe they have been discriminated against on the basis of their disability by federal contractors or subcontractors, may file complaints with OFCCP. Disability discrimination complaints may also be filed by the authorized representatives of the person or persons affected. The complaints must be filed within **300** days from the date of the alleged discrimination, unless the time for filing is extended by OFCCP for good cause. Complaints may be filed directly with any of

OFCCP's regional or district offices throughout the country, or with OFCCP in Washington, D.C.

Disability discrimination complaints filed with OFCCP will be considered charges filed simultaneously under the ADA whenever the complaints also fall within the ADA's jurisdiction. OFCCP will act as EEOC's agent in processing the ADA component of the charge. OFCCP will transfer to EEOC all disability discrimination complaints over which it does not, but EEOC may, have jurisdiction. OFCCP will investigate and process all of the Section 503/ADA complaints not transferred to EEOC. If OFCCP's investigation reveals a violation, the agency will attempt to conciliate with the contractor, often entering into a conciliation agreement. A conciliation agreement may include a job offer, back pay, reinstatement, promotion or reasonable accommodation.

If the investigation results in a finding of no violation, OFCCP will issue both a finding of no violation and a right-to-sue letter under the ADA, and will close the complaint. Complainants may request a right-to-sue letter earlier in the process.

Compliance Reviews

OFCCP also investigates the employment practices of Government contractors by conducting compliance reviews. During a compliance review, a compliance officer checks personnel, payroll, and other employment records; interviews employees and company officials; and investigates virtually all aspects of employment. The investigator also checks to see whether the contractor is making special efforts to achieve equal opportunity through affirmative action. If problems are uncovered, OFCCP will recommend corrective action and suggest ways to improve the company's equal opportunity efforts.

Enforcing Contract Compliance

When a compliance review or complaint investigation discloses problems, and conciliation efforts are unsuccessful, OFCCP refers the case to the Office of the Solicitor for enforcement through administrative enforcement proceedings. Contractors cited for violating their EEO and affirmative action requirements may have a formal hearing before an administrative law judge. If conciliation is not reached before or after the hearing, sanctions may be imposed. For example, contractors could lose their government contracts or subcontracts or be debarred, i.e., declared ineligible for any future government contracts.

Further Information

For more information about filing disability discrimination complaints or compliance reviews, contact any of OFCCP's regional or district offices. All offices are listed in telephone directories under U.S. Department of Labor, Office of Federal Contract Compliance Programs.

Built-In System Headwinds – Systematized Discrimination:

Griggs v. Duke Power Co., 401 U.S. 424 (1971)

Connecticut v. Teal, 457 U.S. 440 (1982)

While these cases did not deal with disabilities and occurred well before the ADA was first passed in 1990, persons with disabilities who encounter built in obstacles to obtaining their ADA accommodations will identify with the basic issues and findings in these cases. The description is worth bringing forward into these cases.

Index

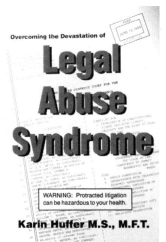
NOTES

_____

_____

_____

_____

_____

_____

_____

_____

_____

_____

NOTES

DR. KARIN HUFFER ALSO PROVIDES:

PUBLIC SPEAKING

- Professional Keynote Speaker, Instructor, and Consultant with Special Experiences in the Areas of Trauma, Post Traumatic Stress Disorder, and Cognitive Disabilities.

- Sunrise Hospital and Medical Center Continuing Medical Education, Regularly Scheduled Lecturer on PTSD and Legal Abuse Syndrome, granting CMEs for Physician licensure. Participating physicians gained expanded skills in diagnosing PTSD, and awareness of their ethical role as to the ADA, and that chronic extreme stress such as litigation as well as acute traumatic incidences precipitate PTSD.

- Speaker on protocols for treatment of PTSD and trauma in schools. Designed and conducted research adapting FBI critical-incident debriefing protocols for children with special needs including PTSD.

- The "Life Span" speakers program and special seminars at Hospital Corporation of America Montevista Psychiatric Hospital in Las Vegas, Nevada.

- International Conference on Violence and Trauma.

- Faculty, Annual Battered Mothers Custody Conference, Albany, New York.

CONSULTING

- Consultant for U.S. Attorney's Office and FBI establishing "FIRST" (Financial Institution Robbery Support Task Force) to assist victims of bank robberies (both customers and employees). Collaboration with FBI field agents developing methods from their Critical-Incident Debriefing method and graphics for use with those under extreme stress with Complex PTSD from non-acute traumatic exposure.

TRAINING

- Instructor in the areas of traumatic stress for Chapman College, La Salle University, and University of Las Vegas Nevada Extension Division.

- Training Manual for PTSD in the Courts with Ethics.

EXPERT WITNESS TESTIMONY

- More than 200 presentations for peer review regarding treatment protocols, potential ethics violations, and inadvertent abuses of those with PTSD in our bureaucratic and legal systems.

- Expert Witness testimony has met Daubert and Frye Standards serving clients in the states of Nevada, California, Michigan, Massachusetts, Alaska, Arizona, Alabama, New York, New Jersey, Colorado, Georgia, Rhode Island, Connecticut, Illinois, Wisconsin. Texas, Virginia, Illinois, Ohio, Oregon, New Hampshire, Pennsylvania, and Florida. Clients also reach to the UK, Ireland, Australia and Canada.

For Information on booking Dr. Huffer or retaining her services mentioned above please visit:
www.DrKarinHuffer.info

NOTES

BECOME A CERTIFIED ADA ADVOCATE - LEVEL 1
BECOME A CERTIFIED FORENSIC DISIBILITY SPECIALIST - LEVEL 2

- Serve litigants with disabilities during litigation

- Open a new career path or income stream

- Serve under the protection of the ADAAA

- Help the judicial system to better serve the public

No pre requisites

Limited Scholarships available, inquire for more details.

18 CEU's and CLE's offered as well as 3 undergraduate and 3 graduate semester credits accredited by King's University. Meets Ethics Requirements.

Must recertify yearly

Includes:

Textbook   Certificate

Syllabus   Identification Badge

Graduates receive ongoing support and updates as to pertinent laws and empirical research. Regular online meetings will be scheduled to keep Advocates updated and to assist with cases. Research opportunities available.

You will learn:

ADAAA Federal Laws mandating equal access

Huffer's 8 Steps for Coaching the client toward self-protection and coping with litigation stress

How to recognize and ease symptoms of PTSD/LAS

How to design and pre arrange ADA Accommodations for clients

How to assist the client during court proceedings

How to be comfortable in the courtroom in the role of advocate

How to assist the court to maintain momentum and protect client functionality while preventing discrimination and exploitation

How to assist in grievances if accommodations are not provided

How to protect client confidentiality under ADAAA and HIPAA

When to refer for medical intervention

To adhere to unwavering ethical obligations regarding disabilities in court

When to recommend Therapeutic Mitigation if litigation and mediation are failing

VISIT WWW.EQUALACCESSADVOCATES.COM

NOTES